Reading Course in American & British News Publications
(Intermediate Level)

美英报刊阅读教程
（中级精选本）
（第六版）

主　编　端木义万　郑志恒

副主编　王慧玉　沈　虹

编著者　张　琦　郭　琼　黄彩梅　黄雅娟
　　　　陈　烨　陈方亚　陈　罡　张　蕊
　　　　李小燕

北京大学出版社
PEKING UNIVERSITY PRESS

图书在版编目(CIP)数据

美英报刊阅读教程：中级精选本 / 端木义万，郑志恒主编. —6版. —北京：北京大学出版社，2023.8
ISBN 978-7-301-34337-1

Ⅰ.①美… Ⅱ.①端… ②郑… Ⅲ.①英语 – 阅读教学 – 高等学校 – 教材 Ⅳ.①H319.37

中国国家版本馆CIP数据核字(2023)第161338号

书　　　名	美英报刊阅读教程(中级精选本)(第六版) MEI-YING BAOKAN YUEDU JIAOCHENG (ZHONGJI JINGXUAN BEN) (DI-LIU BAN)
著作责任者	端木义万　郑志恒　主编
责任编辑	刘　爽
标准书号	ISBN 978-7-301-34337-1
出版发行	北京大学出版社
地　　　址	北京市海淀区成府路205号　100871
网　　　址	http://www.pup.cn　新浪微博:@北京大学出版社
电子邮箱	编辑部 pupwaiwen@pup.cn　总编室 zpup@pup.cn
电　　　话	邮购部 010-62752015　发行部 010-62750672　编辑部 010-62759634
印　刷　者	河北滦县鑫华书刊印刷厂
经　销　者	新华书店
	787毫米×1092毫米　16开本　21.75印张　700千字 1999年9月第1版 2023年8月第6版　2023年8月第1次印刷
定　　　价	69.00元

未经许可，不得以任何方式复制或抄袭本书之部分或全部内容。
版权所有，侵权必究
举报电话：010-62752024　电子邮箱：fd@pup.cn
图书如有印装质量问题，请与出版部联系，电话：010-62756370

主编主要著作介绍

本书主编端木义万系中国人民解放军国防科技大学国际关系学院英语资深教授、博士生导师、全国优秀教师、享受政府特殊津贴专家,从事外报外刊教学与研究近五十年,其主要著作如下:

一、教材系列

*《美英报刊阅读教程(高级精选本)》(北京大学出版社,已2版)
**《美英报刊阅读教程(中级精选本)》(北京大学出版社,已6版)
▲《大学英语外报外刊阅读教程》(北京大学出版社,已2版)
*《美英报刊阅读教程》(南京大学出版社,已3版)
***《美英报刊阅读教程(普及本)》(南京大学出版社,已2版)
《新编美英报刊阅读教程(中级本)》(中国社会科学出版社,1999)
《新编美英报刊阅读教程(普及本)》(世界图书出版公司,2005)
《大学英语报刊阅读教程:英文〈21世纪报〉精华本》(世界图书出版公司,2005)

(以上标有*的书曾列为国家级教学成果二等奖主干教材;标有**的书被评定为普通高等教育"十一五"国家级规划教材;标有***的书获中国大学出版社优秀教材一等奖;标有▲的书为全国教育科学"十一五"规划2010年度教育部重点课题结题成果。)

二、专著系列

《传媒英语研究》(中国社会科学出版社,2000)
《美国传媒文化》(北京大学出版社,2002)
《美国社会文化透视》(南京大学出版社,1999)

三、论文集系列

《高校英语报刊教学论丛》(北京大学出版社,2000)
《高校英语报刊教学论丛》(第二版)(北京大学出版社,2006)
《高校英语报刊教学论丛》(第三版)(北京大学出版社,2010)
《高校英语报刊教学论丛》(第四辑)(北京大学出版社,2017)

四、学术论文59篇

前　言

我主编的《美英报刊阅读教程(中级精选本)》(北京大学出版社)承蒙广大高校师生和读者厚爱,自1999年出版以来,已先后出过五版,连续印刷了三十多次。最近几年国际风云变幻,我国高校英语报刊教学界十分活跃,理念不断更新和改进。为了进一步跟上时代步伐,更好地体现科学、先进的教学理念,我决定出版第六版《美英报刊阅读教程(中级精选本)》。

我从事高校英语报刊教学近五十年,多年的教学实践证明,英语报刊是十分理想的教学资料。

报刊具有贴近时代、贴近大众、贴近现实、贴近生活的特点。作为教学资料,英语报刊具有以下四点显著优势:内容新颖、语言现代、资料丰富、词语实用。

伴随我国国际交流的迅猛发展,英语报刊课程的重要性日趋突出,越来越多的高校为英语专业和非英语专业学生开设了这门课程。

教育部对英语报刊教学给予高度重视。教学大纲的四、六、八级阅读部分都明确将阅读英美报刊水平作为评定阅读能力的标准。

为了适应形势的需要,自20世纪90年代初我们先后编写出版了针对大学不同层次学生的英语报刊系列教材(详情请见"主编主要著作介绍")。这套教材的共同之处在于突出对学生能力的培养。

选材所坚持的标准是:专题为线布局、题材面域广泛、文章内容典型、语言质量上乘、知识含量丰富、使用时效较长。

为了突出能力培养,本书每篇课文之后共设7个部分的内容:

1. 课文生词(New Words)

2. 知识介绍(Background Information)

3. 难点注释(Notes to the Text)

4. 语言简说(Language Features)

5. 内容分析(Analysis of Content)

6. 问题思考(Questions on the Article)

7. 话题讨论(Topics for Discussion)

教材除保留一般英语报刊教材所设的"课文生词""难点注释"和"问题思考"部分外,还特设了"知识介绍""语言简说""内容分析"和"话题讨论"四个部分。

"知识介绍"部分根据课文简明系统地提供文章相关专题的内容,旨在拓宽读者社会文化和科技等方面的知识面域。"语言简说"部分结合课文语言简要介绍报刊英语和现代英语的常见语言现象,意在帮助读者熟悉外报外刊语言的规律和特点。这两个部分有助于学生构建和丰富外报外刊语言和文化的认知结构,引导他们步入轻松自如阅读英语报刊的理想境界。"内容分析"部分提供课文内容和语言的多项选择练习,目的在于帮助学生培养深入理解、分析推断和综合归纳能力。"话题讨论"部分提供与课文内容相关、有一定深度的宏观讨论题,意图是培养学生的问题思辨能力、观点表述能力,增加口头交际实践的机会。

这是一本体现媒介素养教育理念的教材。为了帮助学生提高媒介素养水平,教材在"语言简说"部分提供了西方常见报刊的简况,系统介绍了西方报刊版面和报刊意识形态表现的形式等。"内容分析"和"话题讨论"部分力图培养学生深层次的分析能力和对作者观点的剖析和批评能力。

为了减轻授课教师的备课负担,本书配有教学课件,课件中不仅有课文练习答案,还提供了(英语)相关背景、难点解释和课文篇章层次分析。请授课教师联系2569452818@qq.com免费索取。

本书凝结着许多人的深情厚谊和汗水心血,高校英语报刊教学界的许多同仁和我指导过的博士生、硕士生们为此书献计献策,我的夫人郭荣娣同志为我创造理想的工作环境,全力保障我的教学和科研。在此,谨向为此书作出贡献的所有人士致以诚挚、深切的谢意。

还有一点需要说明:教材中有的课文个别地方值得商榷,主编不揣鄙陋提出修改拙见。为表示对原文作者的尊重,主编保留原文用词,而在认为有问题的用词之后的括号内用黑体字标出修改建议,以供老师和读者们鉴别选择。

由于功力不深、锤炼不足,书中定有不少疏漏和错误,竭诚欢迎并殷切期望广大读者提出宝贵意见。

端木义万
2023年春

Contents
目　录

Unit 1
第一单元　社会群体

Lesson 1　Why Haven't You Gotten Deported? ……………………………………1
　　　　知识介绍：移民之国
　　　　语言简说：新闻英语总体特色

Lesson 2　Silent No More ………………………………………………………………13
　　　　知识介绍：美国社会的种族歧视
　　　　语言简说：词语文化内涵

Lesson 3　The End of Men ……………………………………………………………23
　　　　知识介绍：美国妇女地位
　　　　语言简说：常用俚语

Lesson 4　Millennials Shift Toward Social Responsibility ………………………35
　　　　知识介绍：美国"千禧代"
　　　　语言简说：词性转化

Unit 2
第二单元　衣食住行

Lesson 5　Food and Obesity ……………………………………………………………45
　　　　知识介绍：饮食与肥胖
　　　　语言简说：《泰晤士报》简介

Lesson 6　The End of Ownership: Why Aren't Young People Buying More Houses ……54
　　　　知识介绍：住房情况
　　　　语言简说：嵌入结构

Lesson 7　When Working from Home Doesn't Work ………………………………63
　　　　知识介绍：远程办公
　　　　语言简说：前置定语

Lesson 8　Seeing the Back of the Car …………………………………………………74
　　　　知识介绍：汽车文化
　　　　语言简说：《经济学人》简介

Unit 3
第三单元　家庭婚姻

Lesson 9　No One Way to Keep Love in Bloom, Experts Say ············ 83
　　知识介绍：美国人的婚姻观念
　　语言简说：《华盛顿邮报》简介

Lesson 10　The New Mommy Track ············ 92
　　知识介绍：工作与家庭
　　语言简说：《美国新闻与世界报道》介绍

Lesson 11　One's a Crowd ············ 102
　　知识介绍：独居风尚
　　语言简说：《纽约时报》简介

Lesson 12　Love in the Age of Like ············ 110
　　知识介绍：美国社会婚恋方式的嬗变
　　语言简说：报刊用喻

Unit 4
第四单元　行为风尚

Lesson 13　Take Your Planet to Work ············ 121
　　知识介绍：节能与环保
　　语言简说：《时代》周刊介绍

Lesson 14　We Need to Talk about Kids and Smartphones ············ 130
　　知识介绍：智能手机对美国青少年的影响
　　语言简说：缩略词

Lesson 15　The Beauty Advantage ············ 140
　　知识介绍：美容风尚
　　语言简说：拼缀词

Unit 5
第五单元　体制观念

Lesson 16　This Corruption in Washington Is Smothering America's Future ············ 150
　　知识介绍：美国政治的腐败
　　语言简说：新闻评论

Lesson 17　East Versus West ············ 159
　　知识介绍：东西方观念和思维的差异
　　语言简说：外刊与文化

Unit 6
第六单元　文教体育

Lesson 18 Reining in the Test of Tests ···168
　　知识介绍：高校招生
　　语言简说：新闻标题的结构

Lesson 19 The COVID-19 pandemic has changed education forever. This is how. ···176
　　知识介绍：线上教育的前景
　　语言简说：类比构词

Lesson 20 Time to Get Moving ···186
　　知识介绍：健康意识
　　语言简说：《新闻周刊》介绍

Unit 7
第七单元　企业经济

Lesson 21 Thinking Outside the Box ··194
　　知识介绍：沃尔玛公司当今面临的挑战
　　语言简说：网络新词

Lesson 22 The Lessons of the GM Bankruptcy ···································204
　　知识介绍：通用汽车公司的破产
　　语言简说：名词定语

Lesson 23 Help Wanted ··213
　　知识介绍：美国就业市场结构变化
　　语言简说：标题句式

Unit 8
第八单元　社会问题

Lesson 24 Social Media March on Wall Street ····································223
　　知识介绍：占领华尔街运动
　　语言简说：外报外刊中的意识形态

Lesson 25 Business Affairs, Bedroom Affairs ····································235
　　知识介绍：工作关系与恋情关系
　　语言简说：委婉语

Lesson 26 A Heartbroken Nation ··245
　　知识介绍：美国枪支问题
　　语言简说："说"意动词

Lesson 27　Rags to Rags, Riches to Riches ·· 254
　　　　知识介绍：美国阶级状况
　　　　语言简说：习语活用

Unit 9
第九单元　科技军事

Lesson 28　Power Revolution ·· 263
　　　　知识介绍：再生能源
　　　　语言简说：词义变化

Lesson 29　The Robots Are Coming ·· 275
　　　　知识介绍：机器人的发展与前景
　　　　语言简说：科技新闻报道语言特色

Lesson 30　A Third Industrial Revolution ·· 286
　　　　知识介绍：数字化制造技术
　　　　语言简说：借　词

Lesson 31　The Dark Side of Recruiting ·· 295
　　　　知识介绍：美国征兵
　　　　语言简说：借　代

Unit 10
第十单元　世界风云

Lesson 32　Warming Arctic Opens Way to Competition for Resources ·················· 304
　　　　知识介绍：北极之争
　　　　语言简说："说"意句式

Lesson 33　Tough Terrain Ahead on Road Map ·· 313
　　　　知识介绍：巴以冲突
　　　　语言简说：新闻报道引语

Lesson 34　Age Invaders ·· 322
　　　　知识介绍：全球人口老龄化趋势
　　　　语言简说：报刊英语翻译常见错误

Lesson 35　Lethal Blast Hits Jakarta Hotel ·· 332
　　　　知识介绍：恐怖主义
　　　　语言简说：倒金字塔结构

Unit 1
第一单元 社会群体

Lesson 1

Why Haven't You Gotten Deported?

By Jose Antonio Vargas[1]

That's usually the first thing people ask me when they learn I'm an undocumented immigrant or, put more rudely, an "illegal." Some ask it with anger or frustration, others with genuine bafflement. At a restaurant in Birmingham, not far from the University of Alabama, an inebriated young white man challenged me: "You got your papers?" I told him I didn't. "Well, you should get your ass home[2], then." In California, a middle-aged white woman threw up her arms and wanted to know: "Why hasn't Obama dealt with you?" At least once a day, I get that question, or a variation of it, via e-mail, tweet or Facebook message. Why, indeed, am I still here?

It's a fair question, and it's been hanging over me every day for the past year, ever since I publicly revealed my undocumented status. There are an estimated 11.5 million people like me in this country, human beings with stories as varied as America itself yet lacking a legal claim to exist here. Like many others, I kept my status a secret, passing myself off as a U.S. citizen—right down to cultivating a homegrown accent.[3] I went to college and became a journalist, earning a staff job at the Washington Post. But the deception weighed on me.[4] When I eventually decided to admit the truth, I chose to come out publicly—very publicly—in the form of an essay for the *New York Times* last June. Several immigration lawyers counseled against doing this. ("It's legal suicide," warned one.) Broadcasting my status to millions seemed tantamount to an invitation to the immigration cops[5]: Here I am. Come pick me up.

So I waited. And waited some more. As the months passed, there were no knocks on my door, no papers served, no calls or letters from U.S. Immigration and Customs Enforcement[6] (ICE), which deported a record 396,906 people in fiscal 2011. Before I came out, the question always at the top of my mind was, What will happen if people find out? Afterward, the question changed to What happens now? It seemed I had traded a largely hidden undocumented life in limbo for an openly undocumented life that's still in limbo.

But as I've crisscrossed the U.S.—participating in more than 60 events in nearly 20 states and learning all I can about this debate that divides our country (yes, it's my country too)—I've realized that the most important questions are the ones other people ask me. I am now a walking conversation that most people are uncomfortable having.[7] And once that conversation starts, it's clear why a consensus on solving our immigration dilemma is so elusive. The questions I hear indicate the things people don't know, the things they think they know but have been misinformed about and the views they hold but do not ordinarily voice.

I've also been witness to a shift (**that**) I believe will be a game changer for the debate: more people coming out.[8] While closely associated with the modern gay-rights movement[9], in recent years the term coming out and the act itself have been embraced by the country's young undocumented population. At least 2,000 undocumented immigrants—most of them under 30—have contacted me and outed themselves in the past year. Others are coming out over social media or in person to their friends, their fellow students, their colleagues. It's true, these individuals—many brought to the U.S. by family when they were too young to understand what it means to be "illegal"—are a fraction of the millions living hidden lives. But each becomes another walking conversation. We love this country. We contribute to it. This is our home. What happens when even more of us step forward? How will the U.S. government and American citizens react then?

The contradictions of our immigration debate are inescapable. Polls show substantial support for creating a path to citizenship for some undocumenteds—yet 52% of Americans support allowing police to stop and question anyone they suspect of being "illegal." Democrats are viewed as being more welcoming to immigrants, but the Obama Administration has sharply ramped up deportations. The probusiness GOP waves a KEEP OUT flag at the Mexican border and a HELP WANTED sign 100 yards in, since so many industries depend on cheap labor.[10]

Election-year politics is further confusing things, as both parties scramble to attract Latinos without scaring off other constituencies. President Obama has as much as a 3-to-1 lead over Mitt Romney[11] among Latino voters, but his deportation push is dampening their enthusiasm. Romney has a crucial ally in Florida Senator Marco Rubio, a Cuban American, but is burdened by the sharp anti-immigrant rhetoric he unleashed in the primary-election battle. This month, the Supreme Court is expected to rule on Arizona's controversial anti-immigrant law. A decision either way could galvanize reform supporters and opponents alike.

But the real political flash point is the proposed Dream Act[12], a decade-old immigration bill that would provide a path to citizenship for young people educated in this country. The bill never passed, but it focused attention on these youths, who call themselves the Dreamers. Both the President and Rubio have placed Dreamers at the center of their reform efforts—but with sharply differing views on how to address them.

ICE, the division of the Department of Homeland Security (DHS)[13] charged with enforcing immigration laws, is its own contradiction, a tangled bureaucracy saddled with conflicting goals. As the weeks passed after my public confession, the fears of my lawyers and friends began to seem faintly ridiculous. Coming out didn't endanger me; it had protected me. A Philippine-born, college-educated, outspoken mainstream journalist is not the face the government wants to put on its deportation program. Even so, who flies under the radar[14], and who becomes one of those unfortunate 396,906? Who stays, who goes, and who decides? Eventually I confronted ICE about its plans for me, and I came away with even more questions.

I am not without contradictions either. I am 31 and have been a working journalist for a decade. I know I can no longer claim to be a detached, objective reporter, at least in the traditional sense. I am part of this evolving story and growing movement. It is personal. Though I have worked hard to approach this issue like any other, I've also found myself drawn to the activists, driven to help tell their story.[15]

This is the time to tell it.

"Why don't you become legal?" asked 79-year-old William Oglesby of Iowa City, Iowa. It was early December, a few weeks before the Iowa caucuses, and I was attending a Mitt Romney town hall at an animal-feed maker[16]. Romney had just fielded questions from a group of voters[17], including Oglesby and his wife Sharon, both Republicans. Addressing immigration, Romney said, "For those who have come here illegally, they might have a transition time to allow them to set their affairs in order and then go back home and get in line with everybody else."

"I haven't become legal," I told William, "because there's no way for me to become legal, sir." Sharon jumped in. "You can't get a green card?" "No, ma'am," I said. "There's no process for me." Of all the questions I've been asked in the past year, "Why don't you become legal?" is probably the most exasperating. But it speaks to how unfamiliar most Americans are with how the immigration process works.[18]

As Angela M. Kelley, an immigration advocate in Washington, told me, "If you think the American tax code is outdated and complicated, try understanding America's immigration code." The easiest way to become a U.S. citizen is to be born here — doesn't matter who your parents are; you're in. (The main exception is for children of foreign diplomatic officials.) If you were born outside the U.S. and want to come here, the golden ticket is the so-called green card, a document signifying that the U.S. government has granted you permanent-resident status, meaning you're able to live and, more important, work here. Once you have a green card, you're on your way to eventual citizenship — in as little as three years if you marry a U.S. citizen — as long as you don't break the law and you meet other requirements such as paying a fee and passing a civics test.

Obtaining a green card means navigating one of the two principal ways of getting permanent legal status in the U.S.: family or specialized work. To apply for a green card on the basis of family, you need to be a spouse, parent, child or sibling of a citizen. (Green-card holders can petition only for their spouses or unmarried children.) Then it's time to get in line. For green-card seekers, the U.S. has a quota of about 25,000 green cards per country each year. That means Moldova (population: 3.5 million) gets the same number of green cards as Mexico (population: 112 million). The wait time depends on demand. If you're in Mexico, India, the Philippines or another nation with many applicants, expect a wait of years or even decades. (Right now, for example, the U.S. is considering Filipino siblings who applied in January 1989.)

Taking the employment route to a green card means clearing a pretty high bar if you have an employer who's willing to hire you.[19] There are different levels of priority, with preference given to people with job skills considered crucial, such as specialized medical professionals, advanced-degree holders and executives of multinational companies. There's no waiting list for those. If you don't qualify for a green card, you may be able to secure one of the few kinds of temporary work visas—

including the now famous H1-B visas that are common in Silicon Valley.[20] For those already in the U.S. without documentation—those who have sneaked across a border or overstayed a temporary visa—it's even more complicated. Options are extremely limited. One route is to marry a U.S. citizen, but it's not as easy as the movies would have you think. The process can take years, especially if a sham marriage is suspected. I couldn't marry my way into citizenship even if I wanted to. I'm gay. Same-sex marriage is not recognized by the federal government—explicitly so, ever since Congress passed the Defense of Marriage Act[21]. From the government's perspective, for me to pursue a path to legalization now, I would have to leave the U.S., return to the Philippines and hope to qualify via employment, since I don't have any qualifying family members here. But because I have admitted to being in the U.S. illegally, I would be subject to a 10-year bar before any application would be considered[22].

The long-stalled Dream Act is the best hope for many young people. The original 2001 version would have created a path to legal status—effectively a green card—for undocumented people age 21 and under who had graduated from high school and resided in the U.S. for five years. As the bill stalled in Congress and Dreamers got older, the age requirement went up, getting as high as 35. Rubio is expected to introduce his own variation, granting nonimmigrant visas so Dreamers could legally stay in the U.S., go to school and work. Its prospects are dim in a gridlocked Congress. Obama, meanwhile, is said to be weighing an Executive Order that would halt deportation of Dream Act — eligible youth and provide them with work permits. Under both Rubio's bill (details of which are not yet confirmed) and Obama's Executive Order (which is being studied), Dreamers could become legal residents. However, both proposals are only the first steps of a longer journey to citizenship.

"Why did you come out?" asked 20-year-old Gustavo Madrigal, who attended a talk I gave at the University of Georgia in late April. Like many Dreamers I've met, Madrigal is active in his community. Since he grew up in Georgia, he's needed to be. A series of measures have made it increasingly tough for undocumented students there to attend state universities.

"Why did you come out?" I asked him in turn. "I didn't have a choice," Madrigal replied. "I also reached a point," I told him, "when there was no other choice but to come out." And it is true for so many others. We are living in the golden age of coming out. There are no overall numbers on this, but each day I encounter at least five more openly undocumented people. As a group and as individuals, we are putting faces and names and stories on an issue that is often treated as an abstraction.

Technology, especially social media, has played a big role. Online, people are telling their stories and coming out, asking others to consider life from their perspective and testing everyone's empathy quotient[23]. Some realize the risks of being so public; others, like me, think publicity offers protection. Most see the value of connecting with others and sharing experiences — by liking the page of United We Dream on Facebook, for example, or watching the Undocumented and Awkward video series on YouTube.

This movement has its roots in the massive immigrant-rights rallies of 2006, which were held in protest of HR4437[24], a Republican-backed House bill that would have classified undocumented immigrants and anyone who helped them enter and remain in the U.S. as felons. Though the bill died, it awakened activism in this young generation. Through Facebook, Twitter and YouTube, I encountered youths who were bravely facing their truths.

"For many people, coming out is a way of saying you're not alone," says Gaby Pacheco of United We Dream. Her parents came from Ecuador and brought her to the U.S. in 1993, when she was 7. Immigration officials raided her home in 2006, and her family has been fighting deportation since. Now 27, she has three education degrees and wants to be a special-education[25] teacher. But her life remains on hold while she watches documented friends land jobs and plan their futures. Says Pacheco: "In our movement, you come out for yourself, and you come out for other people."

The movement, as its young members call it, does not have a single leader. News travels by tweet and Facebook update, as it did when we heard that Joaquin Luna, an undocumented 18-year-old from Texas, killed himself the night after Thanksgiving and, though this is unproved, we instantly connected his death to the stresses of living as a Dreamer. Some Dreamers, contemplating coming out, ask me whether they should pretend to be legal to get by. "Should I just do what you did? You know, check the citizenship box [on a government form] and try to get the job?" a few have asked me. Often I don't know how to respond. I'd like to tell them to be open and honest, but I know I owe my career to my silence for all those years. Sometimes all I can manage to say is "You have to say yes to yourself when the world says no."

"What next?" is the question I ask myself now. It's a question that haunts every undocumented person in the U.S. The problem is, immigration has become a third-rail issue[26] in Washington, D.C. — more controversial even than health care because it deals with issues of race and class, of entitlement and privilege, that America has struggled with since its founding. As much as we talk about the problem, we rarely focus on coming up with an actual solution — an equitable process to fix the system.

I am still here. Still in limbo[27]. So are nearly 12 million others like me — enough to populate Ohio. We are working with you, going to school with you, paying taxes with you, worrying about our bills with you. What exactly do you want to do with us? More important, when will you realize that we are one of you?

From *Time*, June 25, 2012

I. New Words

bafflement	[ˈbæflmənt]	n.	困惑
civics	[ˈsiviks]	n.	公民学,公民课
code	[kəud]	n.	a system of laws and rules
consensus	[kənˈsensəs]	n.	a general agreement
constituency	[kənˈstitjuənsi]	n.	选区中的全体选民

contemplate	[kənˈtempleit]	v.	to think about whether you should do sth or how you should do sth
controversial	[ˌkɔntrəˈvəːʃəl]	adj.	causing much disagreement or argument
crisscross	[ˈkriskrɔs]	v.	to come and go across
crucial	[ˈkruːʃəl]	adj.	of deciding importance
deport	[diˈpɔːt]	v.	to send sb (who is not a citizen) out of a country
detached	[diˈtætʃt]	adj.	不带感情的, 不偏不倚的
Ecuador	[ˈekwədɔː]	n.	厄瓜多尔(南美洲西北部国家)
eligible	[ˈelidʒəbl]	adj.	fulfilling the necessary conditions
elusive	[iˈluːsiv]	adj.	difficult to find
embrace	[imˈbreis]	v.	to accept an idea
encounter	[inˈkauntə]	v.	*formal* to be faced with
entitlement	[inˈtaitlmənt]	n.	an official right to have or do sth
equitable	[ˈekwitəbl]	adj.	fair and just
felon	[ˈfelən]	n.	a person who has committed a serious crime
fraction	[ˈfrækʃn]	n.	a small part or amount of sth
frustration	[frʌˈstreiʃən]	n.	feeling of annoyed disappointment or dissatisfaction
galvanize	[ˈɡælvənaiz]	v.	to shock sb into action
gridlock	[ˈɡridlɔk]	v.	使陷入瘫痪/僵局
inebriated	[iˈniːbrieitid]	adj.	*formal or humorous* drunk
Latino	[læˈtiːnəu]	n.	(尤指居住在美国的)拉丁美洲人
Moldova	[mɔlˈdɔːvə]	n.	摩尔多瓦(欧洲东南部国家)
navigate	[ˈnævigeit]	v.	to find the right way to deal with a difficult situation
outdated	[autˈdeitid]	adj.	no longer useful because of being old-fashioned
petition	[pəˈtiʃən]	v.	to make a formal request for
principal	[ˈprinsəpl]	adj.	most important
raid	[reid]	v.	(警察等)突入查抄/搜捕
ramp	[ræmp]	v.	~ sth up to make sth increase
rhetoric	[ˈretərik]	n.	speech or writing that is intended to influence people
scramble	[ˈskræmbl]	v.	to compete with others in order to get sth
stall	[stɔːl]	v.	to stop sth from making progress
substantial	[səbˈstænʃl]	adj.	large in amount
tweet	[twiːt]	n.	在"推特"社交网站上发的信息
undocumented	[ʌnˈdɔkjuməntid]	adj.	无证明文件的

| unleash | [ʌnˈliːʃ] | v. | 发出；发动 |
| variation | [ˌveəriˈeiʃn] | n. | a changed form |

II. Background information

移民之国

  美国是个典型的移民国家，其移民史最早可追溯到1620年，经过近四百年的移民，美国已由民族种类较为单一的国家变为由一百多个民族组成的国家。美国迄今共有四次移民潮。

  第一次移民潮（1820—1860）。移民人数多达500万。拿破仑战争结束后，欧洲重获和平，随着大批军人复员，欧洲各国失业现象严重。与此同时，美国国内建设需要大量劳力。美国政府改变了建国初期的限制移民政策，于是欧洲人移居美国的数量迅猛增加。1848年欧洲革命后，动荡局势和政治、宗教迫害使大批德国人离欧赴美。1846—1851年期间爱尔兰出现的饥荒和疾病迫使100多万人移居美国。

  第二次移民潮（1861—1880）。南北战争结束后，美国迎来了工业化高峰期，劳动力需求强烈。美国政府为了吸引移民，颁布了《鼓励外来移民法》。美国企业界采取许多有效措施，提供种种优惠条件吸引欧洲人移居美国。这一时期，移民总数超过500万。

  第三次移民潮（1881—1920）。移民人数约2350万。美国工业化和城市化步伐加快，劳力需求持续旺盛，吸引了大批欧洲人移居美国。这次移民潮的前半段大部分移民来自北欧和西欧。后半段北欧和西欧移民所占比例下降，大部分移民来自东欧和南欧。

  从1820年到1920年的100年间，美国移民总数为3350万。1920年美国人口增加到1亿，移民给美国带来的不仅是劳力，还有资金、技术和知识。移民为美国经济发展做出了重大贡献，正是在他们的推动下，美国变成了一个强大的国家。

  第四次移民潮（1965— ）。1965年美国颁布了《移民与国籍法》（the Immigration and Nationality Act）。此项法案取消了国家配额制（quota system）。新的法案把对美国有用的人才引进和美国公民家属团聚放在优先地位。美国再次出现移民潮。这次移民潮不仅规模庞大，而且移民来自更广的区域，在群体类别、教育技能、居住分布等方面出现了新的特点。

  数据显示，从1965年到2015年美国移民数量高达4320万。仅以亚洲为例，1901—1930年亚洲移民所占移民总数的比例仅为3.7%。1970年这一比例上升到8.6%，2016年又增加到27%，大致与来自墨西哥的移民相等。来自欧洲和加拿大的移民所占比例约为14%，来自加勒比海地区的移民约占10%，来自中美洲和南美洲的移民所占比例分别为8%和7%，还有来自中东的比例约为4%，来自撒哈拉沙漠以南非洲地区的比例约为4%。

  美国合法移民分为两大类：亲属移民和非亲属移民。美国公民可为配偶、子女、父母，以及兄弟姐妹申请移民；永久居民可为配偶和未婚子女申请移民。非亲属移民有三种:1.职业移民,分为特殊人才、持高等教育学历和特别能力的专业人士、技术工人等;2.投资移民;3.抽奖移民。

美国社会还有数量近1200万的非法移民。非法移民可分为三类:第一类是非法途径进入(illegal entry);第二类是签证逾期滞留(visa overstay);第三类是违背入境卡规定滞留(border crossing card violation)。有关资料显示墨西哥是非法移民最大来源地。为了阻止墨西哥人偷渡,布什总统2006年签署了《安全围墙法案》,决定在美墨边境建造一道1126千米的隔离墙。特朗普就任总统之后对造墙之事更为卖力。据报道,2020年10月底,美墨边境墙已完成近645公里。

非法移民不具有合法身份,无法享受公民权益,生活无保障,不安全。许多经济条件较差者只得放弃求学机会。据统计,25—65岁的非法移民中有三分之一的人受教育程度还不到9年级。没有合法身份就难以接受良好教育,未接受良好的教育就难以摆脱经济贫困,不能改变"非法"身份,这样便陷入了恶性循环之中。

III. Notes to the Text

1. Jose Antonio Vargas—前《华盛顿邮报》记者,其2007年弗吉尼亚理工大学枪击案的报道获得普利策新闻奖。

2. get your ass home—a rude way of saying "go home"

3. I kept my status a secret, passing myself off as a U.S. citizen—right down to cultivating a homegrown accent. —我隐瞒自己的身份,冒充是美国公民,甚至学讲地道的美国音。(① to pass off—to present falsely;② cultivate —to develop a way of talking)

4. But the deception weighed on me. —但是这种欺骗构成了我的心理负担。(weigh on sb—to make sb anxious or worried)

5. Broadcasting my status to millions seemed tantamount to an invitation to the immigration cops... —把我的身份告诉数百万人似乎是在招引移民局警察上门(tantamount to—having the same bad effect as sth else)

6. U.S. Immigration and Customs Enforcement—美国移民和海关执法署

7. I am now a walking conversation that most people are uncomfortable having. —我现在成了被大多数人常常谈论而又谈起来感到不舒服的话题。(walking—used here in a humorous way to emphasize the fact that the author has become a hot topic of conversation)

8. I've also been witness to a shift (that) I believe will be a game changer for the debate: more people coming out. —我也看到了我相信会改变这场辩论局面的形势变化:越来越多的人亮明自己的身份。

9. gay-rights movement—同性恋权利运动(美国同性恋权利运动始于20世纪60年代,经过半个多世纪取得了巨大进展。2015年美国最高法院裁定同性婚姻合法。)

10. The probusiness GOP waves a KEEP OUT flag at the Mexican border and a HELP WANTED sign 100 yards in, since so many industries depend on cheap labor. —支持企业的老大党在美

国与墨西哥的边境挥舞"禁止入境"大旗,而又在离边界100码境内打出招工广告,因为许许多多企业要依赖廉价劳力。(① GOP—the Republican political party in the U.S.; ② HELP WANTED sign—an advertisement for jobs that an employer is seeking to fill)

11. Mitt Romney—an American businessman, politician, the Republican Party's nominee for President of the U.S. in the 2012 election

12. But the real political flash point is the proposed Dream Act...—但是,真正引发政治冲突的导火线是已提交的"梦想法案"[① Dream Act—Dream 是"Development, Relief, and Education for Alien Minors"的缩略词。"梦想法案"旨在为16岁以前随父母非法赴美、在美连续生活5年、无案底的非法移民提供一条入籍途径。要取得资格,他们必须从美国高中毕业或获得GED(一般教育发展)考试证书,完成两年大学学业或至少服兵役两年,且满足年龄不得超过35岁、道德良好等要求,此类群体估计数量为210万。② flash point—a point at which violent action starts and cannot be controlled.]

13. Development of Homeland Security (DHS)—国土安全部(略作DHS)(该部成立于2002年,其职责是应对类似2001年所发生的恐怖组织发起的攻击,保卫美国本土安全。)

14. who flies under the radar —who has not been found (as an illegal immigrant)

15. I've also found myself drawn to the activists, driven to help tell their story. —我还发现自己被这些积极分子所吸引,情不自禁地帮忙介绍他们的情况。(① draw—to attract; ② drive—to force sb to act in a particular way)

16. an animal-feed maker—动物饲料加工厂

17. Romney had just fielded questions from a group of voters...—罗姆尼刚刚巧妙地回答了一群选民所提出的问题(field—to answer a difficult question cleverly and skillfully)

18. But it speaks to how unfamiliar most Americans are with how the immigration process works. —但这说明大部分美国人对于移民程序如何运作是何等无知。(speak to—to show or prove)

19. Taking the employment route to a green card means clearing a pretty high bar if you have an employer who's willing to hire you.—通过工作途径获取绿卡意味着在有人愿意雇佣你的前提下(或情况下)还得越过相当高的障碍。(① clear—to jump over; ② bar—a thing that stops sb from doing sth)

20. H1-B visas that are common in Silicon Valley — 硅谷常见的H1-B签证(H1-B—美国为引进国外专业技术人员所提供的一种工作签证)

21. the Defense of Marriage Act—《婚姻保护法案》(该法案1996年颁布,将"配偶"定义为异性之间的婚姻关系,规定同性婚姻在联邦层面不被认可。)

22. I would be subject to a 10-year bar before any application would be considered—在我的移民申请被审批之前我得接受10年禁止出境的惩罚(① subject to sth—to make sb suffer; ② bar—anything that blocks the way or prevents progress, here, referring to the law that forbids the author from leaving his homeland)

23. empathy quotient—共情商(a psychological self-report intended to measure how easily you pick up on other people's feelings and how strongly you are affected by other people's feelings)

24. HR4437——HR4437法案,要点包括强化边境管控,没有合法文件入境美国将以犯罪论处,雇主不得雇佣非法移民,违者罚款,加速将犯罪的非法移民递解出境等。
25. special-education——the education of children who have physical or learning problems
26. a third-rail issue——a controversial issue avoided by politicians
27. in limbo——in a state of uncertainty

IV. Language Features

新闻英语总体特色

英语新闻报刊多种多样:有纸质新闻报纸、纸质新闻杂志,还有电子报纸(electronic newspaper,简称 e-paper)和电子杂志(electronic magazine,简称 e-zine)。报纸可细分为日报、晨报、晚报、半周报(semiweekly)、周报(weekly)和双周报(biweekly),城市报(metropolitan newspaper)、郊区报(suburban newspaper)和乡村报(rural newspaper),大报(quality newspaper)和通俗小报(tabloid)。

新闻英语主要受以下五个因素制约:大众性、节俭性、趣味性、时新性和客观性。

报刊是大众传媒,写作必须符合广大读者水平,语言必须通俗易懂。

报业十分珍惜版面,要求新闻写作人员在有限的篇幅内提供尽可能多的信息。读者看报珍惜时间,希望在很短的时间得到所要的信息,这就迫使新闻写作人员养成文字简洁的风格。

西方新闻界一向注重趣味性,报刊又面临电视、广播、网络传媒的巨大挑战,要稳住报业市场就得加强趣味性,因而新闻报道必须写得生动有趣。

时新性是新闻价值之一。新闻报道在提供最新消息的同时也传播了相关的新词。此外,不少新闻写作人员为了增加文章的吸引力,在语言上刻意求新,因而新闻英语具有新颖活泼的特色。

客观性是纯新闻报道所遵循的准则,没有客观性报道就要丢掉可信性,也就会失去读者。客观性要求新闻报道文字准确具体,避免用情感词语和夸张手法。

初读美英报刊的人往往会遇到很多困难,主要是因为他们对西方社会文化与新闻文化和报刊英语特点了解不够。西方主要报刊渗透了垄断资本主义集团的意识形态和价值观念。这些意识形态和价值观念表现在语言的各个层面上。不知道这些表现形式就容易被误导。报刊写作具有自身规律和语言特点。不熟悉这些规律和特点就会形成理解障碍。譬如,新闻标题短小精悍,在句式和用词上都有相应的省略手段。又如,新闻报道为了节约篇幅,采用一系列浓缩手段、精练句式。较常见的有前置定语、名词定语、身份同位语前置、词性转化、借代、缩略词等。再如,为使语言生动、活泼,报刊常常使用比喻和成语活用手段。新闻刊物不仅是报道新闻的媒介,而且是"使用新词的庞大机器和杜撰新词的巨大工厂"。这些特点会给读者带来理解上的困难。为了帮助读者克服这些困难,本书把新闻英语特色分成若干细目,结合每篇课文,逐一进行介绍。

V. Analysis of Content

1. The author's essay in the *New York Times*, June, 2011, was intended to _____.
   A. gain his personal fame
   B. mobilize a come-out movement
   C. arouse the U.S. government's concern for undocumented young people
   D. seek relief from deception

2. The term "come out" in the article means _____.
   A. to appear
   B. to declare oneself openly to be a homosexual
   C. to make it known to the public about one's undocumented status
   D. to get published

3. It can be seen from the article that the Dream Act is focused on _____.
   A. elderly people seeking better care and treatment
   B. young undocumented immigrants educated in the U.S.
   C. poor people wishing to improve their life
   D. all undocumented immigrants seeking legal status

4. According to the author, the easiest way to become a U.S. citizen is to _____.
   A. be born in the U.S.
   B. marry a U.S. citizen
   C. have crucial job skills
   D. gain a green card

5. The author's view on the U.S. Immigration and Customs Enforcement is _____.
   A. objective   B. highly critical
   C. biased   D. unknown

VI. Questions on the Article

1. How did the author reveal his undocumented status?
2. Has the U.S. Immigration and Customs Enforcement taken any action against him? What kind of situation has he been living in?
3. Why is a consensus on solving the immigration dilemma so illusive once conversation about the issue starts?
4. What are the inescapable contradictions of the U.S. immigration debate?
5. What is the Dream Act?
6. Why does the author say ICE is its own contradiction?
7. What kind of document is the U.S. green card?
8. What are the two principal ways of obtaining a U.S. green card?

9. What role has technology played in the come-out movement?

10. Why has immigration become a third-rail issue in Washington D.C. ?

VII. Topics for Discussion

1. Is the Dream Act an effective solution to the problem faced by America's undocumented young people?

2. Should all the undocumented people be deported?

Lesson 2

Silent No More

A tragedy in Atlanta and America's long history of violence against Asians

By Cady Lang

It was heart-breaking and horrifying—but to many, it wasn't a surprise.
The news that eight people, six of them Asian American women, were killed at businesses in the Atlanta area on March 16 came after a year of intense anti-Asian racism in the U.S. On the platforms where news arrives first, and quickly attaches to feelings, emotions were already raw[1].

"This mass shooter was targeting Asian women and their businesses. This isn't an isolated incident. There have been 500+ hate crimes targeted at Asian people this year alone," social media specialist Mark Kim wrote on Twitter. "This Atlanta tragedy lies at an intersection of race, gender, class and the legacy of America's history of colonization and violence in Asia[2]," journalist Elise Hu said on the site. "I don't have the words. I'm just despondent. Protect Asian women, solidarity with sex workers, #StopAsianHate."

And as posts went viral, with comments affirming their calls for change, the news kept coming[3]. "Atlanta shooting suspect told investigators that killings of Asian women weren't racially motivated, police say," said a Washington Post news alert. A quote from a Daily Beast story described the alleged shooter—who was charged on March 17 with eight counts of murder—as the son of a pastor who was "very innocent seeming." Meanwhile the victims remained nameless. Later in the day, four were identified: Delaina Ashley Yaun, 33; Paul Andre Michels, 54; Xiaojie Yan, 49; and Daoyou Feng, 44. Additionally, Elcias R. Hernandez-Ortiz, 30, was injured in the attack. (Officials from the Atlanta police department are not naming the other victims until their families are notified.) By the time their names were made public, the suspect would already be accounted for by a member of the Cherokee County sheriff's office who, in a video that was widely circulated, said: "Yesterday was a really bad day for him and this is what he did."

In the dissonance was confirmation of what many Asian Americans already knew: the violence that has long targeted their community is rarely seen for what it is.[4] Since the start of the pandemic last spring, Asian Americans have faced racist violence at a much higher rate than in previous years. Stop AAPI Hate, a reporting database created at the beginning of the pandemic as a response to the increase in racial violence, received 3,795reports of anti-Asian discrimination between March 19, 2020, and Feb. 28, 2021; women reported hate incidents at 2.3 times the rate of men.

After his capture, the police noted that the shooter said he was seeking to address a "sexual addiction" and "was not racially motivated." But for Asian women, racism and misogyny are deeply intertwined. A 2018 report from the American Psychological Association outlined the ways in which Asian American women are exoticized and objectified in media and popular culture, depicted as "faceless, quiet and invisible, or as sexual objects."[5] The survey said these stereotypes "contribute to experiences of marginalization, invisibility and oppression" for Asian American women. On March 16, America saw that reality manifest in the most brutal way.

From the time the first wave of Chinese immigrants arrived as laborers in the U.S. in the 1850s, Asian Americans have always been subject to racist violence. As a source of cheap labor to build railroads, Asian immigrants came to be seen as threats to white jobs and scapegoated as dirty and disease-ridden. The "yellow peril" ultimately led to the Chinese Exclusion Act of 1882, the first time the U.S. had ever barred a specific ethnic group from the country[6].

The brutality runs through more than two centuries of U.S. history, from the incarceration camps of World War II, when over 100,000 Japanese Americans were rounded up and imprisoned because of xenophobic fears, to the 1982 murder of Vincent Chin, who died after being beaten by white men in a racially motivated attack in Detroit.

Yet while racial violence has been an undeniable part of the history of Asian Americans in the U.S., the pervasive "model minority"[7] myth has helped to obscure it. That false idea, constructed during the civil rights era to stymie racial-justice movements, suggests that Asian Americans are more successful than other ethnic minorities because of hard work, education and inherently law-abiding natures. Racial-justice educator Bianca Mabute-Louie emphasizes the connection between this damaging stereotype and the violence we've seen on the news—videos featuring Asian American elders shoved to the ground. "This contributes to erasing the very real interpersonal violence that we see happening in these videos, and that Asian Americans experience from the day-to-day, things that don't get reported and the things that don't get filmed," she says.

Because the myth suggests upward mobility, it creates a fallacy that Asian Americans don't experience struggle or racial discrimination[8]. In reality, the community is America's most economically divided: a 2018 study by the Pew Research Center found that Asian Americans experience the largest income-inequality gap as an ethnic and racial group in the U.S.

The current surge in anti-Asian hate crimes was exacerbated by the xenophobic rhetoric of former President Donald Trump, who has continued to refer to COVID-19 as "the China virus," blaming the country for the pandemic. Trump's choice of words followed a long American history of using diseases to justify anti-Asian xenophobia—one that has helped to shape perception of Asian Americans as "perpetual foreigners."[9] "There's a clear correlation between President Trump's incendiary comments, his insistence on using the term *Chinese virus*, and the subsequent hate speech spread on social media and the hate violence directed toward us," says Russell Jeung, a co-founder of Stop AAPI Hate and a professor of Asian American studies at San Francisco State University.

Anti-Asian racism also surged during the pandemic in Britain and Australia, with incidents of discrimination and xenophobia reported last summer by Human Rights Watch in Italy, Russia and Brazil. The news from Atlanta landed hard in Asian communities already feeling extraordinarily vulnerable[10]. "We're all feeling a collective trauma[11] at the moment," says Mai-Anh Peterson, co-founder of besea.n (Britain's East and South East Asian Network). "We know that this isn't just a problem for North America."

President Joe Biden has sought to undo the damage wrought by his predecessor. Shortly after taking office in January, he signed an Executive Order[12] denouncing anti-Asian discrimination. During a March 11 speech on the anniversary of the COVID-19 pandemic, he said that hate crimes against Asian Americans are "un-American" and that they "must stop."[13] Five days later, the gunman started shooting. The President was not alone. One day before the shootings, Dr. Michelle Au, a state senator of East Asian descent in Georgia, spoke out on the imminent danger faced by the Asian community during the pandemic. "Asian Americans are part of our country's plurality," she said. "Recognize that we need help, we need protection, and we need people in power to stand up for us against hate."

What form that protection takes has been part of a heated debate among Asian Americans, particularly in the wake of a national reckoning over systemic racism and police brutality after the killing of George Floyd in May[14]. During a recent surge in physical violence ahead of Lunar New Year, actors Daniel Dae Kim and Daniel Wu shared on Twitter a video of a 91-year-old man being pushed down in Oakland, Calif., Chinatown. They offered a $25,000 reward to anyone who could provide information about the attacker, who had also pushed down a 60-year-old man as well as a 55-year-old woman, who was left unconscious from the attack.

Kim's tweet brought up mixed feelings within the AAPI community: his attempt to raise awareness tapped into a longtime grievance of many Asian Americans—that violence against them has often been downplayed or ignored. At the same time, the offer of a reward—particularly in a situation where the alleged attacker was a Black man—underscored the difficulty of tackling anti-Asian violence without relying on law-enforcement institutions that have historically targeted Black and brown communities.[14] (The Oakland police charged 28-year-old Yahya Muslim with assault, battery and elder abuse.) "This looks a lot like a bounty on a Black person funded by Asian American celebrities," wrote writer and consultant Kim Tran. "I have major, major doubts."

Rather than turning to additional policing, community leaders have stressed the importance of grassroots organizing at this time, as well as the need for cross-community solidarity. "We know that this is an issue that affects all our communities, and we have to break the cycle of violence," says Jeung, the Stop AAPI Hate co-founder.

Additional policing doesn't pose a threat just to Black and brown communities; people of Asian descent have also suffered disproportionately at the hands of law enforcement. In the aftermath of the March 16 killings, many were reminded of the 2017 death of Yang Song, a massage-parlor worker who fell to her death while trying to escape a police raid in Flushing, Queens: "Don't tell me increased police presence will save us," tweeted writer Mia Sato. For activists, stories like Song's are a reminder of the need to build solidarity across racial, economic and social lines. "Asians with power and visibility should be appalled that white men are targeting our most vulnerable groups—poor, immigrant women," writer and activist Roslyn Talusan said on Twitter. "Protecting and advocating for Asian sex workers should be the founding pillars of any movement for racial justice in Asian communities."

Details of the Atlanta crimes are still being gathered. But at ground level, the impact was immediate[16]. "We're closed today because everybody is afraid," Grace Wang, manager of a local Atlanta spa, says. "All employees are worried to come to work, and customers too and we decided to close until we find out what happened."

There are no quick solutions to racial violence. What Biden calls "un-American" is, after all, deeply rooted in American history. Ending anti-Asian racism in the U.S. means confronting centuries of discrimination, violence and oppression, and recognizing how it manifests in the present day.[15] As Au noted in her statements this week, "This is a new chapter in a very old story." In order to write a new story, we have to acknowledge the ugly past that brought us here.

From *TIME*, March 29, 2021

I. New Words

addiction	[əˈdikʃən]	n.	瘾
despondent	[diˈspɔndənt]	adj.	sad, without much hope
exacerbate	[igˈzæsəbeit]	v.	to make sth worse
exoticize	[igˈzɔtiˌsaiz]	v.	to make excitingly different
fallacy	[ˈfæləsi]	n.	谬论
motivate	[ˈməutiveit]	v.	to stir to action or feeling
misogyny	[maiˈsɔdʒini]	n.	hatred of women
pandemic	[pænˈdemik]	n.	全国[世界]性的流行病
pillar	[ˈpilə]	n.	支柱
racism	[ˈreisizəm]	n.	种族歧视
ridden	[ˈridn]	adj.	penetrated, full
solidarity	[ˌsɔliˈdæriti]	n.	团结一致
sheriff	[ˈʃerif]	n.	县治安官
scapegoat	[ˈskeipgəut]	v.	使成为……的替罪羊
stymie	[ˈstaimi]	v.	妨碍;阻挠
trauma	[ˈtrɔːmə]	n.	damage to the mind caused by a terrible experience
wrought	[rɔːt]	v.	(used only in the past tense) caused sth to happen
xenophobic	[ˌzenəˈfəubiə]	adj.	恐惧或憎恶外国人的;恐外的

II. Background Information

美国社会的种族歧视

美国少数族裔长期遭受普遍性、系统性歧视,这已成为美国社会根深蒂固的顽疾。包括非洲裔、原住民、拉丁裔、亚裔等在内的各少数族裔深受种族歧视之害。

美国的发展史实际上也是一部"印第安人的血泪史"。早期,白人殖民者通过武力

第一单元 社会群体

镇压将印第安人驱赶至密西西比河以西的荒芜地区后,又通过保留地政策进一步压缩印第安人生存空间。如今,印第安人依然生活在美国社会的最底层。2019年,约25%的印第安人生活在贫困中,为全美平均水平的2.5倍。在印第安人保留地(Indian reservations),这一比例甚至更高。许多低收入的印第安人社区遭受核废料有毒环境影响,罹患癌症和心脏病比率很高。很多印第安人生活在危险废物处置场附近,婴儿出生缺陷率很高。同时,印第安人文化和语言也遭到吞噬。目前在美国使用的115种原住民语言中,只有两种处于健康状态,有34种处于濒危状态,79种预计将在一代人的时间里消失。

黑人来到美洲大陆之日便被烙上了奴隶的身份。饱受凌辱的他们不断抗争,打破了奴隶制枷锁,迫使政府废除种族隔离制度,最终获得公民权利。但是,非洲裔至今依然深受种族歧视之苦。目前,黑人生活在贫困线以下的比例是白人的两倍多。超过1/5的黑人家庭面临食物匮乏,这一比例超过白人家庭3倍多;50年前黑人失业率为6.7%,2018年为7.5%。非洲裔在就业中也遭到歧视。报酬较好的职业黑人所占比例大大低于白人:企业管理白人与黑人比例为10∶1;计算机领域8∶1;法律领域12∶1。美国司法领域也存在针对非洲裔的系统性歧视。虽然非洲裔人口仅占人口总数的13%,却占监狱囚犯总数的1/3。

同非洲裔、原住民一样,美国拉美裔在教育、就业和收入等方面全方位落后于白人,长期深陷贫困的代际循环。占美国总人口19%的拉美裔只拥有2%的财富。据美国劳工局统计,拉美裔的失业率通常比白人高出40%,美国4500万贫困人口中28.1%是拉美裔,1450万贫困儿童中37%为拉美裔。皮尤中心研究发现,57%的拉美裔美国人表示自己的肤色会影响日常生活。

美国对亚裔的歧视由来已久。19世纪,美国出台《排华法案》,使当时美国国内歧视侮辱华人合法化,令地方政府和民众对华人的歧视和排斥更加肆无忌惮。如今,亚裔在美国被冠以"模范少数种族"(model minority)的称号。这一"神话"(myth)无视亚裔美国人收入差距在美国各种族中最为悬殊的严酷现实,掩盖了许多中下层亚裔人生活极为贫困的阴暗面。同时,这也导致种族矛盾激化,使不明真相的其他少数种族人强烈嫉恨。特朗普执政期间,美国政府出台臭名昭著的"中国行动计划",给针对亚裔特别是华裔的种族歧视行为火上浇油。同时,新冠疫情在美国爆发后,特朗普借病毒污名化中国,将其称为"中国病毒",导致针对亚裔的歧视行为屡见不鲜。"停止对亚裔仇恨组织"发布《2020—2021国家安全报告》,统计了2020年3月—2021年6月发生的9081件针对亚裔美国人的歧视和骚扰事件。根据该报告,针对亚裔美国人的歧视形式包括口头骚扰、身体攻击、线上攻击等,其中口头骚扰占比最高,64%的申报人表示受到了诸如"滚回中国""病毒中国人"等具有侮辱性的言辞对待;超过13%的人遭到了不同程度的身体攻击,如当街被扔玻璃瓶、在公共场合被恶意撞击等。2021年,美国各地仇恨亚裔犯罪案比2020年增加了339%。美国南加州大学新闻学院上周的最新民调显示,由于受到反亚裔暴力活动和反华政治言论影响,71%的亚裔受访者感到孤立和备受歧视。有美国媒体报道,美国警方在处理涉亚裔等少数族裔仇恨犯罪案件中,习惯性偏袒施暴者。

当今美国少数族裔面临的种族歧视及暴行是系统性的国家悲剧,反映了美国针对少数族裔的系统性种族歧视。深嵌于美国建国理念中的民粹主义和白人至上主义是目前导致美国少数族裔遭受歧视的根本原因。

III. Notes to the Text

1. ...emotions were already raw. ——(人们)情绪已经激奋。(raw — not controlled)

2. This Atlanta tragedy lies at an intersection of race, gender, class and the legacy of America's history of colonization and violence in Asia. ——亚特兰大的这起悲剧事件同时体现了种族、性别、阶级以及美国对亚洲殖民和暴力的历史影响。

3. And as posts went viral, with comments affirming their calls for change, the news kept coming. ——随着伴有支持其变革呼吁评论的帖子疯传,新闻不断传来。(①go viral — to quickly and widely circulate on the Internet, as of a video, picture, or post;②affirm — to state firmly and publicly that you support sth. strongly)

4. In the dissonance was confirmation of what many Asian Americans already knew: the violence that has long targeted their community is rarely seen for what it is. ——观点不同的言论证实了许多亚裔美国人本已知道的事实:长期以来针对他们社区的暴力行为很少被人真正了解。(dissonance — lack of agreement)

5. A 2018 report from the American Psychological Association outlined the ways in which Asian American women are exoticized and objectified in media and popular culture, depicted as "faceless, quiet and invisible, or as sexual objects." ——美国心理学会2018年的一份报告概述了亚裔美国妇女是如何在媒体和流行文化中被异化和物化的,她们被描绘成"缺乏个性、性格文静、不爱露面,或者被描述为性对象"。(faceless — without individuality)

6. The "yellow peril" ultimately led to the Chinese Exclusion Act of 1882, the first time the U.S. had ever barred a specific ethnic group from the country. ——"黄祸论"最终导致1882年《排华法案》的颁布,这是美国第一次禁止某一特定民族进入美国。(① yellow peril — the alleged danger posed by Asian peoples to the supremacy of Whites or Western interests; ② Chinese Exclusion Act — U.S. federal law enacted in 1882 that suspended immigration of Chinese laborers)

7. model minority ——模范少数民族(Asian Americans are commonly seen as the "model minority." This stems from stereotypes surrounding the Asian population and it perpetuates a narrative that Asian Americans are more likely to achieve the American dream and have "made it.")

8. Because the myth suggests upward mobility, it creates a fallacy that Asian Americans don't experience struggle or racial discrimination. ——因为这个神话暗示了(地位)向上流动性,故而产生了一种谬论,即亚裔美国人没有经历奋斗或种族歧视。(upward mobility — the

capacity or facility for rising to a higher social or economic position)

9. Trump's choice of words followed a long American history of using diseases to justify anti-Asian xenophobia—one that has helped to shape perception of Asian Americans as "perpetual foreigners." —— 特朗普的措辞与美国长期以来以疾病为由为反亚裔仇外情绪辩护的历史一脉相承——这种仇外情绪有助于形成人们把亚裔美国人当作"永久外国人"的看法。

10. The news from Atlanta landed hard in Asian communities already feeling extraordinarily vulnerable. —— 来自亚特兰大的消息使得本已感到特别脆弱的亚裔社区遭受重创。

11. Executive Order —— 行政命令（An executive order is a signed, written, and published directive from the President of the United States that manages operations of the federal government.）

12. During a March 11 speech on the anniversary of the COVID-19 pandemic, he said that hate crimes against Asian Americans are "un-American" and that they "must stop." —— 3月11日，拜登在新冠疫情一周年纪念日的演讲中说，针对亚裔美国人的仇恨犯罪"不符合美国特性"，"必须停止"。（① hate crime —— a crime committed against people only because they belong to a particular race, religion etc.; ② un-American —— not characteristic of or consistent with American customs, principles, or traditions）

13. What form that protection takes has been part of a heated debate among Asian Americans, particularly in the wake of a national reckoning over systemic racism and police brutality after the killing of George Floyd in May. —— 采取何种保护形式一直是亚裔美国人热议的话题，特别是在去年5月份乔治·弗洛伊德被杀，全国对系统性种族主义和警察暴行刚进行清算之后。（① in the wake of —— right after; ② systemic racism —— racism that is perpetuated by the systems in place; ③ George Floyd —— 非裔美国人，2020年5月遭美国警察过度暴力致死）

14. At the same time, the offer of a reward—particularly in a situation where the alleged attacker was a Black man—underscored the difficulty of tackling anti-Asian violence without relying on law-enforcement institutions that have historically targeted Black and brown communities. —— 同时，悬赏——特别是在嫌疑犯是一名黑人的情况下——突显了在不依靠历来针对黑人和拉美裔社区的执法机构的情况下解决反亚裔暴力问题的困难。（brown community —— Latino community）

15. Ending anti-Asian racism in the U.S. means confronting centuries of discrimination, violence and oppression, and recognizing how it manifests in the present day. —— 终结美国反亚裔种族主义意味着正视几个世纪以来的歧视、暴力和压迫，并认识到它在当今美国社会的表现形式。（manifest —— show itself/themselves; appear）

IV. Language Features

词语文化内涵

"sex worker"(性工作者)和"sex industry"(性产业)是美国官方用于掩盖社会问题、粉饰社会阴暗面而使用的"委婉语"。

语言与文化存在血肉相连的关系。语言是文化的载体,语言中渗透着文化。因此,我们在学习一门外语时,必须熟悉这门语言的相关文化。

美英报刊题材广泛,内容丰富,涉及政治、经济、军事、宗教习俗、社会风尚、价值观念、家庭观念、人际关系和生活方式等方面,各个方面的文化差异必然影响对外刊的理解。

由于文化差异,英语、汉语中有不少词语虽然概念意义相同,但却具有不同的关联意义,富有不同感情色彩,不了解这些关联意义和感情色彩就会产生误解。

譬如:英语中,peasant, politics, propaganda 这三个词常常带有贬义,而汉语中的对应词却毫无贬义。

此外,英语中有些词含有丰富的关联意义,cowboy 所包含的意思绝非词典中注释的"放牛娃"或"牛仔"所能准确表达的,它还具有以下关联意义:吃苦耐劳、酷爱自由、敢于冒险。再如 sin taxes 并非指对犯罪者征税,而是特指(对烟、酒、赌博所征收的)罪孽税。

外刊中这类情况甚多,大量词语看上去与某些汉语词相似,但实际上是"貌合神离"。不了解这些词语的真正内涵,根据结构望文生义就会产生误解。

例:political campaign≠政治运动,而是竞选运动
　　senior citizens≠地位高的公民,而是老年公民
　　street-walker≠街道散步的人,而是街头拉客的妓女
　　do-gooder≠做好事的人,而是不现实的慈善家
　　baby-kisser≠亲吻孩子的人,而是善于笼络人心的政客
　　easy meat≠可嚼的肉,而是容易上当受骗的人
　　open housing≠开放式的住房,而是住房方面取消种族隔离
　　call-girl≠传呼姑娘,而是电话应召女郎/妓女
　　red power≠红色(革命)权力,而是印第安人政治权力
　　black-hat≠黑帽子,而是歹徒、坏人
　　whistle-blower≠吹哨者,而是告密者
　　busybody≠大忙人,而是爱管闲事的人
　　junk food≠垃圾箱的食品,而是营养价值低、高热量的食品
　　hard money≠硬币,而是合法政治选金
　　gay marriage≠幸福的婚姻,而是同性婚姻
　　rest room≠休息室,而是公共厕所

V. Analysis of Content

1. According to the article, the most vulnerable group of Asian Americans is _____.
   A. poor immigrant women
   B. poor elderly people
   C. people unable to speak English
   D. people without jobs
2. Which of the following statements about Asian Americans is NOT true?
   A. Asian Americans have suffered disproportionately at the hands of law enforcement.
   B. Asian Americans have always been subject to racist violence.
   C. Asian Americans are more successful than other ethnic minorities because of hard work, education and law-abiding nature.
   D. Asian Americans knew that the violence that has long targeted their community is rarely seen for what it is.
3. Which of the following races in the U.S. experience the largest income-inequality gap?
   A. White people   B. Hispanics
   C. Afro-Americans   D. Asian Americans
4. Violence against Asian Americans has often been _____.
   A. downplayed   B. underscored
   C. put in priority   D. stopped by the police
5. It is implied in the last paragraph that _____.
   A. the Atlanta crimes did not impact Asian Americans' daily life
   B. anti-Asian racism is a new issue in the American society
   C. ending racial violence in America will take a long time
   D. anti-Asian racism will never end

VI. Questions on the Article

1. What occurred in the Atlanta area on March 16, 2021?
2. According to Mark Kim, what was the nature of the crime?
3. What was the image of Asian American women produced by media and popular culture? What is the effect of the stereotypes on Asian American women?
4. What ultimately led to the Chinese Exclusion Act of 1882?
5. What effects does the "model minority" myth have on Asian Americans? What accounts for those effects?
6. What remarks has former President Donald Trump made about Covid-19? What effects have his remarks produced?
7. What measure did Joe Biden take in the hope of reducing anti-Asian racism?

8. Do Asian Americans count on additional policing for protection? Why or why not?

9. What does the *ugly past* refer to in the last sentence?

VII. Topics for Discussion

1. What measures should be taken to eliminate anti-Asian racism?
2. Is it possible for the United States to put an end to racism?

Lesson 3

The End of Men

(Abridged)

By Hanna Rosin

In the 1970s the biologist Ronald Ericsson came up with a way to separate sperm carrying the male-producing Y chromosome from those carrying the X[1]. He sent the two kinds of sperm swimming down a glass tube through ever-thicker albumin barriers. The sperm with the X chromosome had a larger head and a longer tail, and so, he figured, they would get bogged down in the viscous liquid. The sperm with the Y chromosome were leaner and faster and could swim down to the bottom of the tube more efficiently. Ericsson had grown up on a ranch in South Dakota, where he'd developed an Old West, cowboy swagger[2].

In the late 1970s, Ericsson leased the method to clinics around the U.S., calling it the first scientifically proven method for choosing the sex of a child. Instead of a lab coat, he wore cowboy boots and a cowboy hat. In 1979, he loaned out his ranch as the backdrop for the iconic "Marlboro Country" ads[3] because he believed in the campaign's central image—"a guy riding on his horse along the river, no bureaucrats, no lawyers," he recalled when I spoke to him this spring. "He's the boss."

Feminists of the era did not take kindly to Ericsson and his Marlboro Man veneer. To them, the lab cowboy and his sperminator portended a dystopia of mass-produced boys.[4] "You have to be concerned about the future of all women," Roberta Steinbacher, a nun-turned-social-psychologist, said in a 1984 *People*[5] profile of Ericsson. "There's no question that there exists a universal preference for sons." Steinbacher went on to complain about women becoming locked in as "second-class citizens" while men continued to dominate positions of control and influence. "I think women have to ask themselves, 'Where does this stop?'" she said. "A lot of us wouldn't be here right now if these practices had been in effect years ago."

Ericsson, now 74, laughed when I read him these quotes from his old antagonist. Seldom has it been so easy to prove a dire prediction wrong. In the '90s, when Ericsson looked into the numbers for the two dozen or so clinics that use his process, he discovered, to his surprise, that couples were requesting more girls than boys, a gap that has persisted, even though Ericsson advertises the method as more effective for producing boys. In some clinics, Ericsson has said, the ratio is now as high as 2 to 1. Polling data on American sex preference is sparse, and does not show a clear preference for girls. But the picture from the doctor's office unambiguously does. A newer method for sperm selection, called MicroSort, is currently completing Food and Drug Administration clinical trials.[6] The girl requests for that method run at about 75 percent.

Even more unsettling for Ericsson, it has become clear that in choosing the sex of the next generation, *he* is no longer the boss. "It's the women who are driving all the decisions," he says—a change the MicroSort spokespeople I met with also mentioned. At first, Ericsson says, women who called his clinics would apologize and shyly explain that they already had two boys. "Now they just call and [say] outright, 'I want a girl.' These mothers look at their lives and think their daughters will have a bright future their mother and grandmother didn't have, brighter than their sons, even, so why wouldn't you choose a girl?"

Why wouldn't you choose a girl? That such a statement should be so casually uttered by an old cowboy like Ericsson—or by anyone, for that matter—is monumental. For nearly as long as civilization has existed, patriarchy—enforced through the rights of the firstborn son—has been the organizing principle, with few exceptions. Men in ancient Greece tied off their left testicle in an effort to produce male heirs; women have killed themselves (or been killed) for failing to bear sons. In her iconic 1949 book, *The Second Sex*[7], the French feminist Simone de Beauvoir suggested that women so detested their own "feminine condition" that they regarded their newborn daughters with irritation and disgust. Now the centuries-old preference for sons is eroding—or even reversing. "Women of our generation want daughters precisely because we like who we are," breezes one woman in *Cookie* magazine. Even Ericsson, the stubborn old goat[8], can sigh and mark the passing of an era. "Did male dominance exist? Of course it existed. But it seems to be gone now. And the era of the firstborn son is totally gone."

Ericsson's extended family is as good an illustration of the rapidly shifting landscape as any other. His 26-year-old granddaughter—"tall, slender, brighter than hell, with a take-no-prisoners personality"—is a biochemist and works on genetic sequencing.[9] His niece studied civil engineering at the University of Southern California. His grandsons, he says, are bright and handsome, but in school "their eyes glaze over. I have to tell 'em: 'Just don't screw up and crash your pickup truck and get some girl pregnant and ruin your life.'" Recently Ericsson joked with the old boys[10] at his elementary-school reunion that he was going to have a sex-change operation. "Women live longer than men. They do better in this economy. More of 'em graduate from college. They go into space and do everything men do, and sometimes they do it a whole lot better. I mean, hell, get out of the way—these females are going to leave us males in the dust."

Man has been the dominant sex since, well, the dawn of mankind. But for the first time in human history, that is changing—and with shocking speed. Cultural and economic changes always reinforce each other. And the global economy is evolving in a way that is eroding the historical preference for male children, worldwide. Over several centuries, South Korea, for instance, constructed one of the most rigid patriarchal societies in the world. Many wives who failed to produce male heirs were abused and treated as domestic servants; some families prayed to spirits to kill off girl children. Then, in the 1970s and '80s, the government embraced an industrial revolution and encouraged women to enter the labor force. Women moved to the city and went to college. They advanced rapidly, from industrial jobs to clerical jobs to professional work. The traditional order began to crumble soon after. In 1990, the country's laws were revised so that women could keep custody of their children after a divorce and inherit property. In 2005, the court ruled that women could register children under their own names. As recently as 1985, about half of all women in a national survey said they "must have a son." That percentage fell slowly until 1991 and then plummeted to just over 15 percent by 2003. Male preference in South Korea "is over," says Monica Das Gupta, a demographer and Asia expert at the World Bank[11]. "It happened so fast. It's hard to believe it, but it is." The same shift is now beginning in other rapidly industrializing countries such as India and China.

Up to a point, the reasons behind this shift are obvious. As thinking and communicating have come to eclipse physical strength and stamina as the keys to economic success, those societies that take advantage of the talents of all the adults, not just half of them, have pulled away from the rest.[12] And because geopolitics and global culture are, ultimately, Darwinian, other societies either follow suit or end up marginalized. In 2006, the Organization for Economic Cooperation and Development devised the Gender, Institutions and Development Database[13], which measures the economic and political power of women in 162 countries. With few exceptions, the greater the power of women, the greater the country's economic success.

In feminist circles, these social, political, and economic changes are always cast as a slow, arduous form of catch-up in a continuing struggle for female equality. But in the U.S., the world's most advanced economy, something much more remarkable seems to be happening. American parents are beginning to choose to have girls over boys. As they imagine the pride of watching a child grow and develop and succeed as an adult, it is more often a girl that they see in their mind's eye.

What if the modern, postindustrial economy is simply more congenial to women than to men? For a long time, evolutionary psychologists have claimed that we are all imprinted with adaptive imperatives from a distant past: men are faster and stronger and hardwired to fight for scarce resources, and that shows up now as a drive to win on Wall Street; women are programmed to find good providers and to care for their offspring, and that is manifested in more nurturing and more flexible behavior[14], ordaining them to domesticity. This kind of thinking frames our sense of the natural order. But what if men and women were fulfilling not biological imperatives but social roles, based on what was more efficient throughout a long era of human history? What if that era has now come to an end? More to the point, what if the economics of the new era are better suited to women?

Once you open your eyes to this possibility, the evidence is all around you. It can be found, most immediately, in the wreckage of the Great Recession[15], in which three-quarters of the 8 million jobs lost were lost by men. The worst-hit industries were overwhelmingly male and deeply identified with macho: construction, manufacturing, high finance.[16] Some of these jobs will come back, but the overall pattern of dislocation is neither temporary nor random. The recession merely revealed—and accelerated—a profound economic shift that has been going on for at least 30 years, and in some respects even longer.

Earlier this year, for the first time in American history, the balance of the workforce tipped toward women, who now hold a majority of the nation's jobs. The working class, which has long defined our notions of masculinity, is slowly turning into a matriarchy, with men increasingly absent from the home and women making all the decisions. Women dominate today's colleges and professional schools—for every two men who will receive a B.A. this year, three women will do the same. Of the 15 job categories projected to grow the most in the next decade in the U.S., all but two are occupied primarily by women. Indeed, the U.S. economy is in some ways becoming a kind of traveling sisterhood[17]: upper-class women leave home and enter the workforce, creating domestic jobs for other women to fill.

The postindustrial economy is indifferent to men's size and strength. The attributes that are most valuable today—social intelligence, open communication, the ability to sit still and focus—are, at a minimum, not predominantly male. In fact, the opposite may be true. Women in poor parts of India are learning English faster than men to meet the demands of new global call centers. Women own more than 40 percent of private businesses in China, where a red Ferrari is the new status symbol for female entrepreneurs. Last year, Iceland elected Prime Minister Johanna Sigurdardottir, the world's first openly lesbian head of state, who campaigned explicitly against the male elite she claimed had destroyed the nation's banking system.

Yes, the U.S. still has a wage gap, one that can be convincingly explained—at least in part—by discrimination. Yes, women still do most of the child care. And yes, the upper reaches of society are still dominated by men. But given the power of the forces pushing at the economy, this setup feels like the last gasp of a dying age rather than the permanent establishment.[18] Dozens of college women I interviewed for this story assumed that they very well might be the ones working while their husbands stayed at home, either looking for work or minding the children. Guys, one senior remarked to me, "are the new ball and chain[19]." It may be happening slowly and unevenly, but it's unmistakably happening: in the long view, the modern economy is becoming a place where women hold the cards.

In his final book, *The Bachelors' Ball*[20], published in 2007, the sociologist Pierre Bourdieu describes the changing gender dynamics of Béarn, the region in southwestern France where he grew up. The eldest sons once held the privileges of patrimonial loyalty and filial inheritance in Béarn. But over the decades, changing economic forces turned those privileges into curses. Although the land no longer produced the impressive income it once had, the men felt obligated to tend it. Meanwhile, modern women shunned farm life, lured away by jobs and adventure in the city. They occasionally returned for the traditional balls, but the men who awaited them had lost their prestige and become unmarriageable. This is the image that keeps recurring to me, one that Bourdieu describes in his book: at the bachelors' ball, the men, self-conscious about their diminished status, stand stiffly, their hands by their sides, as the women twirl away.

The role reversal that's under way between American men and women shows up most obviously and painfully in the working class. In recent years, male support groups have sprung up throughout the Rust Belt[21] and in other places where the postindustrial economy has turned traditional family roles upside down. Some groups help men cope with unemployment, and others help them reconnect with their alienated families. Mustafaa El-Scari, a teacher and social worker, leads some of these groups in Kansas City. El-Scari has studied the sociology of men and boys set adrift, and he considers it his special gift to get them to open up and reflect on their new condition.

The day I visited one of his classes, earlier this year, he was facing a particularly resistant crowd.

None of the 30 or so men sitting in a classroom at a downtown Kansas City school have come for voluntary adult enrichment. Having failed to pay their child support, they were given the choice by a judge to go to jail or attend a weekly class on fathering, which to them seemed the better deal. This week's lesson, from a workbook called *Quenching the Father Thirst*, was supposed to involve writing a letter to a hypothetical estranged 14-year-old daughter named Crystal, whose father left her when she was a baby. But El-Scari has his own idea about how to get through to this barely awake, skeptical crew, and letters to Crystal have nothing to do with it.

Like them, he explains, he grew up watching Bill Cosby[22] living behind his metaphorical "white picket fence"—one man, one woman, and a bunch of happy kids. "Well, that check bounced a long time ago[23]," he says. "Let's see," he continues, reading from a worksheet. What are the four kinds of paternal authority? Moral, emotional, social, and physical. "But you ain't none of those in that house. All you are is a paycheck, and now you ain't even that. And if you try to exercise your authority, she'll call 911[24]. How does that make you feel? You're supposed to be the authority, and she says, 'Get out of the house, bitch.' She's calling you 'bitch'!"

From *The Atlantic*, July/August, 2010

I. New Words

abuse	[əˈbju:z]	v.	to treat sb in a cruel or immoral way
albumin	[ˈælbjumin]	n.	清蛋白,白蛋白
antagonist	[ænˈtæɡənist]	n.	a person who strongly opposes sb/sth
arduous	[ˈɑ:djuəs]	adj.	needing hard and continuous effort
attribute	[ˈætribju:t]	n.	a quality or feature of sb/sth
biochemist	[baiəuˈkemist]	n.	生物化学家
backdrop	[ˈbækdrɔp]	n.	background
bog	[bɔg]	v.	to prevent sb from making progress in an activity
chromosome	[ˈkrəuməsəum]	n.	[生]染色体
congenial	[kənˈdʒi:niəl]	adj.	agreeable; suitable
crumble	[ˈkrʌmbl]	v.	to break into small pieces; to become ruined
Darwinian	[dɑ:ˈwiniən]	adj.	进化论的;优胜劣汰的
dire	[ˈdaiə]	adj.	very serious; very hard
dislocation	[disləˈkeiʃən]	n.	脱位
enrichment	[inˈritʃmənt]	n.	the act of improving quality by adding sth
explicitly	[ikˈsplisitli]	adv.	clearly and openly
Ferrari	[fəˈrɑ:ri]	n.	法拉利(意大利著名跑车品牌)
filial	[ˈfiliəl]	adj.	of a son or daughter
flail	[fleil]	v.	to move around without control

glaze	[gleiz]	v.	to become dull and lifeless
geopolitics	[ˌdʒiːəuˈpɒlitiks]	n.	地缘政治学
heir	[ɛə]	n.	继承人
lesbian	[ˈlezbiən]	adj.	女性同性恋的
Liberia	[laiˈbiəriə]	n.	利比里亚（西非国家）
masculinity	[ˌmæskjuˈliniti]	n.	男性
maternal	[məˈtəːnəl]	adj.	of, like a mother
monumental	[ˌmɔnjuˈmentl]	adj.	very important and having a great influence
nun	[nʌn]	n.	修女
nurture	[ˈnəːtʃə]	v.	to give care and food to
obligate	[ˈɔbligeit]	v.	使感觉负有责任/义务
outright	[ˈautrait]	adv.	directly and openly
patriarchy	[ˈpeitriɑːki]	n.	父权制
plummet	[ˈplʌmit]	v.	to fall steeply or suddenly
reverse	[riˈvəːs]	v.	使反向，使倒转
screw	[skruː]	v.	~ up to do sth badly or spoil sth
shun	[ʃʌn]	v.	to avoid sb/sth
sperm	[spəːm]	n.	精液
unsettling	[ʌnˈsetliŋ]	adj.	making you feel upset, nervous or worried
veneer	[vəˈniə]	n.	an outer appearance of a particular quality hiding the true nature of sb
viscous	[ˈviskəs]	adj.	(of a liquid) thick and sticky
worksheet	[ˈwəːkʃiːt]	n.	工作单；备忘录

II. Background Information

美国妇女地位

美国妇女原先社会地位卑微，其角色仅限于生儿育女、操持家务、干农活。

19世纪上半叶的废奴运动促使美国妇女对自己不公平境遇展开思索，并逐步把她们推上了女权运动的道路。女权运动（Women's Rights Movement）是反对性别歧视，使女性获得应有的社会地位和权利，实现两性权利完全平等的运动。美国妇女曾开展两次规模较大的女权运动：第一次是从19世纪中叶延续到20世纪20年代，主要目的是争取选举权；第二次起始于20世纪60年代，旨在获得各个方面的权益。经过长期不懈的努力，美国妇女在各方面的地位有了很大提高。

在政治方面，美国妇女获得了选举权和参政权。不少妇女获得了高层领导地位，有的成为市长、州长、国会议员甚至副总统、议长。

在经济方面,妇女发挥的作用越来越大。2016年,美国女性占美国劳工总数的比例是46.8%。

在教育方面,美国女性普遍享有受教育的权利,并且取得了十分惊人的成绩。近几十年,美国女性接受高等教育人数持续增长。原先大学男生比例一直高于女生。可是1979年情况出现了大逆转:女生数量首次超过男生。自此以后,美国大学女生数量优势越来越明显,2021年女生所占比例高达59%。除此之外,女生获得学士、硕士和博士学位的人数也出现同样趋势。1990年,女生获得学士学位人数为56万,男生只有49万。2021年,获得学士学位、硕士学位和博士学位的女生所占比例分别为57%、61%、55%。

教育水平的提高促使女性素质的提高,就业竞争力的增强,也有助于女性社会地位的提高和家庭模式的重塑。目前,专职母亲人数正在稳步下降,家庭主夫(househusbands)人数呈现上升趋势。有的社会学家甚至断言,美国传统的"男主外女主内"(breadwinning-daddy-and-homemaking-mommy)模式即将结束。

虽然美国妇女地位近几十年有了明显提高,但与许多国家相比还依然存在不小的差距。联合国人权专家在2016年1月3日所发布的调查报告中说,自由女神是女性和自由的象征。然而美国妇女并没有获得其作为公民的正当地位。妇女在公共和政治领域的任职率、经济和社会权利及其健康和安全保护的国际标准方面处于落后地位。美国是尚未批准《消除对妇女一切形式歧视公约》的七国之一。

统观美国几十年的就业状况,可以看出三大问题。其一是同工不同酬。干同样工作的妇女一般只赚男性80%的工资。歧视严重的行业差距更大,如理财顾问,女性平均工资只有男性的61.3%,女性医生的平均薪金是男性的62.2%。其二是传统上男性占优势的STEM(科学、技术、工程和数学)领域女性比例依然较低,2019年女性在计算机和数学领域所占比例是27%。其三是女性职位晋升存在隐形障碍(glass ceilings)。2021年统计数据显示,美国财富500强企业中CEO的女性比例仅是8.1%,企业高管中女性比例为15.2%。

在维护妇女地位和权益方面,美国还存在不少问题。在家中,妇女要干很多的家务。据统计,美国男性只有38%会分担部分家务。此外,她们常常遭受丈夫或伴侣的家暴,平均每三名妇女中就有一人是家暴受害者。在职场,她们经常遭到性骚扰。美国平等就业委员会的一项报告显示:60%的女性在工作中遭到性骚扰。许多受害者担心失业或被报复,只能保持沉默,苦苦忍受。

美国是"经合组织"国家中唯一在联邦层面不保证为职工提供带薪产假的国家。此外,美国妇女的堕胎自主权得不到保证。2022年,最高法院推翻了原先维护女性堕胎自主权的决议,从而剥夺了女性选择堕胎的自由。

综上所述,美国妇女地位与理想境界还有较大距离,美国社会为消除男性主宰局面还要做出许多努力。

III. Notes to the Text

1. separate sperm carrying the male-producing Y chromosome from those carrying the X—把带有生育男性Y染色体精子和带有X染色体精子分开（1905年美国细胞学家威尔逊等人发现女性的性染色体为XX，男性的性染色体为XY。精子有两种：一种带有X染色体，另一种带有Y染色体。受精时，如果带有X染色体精子与卵结合，则成为XX核型的受精卵，它将发育成为女性；如果带有Y染色体精子与卵结合，则成为XY核型的受精卵，它将发育成为男性。）

2. an Old West, cowboy swagger—老西部牛仔趾高气扬的步姿（①Old West—also Wild West, which centers on a nomadic cowboy or gunfighter who rides a horse; ②swagger—walking with a swinging movement in a way that shows too much self-confidence and self-importance）

3. In 1979, he loaned out his ranch as the backdrop for the iconic "Marlboro Country" ads...—1979年他把自己的牧场出租用作拍摄象征"万宝路郊野"广告的背景（①loan out—to lend; ②iconic—acting as a sign or symbol; ③Marlboro—a type of cigarette made by the U.S. tobacco company Philip Morris. Marlboro ads often show impressive outdoor scenes with a tough-looking, horse-riding cowboy, who often carries a gun. The ads project the image of machismo, toughness and freedom.）

4. To them, the lab cowboy and his sperminator portended a dystopia of mass-produced boys.—在她们看来，这个实验室牛仔和他杀死精子的做法预示着大批生育男孩的恐怖局面的来临。（①lab—laboratory; ②sperminator—a blend formed from sperm and terminator; ③dystopia—an imaginary place where everything is extremely bad; ④portend—to be a sign or warning of sth bad going to happen）

5. *People*—an American weekly magazine of celebrity and human interest stories

6. A newer method for sperm selection, called MicroSort, is currently completing Food and Drug Administration clinical trials.—美国食品药物管理局目前正在完成对一种更加新的精子选择法"微选"的临床试验。（MicroSort—a scientifically proven preconception process that improves the chances that the baby you conceive will be of the desired gender）

7. *The Second Sex*—a 1949 book by Simone de Beauvoir which discusses the treatment of women throughout history

8. old goat—an unpleasant old man

9. His 26-year-old granddaughter—"tall, slender, brighter than hell, with a take-no-prisoners personality"—is a biochemist and works on genetic sequencing.—他的26岁孙女"亭亭玉立，聪明过人，争强好胜"。她是生物化学家，研究基因测序。（①take-no-prisoners—used to say that someone is determined to succeed and will not let anyone stop him/her; ②genetic sequencing—一种新型基因检测技术，能从血液或唾液中测定基因全系列，预测患多种疾病的可能，锁定个人病变基因，从而提前预防和治疗）

10. old boys—男校友

11. Asia expert at the World Bank—世界银行亚洲问题专家（the World Bank—the International

Bank of Reconstruction and Development)

12. As thinking and communicating have come to eclipse physical strength and stamina as the keys to economic success, those societies that take advantage of the talents of all the adults, not just half of them, have pulled away from the rest. —由于思维与交际的能力已经超越体力和耐力,成为获得经济成功的关键,那些利用所有人而不是一半人才智的社会已经拉开了与其他社会的距离。(①eclipse—to do or be much better than; ②stamina—physical or mental strength that enables you to do sth difficult for a long time)

13. the Organization for Economic Cooperaration and Development devised the Gender, Institutions and Development Database —经济合作发展组织设计出性别、机构与发展数据库(the Gender, Institutions and Development Database—The database, with more than 60 data indicators of gender equality, helps researchers and policymakers determine and analyze obstacles to women's social and economic development.)

14. For a long time, evolutionary psychologists have claimed that... and that is manifested in more nurturing and more flexible behavior... —长期以来,进化心理学家声称我们身上都体现了人类自古以来必须顺应和遵从的规则:男人动作更快,力气更大,生来就能争夺供不应求的资源。这种特性现在表现在华尔街金融业为取胜打拼的那股劲头上。女人生来就得找能够养家的男人,自己在家照看孩子,这种特性表现为她们更会照顾人,更加温顺的行为。(①imprint—to print a design on a surface; ②hardwire—to build computer functions into the permanent system; ③program—to give a machine instructions; ④imperative—sth that must be done)

15. the Great Recession— 大衰退(It refers to the period of general economic decline in world markets during the late 2000s and early 2010s. The recession stemmed from the collapse of the U.S. real estate market.)

16. The worst-hit industries were overwhelmingly male and deeply identified with macho: construction, manufacturing, high finance. —受打击最严重的企业是以男性为主体、社会普遍认为应该男性从事的企业:建筑业、制造业和高级融资业。(①macho—male quality of being strong and aggressive; ②high finance—large and complex financial transactions)

17. the U.S. economy is in some ways becoming a kind of traveling sisterhood —美国就业市场在某些方面正在成为一种女性工作流动圈(sisterhood—a society of women)

18. But given the power of the forces pushing at the economy, this setup feels like the last gasp of a dying age rather than the permanent establishment. —但是考虑到推动经济发展群体所具有的力量,这种情况看来只是一个正在衰亡的时代奄奄一息而不是永久性的局面。(①setup—an arrangement; ②establishment—permanent position)

19. ball and chain—拖累(The phrase originally referred to a heavy metal ball and a piece of of chain attached to the leg of a prisoner to prevent escape. It is commonly used jocularly in the sense of a spouse by a husband of his wife. Here, it is used in reference to men.)

20. *The Bachelors' Ball*—The book's full title is *The Bachelors' Ball: The Crisis of Peasant Society in Bearn*. It gives an account of the way the influence of urban values has precipitated a crisis of male peasants. Tied to the land through inheritance, the bachelors find themselves with little to offer the women of Bearn, who abandon the country for the city in groups.

21. Rust Belt—an area in the northern U.S., including parts of the states such as Illinois, Michigan, Indiana, Ohio and Wisconsin, where many large older industries, especially the steel and car industries, have been less successful and many factories have closed down.

22. Bill Cosby—比尔·考斯比(20世纪80年代美国人最熟悉的情景喜剧《考斯比一家》的主角,该剧多次获奖,剧情聚焦于一个上中产阶级黑人家庭。)

23. Well, that check bounced a long time ago... —哎呀,那张支票早就被银行拒付退回了(这里意思是:那种形象早就过时了。)

24. she'll call 911 —她会打报警电话(911—the telephone number used in the U.S. for calling the police, fire ambulance services in an emergency)

IV. Language Features

常用俚语

俚语是现代英语词汇中不可缺少的一部分。《美国俚语词典》编者弗莱克斯纳(S. B. Flexner)在该词典的前言中写道:"普通美国人的词汇量一般为10000—20000……据我的保守估计,其中有2000个词是俚语,它们是最经常被使用的词汇的一部分。"换句话说,俚语占常用词语的十分之一以上。可见,俚语在英语中是起重要作用的。

20世纪被称为"普通人的世纪",过于高雅的语言往往使读者望而生厌。为了迎合读者口味,缩短与大众之间的情感距离,许多报刊文章采用通俗口语体语言,使语言亲昵、自然、幽默、活泼,"产生共同情感联系"(create the common touch)。较为常见的俚语有:

buck(美元);bust(降职,降级);kneejerk(不假思索的);pro(专业人员);poor mouth(哭穷);jawbone(施加压力);cool(酷,时髦,帅);lowdown(内幕,真相);ego trip(追名逐利);yuck(令人厌恶的事物);green(钱);mugger(抢劫犯);pink slip(解雇通知单);buddy(哥们儿);nerd(讨厌的人);jack up(抬高物价);hype(促销);turn-on(使人兴奋的事);quick fix(权宜之计);upscale(高档消费层次的);sobstuff(伤感文章);nab(抓住,捉拿);nuts(疯狂的;古怪的);goody-goody(正人君子);binge(狂欢);goof(傻瓜);prof(教授);uptight(紧张的);nuke(核武器);posh(豪华的);savvy(精明的);muckraking(揭丑新闻);yuppies(雅皮士);go-go(兴隆的,精力充沛的);odds-on(大有希望的);whopping(巨大的);come-on(诱饵);foodie(美食家);killer(迷人的事);rookie(新手);hype(大肆宣传)。

必须指出的是,对待俚语应该持慎重态度。使用得当可以产生新颖时髦、生动诙谐、形象有力的效果,但使用不当则有损效果,给人以轻佻之感,或使人觉得怪诞可笑,不伦不类。

V. Analysis of the Content

1. It can be seen from the article that the iconic "Marlboro Country" ad is focused on_____.
   A. the cowboy's horseriding skill　　　　B. the beauty of country scenery
   C. the sense of freedom　　　　　　　　D. the joy of horseriding
2. Which of the following is NOT listed among the most valuable attributes today?
   A. social intelligence　　　　　　　　　B. stamina
   C. ability to sit still and focus　　　　　D. open communication
3. The author's purpose in citing the example of Bearn is to show_____.
   A. the attraction of France's country
   B. men's sense of the obligation to tend the land
   C. men's unchanged love for their wives
   D. role reversal and men's status decline
4. Which of the following terms is NOT used in the author's reference to Ericsson?
   A. professor　　　B. cowboy　　　C. sperminator　　　D. biologist
5. The role reversal between men and women in the U.S. is most obvious_____.
   A. in the middle class　　　　　　　　　B. in the upper class
   C. in the white people　　　　　　　　　D. in the working class

VI. Questions on the Article

1. What was Ericsson's way of separating sperm carrying the male-producing Y chromosome from those carrying the X chromosome? How did it work?
2. What did Ericsson do about the method of sperm separation in the late 1970s?
3. How did feminists of the era take to Ericsson?
4. Why did Ericsson feel surprised when he looked into numbers for the clinics that used his process in the 1990s?
5. What made women decide to have girls?
6. What are the reasons for the erosion of patriarchy?
7. What do American feminists always think of these social, political and economic changes?
8. What kind of thinking frames people's sense of the natural order?
9. Where can the evidence be found to prove that post-industrial economy is more congenial to women than to men?
10. What kind of change is underway between American men and women? Where does the problem show up most obviously?
11. According to Mustafaa El-Scari, what has happened to paternal authority?

VII. Topics for Discussion

1. Is the modern, post-industrial society better suited to women?
2. Will men lose their dominant position in the near future?

Lesson 4

Millennials Shift Toward Social Responsibility

"It does not have to be the basic tenet upon which a company is founded, but social responsibility must be a core value in order for millennials to believe that a company is genuine and therefore worthy of their almighty dollar."

By Brian Peavey

MILLENNIALS are the future; there is no doubt about that, but it has been said time and time again that they do not have a good work ethic nor care about things like other generations. They also have been labeled as egocentric, entitled, and, at times, outright lazy. However, these traditional views of millennials are changing and our approach in marketing to them must change as well.

It is not that we were all wrong about millennials, but guess what?—they grew up. Just like generations past, they have emerged from their self-absorbed, coddled, little worlds to become part of society. Granted, it has not been without some growing pains and fretting along the way, but yes, they now are at the age where they have solid jobs—although they still are prone to bouncing around on the career path—and are starting families.[1] They took longer than prior generations to come to the conclusion that having a (somewhat) settled life can be pleasing, but they are arriving nonetheless.

As the millennials have grown into their definition of maturity[2], they have discovered that they do care about things other than themselves; they just do not care about things the same way as their predecessors. They are just as passionate about what they believe in; their objectives and causes simply are different.

Once they identify their causes or projects, they actually are quite dedicated to reaching their goals. They are creative and tech savvy, so they are able to develop and/or research their way to find solutions. They do not particularly enjoy standard work hours, but their drive does not diminish at 5 p.m.[3]—in fact, quite the opposite. They may continue to toil well past the traditional 40-hour workweek if they are passionate about the job. The key is to identify the employees that align with your company's beliefs and vision and then turn them loose.[4]

Millennials are looking to make a difference in this world, not just with their work but with their dollars, whether that be the brand of dish soap they purchase or the political candidates they support. They want change and they support those brands and people that align with their interests. Some 70% of millennials will spend more on brands supporting causes they care about. Moreover, *Forbes*[5] reports that by 2020, millennials will represent nearly half of the working population, and they currently control 2.5 trillion dollars in spending power. It is worth paying attention to this demographic.

Companies are learning to garner the support of millennials. However, this change cannot be disingenuous. Millennials grew up dissecting volumes of data via their Facebook, Instagram, other social media and Internet searches. If the data isn't glaring and substantial, they intuitively can tell your heart isn't in your "cause." It takes a real core commitment to equal their passion.

When I started my home flipping/real estate company[6], ProfitShare, I wanted to weave ethics into the very core of the business. While the traditional model of house flipping often preys on people in financial crisis and frequently takes advantage of the original homeowner, I found a way to partner with these home owners and include them in the success of the deal. ProfitShare buys, renovates, and resells homes, and then shares the profit with owners. It took a long while to get to where we are now, but this millennial-friendly business model has paid off.

I learned some hard lessons about how to keep the moral, millennial-mind interested:

Appealing to Millennials doesn't need to be sexy[7]. A lot of people think getting ahold of Millennials requires Tony Hawk on a skateboard jumping off a cliff for climate change, but this is not the case.[8] Millennials want to make a difference in the world. So, give them opportunities to do so. As long as your mission or goals are realistic, it will work. We did this in the real estate world and, let me tell you, there is not an industry that is more boring to Millennials than real estate. However, if your core values are ethical and promote a better future, then that is all you need.

Link your business with a social cause. Remember, though, finding the right cause is important. Look at your company's mission statement[9] and find a charity that aligns with your core message. You want this charity or organization to give you exposure in a way that will convey a meaningful message to the masses. For instance, if your are in the real estate business, you may want to focus on "giving back" through outlets of shelter. Shelter is a basic necessity that even we in the real estate business tend to take for granted. Donating company time, money, and resources to a specific shelter, or providing information for consumers on how to donate, is a great way to help the cause.

Put your money where your principles are. It may go without saying, but if you are going to have a business model that gives back to society, or you are going to donate to a cause, you have to actually give back in a substantial way. Millennials will be able to detect if you are just pandering and trying to get more credit than you deserve.

Get involved with the charity or movement. This does not necessarily mean you need to donate all of your profits to this movement. There are many ways to get involved without hurting your bottom line.[10] For example, you can provide donation opportunities to your customers and employees by posting information on your website or social media.

Another way to give back is by donating your time. After all, your expertise and talent are more valuable than your money. Identify a couple of impact organizations[11] that you believe in and offer them an hour of your expertise. Depending on the nature of your business, you might consult on marketing, evaluate their business plan, or review their finances.

Social responsibility can make money. When a business decides to be socially responsible, there is a common assumption that they are going to lose money, but I am living proof that the decision to be socially responsible pays off financially. People want to work with businesses that are socially responsible. As long as it can work for your business model, it can be the best decision you ever make.

Once you take the steps to incorporate ethical elements into your business practice, get the news out there. Promote your involvement with the charity through social media posts, pictures, newsletters, and blogging.[12] Reach out to a large audience with your message, and I promise you that you will be pleasantly surprised by the results.

People, especially millennials, like to work for a cause, and they become readily willing to invest in it. Reaching out to people with your ideas and plans will help your brand spread organically.[13] The more millennials see you put effort into the cause you are working for, the more they will stand behind you and pledge their business.

Identify their sizzle points.[14] Communicating with potential customers never has been easier thanks to the Internet. Do your research and utilize focus groups[15] to identify what makes millennials interact (or not) with your brand. A hallmark trait of the ethical millennial mind is honesty. This generation will tell you its wants and needs if you ask, and the answers may surprise you.

For instance, in my own business I assumed wrongly that bigger (yet affordable) houses always were the ideal. I found that millennials actually are attracted to smaller lot sizes[16] because there is less maintenance involved. Research and communication is key to targeting this group effectively because they speak their mind, and it may be that their needs are counterintuitive to past generations.[17]

Use the Internet to your advantage. Ask for consumer participation and input by posting questions on Facebook and Twitter. Search current trends and issues, and figure out how to combine these elements and incorporate them in your business model[18]. Current trends promise to capture millennial's attention. This attention is what your business needs to thrive in our current society.

Which of these trends are most relevant to the business that you are conducting? How can you promote your products through the use of these trends? Current issues also capitalize on the millennial brains. The younger members of our society are gung-ho on fighting the accumulating injustices we seem to be facing. Incorporating these millennial triggers will help guarantee you their business.[19]

Be patient. millennials (**Millennials**) grew up spoon fed, yet at the same time they desire to sort things out on their own. This combination often makes them appear lazy and slow to react but, in contrast, millennials thoughtfully are navigating through information on their own. Sometimes they are not as likely to be on top of documentation[20], or extrapolating how long or important a process may be. (I cannot tell you how many times buyer's (**buyers'**) parents have had to turn in W2s[21] to their child's lender (**children's lenders**) because they simply did not think it was important.) So, be patient with prospective millennial customers. Explain finite details and follow up along the way to make sure tasks get accomplished.

Millennials are the buying force of the future, and companies across the nation need to adapt their marketing if they want to stay relevant.[22] If millennials are shifting towards social responsibility, that means businesses must follow suit.

The National Association of Realtors reports that two-thirds of millennials have not yet reached the average first-time home buying age of 32. So, this means the home ownership trend by millennials is just getting started and businesses related to this industry have to take action now if they want to capture the millennial's dollars. Businesses like rental companies, remodelers, flippers, realtors, lenders, etc. must adjust their business models and marketing strategies now to be ahead of the curve.

Not every business can adhere to the ProfitShare model. However, it is this kind of forward-millennial-friendly thinking[23] that is needed for a company to survive. It does not have to be the basic tenet upon which a company is founded, but social responsibility must be a core value in order for millennials to believe that a company is genuine and therefore worthy of their almighty dollar[24].

From *USA TODAY*, January, 2018

I. New Words

coddle	[ˈkɒdl]	v.	to take too much care of a person
demographics	[ˌdeməˈɡræfiks]	n.	data about a particular age group
disingenuous	[ˌdisinˈdʒenjuəs]	adj.	dishonest, insincere
dissect	[diˈsekt]	v.	to examine carefully and critically
documentation	[ˌdɒkjumənˈteiʃən]	n.	文件证据
egocentric	[ˌiːɡəuˈsentrik]	adj.	thinking only of one's own interests
expertise	[ˌekspəˈtiːz]	n.	专门知识, 专长
extrapolate	[ikˈstræpəleit]	v.	to guess from facts already known
finite	[ˈfainait]	adj.	having limits in size, space or time
fret	[fret]	v.	to worry
garner	[ˈɡɑːnə]	v.	to collect or gather
glaring	[ˈɡlɛəriŋ]	adj.	obvious
gung-ho	[ˌɡʌŋˈhəu]	adj.	*informal* very eager to do sth
hallmark	[ˈhɔːlmɑːk]	n.	a typical feature
input	[ˈinput]	n.	(信息的)输入, 提供
incorporate	[inˈkɔːpəreit]	v.	to include as part of a larger unit
lot	[lɒt]	n.	an area of land used for building on
outright	[ˈautrait]	adv.	completely
pander	[ˈpændə]	v.	一味讨好, 迎合
prey	[prei]	v.	~on to live by getting money from
renovate	[ˈrenəveit]	v.	to put back into good condition by repairing, building etc.
savvy	[ˈsævi]	adj.	having practical knowledge or understanding of sth
self-absorbed	[ˌself əbˈsɔːbd]	adj.	自我专注的
tenet	[ˈtenit]	n.	a principle on which a belief or doctrine is based
trait	[treit]	n.	a particular quality, especially of a person

第一单元 社会群体

II. Background Information

美国"千禧代"

美国"千禧代"(Millennials)通常是指1981年到1996年出生的美国人,由于出生临近世纪末而得此名。这代人是紧随Generation X（无名代）之后的一代,故常被称为Generation Y（Y代）。此外,因为这代人大多数是在20世纪80年代生育高峰期出生,人数与"婴儿潮代"相似,故又被称为"回声潮代"(Echo Boomers)。

"千禧代"是在互联网和信息技术爆炸时代成长的。他们擅长使用网络,因而还被称为"网络代"(Net Generation)。网络的广泛使用影响着这一代人的购物行为,他们当中许多人习惯网上购物。一项调查显示,"千禧代"对网上下单、线下取单这种消费方式的使用率是47%,大大高于"无名代"(30%)和"婴儿潮代"(Boomers)(13%)。他们多半喜欢观看视频节目。这一代人中将近98%拥有智能手机,比率明显高过其他年龄群体。

这一代人比父辈更为重视教育,所受教育水平高于父辈。2015年的一项调查结果显示,25—29岁的美国人中拥有大学学历者的比率为35.5%。而在1990年,这个比率仅为23.2%。

"千禧代"虽然受教育水平高于父辈,但是收入却低于父辈。2016年的一项调查报告称,1950年出生的美国人中有79%的概率比父辈赚更多钱。然而对于1981年出生的美国人而言这一概率却只有50%。有项调查将2013年25—34岁年龄段的"千禧代"人和1989年同一年龄段的"婴儿潮代"人进行比较,结果发现"千禧代"人收入中位数为40581美元,比同年龄段的父辈少20%。据美国《财富》杂志网站报道,美国有71%的"千禧代"人为财务状况焦虑,其中教育费用所构成的压力最大。现在的大学毕业生平均带着3万美元的学贷债务踏上工作岗位。2013年,美国有41%的年轻人家庭需要偿还教育贷款。而在1989年这一比率仅为17%。美国心理协会的一份研究报告称这一代是美国心理压力最大的群体。调查发现超过三成的"千禧代"人说心理压力导致他们夜不能寐(keeping them awake at night)。

沉重的经济压力促使许多"千禧代"人推迟进入结婚、生子和购房的成年期。20世纪80年代,25—34岁的群体中有将近七成的人已经结婚生子。而如今,这个年龄段的"千禧代"似乎离传统婚姻越来越远。他们中有许多人成为"啃老族"(boomerang kids)。2015年的一份美国统计局报告显示,年轻人"啃老"比例比十年前猛增。2005年,18—34岁的美国人中仅有四分之一住在家里。如今,这一比例高达34%。这些年轻人中只有35%的人象征性地向父母交点儿房租和伙食费,有25%的人分文不出。当今,这个年龄段的年轻人中经济独立无需父母帮助者比率仅为40.7%,与十年前相比减少了十个百分点。

"千禧代"还被称作"跳槽代"(job-hopping generation)。他们不爱固定在一家公司,一种工作,有六成的人在想着跳槽。2016年的一份盖洛普调查报告显示,"千禧代"

受访者中承认过去一年换了工作的人所占百分比是60%,高出非"千禧代"人15个百分点;考虑下一年如果就业形势好转就换单位的比率是36%,也高出非"千禧代"人15个百分点。

这一代人对政治和宗教的热情较低。他们在自我界定时很少称自己是"信徒"和"爱国者"。皮尤(PEW)研究中心调查显示,他们中的半数以上自称政治独立分子,29%不是任何宗教信徒。"千禧代"所表现出的对政治和宗教方面的疏离令人震惊。受访的年轻人中有半数不愿追随任何党派,31%的人认为民主党和共和党没有什么区别。

III. Notes to the Text

1. Granted, it has not been without some growing pains and fretting along the way, but yes, they now are at the age where they have solid jobs—although they still are prone to bouncing around on the career path—and are starting families.——即便如此,他们成长过程中并非没有痛苦和烦恼。然而现在,虽然他们常常跳槽,但是已到了成家立业的时候了。(bounce around on the career path—to frequently change jobs)

2. As the millennials have grown into their definition of maturity...——当"千禧代"人步入具有自己特色的成熟期

3. but their drive does not diminish at 5 p.m.——但是他们的工作劲头到了下午5点没有减退(drive—a special effort made by someone for a particular purpose)

4. The key is to identify the employees that align with your company's beliefs and vision and then turn them loose.——关键是找出那些与你公司志同道合的雇员并且让他们放手去干。(①align—to be in agreement with; ②turn them loose—to allow them to do things in their own way)

5. *Forbes*——《福布斯》杂志(美国一家每两周发行一次的商业杂志,以金融、工业、投资和营销等主题的原创文章著称)

6. home flipping/real estate company——旧房翻新转卖房地产经营公司(flipping—a term used primarily in the U.S. to describe purchasing a revenue-generating asset, renovating and reselling it for a profit.)

7. Appealing to Millennials doesn't need to be sexy.——要取得"千禧代"人的好感不必非得有很大魅力。(sexy—holding a lot of attention and interest)

8. A lot of people think getting ahold of Millennials requires Tony Hawk on a skateboard jumping off a cliff for climate change, but this is not the case.——许多人认为要赢得"千禧代"的人心就得有滑板大师托尼·霍克为改变气候而表演踩滑板、跳悬崖的那种绝技,但是实际情况并非如此。(①Tony Hawk— an American skateboarder and owner of skateboard company Birdhouse; ②get ahold of—to get control of)

9. company's mission statement——公司的宗旨

10. There are many ways to get involved without hurting your bottom line.——不减少公司利润的

(慈善活动)参与方式有很多。(① get involved—to take part in; ② bottom line—the net profit of a company)

11. impact organizations—organizations which have great influence

12. Promote your involvement with the charity through social media posts, pictures, newsletters, and blogging. —采用社交媒体帖子、图片、新闻通信和博客宣扬你参与慈善事业。(promote—to make it known to the public)

13. Reaching out to people with your ideas and plans will help your brand spread organically. —让人们了解你的理念和计划会自然而然促进你的品牌传播。(organically—in a natural and healthy way)

14. Identify their sizzle points. —Find those things which arouse their great interest.

15. focus groups —smaller groups of people chosen to represent different social classes who are asked questions by people doing market research

16. smaller lot sizes —(住房面积)较小户型

17. Research and communication is key to targeting this group effectively because they speak their mind, and it may be that their needs are counterintuitive to past generations. —销售要有效针对这一群体的关键在于调研和交流,因为他们实话实说,还有可能因为他们的需求与过去几代人相反。(counterintuitive—the opposite of what you would expect)

18. business model—商业模式(指企业与企业之间、企业的部门之间,乃至企业与顾客之间、与渠道之间都存在的各种各样的交易关系和连接方式)

19. Incorporating these millennial triggers will help guarantee you their business. —把这些能激起"千禧代"人反应的元素融入促销中会帮助你做成他们的生意。(trigger—any event that sets a course of action)

20. on top of documentation—对文件证明十分熟悉(①on top of—to be in complete control of; ②documentation—proof in the form of documents)

21. W2s—wages and tax statements (The form is prepared by employers each year for employees, showing the employee's total gross earnings and withholdings)

22. Millennials are the buying force of the future, and companies across the nation need to adapt their marketing if they want to stay relevant. —"千禧代"是未来重要的购物群体。全国各地的公司如果想要做他们的生意就得改变其经营方式。[relevant—directly connected (in business)]

23. forward-millennial-friendly thinking —眼光长远、对"千禧代"人友好的思维

24. worthy of their almighty dollar —值得他们花大把钱(almighty—very great in extent)

IV. Language Features

词性转化

本文"millennial"一词原为形容词,意思为"千禧年的",如"the Millennial Generation"(千禧代),而在课文标题和文章多处都被用作名词,表示"千禧代人"之意。

在英语的发展过程中,词尾基本消失,各种词逐渐失去词类标志。现代英语中各类词之间形态上没有多大区别,因此许多词可以不改变形态,从一种词类转化为另一种词类,从而具有新的意义和作用,成为新词。这种构词法的特点是不需要借助词缀就实现词类的转换,故称之为零位派生法(zero derivation)。

词性转化(conversion)可以节约篇幅,并可使语言生动有力,因而在新闻写作中经常使用。常见的词性转化类型有:

一、名词转化为动词

He mouthed fine words about friendship. 他满口是关于友谊的漂亮话。

The White House press secretary is once more backgrounding newsmen for the president. 白宫新闻秘书再次代表总统向新闻记者介绍背景情况。

二、动词或动词词组转化为名词

Like today's haves and havenots, we will have a society of the knows and knownots. 就像今天社会上有富人和穷人一样,将来社会上会出现有知识的人和无知识的人。

(Computer Gap...) These aging choose-nots become a more serious issue when they are teachers in schools. 这些日益变老,又不愿学习使用电脑的人如果在学校当教师的话,那么问题就更为严重了。

kickback 回扣　　　　　　　　(car) pile-up 撞车

三、形容词转化为名词

这种现象十分普遍,在新闻刊物中常常见到舍去名词而将其形容词修饰语用作名词的做法。例如:

undesirables 不受欢迎的人或物　　perishables 易腐败的东西
pin-ups 钉在墙上的美女照　　　　variables 易变的东西
unreadables 无法读懂的东西　　　gays 同性恋者
undecideds 未下决心的人　　　　never-marrieds 从未结婚的人
retireds 退了休的人　　　　　　unwanteds 不想要的人或物
electives 选修课　　　　　　　　locals 当地人

V. Analysis of the Content

1. The word "promote" in the sentence "Promote your involvement with the charity through social media posts...."(Para. 14)means _____.
   A. to encourage
   C. to help
   B. to make it known to the public
   D. to raise to a higher point
2. The typical trait of the ethical millennial mind is _____.
   A. independence
   C. thrift
   B. hard work
   D. honesty
3. The way suggested by the author for market research is the use of _____.
   A. the Internet
   C. the telephone
   B. the newspaper
   D. the magazine
4. Which of the following statements is NOT true about millennials?
   A. They have firm control of documents and are clear about minute details.
   B. They have grown up into maturity.
   C. They are creative and tech savvy.
   D. They like businesses which show social responsibility.
5. The article is mainly intended to _____.
   A. eulogize millennials
   B. advise millennials about how to spend their money
   C. advise companies about how to market to millennials
   D. advise the society about how to treat millennials

VI. Questions on the Article

1. What were the traditional views of millennials?
2. Why are the traditional views of millennials changing?
3. How do millennials treat their work?
4. According to the article, what kind of millennials should companies employ?
5. What difference exists in millennials' way of spending money?
6. Why are millennials becoming increasingly important to the society?
7. According to the author, what is the difference between ProfitShare and the traditional model in house flipping?
8. What kind of companies appeal to millennials?
9. What are the ways suggested by the author for companies to give back to the society?
10. Does social responsibility necessarily mean loss of profits for a company? Why or why not?
11. How can companies use the Internet to their advantage?

12. Why do companies have to be patient with millennials?
13. What is the author's advice to real estate-related businesses?

VII. Topics for Discussion

1. Are millennials to blame for their late maturity?
2. Should social responsibility be a basic tenet upon which a company is founded?

Unit 2
第二单元 衣食住行

Lesson 5

Food and Obesity

Being fat is becoming the norm for Americans. As it will soon become in this country, I have seen the future, and it's extra large.

By Joan Smith

    A FRIEND WHO happens to be both American and a superb cook—his *poulet de Bresse en deuil*[1] is one of the most memorable dishes I have tasted—called me a couple of days ago, enthusing about a lecture he had just attended. The thesis, he said, was that the human body has changed irrevocably over the last quarter of a century and that the physical environment—chairs, beds, airline seats—will gradually adapt to accommodate the new shape. It is, of course, in the US, where my friend no longer lives, that this evolutionary experiment is most advanced; for years now, millions of people have been gorging themselves on vast helpings of fast food[2], with the consequence that about 60 per cent of the population is overweight.

    According to Greg Critser, author of *Fat Land: How Americans Became the Fattest People in the World*[3], none of this has happened by accident. Critser argues that the challenge to the US food industry in the 1970s was that the population was growing more slowly than the food supply, so people had to be persuaded to change their eating habits. Fast food, invented after the Second World War as an affordable way of getting families to eat together, became a means of selling surplus fat and sugar to the far-from-unwilling masses. This is a social revolution on a grand scale as scarcity, with which most human beings have had to struggle throughout history, has given way to an apparently permanent state of plenty.

    It may also help to explain why the magician David Blaine, suspended without food in a Perspex box beside Tower Bridge, has such a grip on people's imaginations.[4] In an astonishingly short period of time, starvation has metamorphosed from a threat to a spectacle, and families are turning out *en masse* at weekends to see how his hunger strike is going.[5] For the fifth of the British population who are obese, and unused to doing without food for more than a few hours, the notion of someone giving it up for 44 days is unthinkable; some normal-size people have turned up to mock, throwing eggs, cooking food and even trying to cut off the water supply to the hungry

American. Perhaps this is the point, that there are so few starving Americans in the world, which makes his self-imposed ordeal appear ludicrously self-indulgent.[6]

Yet it is possible to take Critser's argument a stage further and suggest that millions of Americans are trapped between two industries, fast food and slimming, which enjoy a cosily symbiotic relationship.[7] Research by a fast-food chain showed that what customers cared about was neither taste nor quality but portion size; what they have come to expect from food, and what their neighbours are beginning to want as well—obesity has increased by 158 per cent in Mexico in a decade, since fast food outlets[8] began to replace the traditional diet—is a feeling of being stuffed to the gills[9]. Cooking has become a spectator sport[10], something to watch famous people do on telly, as the populations of affluent countries rely increasingly on supermarket meals and takeaways. For many people, eating has become an addiction rather than a pleasure, and going on a diet merely replaces one morbid habit with another.[11]

In the circumstances, it is not really surprising that people are confused and angered by Blaine, whose stunt highlights the disordered relation to eating which has become habitual in Western societies. Far from being an object of derision as his body enters ketosis, the state in which it starts to consume itself, he should logically be the envy of all those individuals who are endlessly trying Atkins and other fashionable diets.[12] We are so used to hearing people go on about the cabbage soup diet or modified Atkins that it is easy to overlook the extraordinary fact that we live in a culture in which people pay to get hungry, turning the condition of starving Africans into a longed-for luxury. There is something shaming about this, and about the extent to which so many people—like Kafka's hunger artist[13], who was addicted to starving—have lost control of their appetites.

Perhaps the thesis my friend described to me on the phone is correct, and houses and cars and planes will just have to get bigger as the human race—the affluent part of it, that is—continues to inflate itself with empty calories. Bizarrely, being fat is fast becoming the norm for Americans, and even in this country it will soon be people like me (5ft 5in and a paltry nine stone[14]) who are the freaks. I have seen the future, and it's extra large.

PLAIN FOOD MOVES UP A CLASS[15]

I WAS SUPPOSED to give a talk myself at the weekend, on food and class, but had to pull out because of an annoyingly persistent throat virus. I was going to discuss "eating above your station", which is something I learnt to do, like many people of my generation, when I went to university. Until then, I had scarcely ever eaten in a restaurant and I had never tried what my family referred to as "foreign muck". Even macaroni cheese was too exotic for my parents, who tipped it into the bin when I came home from cookery class with a Pyrex dish full of overcooked pasta and melted cheddar.[16]

Food was plain, served on a plate with thick portions of gravy or custard, and the idea of helping yourself from serving dishes seemed the height of sophistication. What strikes me now, looking back on that traditional working-class diet, is that it was unadventurous but it didn't do me any harm. My father grew vegetables, my mother shelled peas and sliced carrots, and I don't recall anyone in my family being overweight. It's hard to eat too much when someone else puts the food on your plate. These days, if a working-class diet can be said to exist, it is superficially much more cosmopolitan—curries, pizzas, the ubiquitous Chinese takeaway—but adapted to satisfy the British appetite for saturated fat[17], salt and sugar.

In a curious reversal, plain food—simple grilled fish with a green salad, such as the wonderful meal I ate in Marbella in the summer—has become the province of the middle class.[18] I am one of those lucky people who changed class at the right time and in the right direction, but the effects of our eating habits—a slender elite, as millions of ordinary people pile on the pounds—suggest that class divisions are as deep as ever[19].

BRING ON THE EURO

I was driving back from a health farm[20] the other day when the friend with whom I had just shared three days of massage, facials and Pilates said rather nervously that she wanted to ask me a question. I naturally assumed that she wanted to talk about men, underwear or the least painful way of shaving your legs, as women do when they know each other well, but it turned out to be something far more intimate. Am I, she asked, in favour of joining the euro?

Oh God, anything but that. Admitting that you feel no attachment to the pound, and would like to use the euro in Waitrose[21], is like telling your friends that you have joined a weird sect. I don't think people spend much time thinking about Gordon Brown's five economic tests[22], but there is a presumption that the British did jolly well to stay out of the eurozone when all those foreigners gave up their currencies almost two years ago. And now we're supposed to admire the Swedes for resoundingly voting "No" at the weekend.

I don't think I've ever confessed this in public before, and I suspect I won't be invited to any smart parties for weeks at the very least.[23] But I really want to join the euro. And since we both came out somewhere on the M1[24]—it was a relief, I can tell you—I now know at least one other person who feels the same.

From *The Times*, September 18, 2003

I. New Words

accommodate	[əˈkɔmədeit]	v.	to provide enough space for sb
affluent	[ˈæfluənt]	adj.	having a lot of money and a good living standard
bin	[bin]	n.	垃圾箱
bizarrely	[biˈzɑːli]	adv.	very strangely, unusually
calorie	[ˈkæləri]	n.	卡(路里)
cookery	[ˈkukəri]	n.	the art or practice of preparing food
cosily	[ˈkəuzili]	adv.	comfortably
cosmopolitan	[ˌkɔzməˈpɔlitən]	adj.	世界性的, 全球(各地)的

curry	[ˈkʌri]	n.	咖喱菜肴
custard	[ˈkʌstəd]	n.	奶油蛋糕,奶油沙司
derision	[diˈriʒən]	n.	嘲笑
enthuse	[inˈθju:z]	v.	to talk in an enthusiastic way
eurozone	[ˈjuərəuzəun]	n.	欧元区
exotic	[igˈzɔtik]	adj.	foreign; intriguingly unusual or different
facial	[ˈfeiʃəl]	n.	面部美容
freak	[fri:k]	n.	a person considered unusual
gorge	[gɔ:dʒ]	v.	~ oneself to eat a lot of food
gravy	[ˈgreivi]	n.	肉汁,肉汤
grill	[gril]	v.	烧烤
helping	[ˈhelpiŋ]	n.	an amount of food given at a meal
irrevocably	[iˈrevəkəbli]	adv.	不能取消地,不能撤回地
ketosis	[kiˈtəusis]	n.	酮症(体内酮体生成过多)
mock	[mɔk]	v.	to laugh at sb in an unkind way
muck	[mʌk]	n.	垃圾
obese	[əuˈbi:s]	adj.	extremely fat; grossly overweight
Perspex	[ˈpə:speks]	n.	珀思佩有机玻璃(商标名称)
resoundingly	[riˈzaundiŋli]	adv.	轰动地,成功地
scarcity	[ˈskɛəsəti]	n.	insufficiency, shortage
shell	[ʃel]	v.	剥……的壳
slimming	[ˈslimiŋ]	n.	减肥,减食
stunt	[stʌnt]	n.	惊人的表演;惊险动作
takeaway	[ˈteikəˌwei]	n.	外卖饭菜
telly	[ˈteli]	n.	*BrE informal* television
tip	[tip]	v.	to dump
ubiquitous	[ju:ˈbikwitəs]	adj.	seeming to be everywhere; very common
virus	[ˈvaiərəs]	n.	病毒
weird	[wiəd]	adj.	very strange and difficult to explain

II. Background Information

饮食与肥胖

　　肥胖已经成为全球性的严重问题。2020年,世界卫生组织(WHO)发布的统计结果表明,全球肥胖症(obesity)患者人数达12.11亿,占人口总数比例为15.62%。世卫组织最近发出的警告称:超重(overweight)与肥胖(obese)是全球引起死亡的第五大风险,全球每年"胖死"的人数至少有280万。除美国、英国、德国这些传统"胖国",亚非国家的肥胖人数也在猛增。据最新统计,美国是发达国家中肥胖和超重人口比率最高的国家,在全球肥胖率最高的30个国家中排名第九。世界卫生组织所定的体重标准也是美国常用的体重检测标准BMI(Body Mass Index体重指数)。这种标准的计算公式是:体重(公斤数)÷[身高(米数)^2],得数在18.5—25之间为理想体重,得数在25—29.9之间为超重(overweight),得数在30以上为肥胖(obese)。按照这套标准,2021年美国成年人中有三分之二超重,其中一半是肥胖者。密西西比州成年人肥胖率最高,为39.7%,而全美平均最苗条的科罗拉多州,成年人胖子数也占了21.5%。

人们普遍认为,肥胖和饮食文化是分不开的。从美国的快餐业(fast food industry)的发达程度就可以看出美国人对快餐的偏爱。在美国的公共场所到处可见可乐和其他饮料和零食自动售货机,使得美国人在看电视、看电影、看球赛以及在其他闲暇时间里吃零食、喝可乐和加糖饮料变得越来越方便。这些快捷的食品都是高热能食品。缺少运动是肥胖的另一个重要原因。美国是一个以车代步的国家(a country on wheels),从车库到车库的生活和高科技的发展让越来越多的人缺少运动。正是这种高热量摄入(high calories in)和低热量消耗(low calories out)导致超重和肥胖病(obesity)。

伴随肥胖而来的是健康危机。心脏病(heart disease)、糖尿病(diabetes)、高血压(high blood pressure)和中风(apoplexy)都是常见的并发症。每年大约有30万美国人死于与肥胖有关的疾病。美国疾病防治中心最近发布的报告称,2014年美国成年人肥胖比例为37.7%。女性更高,比例为38.2%。肥胖的种族差异更大,亚裔美国人中只有九分之一被列入肥胖,非洲裔比例最高(48%),西语裔比例是43%,白人比例是35%。

专家们呼吁抵制垃圾食品(junk food),改变不健康的饮食与运动习惯,加强体育锻炼,控制体重,增进健康。

III. Notes to the Text

1. *poulet de Bresse en deuil*—布雷斯松鸡(一种法国特色美食)
2. millions of people have been gorging themselves on vast helpings of fast food—数百万人拼命大吃快餐(gorge oneself on sth—to eat a lot of sth)
3. Greg Critser, author of *Fat Land: How Americans Became the Fattest People in the World*—《肥胖之国:美国人是怎样变成世界上最胖的人》的作者格莱格·克里瑟(① Greg Critser—a journalist who writes for *USA Today*, including cover stories dealing with medical, health and nutrition topics; ② *Fat Land*—It is published by Houghton Mifflin in January, 2003. In this book, Greg Critser deals with every aspect of American life—class, politics, culture, and economics—to show how Americans have made themselves the second fattest people on the planet after South Sea Islanders.)
4. It may also help to explain why the magician David Blaine, suspended without food in a

Perspex box beside Tower Bridge, has such a grip on people's imaginations.—这也许有助于解释为什么吊在塔桥旁有机玻璃箱里绝食的魔术师大卫·布莱恩引起了人们极大的关注。(① David Blaine—born April 4, 1973, an American magician, endurance artist and Guinness Book of Records world record-holder. He made his name as a performer of street and close-up magic. ② Tower Bridge—a bridge in London, England, over the River Thames. It is close to the Tower of London, which gives it its name. It has become an iconic symbol of London. ③ has such a grip on people's imaginations—is so interesting that people give it a lot of attention)

5. In an astonishingly short period of time, starvation has metamorphosed from a threat to a spectacle, and families are turning out *en masse* at weekends to see how his hunger strike is going.—在一段很短的时间里,饥饿已经从生命威胁变成观赏奇观,许许多多的人周末全家来观看他的绝食进展情况。[① metamorphose—*formal* to change into sth completely different; ② *en masse*—(from French) altogether, and usually in large numbers]

6. Perhaps this is the point, that there are so few starving Americans in the world, which makes his self-imposed ordeal appear ludicrously self-indulgent.—也许问题在于,现今世界中的美国人挨饿的很少,使得他强加给自己的饥饿苦难显得自我放纵、荒唐可笑。

7. Yet it is possible to take Critser's argument a stage further and suggest that millions of Americans are trapped between two industries, fast food and slimming, which enjoy a cosily symbiotic relationship.—然而,可以将克里瑟的论说向前推进一步,说明:数百万美国人已被快餐业和减肥业所困,这两种企业之间存在亲密的共生关系。(symbiotic relationship—the relation between two different living creatures that live close together and depend on each other)

8. fast food outlets—快餐店(outlet—a shop/store that sells goods)

9. a feeling of being stuffed to the gills—一种吃撑的感觉 [① to the gills—*informal* completely full; ② stuff (oneself with)—to eat too much food]

10. Cooking has become a spectator sport—烹饪已经成为一种观赏性的活动(spectator sport—a sport that many people watch)

11. For many people, eating has become an addiction rather than a pleasure, and going on a diet merely replaces one morbid habit with another.—对于许多人来说,吃不再是乐事而是成瘾了,节食只是一种病态习性取代另一种病态习性。(① addiction—the condition of having a very strong desire for sth and being unable to stop taking it; ② morbid—having a strong interest in sth unpleasant)

12. Far from being an object of derision as his body enters ketosis, the state in which it starts to consume itself, he should logically be the envy of all those individuals who are endlessly trying Atkins and other fashionable diets.—从逻辑上说,当他体内酮体生成过多,身体进入自我消耗状态时,他根本不应该是人们嘲笑的对象,而应该是所有无休止试图通过阿特金斯节食法或其他时新节食法减肥者的羡慕对象。(Atkins diet—阿特金斯节食法,一种提倡以高蛋白、低碳水化合物的饮食来减肥的方法)

13. Kafka's hunger artist—卡夫卡书中描述的绝食艺术家 [① Kafka—(1883—1924) one of the major fiction writers of the 20th century; ② hunger artist—a short story by Franz Kafka published in *Die Neue Rundschau* in 1922. The main character is an archetypical creation of Kafka, an individual marginalised and victimised by society at large.]

14. 5ft 5in and a paltry nine stone—身高5英尺5英寸,体重仅有9英石(① paltry—too small in amounts;② 1 stone—6.35kg)

15. PLAIN FOOD MOVES UP A CLASS—清淡食物地位上升一个阶层

16. Even macaroni cheese was too exotic for my parents, who tipped it into the bin when I came home from cookery class with a Pyrex dish full of overcooked pasta and melted cheddar. —干酪通心面布丁即使对我父母而言也是味道太怪,每当我从烹饪班带回一玻璃盘煮过头的意大利细面和融化了的切达干酪时,他们都会把它倒进垃圾桶。(Pyrex dish—派莱克斯耐热玻璃盘)

17. saturated fat—饱和脂肪(医学界认为这种脂肪的增加对心脑血管有害)

18. In a curious reversal, plain food—simple grilled fish with a green salad, such as the wonderful meal I ate in Marbella in the summer—has become the province of the middle class.—现在情况奇怪地颠倒过来,清淡食物(像我夏季在Marbella吃的那顿美餐,简单的烤鱼加上绿色的凉拌菜)已经进入中产阶级的饮食范畴。(Marbella—位于西班牙南部的阳光海岸,是个著名的游艇港,四季皆宜的气候让这里成为全球富豪休闲、度假、展现惊人财力的地方。)

19. the effects of our eating habits—a slender elite, as millions of ordinary people pile on the pounds—suggest that class divisions are as deep as ever—我们饮食习惯所造成的结果是上层人士苗条起来,而数百万的普通人体重却在迅速增加,这种情况显示阶级的差别和以往一样严重(pile on—to increase quickly)

20. health farm—an establishment, usually in the country, where rich or fashionable people go when they want to lose weight

21. Waitrose—英国一家连锁超市

22. Gordon Brown's five economic tests—戈登·布朗的五条经济检验标准(① Gordon Brown—a British Labour politician and the Prime Minister of the United Kingdom of Great Britain and Northern Ireland; ② five economic tests—the criteria defined by the United Kingdom Government that are to be used to assess the UK's readiness to join the Economic and Monetary Union of the European Union, and so adopt the euro as its official currency)

23. I suspect I won't be invited to any smart parties for weeks at the very least.—我料想至少几个星期我将不会被邀请参加任何时髦社交聚会。(smart—connected with fashionable, rich persons)

24. we both came out somewhere on the M1—我们两人都对货币供应量表明了自己的看法 [① come out—to declare oneself in some way; ②M1—(经)货币供应量]

IV. Language Features

《泰晤士报》简介

《泰晤士报》(*The Times*)创刊于1785年1月1日,是世界上最早的报纸之一。该报原名为《世鉴日报》(*Daily Universal Register*),1788年正式更名为《泰晤士报》(*The*

Times)。

《泰晤士报》创办人兼总编是约翰·沃尔特(John Walter)。第一期只有4页,发行量1000份。目前,该报每期通常为48—52页,发行量在45万份左右,平日版售价为1镑。

《泰晤士报》是英国历史最悠久、最权威、消息灵通可靠、政治影响很大的报纸。在英国帝国主义"鼎盛"时期,该报的社论有时能够引起欧洲小国的阁潮。该报自称,它的办报方针是"独立地、客观地报道事实"。然而,200多年的历史证明,该报是英国政府的喉舌,在重大国内外问题上反映统治集团的意图。该报自创刊后的很长时期,一直被控制在沃尔特家族手中。1908年北岩爵士购得该报后,数次易主。1966年由隶属于肯尼斯·汤姆森集团的加拿大出版商罗伊·汤姆森的公司购得。1981年又由英国报业大亨美籍澳大利亚人罗伯特·默多克收购。

默多克购得《泰晤士报》后虽然一再声称不会干预该报编辑方针(editorial policies),但该报的风格和内容都出现了一些变化:报纸图片增多,人情味(human interest)新闻、犯罪内容报道比例明显增加。自2004年11月1日开始,该报为了提高发行量改为4开版"小报"形式。

每期《泰晤士报》的首页上端以彩色照片和标题形式介绍当日和次日趣闻,中部以大幅彩照和粗体标题介绍当日重要新闻并刊登文章前几段。首页左下角是索引,介绍版面安排。其他篇幅刊登一些报道的前几个段落,末尾注明剩下部分所在页码。此外,每期还有今日要闻页(The Times Today),这一页一般是第26页或第28页。浏览首页和要闻页便可了解一期报纸的主要内容。

《泰晤士报》主要有如下版面:国内新闻(Home News)、国外新闻(Overseas News)、商业(Business)、运动(Sport)、读者来信(Letters)、艺术(Arts)、评论(Comment)、舆论(Opinion)、服饰(Style)、教育(Education)、司法与社会(Court & Social)等。

该报主要读者是政府官员、议员、企业界和上层知识界。其政治观点倾向保守党。

《泰晤士报》的网址是www.thetimes.co.uk。

V. Analysis of Content

1. The word "station" in the sentence " I was going to discuss 'eating above your station'" (Para.7) means _____ .

    A. a place for a train to stop

    B. a place where service is provided

    C. social rank

    D. position for doing something

2. The author believes that the relationship between fast food and slimming is _____ .

    A. parallel

    B. interdependent

    C. interchangeable

    D. non-existent

3. According to research done by a fast food chain, what customers cared about was _____.

   A. taste of the food

   B. quality of the food

   C. quantity of the food

   D. time saved in eating

4. It can be seen from the article that middle-class people in the western society today prefer _____.

   A. fast food

   B. self-cooked food

   C. plain food

   D. Chinese food

5. The reason why the author's friend was nervous in asking the question was that _____.

   A. the question was about the author's private life

   B. the question would sound silly to the author

   C. the euro was a topic avoided by British people

   D. the euro was an exciting topic

VI. Questions on the Article

1. What did the author's American friend talk about over the phone?
2. What was the reason for Americans' overweight according to Greg Critser?
3. How did the British respond to David Blaine's starvation stunt? Why did they behave this way?
4. What is the impact of fast food on Mexicans?
5. How does fast food affect cooking?
6. What kind of diet are people in western societies trying in order to slim down?
7. What is the difference between the traditional working class diet and present-day working class diet?
8. What is the result of westerners' reversal of eating habits?
9. What is the author's attitude towards the use of the euro?

VII. Topics for Discussion

1. Is fast food solely to blame for westerners' obesity?
2. Is fast food a curse or a boon?

Lesson 6

The End of Ownership: Why Aren't Young People Buying More Houses

Richer couples! Cheaper mortgages! Millions of unwanted houses! Despite all this, young home owners declined for 30 years, even before the Great Recession[1]. Here's how the American Dream[2] shrank.

By Derek Thompson

When older generations wonder what's the matter with Millennials[3], they often judge their younger cohorts against such financial and social benchmarks as finding a job, getting married, and buying a home. These observations often come wrapped in weak science—"blame Facebook for their indolence"—or dripping with judgment—"blame their parents for making them weak."[4] The science is weak, but the observations are true. Fewer young people are finding jobs. Fewer young people are getting married. Fewer young people are buying homes.

Between 1980 and 2000, the share of late-twenty-somethings[5] owning homes had declined from 43% to 38%. The share of early-thirty-something home owners[6] slipped from 61% to 55% in that time. After the boom and bust were over, both rates kept falling.[7] The rate of young people getting their first mortgage between 2009 and 2011 was chopped in half from just 10 years ago, according to a recent study from the Federal Reserve[8].

One headwind is student debt. "Close to $1 trillion, America's mounting pile of outstanding student debt is a growing drag on the housing recovery, keeping first-time home buyers on the sidelines and limiting the effectiveness of record-low interest rates,[9]" Bob Willis reported in *Bloomberg Businessweek*[10].

This is good news and bad. Rising student debt is a sign of more students. We should want (and expect) more people to go to school in a recession. But the trepidation of first-time home buyers hurts housing sales, feeding a pernicious cycle[11]. Bad housing numbers circulate back through the economy in the form of low residential investment, scant construction, and fewer housing services.

The decline in young home owners is a puzzling trend. Interest rates have steadily declined over the last 30 years. Mortgage lending has loosened. Women have ascended in the workplace and supplemented their spouse's earnings. How in the face of all of these positive developments did home ownership among the young keep falling?

To understand why young people are buying fewer homes, begin by asking yourself: *What do you need to buy a home?* We'll start with three basics. You need a mortgage. You need income for the downpayment. And you probably need a spouse. Controlling for income, gender, and education, a married person is 23% more likely to own compared to someone who is not married[12], and many more couples buy a home as they are preparing to wed.

"The 1980—2000 decline in young home ownership occurred as improvements in mortgage opportunities made it easier to purchase a home," Martin Gervais and Jonas D.M. Fisher write in their seminal paper "Why Has Home Ownership Fallen Among the Young?" So we can't begin by blaming too few available mortgages. Government interventions and mortgage innovations (remember subprime lending[13]?) should have meant more young couples buying houses. With the rising employment and earnings of women, households should have gotten richer. That, too, should have increased homeownership. It didn't.

Instead, we can begin by blaming a shortage of couples. The decline of marriage and the increase in "household earnings risk" account for practically all of the decline in young home ownership, Gervais and Fisher conclude. So, to understand the decline of young home ownership, we have to understand the decline of marriage.

Unfortunately, the decline of marriage isn't an easier trend to unpack. I offered some thoughts here, which I'll try to sum up in a sentence: Higher college-graduation rates have delayed marriage for many, and as women moved toward financial equality with men (and as technology made it easier to be alone) financially motivated marriages went down, and contently single ladies went up.[14] "A decline in the incidence of marriage mechanically lowers home ownership," Gervais and Fisher write.

But that's not all. It's not just the marriages. It's also the money.

Marriage rates for the 25—44 set fell by 15 percentage points between 1980 and 2000. But this only accounts for half of the decline in Gervais and Fisher's model. The other half comes from stagnating wages, and the worry that the dynamic economy will destroy a couple's earnings with inflation, recession, or job loss. Basically: People aren't buying homes because they're freaked out about the economy.[15]

The freak-out transcends gender and class, and it crystallized within a generation.[16] In one survey comparing early Boomers (born in the late-40s and-50s) and late Boomers (born in the late-50s and -60s), overall economic uncertainty in the second group rose by 11% for college graduates and 52% for high school graduates. Uncertainty about the value of college rose, too.

It's not all in their heads. Between 1950 and 1970, wage growth was something special. Earnings grew 44 percent per decade—more than three times faster than they've grown over the last 30 years. If that trend had continued, the typical working guy would be earning a $194,000 per year today. (He's not.) Michael Greenstone, the director of the Hamilton Project[17], prepared for us this graph to illustrate the difference between where median earnings for men were headed, and where they've really gone. This is what the uncertainty gap looks like.

Houses are expensive. I'm not going to win an award for this observation, but there it is. The problem with expensive things, like houses, is that you can't buy them with only your own money. You need somebody else's money, too. This is why mortgages exist.

In the years before the Great Recession, mortgages bloomed thanks to financial innovation. This was creative destruction, in that order.[18] First came creation. The subprime boom was, in Karl Smith's words, "a technological innovation that allowed millions of households to switch out of the market for multi-family homes [like duplexes] and mobile homes and into the single family market ... [pushing] up the price of existing single family homes."[19] Then came destruction.

Before the Great Recession, we spread apart—out of cities and into the suburbs and single-family homes. After the Great Recession, we came together. A quarter of young adults have moved back in with their parents for a significant period of time. More have shacked up in apartments and tripled up on roommates to split the costs.[20] In the last three years, mortgage interest rates have fallen tremendously, creating a good opportunity for people with means to get in on a house. But who's got the means and opportunity? Unemployment for twenty-somethings is twice as high as the national average. Banks have tighter credit conditions on all but the highest-quality borrowers.

You can focus on the loudest numbers and conclude that young peoples' aversion to home owning is an overreaction to a unique recession.[21] Housing prices have fallen by a third in some cities. Couples have had a few years to pay off their debts. Mortgage interest rates are historically tiny. Could there possibly be a better time to buy?

Maybe not. But if the last 30 years have taught us anything, it's that planning for the future is an act of faith. Supply chains and software eat our jobs.[22] Financial wizardry eats our savings. The cost of insuring against these risks—that is, both college and literal insurance—is rising. "It feels like anytime we hit around $20,000 something terrible or some unexpected thing happens," Steve Kinney, a Brooklyn[23] resident, told *The New York Times* last year. He's part of a new renters society, and rental prices are rising now that housing prices aren't. Three in five net jobs in the last two years have gone to people in their twenties and lower-thirties, "a crucial rental group," according to an analysis of Labor Department[24] data by G. Ronald Witten, an apartment firm consultant.

It's no wonder that in an environment that punishes the long-term faithful, more young people are planning month to month.

From *The Atlantic*, February, 2012

I. New Words

apart	[əˈpɑːt]	adv.	separated by a distance
ascend	[əˈsend]	v.	to rise
aversion	[əˈvɜːʃən]	n.	a strong dislike
benchmark	[bentʃmɑːk]	n.	standard
chop	[tʃɔp]	v.	to cut, to reduce
cohort	[ˈkəuhɔːt]	n.	a group of people who share a common feature
downpayment	[daunˈpeimənt]	n.	（分期付款购物的）首期付款
drag	[dræg]	n.	阻力，障碍
duplex	[ˈdjuːpleks]	n.	复式公寓
dynamic	[daiˈnæmik]	adj.	有活力的
graph	[græf]	n.	图表

第二单元 衣食住行

headwind	[ˈhedwind]	n.	逆风,阻力
indolence	[ˈindələns]	n.	*formal* laziness
mortgage	[ˈmɔːgidʒ]	n.	抵押贷款,按揭
pernicious	[pəˈniʃəs]	*adj.*	*formal* very harmful or evil
scant	[skænt]	*adj.*	(仅用于名词前)不足的,缺乏的
seminal	[ˈseminl]	*adj.*	*formal* very important and influential
spouse	[spaus]	n.	配偶
stagnate	[ˈstæɡneit]	v.	to stop developing or making progress
transcend	[trænˈsend]	v.	to go above or beyond the limits of something
trepidation	[trepiˈdeiʃən]	n.	anxiety, fear
trillion	[ˈtriljən]	n.	万亿
unpack	[ʌnˈpæk]	v.	to separate sth into parts so that it is easier to understand
wed	[wed]	v.	to marry
wizardry	[ˈwizədri]	n.	a very impressive ability, great skill

II. Background Information

住房情况

　　美国人的住房大致分为三类：独立式住房（detached dwellings）；半独立式住房（semi-detached dwellings）；附联式住房（attached dwellings），公寓楼房（apartment buildings）是其主要类型。

　　2021年美国已居住的住房单位（occupied housing units）中有接近2/3的住户是房主，其他为租房户（tenants）。美国的房租主要根据面积大小、内部设施和坐落位置而定。设有厨房、浴室、储藏室，配有齐备的厨具及空调装置的两室一厅套房，一般月租金在1000美元以上。纽约市曼哈顿地区租金在3800美元以上。

　　许多美国人喜欢自己买房子住，他们认为这是一种划算的投资。美国房价上涨很快。1963年一套独立式住房平均售价为1.9万美元，1983年上升到9万美元，2007年增长到31.36万美元，2021年又上涨到36.8万美元。美国房价因地区而异，例如加州地区房价偏高，2020年该州独立式住房价格中位数为81.4万美元。

　　由于购房耗资巨大，美国人购房筹资通常采用抵押贷款（mortgage）的办法。买主通常是向银行贷款，只需先支付一部分（20%或更少）作为第一次付款，其余的以分期付款方式每月偿还本利，30年还清。一般情况下，抵押贷款每月偿还金比租金贵不了多少，因而这种方式颇受欢迎。美国人抵押贷款购房负债十分惊人，1990年全国这一项负债总额为37640亿美元，2022年增至11.4万亿美元。

　　近几十年来，美国人的住房情况有了较大改善。

1950年美国人均只拥有1.5个房间,而到1981年已增加到接近2个房间。按照美国公认标准,如果每个房间所住人数超过1人,就被定为过分拥挤(over-occupied)。依据这一标准,1940年美国过分拥挤户为20.3%,而到1980年这种家庭已减少到4.2%。

虽然美国人的居住条件总的说来比其他国家优越,但还存在两大问题:1. 住房分配不均;2. 住房费用偏高。一方面,巨富们占有的是大庄园,住的是豪宅,住房大大超出实际需要;而另一方面又有不少人为住房而发愁。根据阿斯彭研究所的数据,美国约有1500万人面临近期可能被逐出住所的危险。

美国家庭住房费用偏高构成家庭沉重的生活负担。1984年美国家庭住房平均开支为6556美元,所占家庭总消费的百分比是29.8%。2019年家庭住房平均开支增加到19884美元,所占家庭消费百分比上升到33.1%。住房费用高导致不少人流落街头。2020年,美国无家可归者人数为58万。其中少数族裔所占比例较高,非洲裔和西语裔分别占39.4%和23.1%。纽约市无家可归者多达8万人,其中儿童数量为1.8万。最近一份研究报告预测,疫情下的失业潮将导致美国无家可归者数量激增,人数将达到惊人的116.8万,超过疫情前的2倍!

III. Notes to the Text

1. Great Recession—also referred to as the Lesser Depression, the Long Recession. It is a marked global economic decline that began in Dec. 2007 and took a particularly sharp downward turn in Dec. 2008. The global recession affected the entire world economy.

2. American Dream—美国梦(the idea that the US is a place where everyone has a chance of becoming rich and successful)

3. Millennials—千禧代人(Please refer to Background Information of L4.)

4. These observations often come wrapped in weak science—"blame Facebook for their indolence"—or dripping with judgment—"blame their parents for making them weak."—这些评论常常缺乏科学根据,例如"年轻人的懒惰得怪脸书网站";或是充满主观判断,例如"他们的能力差要怪其父母"。(① wrapped—covered completely;② drip—to contain a lot of sth)

5. late-twenty-somethings—将近三十岁的人

6. early-thirty-something home owners—三十岁出头的房主

7. After the boom and bust were over, both rates kept falling.—经济繁荣期和萧条期之后,这两项比率均继续下跌。

8. Federal Reserve—(美国)联邦储备委员会

9. Close to $1 trillion, America's mounting pile of outstanding student debt is a growing drag on the housing recovery, keeping first-time home buyers on the sidelines and limiting the effectiveness of record-low interest rates —美国学生的高额负债日益增加,数额接近一万亿美元,这对房地产业复苏是不断增大的阻力,把首次购房者拒之门外,限制了最低利率所

第二单元 衣食住行

起的作用。(① drag—sth stopping progress;② on the sidelines—not taking part in an activity even though you want to or should do)

10. *Bloomberg Businessweek*—《商业周刊》(又名《彭博商业周刊》,由美国彭博出版社出版发行,是全球销量第一的商业杂志)

11. feeding a pernicious cycle—助长了恶性循环

12. Controlling for income, gender, and education, a married person is 23% more likely to own compared to someone who is not married... —把收入、性别和教育水平因素考虑在内,已婚者比未婚者买房的可能性要高23%。(controlling for—considering)

13. subprime lending—次级抵押贷款(简称"次贷",是银行或贷款机构为信用评级较差,无法从正常渠道借贷的人所提供的贷款,利率一般比正常贷款要高,常常可以大幅上调,因而对借款人有较大风险)

14. financially motivated marriages went down, and contently single ladies went up.—出于经济目的而结婚的人减少了,甘愿单身的女性增加了。

15. Basically: People aren't buying homes because they're freaked out about the economy.—从根本上说,人们不购买房产是因为他们对经济形势感到担忧。(freak out—to make someone very anxious, upset or frightened)

16. The freak-out transcends gender and class, and it crystallized within a generation.—这种恐惧超越了性别与阶层,整个一代人都产生了这种感觉。(① transcend—to go beyond the usual limits of;② crystallize—to become clear and fixed)

17. Michael Greenstone, the director of the Hamilton Project—汉密尔顿项目主管迈克尔·格林斯通(① Michael Greenstone—麻省理工学院环境经济学教授;② Hamilton Project—launched in April 2006 as an economic policy initiative at the Brookings Institution by a unique combination of leading academics, business people, and public policy makers who wanted to develop a serious, systematic strategy to address the challenges that American economy faces)

18. This was creative destruction, in that order.—它(抵押贷款的迅猛发展)类似创造性破坏。(① in the order of—approximately, like;② creative destruction—这一术语由美籍奥地利经济学家约瑟夫·熊彼特在20世纪50年代提出,意指资本主义不仅包括创新,也包括打破旧的、低效的工艺和产品,现已成为企业变革的核心概念。)

19. The subprime boom was, in Karl Smith's words, "a technological innovation that allowed millions of households to switch out of the market for multi-family homes [like duplexes] and mobile homes and into the single family market ... [pushing] up the price of existing single family homes."—卡尔·史密斯曾说过:次贷的繁荣是"一种技术创新,使数百万的家庭由多户式住宅(如复式公寓)或活动住房市场转向独户住房市场……抬高了现有独户住房的价格"。(① Karl Smith—assistant professor of public economies and government at the School of Government at the University of North Carolina at Chapel Hill;② switch out of—to change from one thing to another, usually suddenly)

20. More have shacked up in apartments and tripled up on roommates to split the costs.—更多的人搬进了公寓,为分担房费三人合住。(① shack up—*informal* to start living with someone

who you are not married to;② triple up—to make sth three times as many)

21. You can focus on the loudest numbers and conclude that young peoples' aversion to home owning is an overreaction to a unique recession.—你会关注最显眼的数据,得出年轻人不喜欢购房是对不寻常经济衰退过度反应的结论。(① loud—outstanding;② unique—very unusual)

22. Supply chains and software eat our jobs.—供应链和软件使用吞噬我们的工作岗位。(supply chains—供应链,指围绕核心企业,通过对信息流、物流、资金流的控制,采购原材料,制成中间产品及最终产品,最后由销售网络把产品送到消费者手中。它是将供应商、制造商、分销商、零售商,直到最终用户连成一个整体的功能网链模式。)

23. Brooklyn—布鲁克林区(纽约市西南部的一区)

24. Labor Department—美国劳工部(美国联邦政府行政部门之一,主管全国劳工事务,成立于1913年3月4日。主要职责是负责全国就业、工资、福利、劳工条件和就业培训等工作。)

IV. Language Features

嵌入结构

本文多处使用了嵌入结构(embedding):

例 1. The cost of insuring against these risks—that is, both college and literal insurance—is rising.

例 2. These observations often come wrapped in weak science—"blame Facebook for their indolence"—or dripping with judgment...

新闻报道为了在有限的篇幅内传达更多的消息,采用了多种手段浓缩、精练句式,大量使用嵌入结构是其中的一种主要方式。插入语是嵌入结构中最为常见的形式,插入语的两头既可用逗号亦可用破折号标明。

例 1. Ken Bush, 54, a state fire marshal, pulled his vehicle onto the shoulder of Route 50 and was struck by two other vehicles.

例 2. People are confounded: which Bible will give a particular person—maybe a scholar or a seeker, a harried parent, a struggling student—spiritual nourishment, moral enlightenment and literary pleasure?

例 3. Watergate Hotel, part of Washington's exclusive and notorious Watergate Complex, has been sold to the investment band Blackstone Group.

例 4. In 1996, the most recent year available, there were about 11.8 million registered boat owners.

从文体效果来看,使用破折号标出插入成分"更具独立性","给人一种随意感"。(*Investigating English Style*, David Crystal & Derek Davy, 1969)

例 1. The mum-and-pop operation—they have two employees besides themselves—is growing at a rate of about 15% a year and last year had sales of $350,000.

例 2. Nevertheless, it's physical evidence—the sticks and stones of murder trials—that delivers crushing blows to a defendant's case, he and other legal experts say.

V. Analysis of Content

1. The word "loud" in the sentence "You can focus on the loudest numbers..." (Para. 17) means ____.
   A. making a great sound
   B. insistent
   C. outstanding
   D. not quiet

2. Which of the following observations is NOT TRUE?
   A. Fewer young people in the U.S. are getting married.
   B. Fewer young people in the U.S. are finding jobs.
   C. Fewer young people in the U.S. are buying houses.
   D. Fewer young people in the U.S. are studying in colleges.

3. According to Martin Gervais and Jonas D.M. Fisher, the first major factor for consideration in home ownership decline among the young is _____.
   A. lack of available mortgages
   B. insufficient supply of houses
   C. a shortage of couples
   D. the high housing price

4. Which of the following statements is TRUE?
   A. Interest rates have steadily declined over the past 30 years.
   B. Housing prices have increased by a third in American cities.
   C. After the Great Recession, Americans moved from cities to suburbs.
   D. House rents are now dropping sharply in America.

5. The article is _____.
   A. an interpretative news report
   B. a straight news report
   C. a news comment
   D. a news feature

VI. Questions on the Article

1. What benchmarks do older generations often use for judging younger cohorts?
2. How did younger people's home ownership change between 1980 and 2000?

3. What effect does American student debt have on the housing market?
4. What are the three basic conditions for buying a house?
5. Was mortgage to blame for young home owners' decrease between 1980 and 2000?
6. How much did marriage rates for the 25—44 set fall between 1980 and 2000? What was its effect on home ownership?
7. What was wage growth like between 1950 and 1970?
8. What does the author mean by creative destruction?
9. Why are more young people planning month to month?

VII. Topics for Discussion

1. Is young people's aversion to home ownership an overreaction to the recession?
2. Which is better, owning a house or renting a house?

Lesson 7

When Working from Home Doesn't Work

IBM pioneered telecommuting. Now it wants people back in the office.

By Jerry Useem

IN 1979, IBM was putting its stamp on the American landscape.[1] For 20 years, it had been hiring the greats of modernism[2] to erect buildings where scientists and salespeople could work shoulder-to-shoulder commanding the burgeoning computer industry. But that year, one of its new facilities—the Santa Teresa Laboratory[3], in Silicon Valley[4]—tried an experiment. To ease a logjam at the office mainframe, it installed boxy, green-screened terminals in the homes of five employees, allowing them to work from home.

The idea of telecommuting was still a novelty. But this little solution seemed effective. By 1983, about 2,000 IBMers were working remotely. The corporation eventually realized that it could save millions by selling its signature buildings and institutionalizing distance work[5]; the number of remote workers ballooned. In 2009, an IBM report boasted that "40 percent of IBM's some 386,000 employees in 173 countries have no office at all." More than 58 million square feet of office space had been unloaded, at a gain of nearly $2 billion. IBM, moreover, wanted to help other corporations reap the same officeless efficiencies through its consulting services. Leading by example was good marketing.[6]

Then, in March of this year, came a startling announcement: IBM wanted thousands of its workers back in actual, physical offices again.

The reaction was generally unsparing. The announcement was depicted, variously, as the desperate move of a company whose revenues had fallen 20 quarters in a row[7]; a veiled method of shedding workers; or an attempt to imitate companies, like Apple and Google, that never embraced remote work in the first place. "If what they're looking to do is reduce productivity, lose talent, and increase cost, maybe they're on to something," says Kate Lister, the president of Global Workplace Analytics[8], which measures (and champions) working from home.

IBM might have seen this coming. A similarly censorious reaction greeted Yahoo when it reversed its work-from-home policy in 2013. Aetna and Best Buy have taken heat for like-minded moves since.[9] That IBM called back its employees anyway is telling, especially given its history as "a business whose business was how other businesses do business." Perhaps Big Blue's decision[10] will prove to be a mere stumble in the long, inevitable march toward remote work for all. But there's reason to regard the move as a signal, however faint, that telecommuting has reached its high-water mark[11]—and that more is lost in working apart than was first apparent.

How could this be? According to Gallup, 43 percent of U.S. employees work remotely all or some of the time. As I look to my left, and then to my right, I see two other business-casual-clad men hammering away on their laptops beside me at a Starbucks just outside Chicago[12]. They look productive. Studies back this impression up. Letting Chinese call-center employees work from home boosted their productivity by 13 percent, a Stanford study reported. And, again according to Gallup, remote workers log significantly longer hours than their office-bound counterparts.

Another batch of studies, however, shows the exact opposite: that proximity boosts productivity. (Don't send call-center workers home, one such study argues—encourage them to spend more time together in the break room[13], where they can swap tricks of the trade.) Trying to determine which set of studies to trust is—trust me—a futile exercise. The data tend to talk past each other.[14] But the research starts to make a little more sense if you ask what type of productivity we are talking about.

If it's personal productivity—how many sales you close or customer complaints you handle—then the research, on balance, suggests that it's probably better to let people work where and when they want. For jobs that mainly require interactions with clients (consultant, insurance salesman) or don't require much interaction at all (columnist), the office has little to offer besides interruption.

But other types of work hinge on what might be called "collaborative efficiency"—the speed at which a group successfully solves a problem. And distance seems to drag collaborative efficiency down. Why? The short answer is that collaboration requires communication. And the communications technology offering the fastest, cheapest, and highest-bandwidth connection is—for the moment, anyway—still the office.

Consider the extremely tiny office that is the cockpit of a Boeing 727. Three crew members are stuffed in there, wrapped in instrument panels. Comfort-wise, it's not a great setup.[15] But the forced proximity benefits crew communication, as researchers from UC San Diego and UC Irvine[16] demonstrated in an analysis of one simulated flight—specifically the moments after one crew member diagnoses a fuel leak.

A transcript of the cockpit audio doesn't reveal much communication at all. The flight engineer reports a "funny situation." The pilot says "Hmmm." The co-pilot says "Ohhhh."

Match the audio with a video of the cockpit exchange and it's clear that the pilots don't need to say much to reach a shared understanding of the problem. That it's a critical situation is underscored by body language: The flight engineer turns his body to face the others. That the fuel is very low is conveyed by jabbing his index finger at the fuel gauge. And a narrative of the steps he has already taken—no, the needle on the gauge isn't stuck, and yes, he has already diverted fuel from engine one, to no avail—is enacted through a quick series of gestures at the instrument panel and punctuated by a few short utterances.

It is a model of collaborative efficiency, taking just 24 seconds. In the email world, the same exchange could easily involve several dozen messages—which, given the rapidly emptying fuel tank, is not ideal.

This brings us to a point about electronic communications technologies. Notionally, they are cheap and instantaneous, but in terms of person-hours spent using them, they are actually expensive and slow. Email, where everything must literally be spelled out, is probably the worst. The telephone is better. Videoconferencing, which gives you not just inflection but expression, is better still. More-recent tools like the workplace-communication app Slack integrate social cues into written languages, leveraging the immediacy of instant-messaging and the informality of emoji, plus the ability to create a channel to bond over last night's #gameofthrones.[17]

Yet all of these technologies have a weakness, which is that we have to choose to use them. And this is where human nature throws a wrench into things. Back in 1977, the MIT[18] professor Thomas J. Allen looked at communication patterns among scientists and engineers and found that the farther apart their desks were, the less likely they were to communicate. At the 30-meter mark, the likelihood of regular communication approached zero.

The expectation was that information technology would flatten the so-called Allen Curve.[19] But Ben Waber, a visiting scientist at MIT, recently found that it hasn't. The communications tools that were supposed to erase distance, it turns out, are used largely among people who see one another face-to-face. In one study of software developers, Waber, working alongside researchers from IBM, found that workers in the same office traded an average of 38 communications about each potential trouble spot they confronted, versus roughly eight communications between workers in different locations.

The power of presence has no simple explanation. It might be a manifestation of the "mere-exposure effect": We tend to gravitate toward what's familiar; we like people whose faces we see, even just in passing. Or maybe it's the specific geometry of such encounters. The cost of getting someone's attention at the coffee machine is low—you know they're available, because they're getting coffee—and if, mid-conversation, you see that the other person has no idea what you're talking about, you automatically adjust.

Whatever the mechanisms at play, they were successfully distilled into what Judith Olson, a distance-work expert at UC Irvine, calls "radical collocation."[20] In the late 1990s, Ford Motor[21] let Olson put six teams of six to eight employees into experimental war rooms[22] arranged to maximize team members' peripheral awareness of what the others were up to. The results were striking: The teams completed their software-development projects in about a third of the time it usually took Ford engineers to complete similar projects. That extreme model is hard to replicate, Olson cautions. It requires everyone to be working on a single project at the same time, which organizational life rarely allows.

But IBM has clearly absorbed some of these lessons in planning its new workspaces, which many of its approximately 5,000 no-longer-remote workers will inhabit. "It used to be we'd create a shared understanding by sending documents back and forth. It takes forever. They could be hundreds of pages long," says Rob Purdie, who trains fellow IBMers in Agile, an approach to software development[23] that the company has adopted and is applying to other business functions, like marketing. "Now we ask: 'How do we use our physical space to get on and stay on the same page?'"

The answer, of course, depends on the nature of the project at hand. But it usually involves a central table, a team of no more than nine people, an outer rim of whiteboards, and an insistence on lightweight forms of communication. If something must be written down, a Post-it Note[24] is ideal. It can be stuck on a whiteboard and arranged to form a "BVC"—big, visual chart—that lets everyone see the team's present situation, much like the 727's instrument panels. Communication is both minimized and maximized.

Talking with Purdie, I began to wonder whether the company was calling its employees back to an old way of working or to a new one—one that didn't exist in 1979, when business moved at a more stately pace. In those days, IBM could decide what to build, plan how to build it, and count on its customers to accept what it finally built at the end of a months-long process. Today, in the age of the never-ending software update[25], business is more like a series of emergencies that need to be approached like an airplane's fuel leak. You diagnose a problem, deliver a quick-and-dirty solution, get feedback, course-correct, and repeat, always with an eye on the changing weather outside.[26]

I asked Purdie whether IBM's new approach could be accomplished at a distance, using all the new collaborative technology out there. "Yes," he said. "Yes, it can. But the research says those teams won't be as productive. You won't fly."

From *The Atlantic*, November, 2017

I. New Words

audio	[ˈɔːdiəu]	adj.	音频的，声频的
avail	[əˈveil]	n.	to little/no~ with little or no success
batch	[bætʃ]	n.	a group
boost	[buːst]	v.	to make sth increase
burgeon	[ˈbəːdʒən]	v.	*formal* to begin to grow or develop rapidly
call center	[ˈkɔːl sentə]	n.	(大公司服务部门的)来电接听中心
censorious	[senˈsɔːriəs]	adj.	highly critical
cockpit	[ˈkɔkpit]	n.	(飞行员的)座舱
collaborative	[kəˈlæbərətiv]	adj.	involving or done by several people working
columnist	[ˈkɔləmist]	n.	专栏作家
depict	[diˈpikt]	v.	to describe sth in words
drag	[dræg]	v.	~ sth down to bring sth to a low level
embrace	[imˈbreis]	v.	to make use of or accept eagerly
gauge	[geidʒ]	n.	测量仪表
geometry	[dʒiˈɔmitri]	n.	(几何)图形
gravitate	[ˈgræviteit]	v.	*formal* ~ toward sb/sth to move towards sb/sth that you are attracted to
hinge	[hindʒ]	v.	~ on sth (of an action, a result etc.) to depend on sth completely
inflection	[inˈflekʃən]	n.	变音，语调的抑扬变化
instantaneous	[ˌinstənˈteiniəs]	adj.	happening immediately
log	[lɔg]	v.	to travel or work for a particular length of time

第二单元 衣食住行

logjam	[ˈlɔgdʒæm]	n.	阻塞
mainframe	[ˈmeinfreim]	n.	[计]主(计算)机
manifestation	[ˌmænifeˈsteiʃən]	n.	*formal* anything that is a sign that sth exists or is happening
maximize	[ˈmæksimaiz]	v.	to increase sth as much as possible
minimize	[ˈminimaiz]	v.	to reduce sth to the lowest possible level
notionally	[ˈnəuʃənəli]	adv.	从理论上讲,从概念上说
novelty	[ˈnɔvlti]	n.	the quality of being new, different and interesting
panel	[ˈpænl]	n.	仪表盘
peripheral	[pəˈrifərəl]	adj.	外围的,边缘的
punctuate	[ˈpʌŋktʃueit]	v.	to break the flow of sth repeatedly
reap	[ri:p]	v.	to obtain sth, especially sth good
replicate	[ˈreplikeit]	v.	*formal* to copy sth exactly
reverse	[riˈvə:s]	v.	to change a decision to the opposite
rim	[rim]	n.	边,缘
shed	[ʃed]	v.	to get ride of
simulated	[ˈsimjuleitid]	adj.	模拟的
stately	[ˈsteitli]	adj.	impressive in size
stuff	[stʌf]	v.	to fill a space or container tightly with
stumble	[ˈstʌmbl]	n.	绊脚,失足
swap	[swɔp]	v.	to exchange
telecommuting	[ˌtelikəˈmju:tiŋ]	n.	(通过计算机网络等设备)远程办公
terminal	[ˈtə:minl]	n.	终端(设备)机
underscore	[ˌʌndəˈskɔ:]	v.	to emphasize
video conference	[ˈvidiəuˈkɔnfərəns]	n.	电视会议
wrap	[ræp]	v.	to cover sth completely in paper or other material
wrench	[rentʃ]	n.	throw a ~ into sth *informal* 阻挠;破坏

II. Background Information

远程办公

　　远程办公(remote work),亦称电子联勤(telecommuting),指借用网络、电话,或移动电话、传真、电子邮件、音频视频软件等通信设备在家或其他非传统办公地点工作的新型办公形式。

　　伴随着通信技术的迅猛发展和经济全球化步伐加快,越来越多的企业为了适应新时代的生存环境,大刀阔斧革新企业管理模式,远程办公便应运而生。

　　远程办公建立网络工作环境可以超越地域限制,提高公司的服务能力和扩大公司的业务范围,精简机构,减少办公租用场地,从而节省经济成本;减少员工通勤时间,缓解交通压力,降低碳排放,有利于环境保护。对于员工而言,远程办公可以让他们自主安排时间,平衡工作与生活。员工的满意度上升,工作积极性提高,对公司的凝聚力增加,反过来也促使公司的生产力提高。

　　正因为具有上述优点,这些年来远程办公模式规模不断扩大。根据盖洛普2015年8月的一份调查报告,美国具有远程办公经历的员工的比例1995年为9%,2006年这一比例增至32%,2015年进一步上升到37%。美国工作人员一个月人均有两天时间远程办公。

　　远程办公与个人的学历、行业和地位有着密切关系。美国劳工部统计局的一项调查发现学历越高者远程工作比例越高。远程工作者在高中毕业的群体中所占比例为13.8%,在具有大专学历或准学士学位的群体中所占比例为17.5%,可是在具有大学本科学历者中却是39%。在各行业中,信息通信行业远程办公最为普遍,该行业的上班族中超过六分之一的人不在办公室工作。紧随其后的是专业性较强的行业以及科研和技术行业。卫生行业中远程办公者比例较低,为十二分之一。教育和零售业远程办公比例更低,仅为十四分之一。在公司里层次越高的管理人员越有可能在家办公,经理在家办公所占比例为五分之一,而级别低的上班族的比例仅是十五分之一。

　　远程办公虽然具有诸多好处,但这种管理模式也带来了以下不可忽视的问题:员工彼此接触减少,交流效果减弱;工作氛围不利于相互启发思维、激发灵感,从而对协作工作效率造成负面影响;引发办公室工作者对在家工作者群体的嫉妒和不满;员工相互交流接触减少导致集体凝聚力降低,公司文化淡化;对于那些缺乏自我控制和自我规划能力的员工会导致工作效率下降,不善于调节心理的员工容易产生孤独感和焦虑感。

　　2016年后,美国出现一股逆流。一些曾经热衷于推行远程办公模式的公司开始废除这一模式,要求员工返回办公室工作。国际商业机器公司是远程办公的鼻祖,早在1979年该公司就开始了这一尝试并取得了可喜的实际效果,故而规模不断扩大。到2009年,这家公司几乎有40%的员工采用了远程办公方式。但在2017年5月,该公司宣布取消这一做法,让数千名远程办公员工回到实体办公场所。雅虎公司首席执行官玛丽萨·迈耶上任后实施的新政之一就是废除远程办公制度,要求工作人员都到办公室上班。迈耶认为,肩并肩一起工作可以使员工更好地交流与合作,能产生更强的凝聚力。该公司人力资源部主管杰奎琳·雷塞斯说:"作为雅虎公司的一员,你们要做的不只是日复一日地工作,它还意味着互动和体验,而这些只能在雅虎办公室里发生。"电子零售商百思买公司也采取类似行动。公司发言人说:"在家工作是权利,现在需要商量,只有经理认为有必要在家工作才会批准申请。"

　　新冠疫情的爆发对远程办公形成了推动力量。2020年5月美国疫情最严重的时候,超过1/3的职工至少部分工作是在家里完成。然而,伴随疫情的逐步缓和,很多公司又开始要求员工返回公司上班。

III. Notes to the Text

1. IN 1979, IBM was putting its stamp on the American landscape. —1979年（美国）国际商业机器公司正在对美国产生不可磨灭的影响。（① IBM—国际商业机器公司,1911年创立,是世界最大的信息技术和业务解决方案公司,在全球拥有30多万雇员,业务遍布160多个国家和地区。② put its stamp on —to produce its lasting effect on ）

2. the greats of modernism—现代主义的（建筑）大师 (great—*informal* a very well-known and successful person)

3. Sante Teresa Laboratory—圣塔特蕾莎实验室

4. Silicon valley—硅谷（位于美国加州,是美国主要微电子公司集中地,因微电子工业主要材料是硅片而得名）

5. selling its signature buildings and institutionalizing distance work—出售其特色办公大楼,使远程办公制度化（① signature—bearing a particular quality that makes sth different; ② institutionalize—to make sth part of an organized system）

6. Leading by example was good marketing.—以自身榜样引领时代具有很好的营销作用。(marketing—the activity of presenting, advertising, and selling a company's products)

7. whose revenues had fallen 20 quarters in a row— (公司的)收入20个季度连续下降（in a row—one after the other without a break）

8. Global Workplace Analytics—全球工作场所分析公司（It is a research-based consulting organization.)

9. Aetna and Best Buy have taken heat for like-minded moves since. —从此,安泰保险公司和百思买集团由于采取同样行动而受到攻击。（① Aetna—美国一家国际医疗保险公司；② Best Buy—美国一家全球最大的家用电器和电子商品零售集团；③ take heat — to receive criticism; ④ like-minded—having similar ideas and interests）

10. Big Blue's decision—国际商业机器公司的决定（Big Blue — 国际商业机器公司的外号,由于该公司的徽标是蓝色的,数以千计的经理都很传统地穿着蓝色衣服而获此称号）

11. high-water mark— a line or mark showing the highest point that the sea or flood water has reached, here used figuratively in the sense of the most successful stage of achievement

12. I see two other business-casual-clad men hammering away on their laptops beside me at a Starbucks just outside Chicago—就在芝加哥市外一家星巴克咖啡店里我看见旁边两个身着商务休闲装的人用便携式电脑在认真工作。（① business-casual —以商务、时尚气息为主调的服装,既体面整洁又偏带休闲味；② hammer away—to work hard）

13. break room—a room in a work place that is set aside for employees to use during a break from work, as to relax, socialize or eat

14. The data tend to talk past each other. —数据相互之间往往缺乏关联性。

15. Comfort-wise, it's not a great setup. —就舒适程度而言,这并非是很理想的安排（comfort-wise—in the way of comfort）

16. UC San Diego and UC Irvine—加州大学圣地亚哥分校和加州大学欧文分校（这两所大学是世界比较著名的公立研究型大学）

17. More-recent tools like the workplace-communication app Slack integrate social cues into written languages, leveraging the immediacy of instant-messaging and the informality of emoji, plus the ability to create a channel to bond over last night's #gameofthrones.—更为新近出现的如Slack一类办公交流软件把社交暗示融入书面语，采用即时通信的实时性和表情符号的非正式性，还具有创建黏合前一夜电视剧《权力的游戏》的渠道的能力。[①Slack——一款提供大型聊天群组、工具集合、文件整合等多种功能的办公交流软件；② social cues—verbal or nonverbal hints which guide conversation or other social interactions; ③ bond over—to join firmly; ④ #gameofthrones—referring to "Games of Thrones"(《权力的游戏》，美国HBO电视网制作的一部中世纪史诗奇幻题材的电视剧，该剧曾获多项电视剧奖);⑤ leverage—to use)]

18. MIT— Massachusetts Institute of Technology (美国)麻省理工学院

19. The expectation was that information technology would flatten the so-called Allen Curve.—当时的期望是信息技术会拉平所谓的"艾伦曲线"。[the Allen Curve—In communication theory, the Allen Curve is a graphical representation that reveals the exponential (呈几何级数的) drop in frequency of communication between engineers as the distance between them increases. It was discovered by MIT professor Thomas J. Allen in the late 1970s.]

20. Whatever the mechanisms at play, they were successfully distilled into what Judith Olson, a distance-work expert at UC Irvine, calls "radical collocation."—不管是什么机制在起作用，这些机制被成功优化为加州大学欧文分校研究远程办公专家朱迪斯·奥尔生所称的"超级搭配"。(radical—*AmE slang*, very good)

21. Ford Motor—Ford Motor Company 福特汽车公司

22. war room—(司令部内的)作战室

23. Agile, an approach to software development— 敏捷方法，一种软件开发方式 [是一种提高软件开发效率的方法，又称轻量级方法(lightweight methodology)]

24. Post-it Note—便利贴/报事贴(a Post-it Note is a small piece of paper with a strip of glue on its back, made for temporarily attaching notes to documents and other spaces.)

25. the age of the never-ending software update—永无止境的软件更新时代

26. You diagnose a problem, deliver a quick-and-dirty solution, get feedback, course-correct, and repeat, always with an eye on the changing weather outside. —确定问题原因，提供应急方案，获取反馈，改变方案，周而复始，永远关注外界形势的变化。(quick-and-dirty — *AmE slang*, used to describe sth that is usually complicated, but is being done quickly and simply in this case)

IV. Language Features

前置定语

本文多处使用前置定语(premodification),例如:high-water mark, green-screened terminals, work-from-home policy, business-casual-clad men, distance-work expert, no-longer-remote workers, quick-and-dirty solution。前置定语不仅可以替代短语,还可以替代定语从句,是精练句式的十分有效的手段。例如:

an all-male club (a club whose members are all male) 男子俱乐部
once-poor farmers (farmers who were once poor) 曾经贫穷的农民
mosquito-breeding place (place where mosquitoes breed) 蚊虫滋生场所

在现代英语中,前置定语使用频率日趋增加。由于它可以浓缩结构,节约篇幅,因而深受新闻写作人员青睐。《美国新闻与世界报道》专栏作家约翰·利奥(John Leo)曾在一篇新闻语言评论文章中称前置定语为"新闻语言的基本成分"。

从结构上看,新闻英语的前置定语大致可分为六类:

1. 名词短语作前置定语

mom-and-pop store	夫妻店
a dead-end job	没有奔头的工作
waste-to-energy power plant	垃圾发电厂
carrot-and-stick policy	胡萝卜加大棒政策
rags-to-riches success story	乞丐成富翁的成功故事

2. 动词短语作前置定语

a stand-up meeting	站着开的会议
start-up costs	启动费用
drive-by shooting	飞车射杀
do-it-yourself repair	自己动手修理
kill-for-a-fix crime	为过吸毒瘾所犯的抢劫杀人罪

3. 形容词短语作前置定语

war-weary citizen	厌倦战争的公民
fire-proof materials	耐火材料
fail-safe system	故障保险系统
power-hungry politician	权欲熏心的政客
sugar-free drink	不含糖饮料

4. 介词短语作前置定语

on-the-job problem	工作时出的问题
on-site service	现场服务
on-the-spot investigation	现场调查
under-the-counter dealings	台下交易
on-duty officer	值班军官

5. 分词短语作前置定语
turned-on audience	激动的观众
sexually-transmitted disease	性渠道传染疾病
land-based missile	陆基导弹
flood-stricken region	洪水袭击的地区
the over-drained clan	掏空族
people-oriented concept	以人为本的理念

6. 句子作前置定语
a seeing-is-believing attitude	眼见为实的态度
the three-strikes-and-you're-out law	"事不过三"法(犯罪三次,终身监禁)

V. Analysis of Content

1. Which of the following communication technologies is the worst according to the author?
   A. email
   B. the telephone
   C. video conferencing
   D. the workplace communication app Slack
2. It can be seen from the article that telecommuting is suitable for _____.
   A. all kinds of jobs
   B. jobs hinging on "collaborative efficiency"
   C. jobs requiring close teamwork
   D. jobs hinging on personal productivity
3. According to the author, reaction to IBM's announcement about reversing remote work was ____.
   A. highly critical
   B. favorable
   C. unknown
   D. supportive
4. Agile is _____.
   A. a name of a place
   B. a name of a person.
   C. a name of a software development approach
   D. a name of a company
5. Which of the following companies never allowed telecommuting?
   A. IBM
   B. Google
   C. Ford Motor
   D. Yahoo

VI. Questions on the Article

1. What experiment did IBM's Santa Teresa Laboratory try? What was the aim?
2. How large was the scale of IBM's tele-commuting in 2009? What effect did it produce?
3. What announcement did IBM make in March, 2017? What was the outside reaction?
4. Why does the author say that IBM's callback of its employees is telling?

5. Is telecommuting out of date in the U.S.?
6. What does the example of a Boeing 727's cockpit prove?
7. What is the weakness that all of these electronic technologies have?
8. What did Thomas Allen's study of communication patterns among scientists and engineers find?
9. What did Ben Waber's study find?
10. Why does Judith Olson caution that the extreme model of "radical collocation" is hard to replicate?
11. How is the new workplace designed to both minimize and maximize communication according to the article?

VII. Topics for Discussion

1. Is telecommuting out of date?
2. Can electronic communication replace face-to-face communication?

Lesson 8

Seeing the Back of the Car[1]

In the rich world, people seem to be driving less than they used to.
(Abridged)

"I'll love and protect this car until death do us part," says Toad, a 17-year-old loser whose life is briefly transformed by a "super fine" 1958 Chevy Impala in "American Graffiti."[2] The film follows him, his friends and their vehicles through a late summer night in early 1960s California: cruising the main drag, racing on the back streets and necking in back seats of machines which embody not just speed, prosperity and freedom but also adulthood, status and sex.[3]

The movie was set in an age when owning wheels was a norm deeply desired and newly achievable.[4] Since then car ownership has grown apace. There are now more than 1 billion cars in the world, and the number is likely to roughly double by 2020. They are cheaper, faster, safer and more comfortable than ever before.

Cars are integral to modern life. They account for 70% of all journeys not made on foot in the OECD[5], which includes most developed countries. In the European Union more than 12m people work in manufacturing and services related to cars and other vehicles, around 6% of the total employed population; the equivalent figure for America is 4.5% of private-sector employment, or 8m jobs. They dominate household economies too: aside from rent or mortgage payments, transport costs are the single biggest weekly outlay, and most of those costs normally come from cars.

Nearly 60m new cars were added to the world's stock in 2011. People in Asia, Latin America and Africa are buying cars pretty much as fast as they can afford to, and as more can afford to, more will buy.

But in the rich world the car's previously inexorable rise is stalling. A growing body of academics cite the possibility that both car ownership and vehicle-kilometres driven may be reaching saturation in developed countries—or even be on the wane, a notion known as "peak car."[6]

Recession and high fuel prices have markedly cut distances driven in many countries since 2008, including America, Britain, France and Sweden. But more profound and longer-run changes underlie recent trends. Most forecasts still predict that when the recovery comes, people will drive as much and in the same way as they ever have. But that may not be true.

As a general trend, car ownership and kilometres travelled have been increasing throughout the rich world since the 1950s. Short-term factors like the 1970s oil-price shock caused temporary dips, but vehicle use soon recovered.

The current fall in car use has doubtless been exacerbated by recession. But it seems to have started before the crisis. A March 2012 study for the Australian government—which has been at the forefront of international efforts to tease out peak-car issues[7]—suggested that 20 countries in the rich world show a "saturating trend" to vehicle-kilometres travelled. After decades when each individual was on average travelling farther every year, growth per person has slowed distinctly, and in many cases stopped altogether.

There are different measures of saturation: total distance driven, distance per driver and total trips made. The statistics are striking on each of these counts even in America, still the most car-mad country in the world. There, total vehicle-kilometres travelled began to plateau in 2004 and fall from 2007; measured per person, growth flatlined sooner, after 2000, and dropped after 2004 before recovering somewhat (see chart). The number of trips has fallen, mostly because of a decline in commuting and shopping (of the non-virtual variety)[8].

Britain, another nation that measures such things obsessively, has a similar arc. Kilometres travelled per person were stable or falling through most of the 2000s. Total traffic has not increased for a decade, despite a growing population. For the past 15 years Britons have been making fewer journeys; they now go out in cars only slightly more often than in the 1970s. Pre-recession declines in per-person travel were also recorded in France, Spain, Italy, Australia, New Zealand and Belgium.

Saturation of car ownership over time is one explanation. The current cohort of retirees—Toad from "American Graffiti", having faked his death in Vietnam, is now 67—is the first in which most people drove. So more retired people drive now than ever before. In Britain 79% of people in their 60s hold licences, which is higher than the figure for the driving-age population as a whole; in America more than 90% of people aged 60—64 can drive, a larger share than for any other cohort. New generations of drivers will replace old ones rather than add to the total number.

Then there is a second trend. All over the rich world, young people are getting their licences later than they used to. Even in Germany, car-culture-vulture of Europe, the share of young households without cars increased from 20% to 28% between 1998 and 2008.[9] Unsurprisingly, this goes along with driving less. American youngsters with jobs drive less far and less often than before the recession. 16- to 34-year-olds in American households with incomes over $70,000 increased their public-transport use by 100% from 2001 to 2009, according to the Frontier Group, a think-tank.

Cost is one factor: fuel prices have risen for all; insurance premiums for the young have soared. Youth unemployment has not helped. But there is also the influence of a new kid on the block: the Internet. A University of Michigan survey of 15 countries found that in areas where a lot of young people use the internet, fewer than normal have driving licences. KCR, a research firm, has found that in America far more 18- to 34-year-olds than any other age group say socialising online is a substitute for some car trips.

Even without changing absolute numbers, however, age can still play a role in patterns of use. Though more older people drive than used to, per person they also tend to drive less. And so, if people keep getting their licenses later, may everyone else. The later people pass their test, the less far they drive even once they can, according to Gordon Stokes of Oxford University. He says people in Britain who learn in their late 20s drive 30% less than those who learn a decade earlier.

Geography matters too. In most rich countries car use has been stable or increasing in rural areas, where driving still offers freedom and convenience. It is in cities, especially their centres, that car ownership and use is declining. And city living is on the rise: the OECD, a rich-country think-tank, expects that by 2050, 86% of the rich world's population will live in urban areas, up from 77% in 2010.

In America the share of metropolitan residents without a car has grown since the mid-1990s: 13% of people in cities of more than 3m people have no car while only 6% in rural areas live without one. In London car ownership has been falling since 1990, with a plateau from 1995 to 2005; the percentage of households without cars has been growing since 1992. In other British cities the proportion of carless households has been growing since 2005. Car use has fallen in many European cities.

There are various reasons for this. Public mass-transit systems[10] are, in the main, faster and more reliable than they used to be, with increased capacity in many cities. This partly reflects increased investment, particularly in rail. For the past 15 years road and rail investment has been about 1% of GDP for OECD countries, but rail's share of that has increased from 15% to 23%, says the International Transport Forum[11].

More recently, private alternatives to car ownership[12], notably car clubs, have been spreading across North America and northern Europe. By some estimates one rental car can take the place of 15 owned vehicles. Zipcar, which is the biggest international car-share scheme, has 700,000 members and over 9,000 vehicles.[13] Buzzcar, a French company set up by the Zipcar founder, has 605,000 members sharing 9,000 cars.

Perhaps most basic, though, is that in terms of urban living the car has become a victim of its own success. In 1994, the physicist Cesare Marchetti argued that people budget an average travel time of around one hour getting to work[14]; they are unwilling to spend more. For decades cars allowed this budget to go farther. But as suburbs grow and congestion increases most cities eventually hit a "sprawl wall" of too-long commutes beyond which they will not spread far.[15] After that, it appears, a significant number of people start to move back towards the city centre. In America, where over 50% of the population lives in suburbs, more than half the nation's 51 largest cities are seeing more growth in the core than outside it, according to William Frey at the Brookings Institution[16].

If car use has peaked, what are the implications? One is that vehicle-makers, which are already having a tough time, will not easily find new markets in the rich world. In America available cars already outnumber licensed drivers. "We are looking at replacement rather than growth in these countries," says Yves van der Straaten of the OICA[17], an international trade body of car manufacturers.

Some niche and luxury brands are thriving and are likely to keep doing so.[18] But manufacturers know that the developing world is the future—sales in China overtook those in America between 2010 and 2011 and rose by 2.6%; those in Indonesia, a younger market, jumped by 17%.

A more radical response from carmakers could be to say that if buyers are less interested in driving, then cars will require less driving from them. Driverless cars—robot-guided vehicles that leave their occupants free to text, work or sleep—could go on sale within the next decade[19], and might meet the mood of the moment. They could be safer and a lot less hassle. Flocking together through clever algorithms, they could cut congestion dramatically.[20] They might further strain the already weakening link between driving and identity and the sense of driving as an expression of self and skill. But they could still be a highly profitable innovation.

The possibility of reaching "peak car" is most evident in the rich world. But emerging-world cities may reach a similar state earlier in their development, reckons David Metz of University College London[21].

Non-OECD countries have higher levels of vehicle ownership now than OECD countries did at similar income levels. This is because their transport infrastructure has developed faster than it did in richer countries, cars are cheaper in real terms and urbanization is happening faster.

Since car use is growing so fast—and urban planning lags behind—cities in poorer countries could hit the "sprawl wall" sooner than those in the rich world did, reckons Mr Newman. Space is already at a premium in dense centres[22] such as Jakarta, where the number of cars is growing ten times faster than the roads available for them to roll on.

Some municipalities in the developing world are already planning for less car use, notably by deploying urban rail systems. The Shanghai metro, mostly built since 2000, ferries 8m people a day and covers 80% of the city. Eighteen Indian cities and several Middle Eastern ones are designing urban rail networks.

But after 50 years of car culture, culture may finally be changing the car. Gone is the nostalgia of "American Graffiti." "Cosmopolis,"[23] released in 2012, also features a cocky young man deeply involved with his car; but it is a near stationary limousine that constrains and isolates him far more than it enhances his possibilities. "I'm looking for more," he protests during his endless journey across Manhattan. The world's once and future car-owners are increasingly inclined to agree.

From *The Economist*, September 22, 2012

I. New Words

apace	[əˈpeis]	*adv.*	at a fast speed
arc	[ɑ:k]	*n.*	弧形
cocky	[ˈkɔki]	*adj.*	狂妄自信的
congestion	[kənˈdʒesʃən]	*n.*	拥塞
defuse	[diˈfju:z]	*v.*	卸除……的引信；缓和，平息
dip	[dip]	*n.*	a decrease in the amount
exacerbate	[igˈzæsəbeit]	*v.*	*formal* to make sth worse
ferry	[ˈferi]	*v.*	渡运，运送
flatline	[ˈflætlain]	*v.*	*informal* to be at a low level and fail to increase
hassle	[ˈhæsl]	*n.*	困难，问题，麻烦
inexorable	[inˈeksərəbl]	*adj.*	*formal* (of a process) that cannot be stopped or changed

infrastructure	[ˈinfrəstrʌktʃə]	n.	基础, 基础设施
integral	[ˈintigrəl]	adj.	~ to sth being an essential part of sth
municipality	[mjuːˌnisiˈpæliti]	n.	市政当局
nostalgia	[nɔˈstældʒiə]	n.	恋旧, 怀旧
outlay	[ˈautlei]	n.	money spent for a purpose
plateau	[ˈplætəu]	v.	to stay at a steady level after a period of growth
saturation	[sætʃəˈreiʃən]	n.	饱和(状态)
stall	[stɔːl]	v.	to stop suddenly because of a lack of power
stationary	[ˈsteiʃənəri]	adj.	not moving
substitute	[ˈsʌbstitjuːt]	n.	代替物
vulture	[ˈvʌltʃə]	n.	[鸟]秃鹫; 贪得无厌者

II. Background Information

汽车文化

在美国, 汽车十分普及, 号称"车轮上的国家"(a country on wheels)。据2010年统计资料, 美国共有两亿五千四百多万辆汽车, 平均每户(household)拥有车辆数为1.9辆。

伴随城市"郊区化"(suburbanization)和"远郊化"(exurbanization), 许多美国人的居住地点离工作场所、文化娱乐设施、医院、学校和购物中心越来越远, 驾车便成了生活中的重要部分, 占去了相当多的时间。据2010年的数据, 美国人一年驾车里程平均约为21688千米, 开车时间每天平均有72分钟; 有三百多万人每天驾车时间在90分钟以上, 属于"极端型通勤者"(extreme commuters)。美国人均花在汽车和汽油上的费用一年平均为5477美元, 每天的费用占一天总消费的14.5%。

从18世纪90年代起, 美国发起了改善公路运输运动。20世纪60年代开始, 政府开始大力修建和完善高速公路网络。经过几十年的发展, 美国高速公路系统已经完备。高速公路和主次干道纵横交错, 辅助设施完整齐备。

美国人领取正式驾照的起始年龄是18周岁, 15岁半可以领取临时驾照(provisional driver license), 这类驾照有不少附加限制。有的州领取临时驾照年龄降至14周岁。

汽车对美国人而言是福也是祸, 既为他们带来自由和方便, 也给他们带来一些灾难和问题。首先是交通事故: 据报道, 2010年美国共发生542万起撞车事故(car crashes), 导致32886人死亡, 230万人受伤。另一大问题是环境污染。据美国能源部发布的数据, 2011年美国汽车耗油总量高达1420亿加仑。汽车排放污染(motor vehicle emissions)十分惊人: 汽车一氧化碳(carbon monoxide)排放量占美国总排放量的二分之一以上, 汽车二氧化氮(nitrogendioxide)排放量占总排放量的三分之一以上,汽车碳氢化合物排放量占总排放量的四分之一以上。除此之外,汽车还排放大量的颗粒物质(particulate matter)、温室气体(greenhouse gases)和其他污染物。美国科学研究人员认为汽车排放污染所造成的美国人死亡人数每年多达三万人。

近年来美国汽车市场呈现饱和状态。2007年下半年,美国步入了经济衰退期。经济不景气使得许多年轻人推迟购车时间;城市扩张步伐放缓,不少人回归市区生活;公交服务质量提高,很多人觉得乘坐公交既方便又经济。上述因素导致美国私家汽车销售数量和使用情况有所下降。

III. Notes to the Text

1. Seeing the Back of the Car — Abandoning the use of the car
2. Toad, a 17-year-old loser whose life is briefly transformed by a "super fine" 1958 Chevy Impala in "American Graffiti." —在《美国风情画》影片中 Toad 是一名17岁的倒霉鬼,可一辆"超级"1958年款雪佛兰羚羊牌车却短暂地改变了他的生活。[① Chevy Impala—a full size automobile built by the division of General Motors; ② American Graffiti—(1973) a U.S. film made by George Lucas about a group of young men in California in the 1960s, who go out at night, drive around in big cars, and try to attract girls. Terry "the Toad" Fields, a member of the group, drives a car borrowed from his friend Steve Bolander, trying to find a girl friend.]
3. ...cruising the main drag, racing on the back streets and necking in back seats of machines which embody not just speed, prosperity and freedom but also adulthood, status and sex. —在主街大道上漫游,偏僻街道上飞奔,车后座位上亲吻,汽车体现的不仅是速度、财富和自由,而且是成年、地位和性感。(① drag—*slang* street; ② neck—to kiss in a sexual way; ③ embody—to represent a quality)
4. The movie was set in an age when owning wheels was a norm deeply desired and newly achievable. —影片背景是拥有汽车已经成为人们内心十分渴求、经济能力新近可以实现的生活目标的时代。(① wheels—referring to cars; ② set—to place the movie in a particular time)
5. OECD—Organization for Economic Cooperation and Development 经济合作与发展组织(简称经合组织,该组织是由36个市场经济国家组成的政府间国际经济组织,成立于1961年,总部设在巴黎。)
6. ...both car ownership and vehicle-kilometres driven may be reaching saturation in developed countries—or even on the wane, a notion known as "peak car." —发达国家汽车拥有量和行驶里程可能快要达到饱和,甚至正在下降,这一概念被称为"汽车峰值"。(① on the wane — growing less; ② peak car—also "peak car use" or "peak car travel," a notion that motor vehicle distance travelled per capita has reached the highest point)
7. ...which has been at the forefront of international efforts to tease out peak-car issues —在世界各国中(澳大利亚)政府一直率先努力搞清汽车峰值问题 (tease out—to spend time trying to find out information or the meaning of sth)

8. shopping (of the non-virtual variety)—referring to the kind of shopping done by going to stores and buying things in person instead of using the Internet

9. Even in Germany, car-culture-vulture of Europe, the share of young households without cars increased from 20% to 28% between 1998 and 2008.—即使在欧洲汽车占有欲望最大的国家德国,年轻的无车户比率也从1998年的20%增长到了2008年的28%。(car-culture-vulture—referring to a society greedy for car ownership)

10. public mass-transit systems—公共交通系统

11. International Transport Forum—国际交通论坛

12. private alternatives to car ownership—取代汽车私有的私营机构

13. Zipcar, which is the biggest international car-share scheme, has 700,000 members and over 9,000 vehicles.—Zipcar是国际上最大的汽车共享机构,它拥有九千多辆车,其成员有70万。(Zipcar—美国一家大型网上租车公司,通过吸收会员、发会员卡运营。会员预约用车,用完后在预定时间开回原地。)

14. In 1994, the physicist Cesare Marchetti argued that people budget an average travel time of around one hour getting to work…—1994年物理学家西泽雷·马凯蒂认为人们每天上班预计花在交通上的时间平均为一小时左右(budget—to plan to spend an amount of time for a particular purpose)

15. But as suburbs grow and congestion increases most cities eventually hit a "sprawl wall" of too-long commutes beyond which they will not spread far.—但是,伴随郊区扩张和交通拥堵情况增加,大部分城市最终达到"扩张极限":通勤距离过长,不能继续扩张。

16. Brookings Institution —布鲁金斯学会(总部设在华盛顿的一个非营利性的政治学与经济学研究所,带有自由主义色彩)

17. OICA —(Organisation Internationale des Constructeurs d'Automobiles)世界汽车组织(成立于1919年,总部设在巴黎)

18. Some niche and luxury brands are thriving and are likely to keep doing so. —一些定位明确的豪华汽车品牌生意兴隆,这种态势可能会持续下去。(niche brand — a brand targeting a particular group of people)

19. Driverless cars—robot-guided vehicles that leave their occupants free to text, work or sleep—could go on sale within the next decade…—无人驾驶汽车,即机器人驾驶汽车,使乘车者能自由发短信、工作或睡觉,此类车可能在未来十年内上市(无人驾驶汽车是一种智能汽车,主要依靠车内的计算机系统为主的智能驾驶仪来实施驾驶)

20. Flocking together through clever algorithms, they could cut congestion dramatically. —通过巧妙的计算程序使汽车成群结队运行,可以大大减少拥堵。(①flock—to go together in large numbers; ②dramatically—greatly; ③algorithm—算法,计算程序)

21. University College London —伦敦大学学院(一所综合性大学,创建于1826年,通常被认为是继牛津、剑桥大学之后英格兰第三古老大学。)

22. Space is already at a premium in dense centres… —在车辆密集的市中心空间已经稀缺(at a premium—there is little of it available)

23. "Cosmopolis" —电影《大都会》(影片讲述一个28岁的孤傲的亿万富翁坐豪华的轿车穿过曼哈顿的繁华市区前去理发途中遇到的形形色色的人和各种怪异的事。由于股市异常,他的全部财产一天之内化作泡影。)

IV. Language Features

《经济学人》简介

《经济学人》周刊创刊于1843年9月,迄今已有170多年历史。该刊创刊人是詹姆斯·威尔逊,现在该刊归经济学家集团所有。该集团是一家私人企业,一半股份由私人股东控制,另一半由《金融时报》拥有。其经济收入一半来自读者订阅,另一半来自广告。

2018年,该刊纸质刊在全世界发行量近86.8万,其中北美所占份额最大,所占比例为56%,英国占18%,欧洲占16%,亚洲占8%,中东和非洲占1%,拉丁美洲占1%。该刊电子刊一年在全球的发行量为79万。

《经济学人》自称是报纸,但其版面却更像是新闻周刊。其创刊的目的是"参与推动社会发展的智慧和阻碍社会发展的卑劣、胆怯的愚昧之间的一场激烈博弈",这句话仍印在每期目录页的左下角处。

该刊一直奉行所刊登文章不署名的做法。据称,这样做的目的是突出"协作成果"和"集体观点"。该刊读者定位是受过高等教育、富有独立见解的精英,声称其读者群中许多是经理和决策者。

自创刊以来,《经济学人》始终保持自己的独特风格:注重数字、图表,强调新闻事实,看重理性分析。它很少刊登广告,这与广告充斥的其他新闻刊物形成了鲜明对照。

《经济学人》每期第5—6页是这期杂志文章的目录,主要有两大部分。一部分是世界政治和时事,下分:亚洲、美国、美洲、国际、欧洲、英国。另一大部分涉及企业、金融和科技。目录页还标出该期杂志的封面故事、重要文章、一周新闻概要、亚洲、美国、南北美洲、中东和非洲、欧洲、英国、商业、金融与经济、科学技术、图书艺术等栏目。此外,还有读者来信等。2012年初,该刊增设了中国栏(China)。

《经济学人》清晰、简洁的写作风格独树一帜,对于复杂的社会问题、世界重大事件,它能以浅显的语言、较短的篇幅、清楚的图表把来龙去脉、前因后果交代出来,条理自然,表达清晰,令人叹服。

美国新闻写作学家卡彭在《美联社写作指南》一书中高度赞赏《经济学人》的文笔:"英国《经济学人》深受称赞,虽然它所报道的是严肃题材,但它所用的文字却简洁明快,许多导语所含句子的平均长度只有16个词,文章大部分句子较短,平均在16至19个词之间。"

《经济学人》的另一大特色是其英国式的幽默与辛辣讽刺。它对美国社会文化的报道、对其政治形势的评论常常夹杂一些讥讽,使得美国知识分子感到不是滋味。

该刊声称坚守超党派立场,前编辑杰弗里·克劳瑟曾说:"极端中立是本刊的传统立场。"《经济学人》常被称为"英国金融界的喉舌,所登文章大都反映出相关的资本主义垄断集团的观点和立场"。

该刊对我国报道镜头往往对准负面,常常表现深刻偏见。

V. Analysis of Content

1. According to the article, the most car-mad country in the world is _____.
   A. America   B. Britain   C. Germany   D. France
2. Car use has been dropping the fastest in _____.
   A. rural areas   B. suburbs   C. metropolitan areas   D. city centers
3. The author's list of measures of car saturation does NOT include _____.
   A. total distance driven   B. total number of cars
   C. total trips made   D. distance per driver
4. Which country has been leading international efforts to find out information about "peak car" issues?
   A. the U.S.   B. Britain   C. Australia   D. Japan
5. The author's use of the movie "Cosmopolis" is intended to show _____.
   A. Americans' nostalgia for speed, prosperity, freedom and status
   B. the prosperity of the U.S.
   C. the richness of metropolitan culture
   D. cars' possible effects of constraining and isolating a person

VI. Questions on the Article

1. How fast has car ownership grown in the world since the 1960s?
2. What role do cars play in the modern life of people in the OECD?
3. What do cars mean to the economy of the rich world?
4. How is the car sale situation in the developing world?
5. Is the car's increase in the rich world continuing?
6. When did the fall in car use start in the rich world?
7. What do the statistics show about car saturation in America?
8. What is the impact of age on driving?
9. What does geography have to do with driving?
10. What are the implications of car saturation for car manufacturers?
11. Why is it possible for emerging world cities to reach "peak car" earlier in their development?

VII. Topics for Discussion

1. Will developing-world cities reach "peak car" earlier in their development?
2. Should developing countries popularize cars as developed countries did?

Unit 3
第三单元 家庭婚姻

Lesson 9

No One Way to Keep Love in Bloom, Experts Say

By Shankar Vedantam

More than a century ago, Russian novelist Leo Tolstoy[1] wrote, "Happy families are all alike; every unhappy family is unhappy in its own way."

The words have become immortalized, and the unhappy story of *Anna Karenina*[2] is considered one of the greatest novels ever written. Recently, however, psychologists and sociologists are starting to question the observation.

"I think Tolstoy was totally wrong," said John Gottman, a professor of psychology at the University of Washington in Seattle[3]. "Unhappy families are really similar to one another—there's much more variability among happy families."

As couples clink wine glasses over candlelit Valentine's Day dinners this week and exchange vows of undying love, Gottman and others are trying to understand why as many as one in two marriages end in divorce, and why so many couples seem to fall out of love and break apart.[4]

Some of the most revealing answers, it turns out, come from the couples who stay together. While conventional wisdom holds that conflicts in a relationship slowly erode the bonds that hold partners together, couples who are happy in the long term turn out to have plenty of conflicts, too. Fights and disagreements are apparently intrinsic to all relationships—couples who stay together over the long haul are those who don't let the fighting contaminate the other parts of the relationship, experts say[5].

"Why do people get married in the first place?" asked Thomas Bradbury, a professor of psychology at the University of California at Los Angeles[6]. "To have someone to listen to—to have a friend, to share life's ups and downs. We want to try to draw attention to what's valuable in their relationship."

Researchers are finding that it is those other parts of relationships—the positive factors—that are potent predictors of whether couples feel committed to relationships, and whether they weather storms and stick together.[7] As long as those factors are intact, conflicts don't drive people apart.

"What we've discovered is surprising and contrary to what most people think," said Gottman, the author of *The Mathematics of Marriage*[8]. "Most books say it's important for couples to fight fair[9]—but 69 percent of all marital conflicts never get resolved because they are about personality differences between couples. What's critical is not whether they resolve conflicts but whether they can cope with them."

"Every couple has irreconcilable differences," agreed Diane Sollee, the founder of smartmarriages.com[10], a Web site devoted to teaching couples skills to improve their relationships. She explained such differences ought to be "managed," instead of being grounds for separations, split-ups and divorce.[11]

Almost 90 percent of Americans marry at some point in their lives. An overwhelming number of those who get divorced marry a second time, meaning that although they may have lost faith in a partner, they have not lost faith in the promise of the institution.

At the same time, changing social mores and expectations have placed stresses on long-term relationships. Two-income couples juggle (**juggling**) demanding jobs and professional advancement can sometimes detract from family and intimate relationships.[12]

Simultaneously, the rising number of women in the workforce has given women the economic security to leave unhappy relationships, the sexual revolution has made sex before and outside marriage common, and the destigmatization of divorce has contributed to the phenomenon of serial monogamy[13].

Despite these pressures and temptations, most Americans still seek lifelong soul mates[14]—and expectations from love and marriage have never been higher.

The juxtaposition of high expectations with the stress and cycles of relationships appears to be an important reason why many relationships don't work, said Ted Huston, a professor of human ecology and psychology at the University of Texas at Austin, who tracked 168 couples over $13\frac{1}{2}$ years.

Huston found that changes in the first two years of marriage often predicted the outcome of relationships. Almost half of all divorces occur within the first seven years of marriage, according to national census data[15], and many of these "early exiters" report a decline in "bliss" right after marriage[16].

"When you look at them as newlyweds, they look like they are mutually enchanted and deeply in love and a prototype of your perfectly wed couple—they hug, kiss, say, 'I love you' all the time," he said. "Two years later—they've lost a lot of that romance. They think, 'We once had this great romance, and now we don't.' "

"People have this fairly unrealistic idea: 'I have got to have bliss and it's got to stay or this is not going to work[17],' " he said. "At some level, you don't need the bliss. The Hollywood romance may not be the prelude to a long-term happy marriage.[18]"

Couples who were happy over the long term reported being content at the start of relationships and still contented two years later. Some of these couples told Huston, "I wasn't sure I was in love because I didn't have the tingly feelings you are supposed to have," he said. "They worried their feelings were positive but not intense.[19]"

Pepper Schwartz, a professor of sociology at the University of Washington in Seattle, said her study of 6,000 couples—heterosexual, gay, lesbian, married and cohabiting—also revealed that couples in long-term relationships tended to have mutual respect, took pride in each other and saw themselves as equals.

"Very successful couples we studied had something besides children that was enjoyable to their relationship," she added. "It could be travel, hospice work, working on a summer place... Those things bring stability because they confer pleasure and identity in the way people live together. If you don't like to be together, and don't like the same friends and don't have the same hobbies, you have a problem."

No scientific study, of course, says much about an individual couple—and the new research underscores that there are a wide variety of happy couples. And factors beyond individual circumstance—social and family supports, socioeconomic status, government and workplace policies—can help and hinder relationships.

For example, said Marilyn Yalom, a cultural historian at the Institute for Research on Women and Gender at Stanford University and the author of *A History of the Wife*[20], the arrival of babies significantly adds to parents' stress. Inexpensive and affordable child care, equitable benefits for gay and lesbian families, and more generous leave policies after the birth of a child can influence how lovers feel about themselves—and each other.

From *The Washington Post*, February 11, 2002

I. New Words

bliss	[blis]	n.	extreme happiness
clink	[kliŋk]	v.	(使)发叮当声
candlelit	[ˈkændl͵lit]	adj.	lit by candles
cohabit	[kəuˈhæbit]	v.	(男女)同居
contaminate	[kənˈtæmineit]	v.	污染
content	[kənˈtent]	adj.	happy and satisfied
ecology	[iːˈkɔlədʒi]	n.	生态;人类生态学
destigmatization	[͵distigmətaiˈzeiʃən]	n.	the act of getting rid of the disgraceful mark
enchant	[inˈtʃɑːnt]	v.	to attract and delight
equitable	[ˈekwitəbl]	adj.	just and impartial
erode	[iˈrəud]	v.	to gradually make sth weaker
exiter	[ˈeksitə]	n.	a person who exits
heterosexual	[͵hetərəuˈseksjuəl]	adj.	异性的;异性恋的
hinder	[ˈhində]	v.	to be or get in the way of
hospice	[ˈhɔspis]	n.	收容所,济贫院
immortalized	[iˈmɔːtəlaizd]	adj.	不朽的,名垂千古的
intact	[inˈtækt]	adj.	not changed or damaged in any way
intrinsic	[inˈtrinsik]	adj.	固有的,内在的
irreconcilable	[iˈrekənsailəbl]	adj.	不能和解的

juxtaposition	[ˌdʒʌkstəpəˈzɪʃn]	n.	并置,并列
lesbian	[ˈlezbiən, -bjən]	adj.&n.	(女性)同性恋的;同性恋的女性
monogamy	[məˈnɒgəmi]	n.	一夫一妻制
mores	[ˈmɔːriːz]	n.	道德观念
newlywed	[ˈnjuːliwed]	n.	a person who has recently married
overwhelming	[ˌəʊvəˈwelmɪŋ]	adj.	very great in number
prelude	[ˈpreljuːd]	n.	先驱;前奏,序幕
prototype	[ˈprəʊtətaɪp]	n.	原型;典型
tingly	[ˈtɪŋli]	adj.	causing a feeling of excitement
underscore	[ˌʌndəˈskɔː]	v.	to emphasize; stress
undying	[ʌnˈdaɪɪŋ]	adj.	不死的,永恒的;不朽的

II. Background Information

美国人的婚姻观念

第二次世界大战前,美国人的婚姻较为牢固,离婚被社会视为一种耻辱。20世纪40年代社会学教科书上写明:"离婚是公认的个人生活失败。"

第二次世界大战后,妇女就业率不断上升。妇女经济独立性的增强使丈夫对妻子的约束力也就减小了。工作使已婚妇女扩大了社会圈子,同时也增加了重新择偶的可能性。

美国进入20世纪60年代之后价值观念发生了很大变化。妇女解放运动增强了她们保护自身权益的意识,性解放运动(Sexual Liberation Movement)对传统性观念造成了重大冲击。个体主义(individualism)价值观的发展使美国人更加崇尚个人幸福和注重个人的选择。

过去,大多数美国人认为,即使夫妻感情不和,为了孩子的利益也得维持婚姻。然而,随着"追求个人欢乐"的观念增强,越来越多的人把个人利益放在首位,夫妇利益放在次位,孩子利益放在末位(self interest first, spousal interest second, and kids' interest last)。有的美国人类学者甚至提倡双方不受约束的"开放式婚姻"(open marriage),认为这样"可使个人获得最大的满足"。美国传媒对婚姻观念的改变起了推波助澜的作用,不少媒体把离婚颂扬为"自我解放"(self-liberation),"获得新生"(rebirth)。

观念的变化导致了法律的更改。1969年加州颁布了"无过失离婚法"(no-fault divorce law),其他一些地区相继仿效,离婚变得越来越容易。婚姻观念的变化也造成了下列四个问题:

1. 同居人数增加(increase of cohabitants)。据最近的调查,美国结婚者中三分之二有过同居经历。同居关系(live-in unions)比婚姻关系(married unions)更加脆弱。

2. 晚婚情况普遍(Late marriage has become more common.)。美国年轻人中晚婚

第三单元　家庭婚姻

者越来越多。1970年女性平均首次结婚年龄为20.8岁，男性为23.2岁。2017年这两个数字分别上升到27.4岁和29.5岁。

3. 离婚率上升(a rise in divorce rate)。20世纪50年代，有90%的新婚可以维系至少10年时间，而到90年代，这一比例已降至50%以下。于是，社会上流行"七年之痒"(seven-year itch)之说。

4. 不忠问题(the problem of infidelity)严重。据美国《结婚与离婚》期刊2019年公布的数据，美国社会已婚者中70%的人曾有过至少一次出轨。

上述问题并非说明美国人对婚姻持否定态度。调查显示：大多数美国人还是肯定婚姻的价值的。目前，美国成年人中有53%已结婚，65%至少结过一次婚。

近些年来，美国政府和社会机构采取了不少积极措施加强婚姻体制(the institution of marriage)，譬如中学开设婚姻价值观课程，为已婚者开办"夫妻交流"(couple communication)讲座和"婚姻技能培训班"(marriage skill workshops)等，有的州还颁布旨在限制离婚的"契约婚姻法"(covenant marriage law)。

III. Notes to the Text

1. Leo Tolstoy—列夫·托尔斯泰(1828—1910，俄国作家，位居世界文学领域最伟大的小说家之列，其杰作有《战争与和平》《安娜·卡列尼娜》和《复活》等。)

2. *Anna Karenina*—《安娜·卡列尼娜》(小说描述公爵夫人安娜·卡列尼娜与沃伦斯基的婚外情，安娜不顾强大社会压力与其私奔，后又遭沃伦斯基的冷淡对待，付出了失去家庭、儿子和社会地位的高昂代价。)

3. the University of Washington in Seattle—华盛顿大学西雅图分校

4. As couples clink wine glasses ... so many couples seem to fall out of love and break apart.—当情侣们在本周情人节的烛光晚餐碰杯、相互海誓山盟的时候，哥德曼与其他人正在试图弄懂为什么多达一半的婚姻都以离婚告终，为什么如此多的夫妻似乎不再相爱，关系破裂。(fall out of—give up)

5. couples who stay together over the long haul are those who don't let the fighting contaminate the other parts of the relationship, experts say—experts say that the long-term couples won't let the conflicts damage other parts of their relationship(over the long haul—for a long period of time)

6. the University of California at Los Angeles—加州大学洛杉矶分校

7. Researchers are finding that it is those other parts of relationships ... whether they weather storms and stick together.—研究者们发现正是婚姻关系中的其他方面，那些积极的因素能有效地预测配偶们是否会忠诚于他们的婚姻，是否能共渡难关，长期相守。(① potent—effective; ② weather storm—to come safely through a difficult period)

8. *The Mathematics of Marriage*—《婚姻数学》(The book is intended to provide the foundation for a scientific theory of marital relations. It applies a mathematical model using different equations.)

9. Most books say it's important for couples to fight fair... —大多数书都说心平气和地解决夫妻之间分歧十分重要(fight fair— to discuss differences in a calm and open-minded way)

10. the founder of *smartmarriages.com*—美国"聪明婚姻"网站(*smartmarriages.com*)的创始人(该网站旨在通过提供夫妻教育和相关信息而维护婚姻和减少家庭破裂)

11. She explained such differences ought to be "managed," instead of being grounds for separations, split-ups and divorce.—她解释说应该处理好这些分歧,而不应使其成为分居、关系破裂和离婚的理由。(grounds—good reasons)

12. Two-income couples juggle (**juggling**) demanding jobs and professional advancement can sometimes detract from family and intimate relationships.—双职工夫妻勉为其难地既要干好费力的工作,同时又要求事业上的发展,这有时会损害家庭和夫妻的亲密关系。(① juggle — to try to fit two or more jobs or activities into one's life; ② demanding—needing a lot of ability, effort, or skill; ③ detract from sth—to make sth less good than it really is)

13. the destigmatization of divorce has contributed to the phenomenon of serial monogamy—离婚不再被视为耻辱,这便促使了系列性一夫一妻制的出现(serial monogamy—指不断离散并与新伴结合而每次维持的时间很短的一夫一妻关系)

14. soul mates—心心相印的伙伴(two persons compatible with each other in disposition, point of view, or sensitivity)

15. national census data—人口普查资料

16. many of these "early exiters" report a decline in "bliss" right after marriage—许多"早离者"说他们刚结婚幸福感就下降了

17. I have got to have bliss and it's got to stay or this is not going to work —我得有幸福感,而且一直得有,否则不行

18. The Hollywood romance may not be the prelude to a long-term happy marriage.—好莱坞式的浪漫并不一定是长期幸福婚姻的序幕。(Hollywood—referring to films produced by Hollywood studios)

19. They worried their feelings were positive but not intense.—他们当初还担心,尽管他们的感情是积极的,但是不够强烈。

20. Marilyn Yalom, a cultural historian at the Institute for Research on Women and Gender at Stanford University and the author of *A History of the Wife* —美国斯坦福大学女性与性别研究所的文化历史学家,《妻子的历史》的作者玛丽莲·亚隆

IV. Language Features

《华盛顿邮报》简介

1877年,斯蒂尔森·哈钦斯(Stilson Hutchins)创办了《华盛顿邮报》。

1933年,美国60位富翁之一,联邦储备委员会主席尤金·迈耶(Eugene Meyer)买下了《华盛顿邮报》。迈耶立志为首都读者提供"全面正确的观点"。为加强社论写作,他专门聘用了社论写作方面获得普利策奖的编辑。此外,他还聘用了一位著名的漫画家。很快,《华盛顿邮报》的社论和国内新闻解释性报道就赢得了社会的赞赏,获得了"富有才智和人情味,观点开明"的良好声誉。在1933年至1943年这段时间里,该报发行量增加了两倍。

1946年迈耶将《华盛顿邮报》发行人职位交给其女婿菲利普·格雷厄姆(Philip Graham)。格雷厄姆加强了报社编辑部力量配备。

50年代初麦卡锡主义猖狂时期,该报持开明态度,很早就公开抨击麦卡锡煽动反共情绪的伎俩。1954年,该报发行量已增加到38万份,成为政府官员、国会议员和驻华盛顿记者的必读报。

1963年,格雷厄姆由于抑郁症自杀,其妻凯瑟林·格雷厄姆担任华盛顿邮报公司总裁。2013年,华盛顿邮报公司把《华盛顿邮报》的业务转让给亚马逊掌门人贝索斯。

1971年《华盛顿邮报》继《纽约时报》之后,刊登了"五角大楼秘密文件"(the Pentagon Papers),揭露美国政府在战争中的欺骗行为,为此而名声大振。1972年,该报两名年轻记者关于"水门丑闻"(the Watergate Scandal)的调查性报道揭露了尼克松总统的重大政治丑闻。这一成功报道使该报荣获1973年普利策公共服务奖。2017年美国三家电影公司以此为剧情制作了影片《华盛顿邮报》("The Post")。该片引起了社会轰动并赢得了最佳影片,最佳男、女主角三项大奖。

1981年,《华盛顿邮报》由于刊登了一篇骗得普利策奖的该报记者珍妮·库克(Janet Cooke)所杜撰的有关一位名叫吉米(Jimmy)的男孩吸食海洛因的虚假报道,而形象受到损害。但是,1983年该报又获两项普利策奖,声誉再度上升。

1986年,该报率先调查美国向伊朗出售武器的丑闻和美国政府为颠覆尼加拉瓜政府而挪用资金支持该政府反对派的事件。

截至2011年,该报记者共获57项普利策奖,仅次于《纽约时报》。

《华盛顿邮报》注重国会和政府活动的新闻报道,国际新闻报道也较多,该报威望较高,影响较大。2015年,该报平日版发行量为35.7万,周日版发行量是83.8万。该报电子报2018年发行量为100万。2015年,平日版有六组文章:A组为国内、国际新闻(National News, World News);B组为本市新闻(Metro);C组为文化娱乐新闻(Style);D组为体育新闻(Sports);E组为商务经济新闻(Business);F组为健康内容(Health)。每期内容有六十多页。

该报政治观点倾向民主党。其网站是www.washingtonpost.com。

V. Analysis of Content

1. According to Gottman, couples who stick together for a long term tend to _____.
   A. fight fair
   B. have no conflicts
   C. manage their differences well
   D. have intense feelings of love
2. Which of the following is NOT on Bradbury's list of reasons for marriage?
   A. Having someone to listen to.
   B. Having a friend.
   C. Having someone share ups and downs.
   D. Having someone look after you.
3. It can be seen from the article that Americans' expectations from marriage _____.
   A. are higher than before
   B. are lower than before
   C. are as high as before
   D. have dropped to the bottom
4. According to the book *The Mathematics of Marriage*, most of marital conflicts never get resolved because they are about _____.
   A. personality differences
   B. age differences
   C. income differences
   D. differences in expectations
5. According to the findings made by psychologists and sociologists, which of the following statements is NOT TRUE?
   A. Every couple has irreconcilable differences.
   B. Couples who stay together over the long term don't let conflicts contaminate the other parts of the relationship.
   C. All happy couples have resolved their conflicts.
   D. Social factors can affect couples' relationship.

VI. Questions on the Article

1. What was Tolstoy's observation on happy and unhappy families?
2. What is Gottman's view on Tolstoy's observation?
3. According to the researchers, what are the potent predictors of whether couples feel committed to relationships?
4. What are the effects of changing social mores and expectations on marriage?
5. What's Huston's finding about the failure of many relationships?
6. How did couples who were happy over the long term feel about marriages according to Huston's study?
7. What did Schwartz find about very successful couples?
8. What are the factors beyond individual circumstance which may affect couples' relationships?

VII. Topics for Discussion

1. Are unhappy families similar to one another?
2. Which is more important for couples, resolving conflicts or managing conflicts?

Lesson 10

The New Mommy Track

More mothers win flextime at work, and hubbies' help (really!) at home.

By Kimberly Palmer

On a Tuesday evening in early summer, a very pregnant Lindsay Androski Kelly walked in her door to exuberant shouts of "Mommy! Mommy!" from her 2-year-old son, George. She dropped her laptop in her home office and listened to the boy tell her about his adventures on the playground.

Kelly, a 30-year-old lawyer on track to become partner at her Washington, D.C., law firm, is now on maternity leave with her baby daughter, Vivian.[1] But when she returns to the office, she'll also go back to working part of her 55-hour week at home so she can spend as much time as possible with her children, who have a nanny. And she'll resume her old routine: rising at 5 a.m. to put in a couple of hours before the kids wake up and logging in for an hour or two after they go to sleep. She'll eat breakfast with her family and be home in time to make dinner.

A generation ago, a lawyer in Kelly's situation would probably have felt pressure to put in early mornings and late nights at the office. But Kelly's firm allows employees to work flexible hours. "As long as you get everything done and meet the clients' needs, you can work whatever time of day you like," she says.

Kelly represents a new generation of American mothers who are rejecting the "superwoman" image from the 1980s as well as the "soccer mom" stereotype of the 1990s.[2] Mothers today are more likely to negotiate flexible schedules at work and demand fuller participation of fathers in child raising than previous generations did, giving them more time to pursue their own careers and interests. Some so-called mompreneurs start their own businesses. Nearly 26 percent of working women with children under 18 work flexible schedules, according to the Bureau of Labor Statistics, compared with 14 percent in 1991.[3]

"Fifteen to 20 years ago, women in suits and sneakers...were playing by the traditional rules of the game, trying to live in a man's world. Now women are saying, 'Screw the rules—the rules didn't work,'" says Kellyanne Conway, president of the Polling Co.[4], a research firm. Conway, 40, the mother of twins who are almost 3 years old, started her business in 1995, allowing her to set her own hours and occasionally work from home.

Not that it's always easy. Heidi Leigh, 34, a former theater sales manager and mother of a 1-year-old in South Plainfield, N.J.,[5] tried to shift her schedule a half-hour earlier in the day so she could get home in time to pick up her son from day care and make dinner. Her boss said no. "He wouldn't allow it, because he didn't want other people to do the same thing," she says.

"More and more companies are hip to [flexibility], but it's still not the norm[6]," cautions Michelle Goodman, author of *The Anti 9-to-5 Guide: Practical Career Advice for Women Who*

Think Outside the Cube[7].

Art of the deal[8]. While balancing work and family is never simple, Goodman and others who have studied the issue say mothers can increase their chances of getting onto this new mommy track by choosing certain careers, partners, and companies. While a handful of workplaces are making it easier for mothers (and fathers) to meld work with family, many women report that they often need to take matters into their own hands, through skillful negotiation with supervisors or, in some cases, quitting office life and starting their own businesses.

On the company front, 31 percent of organizations allow employees to work from home or off site on a regular basis, and 73 percent allow extended career breaks for family responsibilities, according to a survey by the Families and Work Institute[9]. Best Buy allows some of its corporate employees to set their own hours and work entirely from home. Last year, PricewaterhouseCoopers, a public accounting firm, launched Full Circle, a program for parents that enables them to temporarily stop working for the company but stay in touch through networking and training events.[10] Keeping connected makes it easier for moms to return to work when they're ready. "The thing we know for sure is that women need choices. Our careers are not as linear as men's[11]," says Jennifer Allyn, managing director in the office of diversity.

The company did not start the program out of a spirit of generosity: In 2001, it faced a 24 percent turnover rate.[12] Allyn estimates the cost of losing a client services' employee, which most are, to be around $80,000. So if Full Circle enables one person to return to the firm, she says, the program has paid for itself. Allyn says the turnover rate has already fallen to 15 percent.

Gina Thoma, 43, one of the 25 female participants in the Full Circle program, worked as a senior manager in PricewaterhouseCoopers's San Francisco office until she had three children, including twins, in less than two years. After a series of nannies didn't work out, she and her husband decided one of them needed to stay home, at least temporarily, to restore order to their home life. Despite her time out, Thoma is still on track to become partner after she returns in 2008 or 2009. "I'm determined to make it work," she says.

Thoma's promise of a job after years off is unusual, and even at a company like Pricewaterhouse Coopers, participation in the Full Circle program is highly selective. That's what inspired Cathleen Benko, managing principal of talent for Deloitte & Touche[13], which provides consulting services, to develop a new model that views flexibility as the norm, instead of an exception.

Deloitte's new approach, laid out in *Mass Career Customization: Aligning the Workplace with Today's Nontraditional Workforce*, coauthored by Benko, personalizes employees' careers to fit their life styles.[14] For example, young 20-somethings might have few travel restrictions or work limitations and then add restrictions during childbearing years. Deloitte has already rolled out the program to about one fifth of its workforce; next year it will apply to the whole firm.

Many agencies within the federal government encourage employees to work from home and to have flexible hours. Daniel Green, deputy associate director in the Office of Personnel Management, says such arrangements increase loyalty and motivation among staff. By January 2005, over 140,000 federal employees, or 19 percent of the workforce, teleworked, almost double the number for 2001.

Opting out. Most women don't have access to such corporate and federal programs, and that leads some of them to decide combining motherhood and work is impossible. A recent survey of almost 2,500 high-achieving women by Sylvia Ann Hewlett found that 37 percent of women stop working for a period, or temporarily "opt out" of the workforce.[15] Most of those women would have preferred to have taken a job with reduced or flexible hours if it had been available, says Hewlett, author of *Off-Ramps and On-Ramps: Keeping Talented Women on the Road to Success*[16].

Leigh, the former theater manager, exemplifies that dilemma. She eventually decided to quit her job to sell advertisements from home on a commission-only basis.[17] She works in the mornings, before her husband leaves for his afternoon shift at a pharmaceutical company. While she'd like to continue to stay home, she isn't sure that will be possible. "Living in New Jersey is really difficult on one income," she says.

Through interviews with women who chose to leave the workplace, Pamela Stone, author of *Opting Out? Why Women Really Quit Careers and Head Home*[18], found that sometimes just small differences, such as the ability to work from home one or two days a month, would have made it possible for women to stay in the workforce. Often, she says, women's flexible arrangements were based on handshake agreements[19] with supervisors; new bosses meant no more flexibility.

Partly as a result of those continuing difficulties, a growing number of mothers are deciding that starting their own business is the answer. On a cool evening in May, dozens of women gathered in lower Manhattan to celebrate the launch of a new magazine, *Hybrid Mom*[20]. It caters to women who are balancing work and motherhood with a special focus on mompreneurs, or mothers who launch their own businesses. Linda Shapiro, cofounder of *Moms-for-Profit*, the company that publishes the magazine, says that two thirds of stay-at-home moms start their own businesses, and they want a place to talk about it.

Low-tech solution. Lori Johnson, 34, is one of those moms. After working more than 80 hours a week as a sales account executive[21] in the semiconductor industry, she quit after having her daughter, Avery, just over two years ago. Not willing to return to such a hectic lifestyle, she decided starting her own business out of her home in Concord, Mass., was a "happy medium."[22] She now designs and sells car seat covers. The idea for Hot Toddies Baby Gear[23] came to her after she became frustrated when people mistook her daughter for a boy because she could find only blue seat covers.

Rachel Thebault, 31, started a bakery, Tribeca Treats, in lower Manhattan after realizing that her investment banking job wasn't conducive to being a mother. "I felt like in the long term that was not going to be a job where I felt like I could commit to being successful at my job and also happily raise a family," she says.

Even though she spends up to 80 hours a week working, she does it according to her own schedule. If her nanny calls in sick, then she brings her daughter, Marin, $2\frac{1}{2}$, to work with her. "I'm at my own beck and call, not someone else's," she says.[24]

"In some cases," says author Goodman, "[self-employment] is the only way they could fit work life with their personal life." One woman she interviewed for her book was divorced with five school-age children. The cost of day care would have been overwhelming, so she worked from home as a marketer and copywriter instead.[25]

Tamara Monosoff, inventor of a device that stops kids from unraveling toilet paper, wrote *Secrets of Millionaire Moms* to explain to other moms how to raise capital, develop a business plan, and balance family time with running a business. She started writing about mompreneurs after discovering a high demand from mothers interested in starting their own businesses.

It's a trend that's likely to continue: A 2006 Lifetime Television[26] poll found that the most popular goal among women ages 18 to 29 was to manage their own companies, with 47 percent of respondents choosing it. Yet becoming president of a major corporation was named by only 10 percent of respondents. "Women are **(not)** trying to have it all but are trying to regain control over their time," says Conway, who helped conduct the poll. "That's why many women are busting out of the traditional workforce and starting their own businesses."

Back at Kelly's house, the pork tenderloin is almost done roasting.[27] Kelly stops **(steps)** into her home office for a quick E-mail check as her husband, George, a real-estate developer, gives their son a bath while speaking to him in his best Sir Topham Hatt impression[28]. For now, at least, Kelly has achieved what she considers an ideal balance.

From *U.S. News & World Report*, September 3, 2007

I. New Words

cater	[ˈkeitə]	v.	~ to to attend to the wants or needs of
caution	[ˈkɔːʃən]	v.	警告，告诫
conducive	[kənˈdjuːsiv]	adj.	favorable; helpful
copywriter	[ˈkɔpiˌraitə]	n.	广告文编写人
customization	[kʌstəmaiˈzeiʃən]	n.	the act of changing sth to suit the needs of the owner
exemplify	[igˈzemplifai]	v.	to illustrate by example
exuberant	[igˈzjuːbərənt]	adj.	full of happiness and excitement
flextime	[ˈflekstaim]	n.	弹性上班制
generosity	[ˌdʒenəˈrɔsiti]	n.	慷慨，大方
high-achieving	[ˈhaiəˈtʃiːviŋ]	adj.	successful
hubby	[ˈhʌbi]	n.	*informal* husband
hybrid	[ˈhaibrid]	adj.	混合的
laptop	[ˈlæptɔp]	n.	便携式电脑
linear	[ˈliniə]	adj.	线的，直线的
log	[lɔg]	v.	~in [计]进入系统
low-tech	[ˈləutek]	adj.	低技术的
maternity	[məˈtəːniti]	adj.	孕妇的，产妇的，产科的
meld	[meld]	v.	*formal* to combine with sth else
mompreneur	[ˌmɔmprəˈnəː]	n.	妈咪企业家

nanny	[ˈnæni]	n.	保姆,奶妈
pharmaceutical	[ˌfɑːməˈsjuːtikəl]	adj.	配药的,制药的
shift	[ʃift]	v.	to move from one position to another
sneaker	[ˈsniːkə]	n.	运动鞋
stereotype	[ˈstiəriəutaip]	n.	铅版;刻板印象
telework	[ˈteliˌwəːk]	v.	to work from home, communicating by telephone or the Internet
tenderloin	[ˈtendəlɔin]	n.	(牛、羊等的)腰部嫩肉
twenty-something	[ˌtwentiˈsʌmθiŋ]	n.	二十来岁的人
unravel	[ʌnˈrævəl]	v.	拆开,解开

II. Background Information

工作与家庭

　　第二次世界大战之后,美国经济发展需要大批劳力,给妇女就业创造了条件。1950—1960年这十年中仅美国服务业就给妇女提供了580万个就业机会。妇女解放运动增强了女性经济独立的意识,使得越来越多的妇女加入了劳动大军(labor force),并从女性传统职业渗入男性一统天下的职业范畴。

　　统计资料显示:1970年美国16岁以上女性就业率为43.3%,2000年上升到61%,与男性当年就业率(71%)差距不大。女性已经成为两大类型行业的主体:一类是教育、卫生和社会救助类行业,女性比例高达68.4%;另一类是金融、保险、房地产、租赁类行业,女性比例为56.3%。1985年女性专业人员(professionals)所占比例是49%,1989年女性管理层工作者所占比例为36%。不少妇女自己创业。据统计,美国共有910万妇女企业主,所雇员工总数多达2750万。

　　然而,自20世纪90年代中期后一段时期,美国妇女就业率呈现下降趋势。对于这一问题形成的原因众说纷纭,大致有以下三种解释:

　　1. 妇女压力已达极限(Women have been stretched to the limit)。不少社会学者认为妇女既要工作又要照顾家庭,压力很大,对于25—54岁有孩子的母亲更是如此。调查显示:2003年工作妇女每周平均花在孩子身上的时间比1975年不工作妇女还要多出15小时,少睡觉3.6小时。这种压力已达极限,不能再持续下去。

　　2. 妇女自愿放弃工作(Women have voluntarily quit their jobs)。另一些社会学者认为有相当数量经济条件较好的妇女更加注重生活质量,把家庭和谐置于个人事业之上,自愿待在家里当贤妻良母。

　　3. 妇女被迫离开公司(Women have been forced to leave companies)。还有的社会学家指出,许多公司依然存在隐形歧视(glass ceilings),妇女晋升比较困难,进入高管职位(high management positions)难上加难。2006年《财富》500强公司(*Fortune* 500)只有10名妇女担任执行总裁(CEO),《财富》1000强公司(*Fortune* 1000)执行总裁中妇女人数只有20名。不少公司对有孩子的妇女缺乏关爱,不愿提供弹性工作制(flextime)。据统计,2002—2003年期间女性全日制员工(full-time workers)薪金下降了0.6%,男性员工薪金保持不变。这些因素迫使女性做出退出公司的决定。持这种观点的学者认为女性员工不是自愿退出(opt out),而是被公司排挤出去的(are pushed out of the companies)。

III. Notes to the Text

1. Kelly, a 30-year-old lawyer on track to become partner at her Washington, D.C., law firm, is now on maternity leave with her baby daughter, Vivian.—凯利是一位30岁的律师,不久将可能成为她所生活的华盛顿特区的律师事务所的合伙人,目前正在家休产假,照看她的小女儿维维安。(be on track to—to be likely to)

2. Kelly represents a new generation of American mothers who are rejecting the "superwoman" image from the 1980s as well as the "soccer mom" stereotype of the 1990s.—凯利代表了新一代的美国母亲,她们正在摒弃20世纪80年代的"女超人"形象以及20世纪90年代的"足球妈咪"模式。(soccer mom—an American mother who spends a lot of her time driving her children to sports practice, music lessons, etc, considered as a typical example of women from the middle to upper class in U.S. society)

3. Nearly 26 percent of working women with children under 18 work flexible schedules, according to the Bureau of Labor Statistics, compared with 14 percent in 1991.—根据劳工统计局的数据,孩子不满18岁的在职妇女享有弹性工作制的比率将近26%,而1991年的比率为14%。(the Bureau of Labor Statistics—the principal fact-finding agency for the Federal Government in the broad field of labor economics and statistics)

4. the Polling Co.—民意调查公司

5. South Plainfield, N.J.—新泽西州南普莱恩菲尔德市

6. More and more companies are hip to [flexibility], but it's still not the norm...—越来越多的公司采用当前流行的弹性工作制,但是这种工作制尚未成为规范(be hip to—to follow what is fashionable)

7. *The Anti 9-to-5 Guide: Practical Career Advice for Women Who Think Outside the Cube*—《摆脱早九晚五固定工作制——创新思维女性求职指南》(① This book is about working outside the typical mind-numbing 9-to-5 office grind, written by freelance writer/editor and blogger Michelle Goodman who shares her own successes and humorous yet sound career advices for would-be entrepreneurs; ② 9-to-5—a work schedule from 9 o'clock in the morning to 5 o'clock in the afternoon; ③ think out of the cube—to think about sth in a way that is new, different or shows imagination)

8. Art of the deal—处理技巧(It specifically refers to the skill of balancing work and family.)

9. the Families and Work Institute—家庭与工作研究所(一家设在纽约的非营利组织)

10. Last year, PricewaterhouseCoopers, a public accounting firm, launched Full Circle, a program for parents that enables them to temporarily stop working for the company but stay in touch through networking and training events.—去年,普华永道会计师事务所启动了一个名为 Full Circle 的项目,旨在帮助孩子母亲能够暂时不上班但仍可通过网络和培训与公司保持联系。[① PricewaterhouseCoopers... —普华永道会计师事务所,是由普华会计师事务所(Price Waterhouse)与永道会计师事务所(Coopers & Lybrand)1998年7月1日合并而成的,合并后公司更名为 PricewaterhouseCoopers。该公司在全球150多个国家拥有800多个办事处。② Full Circle—If a PwC employee decides to leave the firm to take care of a new baby or sick or ageing family member for an extended period of time (up to five years), the Full Circle program encourages them to remain connected to the firm in the event they want to come back to work. They remain connected in a variety of ways. PwC reimburses Full Circle participants for any work-related training and credentialing they pursue while away from the firm.]

11. Our careers are not as linear as men's...—我们的职业生涯不像男士们那样能够持续发展。(linear career—the type of career in which sb stays in a certain field and works his/her way to the expected objective)

12. The company did not start the program out of a spirit of generosity: In 2001, it faced a 24 percent turnover rate.—该公司启动这个项目并不是出于慷慨:2001年,该公司面临24%的人员更替率(turnover rate—the rate at which employees leave a company and are replaced by other people)

13. managing principal of talent for Deloitte & Touche—德勤会计师事务所人才事务总管[该所是世界四大会计师事务所之一,是德勤全球(Deloitte Touche Tohmatsu)在美国的分支机构。]

14. Deloitte's new approach, laid out in *Mass Career Customization: Aligning the Workplace with Today's Nontraditional Workforce*, coauthored by Benko, personalizes employees' careers to fit their life styles.—Benko 与他人合著的《大众职业个性化:调整职场,适应当今非传统职工需求》展示了德勤咨询公司的新方法,该方法使得雇员的职业个性化与他们的生活方式相适应。(align—to change sth slightly so that it is in the correct relationship to sth else)

15. A recent survey of almost 2,500 high-achieving women by Sylvia Ann Hewlett found that 37 percent of women stop working for a period, or temporarily "opt out" of the workforce.—西尔维亚·安·休利特最近对近2500位成功女士做了调查,她发现,其中37%的女性决定一段时间不工作或者暂时离开工作岗位。(① Sylvia Ann Hewlett—the founding president of the New York-based Center for Work-Life Policy and the leader of the gender and policy program at the School of International and Public Affairs at Columbia University; ② opt out—to choose not to take part in)

16. *Off-Ramps and On-Ramps: Keeping Talented Women on the Road to Success*—《下岗与上岗:不让有才能的妇女离开成功之路》(① 该书作者为 Sylvia Ann Hewlett,由加州大学出版社于2007年出版;② off-ramps—referring to professional women who leave jobs to be stay-at-home moms)

17. She eventually decided to quit her job to sell advertisements from home on a commission-only basis.—她最后决定辞去工作在家销售广告,从中只提取佣金。
18. *Opting Out? Why Women Really Quit Careers and Head Home*—《主动辞职? 妇女放弃职业回归家庭的真正原因》
19. handshake agreement—口头协议
20. *Hybrid Mom*—《多重身份的妈咪》(a magazine for moms and by moms, a new generation of moms who embrace their multiple identities)
21. sales account executive—销售业务经理
22. Not willing to return to such a hectic lifestyle, she decided starting her own business out of her home in Concord, Mass., was a "happy medium."—由于不愿意再回到这样繁忙的生活方式,她决定采取折中办法,在住地马萨诸塞州的康科德城开办自己的公司。(① hectic—very busy; ② happy medium—a way of doing sth that is half way between two possible opposite ways)
23. Hot Toddies Baby Gear—a company which produces car seats for babies
24. If her nanny calls in sick, then she brings her daughter, Marin, 2½, to work with her. "I'm at my own beck and call, not someone else's," she says.—如果她的保姆打电话请病假的话,她就带两岁半的女儿马林去工作。她说:"我现在是自己指挥自己,而不是听其他人的使唤。"(① call in sick—to ask for sick leave by telephone; ② to be at one's beck and call—to be always ready to obey sb's orders)
25. The cost of day care would have been overwhelming, so she worked from home as a marketer and copywriter instead.—日托的费用难以承受,所以她就在家干活,从事营销和广告撰稿工作。(day care—托儿所的日托)
26. Lifetime Television—a U.S. cable TV network for women
27. Back at Kelly's house, the pork tenderloin is almost done roasting.—回到凯利家,猪里脊肉差不多烤好了。
28. ...speaking to him in his best Sir Topham Hatt impression—尽可能学着Topham Hatt先生的样子对他说话(Sir Topham Hatt—also known as "The Fat Controller". He is the head of the railway in the TV series *Thomas the Tank Engine and Friends*. He might be described as "firm but fair and kind" leader.)

IV. Language Features

《美国新闻与世界报道》介绍

辛迪加专栏作家大卫·劳伦斯(David Lawrence)于1933年创办了《美国新闻》(*US News*),1946年又创办了《世界报道》(*World Report*)。1948年,劳伦斯将这两个刊物与《美国周刊》(*US Weekly*)三合为一,更名为《美国新闻与世界报道》(*US News & World Report*)。

在美国三大新闻周刊中,《美国新闻与世界报道》一直屈居第三,无法与其他两家杂志抗衡。

1995年,为了顺应时代发展,该刊开设了电子版。电子版《美国新闻与世界报道》内容比纸质版丰富得多,网页超过10万。此外,电子版的信息不断更新。这些优势使得电子版的读者数量不断增加。据2008年统计,该刊电子版每月读者数量为500万,是纸质版的3倍。

该刊报纸版从2008年7月改成双周刊,2009年2月又改为月刊。与此同时,该刊在版面、风格方面也有重大变化。《美国新闻与世界报道》的月刊报道具有主题单一、重点突出、深度加大的特色。例如:2009年9月期刊所有文章围绕大学教育专题。"编者按"(Editor's Note)谈的是消费者选择大学必须谨慎。"正反观点栏"(Two Views)的辩论题是:高考是否必要?该期报道内容下分四个子题:1. 如何改进大学教育(How to Fix Higher Education);2. 大学面貌变化(Changing Face of College);3. 大学教育费用的支付(Paying for College);4. 大学排行榜(The Rankings)。每一子题包含一组文章,报道该子题各方面的情况。读者通过这一期文章的阅读可以获得美国高等教育专题较为完整、全面、清晰的画面。电子版的《美国新闻与世界报道》版面较为固定,每期都设有:国内外新闻版(Nation & World)、观点版(Opinion)、金融商务版(Money & Business)、健康卫生版(Health)和教育版(Education)。有时根据形势发展,电子版还会增设其他版面。总的说来,改版后的纸质版《美国新闻与世界报道》的语言更为简明,阅读起来更加轻松,内容更强调服务性、实用性。

从2011年1月开始,《美国新闻与世界报道》停止发行纸质版,只发行电子版。其电子版仍然保留原先实用性、服务性的特色。

该刊在政治观点上支持共和党右翼;经济方面反对增税,反对增加联邦政府权力;军事方面主张加强美国军事实力。

《美国新闻与世界报道》的网址是www.usnews.com。

V. Analysis of Content

1. According to the article, the stereotype of American mothers in the 1980s was the _____.

   A. soccer mom

   B. superwoman

   C. homemaking mom

   D. mompreneur

2. The subhead "Art of the deal" in the article refers to _____.

   A. skill of balancing work and family

   B. creative power of making arrangements

   C. businessmen's skill in making money

   D. skill in doing business

3. It can be seen from Paragraphs 9 and 10 that PricewaterhouseCoopers launched the program of Full Circle in order to _____.

   A. show the spirit of generosity

   B. keep turnover rate at a lower level

   C. make employees happy

   D. keep the good image of the firm

4. We can infer from the article that women's main purpose in starting up their own business is to _____.

   A. become a boss

   B. break off husbands' control

   C. regain control over their time

   D. earn more money to support the family

5. Which of the following statements is FALSE?

   A. It is still not easy for most women to win flexible schedule.

   B. More and more companies offer flexible schedule.

   C. Most of American women are eager to launch their own business.

   D. Flexible schedule is the norm in America today.

VI. Questions on the Article

1. Why could Kelly work at home, taking care of her 2-year-old son?
2. According to the article, what are American mothers more likely to do today?
3. To Goodman's mind, how can mothers increase their chances of getting onto the new mommy track?
4. What kind of program is Full Circle? What is its aim?
5. In what way is Full Circle different from Deloitte's new approach?
6. Why do many women leave the workforce?
7. What did Pamela Stone find would have made it possible for women to stay in the workforce?
8. What kind of magazine is *Hybrid Mom*?
9. What was Tamara Monosoff's purpose in writing *Secrets of Millionaire Moms*?

VII. Topics for Discussion

1. Does it work in the interest of a company to offer women flexible schedule?
2. Should all companies offer flexible schedule to women?

Lesson 11

One's a Crowd[1]

By Eric Klinenberg[2]

MORE people live alone now than at any other time in history. In prosperous American cities—Atlanta, Denver, Seattle, San Francisco and Minneapolis—40 percent or more of all households contain a single occupant. In Manhattan and in Washington, nearly one in two households are occupied by a single person.

By international standards, these numbers are surprising—surprisingly low. In Paris, the city of lovers, more than half of all households contain single people, and in socialist Stockholm[3], the rate tops 60 percent.

The decision to live alone is common in diverse cultures whenever it is economically feasible. Although Americans pride themselves on their self-reliance and culture of individualism, Germany, France and Britain have a greater proportion of one-person households than the United States, as does Japan. Three of the nations with the fastest-growing populations of single people—China, India and Brazil—are also among those with the fastest growing economies.

The mere thought of living alone once sparked anxiety, dread and visions of loneliness. But those images are dated. Now the most privileged people on earth use their resources to separate from one another, to buy privacy and personal space.

Living alone comports with modern values.[4] It promotes freedom, personal control and self-realization—all prized aspects of contemporary life.

It is less feared, too, for the crucial reason that living alone no longer suggests an isolated or less-social life. After interviewing more than 300 singletons (my term for people who live alone) during nearly a decade of research, I've concluded that living alone seems to encourage more, not less, social interaction.

Paradoxically, our species, so long defined by groups and by the nuclear family, has been able to embark on this experiment in solo living[5] because global societies have become so interdependent. Dynamic markets, flourishing cities and open communications systems make modern autonomy more appealing; they give us the capacity (**not only**) to live alone but to engage with others when and how we want to and on our own terms.[6]

In fact, living alone can make it easier to be social, because single people have more free time, absent family obligations, to engage in social activities.

Compared with their married counterparts, single people are more likely to spend time with friends and neighbors, go to restaurants and attend art classes and lectures. There is much research suggesting that single people get out more—and not only the younger ones. Erin Cornwell, a sociologist at Cornell, analyzed results from the General Social Survey[7] (which draws on a nationally representative sample of the United States population) from 2000 to 2008 and found that single people 35 and older were more likely than those who lived with a spouse or a romantic partner to spend a social evening with neighbors or friends. In 2008, her husband, Benjamin Cornwell (also a sociologist at Cornell), was lead author of "The Social Connectedness of Older Adults," a paper in the *American Sociological Review*[8] that showed that single seniors had the same number of friends and core discussion partners as their married peers and were more likely to socialize with friends and neighbors.

SURVEYS, some by market research companies that study behavior for clients developing products and services, also indicate that married people with children are more likely than single people to hunker down at home. Those in large suburban homes often splinter into private rooms to be alone. The image of a modern family in a room together, each plugged into a separate reality, be it a smartphone, computer, video game or TV show has become a cultural cliché.[9]

New communications technologies make living alone a social experience, so being home alone does not feel involuntary or like solitary confinement. The person alone at home can digitally navigate through a world of people, information and ideas. Internet use does not seem to cut people off from real friendships and connections.

The Pew Internet Personal Networks and Community Survey[10]—a nationally representative survey of 2,512 American adults conducted in 2008 that was the first to examine how the Internet and cellphones affect our core social networks—shows that Web use can lead to more social life, rather than to less. "Social Isolation and New Technology," written by the Rutgers University communications scholar Keith Hampton[11], reveals that heavy users are more likely than others to have large and diverse social networks; more likely to visit parks, cafes and restaurants; and more likely to meet diverse people with different perspectives and beliefs.

Today five million people in the United States between ages 18 and 34 live alone, 10 times more than in 1950. But the largest number of single people are middle-aged; 15 million people between ages 35 and 64 live alone. Those who decide to live alone following a breakup or a divorce could choose to move in with roommates or family. But many of those I interviewed said they chose to live alone because they had found there was nothing worse than living with the wrong person.[12]

In my interviews, older single people expressed a clear preference for living alone, which allowed them to retain their feelings of independence and integrity, and a clear aversion to moving in with friends or family or into a nursing home.[13]

According to research by the Rutgers sociologist Deborah Carr, at 18 months after the death of a spouse, only one in four elderly men and one in six elderly women say they are interested in remarrying; one in three men and one in seven women are interested in dating someday; and only one in four men and one in 11 women are interested in dating immediately.

Most older widows, widowers and divorced people remake their lives as single people.[14] A century ago, nearly 70 percent of elderly American widows lived with a child; today—thanks to Social Security[15], private pensions and wealth generated in the market—just 20 percent do. According to the U.C.L.A.[16] economist Kathleen McGarry: "When they have more income and they have a choice of how to live, they choose to live alone. They buy their independence."

Some unhealthy old people do become dangerously isolated, as I learned when I researched my book about the hundreds of people who died alone in the 1995 Chicago heat wave[17], and they deserve more attention and support than we give them today. But the rise of aging alone is also a social achievement. The sustained health, wealth and vitality that so many people over age 65 enjoy allow them to maintain domestic independence far longer than previous generations did. What's new today is that the great majority of older widows, widowers and divorced people prefer living alone to their other options, and they're willing to spend more on housing and domestic help for the privilege. Some pundits predicted that rates of living alone would plummet because of the challenged economy: young people would move into their parents' basements; middle-aged adults would put off divorce or separation for financial reasons; the elderly would move in with their children rather than hold on to places of their own.

Thus far, however, there's little evidence that this has happened. True, more young adults have moved in with their parents because they cannot find good jobs; but the proportion of those between 20 and 29 who live alone went down only slightly, from 11.97 percent in 2007 to 10.94 percent in 2011. In the general population, living alone has become more common—in absolute and proportional terms.[18] The latest census report estimates that more than 32 million Americans live alone today, up from 27.2 million in 2000 and 31 million in 2010.

All signs suggest that living alone will become even more common in the future, at every stage of adulthood and in every place where people can afford a place of their own.[19]

From *The New York Times*, February 4, 2012

I. New Words

appealing	[ə'pi:liŋ]	adj.	attractive
autonomy	[ɔ:'tɔnəmi]	n.	the ability to act or make decision without being controlled
aversion	[ə'və:ʃn]	n.	~ to sth a strong feeling of not liking sth
basement	['beismənt]	n.	地下室
café	['kæfei]	n.	小餐馆,咖啡馆
cellphone	['selfəun]	n.	手机,移动电话
confinement	[kən'fainmənt]	n.	限制;被幽禁,禁闭
dated	['deitid]	adj.	belonging to a time in the past
dread	[dred]	n.	a feeling of great fear
feasible	['fi:zəbl]	adj.	that is possible and likely to be achieved
hunker	['hʌŋkə]	v.	蹲坐
involuntary	[in'vɔləntəri]	adj.	非自愿的
occupant	['ɔkju:pənt]	n.	(房屋等的)占有者,所有人
paradoxically	[pærə'dɔksikəli]	adv.	似是而非地;自相矛盾地

perspective	[pəˈspektiv]	n.	视角,观点,看法
plug	[plʌg]	v.	(将插头插入插座)给……接通电源
plummet	[ˈplʌmit]	v.	to fall suddenly and quickly from a high level
pundit	[ˈpʌndit]	n.	专家;学者
prized	[praizd]	adj.	very valuable
promote	[prəˈməut]	v.	to help sth to develop
solitary	[ˈsɔlitəri]	adj.	alone, with no other people around
spark	[spɑ:k]	v.	to cause sth to develop
splinter	[ˈsplintə]	v.	to break or cause to break into small sharp fragments
spouse	[spauz]	n.	配偶
sustain	[səsˈtein]	v.	to make sth continue for sometime
widower	[ˈwidəuə]	n.	鳏夫

II. Background Information

独居风尚

1900年美国独身者所占比例仅是5.1%。2018年统计数据显示,超过50%的美国成年人单身,其中3100万人独自一人生活,美国独居者占全国人口总数的28%。这意味着独居者现已成为仅次于无子女的夫妻家庭的第二大家庭形式,数量远远超过核心家庭、多代复合式家庭、室友同居以及老人之家等其他形式。调查发现,独居是一种比较稳定的居住和生活方式,独居5年以上者更有可能维持同样状态不变。

美国人口普查局(Census Bureau) 2010年9月28日公布的数据显示,2009年25岁到34岁的人群中,从未结婚的人数首次超过处于结婚状态的人数——前者占该群体的比例为46.3%,而后者占44.9%。

自20世纪60年代起,美国人的婚姻观念和家庭关系发生了结构性的转变,单身人数后来居上正是这一趋势发展的具体表现。50年代,70%美国成年人都有配偶,现在已经不到一半。婚姻观念的变化在那些教育水平不高的人群中最为盛行。据美国人口普查局的数据,从2000年到2010年,没上过大学的已婚年轻人比率下跌了10个百分点,为44%。与此形成对比的是,在同一年龄组中,大学学历以上的已婚年轻人比例同期下跌4%,为52%。也有一些情况与历史趋势不同。以往,大学毕业生更有可能推迟结婚,以便把注意力集中在事业发展或进一步深造方面;但现在,没有读过四年大学的人群推迟结婚的情况更普遍。

单身独居最大的优势莫过于自由。独居者可以在自己愿意的时候,做自己想要做的事,觉得生活更加充实、更有趣味。有些学者认为,现代科技弥补了单身孤立的缺憾,网络和过去的电话一样,改变了人类互动行为。医疗技术进步使人们的健康状况优于实际年龄,美国老年医疗护理服务趋于周到成熟,大大减少了独身和独居者的后顾之忧。这些都是单身独居数量增加的因素。

一些调查结果显示,单身独居者比已婚有家者更有可能参与社会活动,有更多时间做运动,享用美食,出席文化活动和当义工。单身独居者未必是埋头工作的过劳一族。研究资料显示,这些人比与亲友或他人同居者有更好的心理健康状态,由于单身独居者多数选择住在市区,他们比住在郊区的家庭生活得更加丰富多彩。比起有家庭者,独居者更加有可能在外就餐,成为健身俱乐部成员,参加聚会和各种课程。他们的消费能力很强,每年消费总额为1.9万亿美元。商界对这一大消费群体十分关注。

然而,不少社会学家认为,长期独居有损健康,导致孤独感,促使免疫力下降。调查发现,单纯的社交网络朋友圈无助于减轻孤独感,在网络上得到再多点赞也不及生活中几个朋友和熟人的寥寥数语。

III. Notes to the Text

1. One's a Crowd—独身者众多 (The headline suggests that living alone has become common in the society.)

2. Eric Klinenberg—埃里克·克利嫩伯格 [纽约大学社会学教授和《单身时代:独居生活方式异常崛起和惊人魅力》(*Going Solo: The Extraordinary Rise and Surprising Appeal of Living Alone*)一书的作者]

3. Stockholm—斯德哥尔摩市(瑞典首都,该市失业率较低,个人收入较高,社会福利保障较为完善,一直被认为是个幸福感较高的城市。)

4. Living alone comports with modern values. —独居符合现代价值观。(comport with—agree with)

5. Paradoxically, our species, so long defined by groups and by the nuclear family, has been able to embark on this experiment in solo living... —十分奇特的是,人类长期以来一直以群体和核心家庭为单位生活,而现在却能开创独居生活方式的尝试 (① our species—referring to the human race; ② define—to characterize; ③ embark on—to start sth; ④ nuclear family—a family unit consisting only of husband, wife and children)

6. Dynamic markets, flourishing cities and open communications systems make modern autonomy more appealing; they give us the capacity (**not only**) to live alone but to engage with others when and how we want to and on our own terms.—市场活跃、城市繁荣以及通信系统畅通使现代独居更具吸引力;这些条件不仅使我们能独立生活,而且能以自己所选的时间和方式按自己所定的条件与其他人交往。

7. the General Social Survey—美国社会综合调查(一项对美国社会全面而系统的、连续性的调查项目)

8. ... lead author of "The Social Connectedness of Older Adults," a paper in the *American Sociological Review*—刊登在《美国社会评论》上题为《老年人的社会交往》论文的第一作者

9. The image of a modern family in a room together, each plugged into a separate reality, be it a smartphone, computer, video game or TV show has become a cultural cliché.—现代家庭虽然同住一房,但却各干各的事,不管是拨弄智能手机、使用电脑、玩电子游戏,还是观看电视节目,这种景象已经是十分常见的社会现象。(a cultural cliché—referring to a common social phenomenon)

10. The Pew Internet Personal Networks and Community Survey—皮尤互联网个人网络和社会调查(Pew Research Center—美国一家独立性民调机构,总部设在华盛顿特区)

11. "Social Isolation and New Technology," written by the Rutgers University communications scholar Keith Hampton...—罗格斯大学传播学学者基思·汉普顿所撰写的《社会隔离与新技术》(the Rutgers University—美国罗格斯大学,全称 Rutgers, The State University of New Jersey,是美国新泽西州最大的高等学府)

12. But many of those I interviewed said they chose to live alone because they had found there was nothing worse than living with the wrong person.—然而,许多被采访者说,他们选择独居是因为他们觉得没有什么能比与不合适的人一起生活更加糟糕的了。

13. a clear aversion to moving in with friends or family or into a nursing home—明确表示讨厌搬到亲朋好友家或者养老院

14. Most older widows, widowers and divorced people remake their lives as single people.—大多数年纪较大的寡妇、鳏夫和离婚者开始独居的新生活。

15. Social Security—(美国的)社会保障(政府对老年或残疾人、贫苦儿童、失业工人等提供最低额救济金)

16. the U.C.L.A.—加利福尼亚大学洛杉矶分校

17. the 1995 Chicago heat wave—1995芝加哥热浪(1995年7月中旬,热浪袭击芝加哥市,导致七百余人中暑死亡)

18. In the general population, living alone has become more common—in absolute and proportional terms.—在人口总数统计中,从绝对数和比例数来看,独居已经变得更为常见。

19. All signs suggest that living alone will become even more common in the future, at every stage of adulthood and in every place where people can afford a place of their own.—所有迹象表明,独居在未来将变得更加常见,在成年期的每一个阶段和人们经济条件许可的任何地方,莫不如此。

IV. Language Features

《纽约时报》简介

《纽约时报》(*The New York Times*),由亨利·雷蒙德于1851年创办。1896年该报被A.S.奥克斯购买。1935年奥克斯去世后,归其婿索尔茨伯格家族所有。1969年起该报从家族企业变为纽约时报公司(The New York Times Company),成为拥有多家美国报纸、杂志、电视台、广播电台和国外联合企业的大报团。它与《华盛顿邮报》(The Washington Post)、《洛杉矶时报》(The Los Angeles Times)并列为美国最有影响的三家报纸。也有不少人称它为美国"第一大报"。该报所获美国新闻普利策奖的数量雄踞榜首,到2012年共获112项奖。

《纽约时报》读者多属于美国上层社会,包括政府官员、国会议员、工商业家和高级知识分子等。它的平日发行量为107万份,星期日发行量为163万份。它的印张最多,平日版有60—100页,星期日版达300页以上。

该报资料雄厚,文章内容充实。20世纪70年代,《纽约时报》进行了一次版面改革,在与社论版相对的一页上设"社论相对版"(Op-ed Page),刊登报外人士评论。报纸平日版(周一至周五)内容由原来的两部分改为四部分:

　　A组——国内新闻、国际新闻、纽约新闻、社论

　　B组——经济新闻

　　C组——文化艺术新闻

　　D组——专题报道,每天刊登一个专题,星期一为体育,星期二为科技,星期三为生活,星期四为家庭,星期五为周末版

有时,周三会增加F组(金融新闻),周四会增加E组(时尚相关新闻)。周日版除了新闻报道之外,还包括许多专栏,如饮食、旅游、艺术和其他文化专题。

星期日版包括两大副刊:《纽约时报杂志》(The New York Times Magazine)和《纽约时报书评》(The New York Times Review)。此外,该报还发行几种郊区版,内容比较庞杂。

阅读《纽约时报》时,首先应看一下A组第一页左下方"内页栏"(Inside),从这一栏可以看出这一天的版面情况。在第二部分,即B组第一页有新闻摘要及索引。一日重大新闻分类归纳在内,并标有页数和栏数。读者可从中找出自己感兴趣的新闻。

该报一贯标榜客观公正,其口号是"刊登一切适合刊登的新闻"(All the news that's fit to print.)。其网站将这一口号改为"All the news that's fit to click."该报风格比较严肃,享有新闻来源较为可靠的声誉。其观点比较自由开放,不时发表一些批评政府政策的报道和评论。1971年,该报曾连续刊登五角大楼秘密文件,揭露政府蓄意扩大越战规模。2004年,该报报道伊拉克战争"情报门事件",挑战攻击伊拉克的正当性。但该报也出现过不少失误,2003年该报承认其记者杰森•布莱尔多年新闻报道作假。2004年5月26日,该报承认在伊拉克战争爆发前的报道错误促使公众进一步相信伊拉克拥有"大规模杀伤性武器"的谎言。该报与东部大财团关系密切,其报道和评论基本代表垄断集团的利益。

V. Analysis of Content

1. Which city has the highest rate of single people?
　　A. Denver.　　　　B. Washington.　　　　C. Stockholm.　　　　D. Paris.

2. Which of the following is NOT on the author's list of benefits offered by living alone?
   A. Giving privacy.	B. Improving health.
   C. Promoting self-realization.	D. Increasing freedom.
3. The Cornwells' studies show that compared with their married counterparts single people are more likely to _____.
   A. spend time with friends and neighbors
   B. avoid social activities
   C. develop loneliness
   D. hunker down at home
4. "Social Isolation and New Technology" reveals that heavy Web users _____.
   A. have small social networks
   B. cut themselves from real friendships
   C. hardly meet diverse people with different perspectives and beliefs
   D. are more likely to have large social networks
5. According to the article, the most important factor in the live-alone decision by widows, widowers and divorced people in western countries is _____.
   A. the political system	B. children's encouragement
   C. the sufficient income	D. the change of marriage concept

VI. Questions on the Article

1. Is the decision to live alone limited to the U.S.?
2. What are the dated images of single people?
3. What is the author's finding after interviewing more than 300 single people?
4. What make the life of single people more appealing?
5. What did Erin Cornwell's research find?
6. What do the surveys made by market research companies find?
7. What are the effects of new communication technologies on living alone?
8. What is Keith Hampton's finding about the effects of Web use on social life?
9. What did the author find through interviews with older single people?
10. According to research by Deborah Carr, do the majority of elderly men and women intend to marry at 18 months after the death of a spouse?
11. What was pundits' prediction about the living-alone style? What does evidence show?

VII. Topics for Discussion

1. Is the increase of single people an inevitable result of economic growth?
2. Is the life of single people happier than the life of married couples?

Lesson 12

Love in the Age of Like[1]

Human beings have never had as many romantic options as they do now. Will that doom love or save it?

(Abridged)

By Aziz Ansari[2]

My parents had an arranged marriage. This always fascinated me. I am perpetually indecisive about even the most mundane things, and I couldn't imagine navigating such a huge life decision so quickly.

I asked my dad about this experience, and here's how he described it: he told his parents he was ready to get married, so his family arranged meetings with three neighboring families. The first girl, he said, was "a little too tall," and the second girl was "a little too short." Then he met my mom. He quickly deduced that she was the appropriate height (finally!), and they talked for about 30 minutes. They decided it would work.[3] A week later, they were married.

And they still are, 35 years later. Happily so—and probably more so than most people I know who had nonarranged marriages. That's how my dad decided on the person with whom he was going to spend the rest of his life.

Today's generations are looking (exhaustively) for soul mates, whether we decide to hit the altar or not[4], and we have more opportunities than ever to find them. The biggest changes have been brought by the $2.4 billion online-dating industry, which has exploded in the past few years with the arrival of dozens of mobile apps[5]. Throw in the fact that people now get married later in life than ever before, turning their early 20s into a relentless hunt for more romantic options than previous generations could have ever imagined, and you have a recipe for romance gone haywire.[6]

In the course of our research, I also discovered something surprising: the winding road from the classified section of yore to Tinder[7] has taken an unexpected turn. Our phones and texts and apps might just be bringing us full circle, back to an old-fashioned version of courting that is closer to what my own parents experienced than you might guess.

Today, if you own a smartphone, you're carrying a 24-7 singles bar in your pocket.[8] As of this writing, 38% of Americans who describe themselves as "single and looking" have used an online-dating site. It's not just my generation—boomers are as likely as college kids to give online dating a whirl.[9] Almost a quarter of online daters find a spouse or long-term partner that way.

It's easy to see why online dating has taken off. It provides you with a seemingly endless supply of people who are single and looking to date. Let's say you're a woman who wants a 28-year-old man who's 5 ft.10 in., has brown hair, lives in Brooklyn, is a member of the Baha'i faith[10] and loves the music of Naughty by Nature[11]. Before online dating, this would have been a fruitless quest, but now, at any time of the day, no matter where you are, you are just a few screens away from sending a message to your very specific dream man.[12]

There are downsides with online dating, of course. Throughout all our interviews—and in research on the subject—this is a consistent finding: in online dating, women get a ton more attention than men. Even a guy at the highest end of attractiveness barely receives the number of messages almost all women get. But that doesn't mean that men end up standing alone in the corner of the online bar. On the Internet, there are no lonely corners. What I'm about to say is going to sound very mean, but Derek is a pretty boring guy. Medium height, thinning brown hair, nicely dressed and personable, but not immediately magnetic or charming. If he walked into a bar, you'd probably go, "Oh, there's a white guy."

At our focus group on online dating in Manhattan, Derek got on OkCupid[13] and let us watch as he went through his options. These were women whom OkCupid had selected as potential matches for him based on his profile and the site's algorithm. The first woman he clicked on was very beautiful, with a witty profile page, a good job and lots of shared interests, including a love of sports. After looking the page over for a minute or so, Derek said, "Well, she looks O.K. I'm just gonna keep looking for a while."

I asked what was wrong, and he replied, "She likes the Red Sox[14]." I was completely shocked. I couldn't believe how quickly he had moved on. Imagine the Derek of 20 years ago, finding out that this beautiful, charming woman was a real possibility for a date. If she were at a bar and smiled at him, Derek of 1993 would have melted. He wouldn't have walked up and said, "Oh, wait, you like the Red Sox?! No thank you!" before putting his hand in her face and turning away. But Derek of 2013 simply clicked an X on a web-browser tab[15] and deleted her without thinking twice. Watching him comb through those profiles, it became clear that online, every bozo could now be a stud.[16]

But dealing with this new digital romantic world can be a lot of work. Answering messages, filtering profiles—it's not always fun. Priya, 27, said she'd recently deleted her Tinder and other online-dating accounts. "It just takes too long to get to just the first date. I feel like it's way more effective utilizing your social groups," she said. "I would rather put myself in those social situations than get exhausted." For Priya, as for so many of the online daters we met in different cities, the process had morphed from something fun and exciting into a source of stress and dread.[17]

Even the technological advances of the past few years are pretty absurd. You can stand in line at the grocery store and swipe through 60 people's faces on Tinder while you wait to buy hamburger buns. That's 20 times as many people as my dad met on his marriage journey. In the history of our species, no group has ever had as many romantic options as we have now.

In theory, more options are better, right? Wrong. Psychology professor Barry Schwartz, famous for his 2004 book *The Paradox of Choice*, divided us into two types of people: "satisficers" (those who satisfy and then suffice) and "maximizers," who seek out the best.

Thanks to smart phones and the Internet, our options are unlimited, whether it's a retail item or a romantic possibility. We have all become maximizers.

It's easy to find and get the best, so why not do it? If you are in a big city or on an online-dating site, you are now comparing your potential partners not just to other potential partners but rather to an idealized person to whom no one could measure up.[18]

But people don't always know what they're looking for in a soul mate, unlike when they're picking something easier, like laundry detergent.

While we may think we know what we want, we're often wrong. As recounted in Dan Slater's history of online dating, *Love in the Time of Algorithms*[19], the first online-dating services tried to find matches for clients based almost exclusively on what clients said they wanted. But pretty soon they realized that the kind of partner people said they were looking for didn't match up with the kind of partner they were actually interested in.

Amarnath Thombre, Match.com's[20] president, discovered this by analyzing the discrepancy between the characteristics people said they wanted in a romantic partner (age, religion, hair color and the like) and the characteristics of the people whom they contacted on the site. When you watched their actual browsing habits—who they looked at and contacted—they went way outside of what they said they wanted.

When I was writing stand-up about online dating, I filled out the forms for dummy accounts on several dating sites just to get a sense of the questions and what the process was like.[21] The person I described was a little younger than me, small, with dark hair. My girlfriend now, whom I met through friends, is two years older, about my height—O.K., slightly taller—and blond. She wouldn't have made it through the filters I set up.

A big part of online dating is spent on this process, though—setting your filters, sorting through profiles and going through a mandatory checklist of what you think you are looking for. People take these parameters very seriously. They declare that their mate "must love dogs" or that their mate "must love the film *Must Love Dogs*," about a preschool teacher (Diane Lane) who tries online dating and specifies that her match "must love dogs." (I looked it up on Wikipedia.)

But does all the effort put into sorting profiles help? Despite the nuanced information that people put up on their profiles, the factor that they rely on most when preselecting a date is looks. In his book *Dataclysm*[22], OkCupid founder Christian Rudder estimates, based on data from his own site, that photos drive 90% of the action in online dating.[23]

Now, of course, we have mobile dating apps like Tinder. Contrary to the labor-intensive user experience of traditional online dating, mobile apps generally operate on a much simpler and quicker scale. As soon as you sign in, Tinder uses your GPS location to find nearby users and starts showing you pictures. You swipe right on their pictures if you might be interested, left if you're not.

Maybe it sounds shallow. But consider this: In the case of my girlfriend, I initially saw her face somewhere and approached her. I didn't have an in-depth profile to peruse or a fancy algorithm.[24] I just had her face, and we started talking and it worked out. Is that experience so different from swiping on Tinder?

"I think Tinder is a great thing," says Helen Fisher, an anthropologist who studies dating. "All Tinder is doing is giving you someone to look at that's in the neighborhood. Then you let the human brain with his brilliant little algorithm tick, tick, tick off what you're looking for."

In this sense, Tinder actually isn't so different from what our grandparents did. Nor is it all that different from what one friend of mine did, using online dating to find someone Jewish who lived nearby. In a world of infinite possibilities, we've cut down our options to people we're attracted to in our neighborhood.

In relationships, there's commitment and *commitment*, the kind that involves a license, usually some kind of religious blessing and a ceremony in which every one of your close friends and relatives watches you and your partner promise to stay together until one of you dies.

Look at my parents: they had an arranged marriage, and they are totally happy. I looked into it, and this is not uncommon. People in arranged marriages start off lukewarm, but over time they really invest in each other and in general have successful relationships.[25] This may be because they bypassed the most dangerous part of a relationship.

In the first stage of a relationship, you have passionate love. This is where you and your partner are just going crazy for each other. Every smile makes your heart flutter. Every night is more magical than the last. During this phase, your brain floods your neural synapses with dopamine, the same neurotransmitter that gets released when you do cocaine.

Like all drugs, though, this high wears off after 12 to 18 months. At a certain point, the brain rebalances itself. In good relationships, as passionate love fades, companionate love arises to take its place. If passionate love is the cocaine of love, companionate love is like having a glass of wine.

In his book *The Happiness Hypothesis*, NYU social psychologist Jonathan Haidt identifies two danger points in every romantic relationship. One is at the apex of the passionate-love phase. People get all excited and dive in headfirst. A new couple, weeks or months into a relationship, high off passionate love, goes bonkers and moves in together and gets married way too quickly. Sometimes these couples are able to transition from the passionate stage to the companionate one. Other times, though, they transition into a crazy, toxic relationship and/or get divorced.

The second danger point is when passionate love starts wearing off. This is when you start coming down off that initial high and start worrying about whether this is really the right person for you.

Your texts used to be so loving: It's hard to focus on anything at work, 'cause all that's in my head is you. Now your texts are like: Let's just meet at Whole Foods. Or: Hey, that dog you made us buy took a dump in my shoe.

But Haidt argues that when you hit this stage, you should be patient. With luck, if you allow yourself to invest more in the other person, you will find a beautiful life companion.

I had a rather weird firsthand experience with this. When I first started dating my girlfriend, a few months in, I went to a friend's wedding in Big Sur, Calif.

The vows in this wedding were powerful. They were saying the most remarkable, loving things about each other. Things like "You are a prism that takes the light of life and turns it into a rainbow" and "You are a lotion that moisturizes my heart. Without you, my soul has eczema." It was the noncheesy, heartfelt version of stuff like that.

After the wedding, I found out about four different couples that had broken up, supposedly because they didn't feel like they had the love that was expressed in those vows. Did they call it off too early, at their danger point? I don't know, but I, too, felt scared hearing that stuff. Did I have what those people had? At that point, no. But for some reason, I felt deep down that I should keep investing in my relationship—as my father did, after those fateful 30 minutes of literally sizing up my mother—and that eventually that level of love would show itself.[26] And so far, it has.

From *Time*, June 22, 2015

I. New Words

absurd	[əbˈsəːd]	adj.	荒谬的，可笑的
anthropologist	[ˌænθrəˈpɔlədʒist]	n.	人类学家
apex	[ˈeipeks]	n.	顶峰
bonkers	[ˈbɔŋkəz]	adj.	*informal* completely crazy
bozo	[ˈbəuzəu]	n.	*informal* a stupid person
browse	[brauz]	v.	（快速，随意地）浏览
bypass	[ˈbaipɑːs]	v.	to go around or avoid a place
commitment	[kəˈmitmənt]	n.	承诺，保证，允诺
compassionate	[kəmˈpæʃənit]	adj.	有同情心的
deduce	[diˈdjuːs]	v.	*formal* 推断
detergent	[diˈtəːdʒənt]	n.	清洁剂，去垢剂
discrepancy	[diˈskrepənsi]	n.	difference, disagreement
dopamine	[ˈdəupəmiːn]	n.	[生化]多巴胺
downside	[ˈdaunˌsaid]	n.	the disadvantages or less positive aspects
eczema	[ˈeksimə]	n.	[医]湿疹
filter	[ˈfiltə]	n.	过滤器
		v.	筛选
flutter	[ˈflʌtə]	v.	(of the heart) beat weakly and irregularly, esp. because of nervous excitement
hypothesis	[haiˈpɔθəsis]	n.	假设
labor-intensive	[ˌleibərinˈtensiv]	adj.	劳动密集型的
indecisive	[ˌindiˈsaisiv]	adj.	unable to make decisions
magnetic	[mægˈnetik]	adj.	attractive
mandatory	[ˈmændətəri]	adj.	required or commanded by authority; obligatory
mundane	[mʌnˈdein]	adj.	ordinary and typically unexciting
navigate	[ˈnævigeit]	v.	to find the right way to deal with a difficult situation
neurotransmitter	[ˌnjuərəˈtrænsˈmitə]	n.	[生化]神经递质

第三单元　家庭婚姻

nuanced	[njuːˈɑːnst]	adj.	细致的
parameter	[pəˈræmitə]	n.	参数
personable	[ˈpəːsənəbəl]	adj.	惹人爱的，个性或外表宜人的
passionate	[ˈpæʃənit]	adj.	having or showing strong feelings
prism	[ˈprizəm]	n.	棱镜
shallow	[ˈʃæləu]	adj.	lacking depth of intellect, emotion, or knowledge
stud	[stʌd]	n.	性欲旺盛的男子
suffice	[səˈfais]	v.	to be enough
swipe	[swaip]	v.	滑动屏幕
tick	[tik]	v.	用记号标出
utilize	[ˈjuːtilaiz]	v.	*formal* to use
yore	[jɔː]	n.	*literary* time long past

II. Background Information

美国社会婚恋方式的嬗变

　　美国西北大学心理学教授芬克尔研究认为，当代美国社会婚恋方式大致经历了三个发展阶段。

　　在很长一段时期里，人们为了实际需求而结婚。1932年，经过对费城5000对夫妇开展问卷测试后发现，受访者中竟有八分之一在婚前曾生活在同一座大楼。当时，地理距离在男女婚恋中几乎起到了决定性作用。熟人介绍或是邻里相识通常是人们选择自己终身伴侣的主要方式。彼时的婚姻更像是生活伴侣的结合。在这种婚姻形态中，男女双方通常有着清晰的分工和角色。丈夫负责赚钱养家，妻子则相夫教子。对于婚姻的满足感通常取决于双方演绎本身角色的程度。所谓爱情，只是生活的附加品。

　　第二次世界大战后，年轻人开始为了爱情而结婚。他们对真爱的渴求和期待逐渐增强，更倾向于想方设法寻找完美的另一半——心灵伴侣(soul mate)。他们期望每次遇见对方时，都能产生怦然心动的感觉。此时的婚姻建立在男女双方的"情爱关系"基础上。女性不再在婚姻中处于从属地位。而这种对爱情的执着追求也直接导致了初婚年龄的推后。

　　60年代，受反主流文化运动(the counter-culture movement)的影响，人们开始注重从基于爱情的婚姻关系转变到现在的"自我实现"式婚姻关系。婚姻不再是步入"成年"的必经之路。步入大学，投入工作，走向社会都意味着个人"成年"的开始。诸如"自我价值""自我发现"等概念在文化中站稳了脚跟。美国人如今在婚姻关系中想要的不仅仅是爱情，同时也在寻找一个能为自己生命赋予更多意义的人，实现自我价值的升华。

20世纪90年代中后期,随着互联网的逐渐普及,网络即时通讯、聊天室、留言板和论坛的兴起进一步拉近了人们之间的距离,有着共同兴趣的单身男女开始通过门户网站在线交流,相识恋爱。1998年,好莱坞浪漫喜剧电影《电子情书》("You've Got Mail")大获成功,由汤姆·汉克斯(Tom Hanks)和梅格·瑞安(Meg Ryan)饰演的男女主角通过美国在线(AOL)电子邮件系统和留言板坠入爱河的故事从侧面表明了互联网已经深刻改变了美国社会传统的恋爱方式。到2007年,相亲网站已经成为美国第二大网络内容付费产业。美国最大、最成功的约会平台Tinder 2019年的收入达到12亿美元。知名婚庆服务网站The Knot公布的一份调查数据显示:有比例高达22%的配偶是通过网站结识的,通过朋友介绍认识的比例为19%,大学时期结识的比例是17%,高中结识的比例是8%,工作时结识的比例为13%,酒吧、音乐会等社交场合结识的比例是11%,青梅竹马从小认识的比例是4%。

　　今天,相对于传统的直接见面相亲方式而言,网恋具有许多优势。比如,单身男女的合意对象选择变得更加广泛,交流方式在电脑和手机的帮助下超越了以往的空间和时间限制,大数据计算甚至帮助用户排除或是选定相应的合适交往对象人群。然而,由此产生的问题也显而易见。首先,过于庞大的交往对象数量导致恋爱似乎成了一种商品。人们仿佛在情爱市场中闲逛,按照特定标准漫不经心地挑选自己中意的商品,对恋爱过程也愈加懒惰和不够投入,久而久之甚至对恋爱成功丧失了信心。其次,通过电脑或手机屏幕上冰冷空虚的文字而得出的个人印象过于片面。甚至为了博取青睐对象的信任和好感,有人可能会刻意隐瞒真实情况或使用虚假信息。这种根据零星信息不断拼凑起来的人物形象很容易令对方产生与实际不相符的期望或想象,从而影响彼此对于未来交往的判断。最后,至今仍无明确证据显示大数据计算配对优于其他恋爱方式。相亲网站在进行电脑比对时,往往侧重于双方性格经历上的相似点和互补性,而这些在一段成功的恋爱关系中却并非是关键因素。更重要的是,计算机无法预测一个人的成长路径和双方在长期交往过程中的性格变化。因此,基于男女双方相识前数据计算得出的配对成功率根本无法左右二人恋爱过程中感情的稳定性和各自内心的满意度。

　　总而言之,在过去15年到20年间,网恋颠覆了美国社会传统的婚恋方式。而未来随着科技的不断发展和人类对爱情的孜孜追求,网恋这一新生事物或许将获得更大程度的改进和认可。

III. Notes to the Text

1. Love in the Age of Like——网恋时代的爱情[作者在此处采用"借代"修辞手段,用事物产生的后果(like)指代相关原因(online dating),从而突显了网恋所产生的共同问题:投入不足,感情不深。]

2. Aziz Ansari——阿齐兹·安萨里,印度裔美国人,作家、导演、喜剧演员,多次获得演出奖和写作奖。

3. They decided it would work. —他们认为可行。(work—If an idea, system, or way of doing something works, it is successful, effective, or satisfactory.)

4. Today's generations are looking (exhaustively) for soul mates, whether we decide to hit the altar or not... —当代人在(竭尽全力地)寻找心灵伴侣，无论最终是否决定结婚……(altar—a holy table in a church or temple. The word is often used in connection with weddings.)

5. mobile apps—手机应用软件

6. Throw in the fact that people now get married later in life than ever before, turning their early 20s into a relentless hunt for more romantic options than previous generations could have ever imagined, and you have a recipe for romance gone haywire. —此外，现在人们结婚比之前任何时代都晚，20出头成了无休止的恋爱对象选择期，可选者数量之多超出前几代人的想象。这种状况必然导致恋爱失控。(① throw in—to add sth to a discussion; ② relentless—never stops or never becomes less intense; ③ a recipe for sth—a way that seemly likely to have a particular result; ④ haywire—out of control)

7. Tinder—美国一款(主要用于男女约会)手机交友软件

8. Today, if you own a smartphone, you're carrying a 24-7 singles bar in your pocket. —如今，拥有一台智能手机，就意味着你的口袋里带着一间每周7天、每天24小时不间断营业的单身酒吧。(singles bar—a bar used as a meeting place, especially for young, single people)

9. It's not just my generation—boomers are as likely as college kids to give online dating a whirl. —不单是我们这代人，"婴儿潮代"的人和大学生一样可能去尝试线上约会。(give sth a whirl—try sth as an experiment, to see if it is suitable, pleasant, etc.)

10. the Baha'i faith—巴哈依教

11. Naughty by Nature—美国新泽西东奥兰治的说唱组合。

12. Before online dating, this would have been a fruitless quest, but now, at any time of the day, no matter where you are, you are just a few screens away from sending a message to your very specific dream man. —在网恋时代之前，这会是一场徒劳的搜寻，但是现在，无论何时何地，你要找自己特定的梦中人只需发一条信息，搜索几个网页就可以做到。

13. OkCupid—美国约会应用软件

14. the Red Sox—"红袜队"(美国波士顿的一支参加美国棒球大联盟比赛的职业棒球队，国内一般称其为红袜队)

15. web-browser tab—网页浏览器标签页

16. Watching him comb through those profiles, it became clear that online, every bozo could now be a stud. —看着他一一浏览那些人的简介，我明白了一件事，在网上，"矮矬穷"都可能变成"高富帅"。(profile—a short description of a person, that contains all the details that someone needs)

17. For Priya, as for so many of the online daters we met in different cities, the process had morphed from something fun and exciting into a source of stress and dread. —对Priya来说，正如我们在不同城市遇到过的很多在线约会者一样，这个过程已经从一件有趣而令人激动的事变成了一种压力和忧虑之源。(① morph—to change into; ② dread—a feeling of great anxiety and fear about something that may happen)

18. If you are in a big city or on an online-dating site, you are now comparing your potential

partners not just to other potential partners but rather to an idealized person to whom no one could measure up. —如果你身处一个大城市或者登录到一处线上约会网站，你不只是将可能的约会对象与其他可能的约会对象进行比较，更会将他(她)们与一个无人能配的理想对象进行比较。(measure up—to be good enough, or as good as someone or something else)

19. *Love in the Time of Algorithms*—《网络时代的婚恋》[作者丹·斯莱特(Dan Slater)，该书审视了网络相亲产业的发展历史和现状。英文 algorithm 原意是"计算机算法"，这里指"网络应用"。]

20. Match.com—线上婚恋交友网站(该网站用8种语言为25个国家提供服务)

21. When I was writing stand-up about online dating, I filled out the forms for dummy accounts on several dating sites just to get a sense of the questions and what the process was like. —当时我正在撰写关于网恋的单口相声稿子，为了了解婚恋网站上常见的问题和操作流程，我在几家婚恋网站上注册了假账号，并填写了表格。(stand-up—a comedy consisting of one person standing in front of an audience and telling jokes)

22. *Dataclysm*—《数据灾难》(a blend formed from *data* and *cataclysm*)

23. ...that photos drive 90% of the action in online dating —线上约会过程中行为驱动力有九成来自照片

24. I didn't have an in-depth profile to peruse or a fancy algorithm. —我并没有一个全面的个人情况介绍来进行仔细研究，也没有一种精细的算法。(① in-depth—very thorough and detailed; ② peruse—to read or examine, typically with great care; ③ fancy—requiring much skill)

25. People in arranged marriages start off lukewarm, but over time they really invest in each other and in general have successful relationships. —包办婚姻的夫妻起初关系都是不温不火的，但是他们在彼此身上投入感情，经过一段时间，一般都能收获成功的夫妻关系。(lukewarm—not eager or enthusiastic)

26. But for some reason, I felt deep down that I should keep investing in my relationship—as my father did, after those fateful 30 minutes of literally sizing up my mother—and that eventually that level of love would show itself. —不知怎么的，我深深地感到，我应该在爱情和婚姻中不断地投入时间与精力——正如我父亲当年经过30分钟对我母亲作出判断后所做的那样——那种层次的爱最终会自然而然地出现。(size up—to form a judgment or an opinion

about sb)

IV. Language Features

报刊用喻

　　为了使语言浅显易懂,生动活泼,新闻报道常用比喻性词语(metaphorical words)。

　　西方报刊在选择消息时往往侧重于"能引起情感联系"的趣味新闻,特别是那些能产生威尔伯·施拉姆博士(Dr. Wiber Schramm)所定名为"瞬即心理报酬"(immediate reward)的新闻。在文字应用上也明显反映了这种倾向,暴力、性爱等相关的比喻表达法常被使用,如:用 courting(求爱)表示 seek friendly relations(寻求友好关系);用 marriage 或 wedding(结婚、联姻)表示 close association 或 union(密切的关系或联盟);用 divorce(离婚)表示 breakup of relationship(关系破裂);用 flirt(调情)表示 make an insincere proposition of friendly relationship(提出并无诚意的友好关系或建议);以 sexy(性感的)表示 attractive(吸引人的)或 interesting(有趣的)等。

　　新闻报道中"暴力""战争"等比喻词语使用也很普遍。"冲突""辩论""争吵""比赛""竞争"都可能被说成是战争,如 war on poverty(向贫穷开战),war on cancer(向癌症开战),war on inflation(向通货膨胀开战),war on corruption(向腐败开战),a war of words(舌战),turf war(争夺势力范围战),trade war(贸易战),propaganda war(宣传战),spy war(间谍战),price war(价格战);其他与暴力相关的比喻词语还有:blitz(闪电战),barrage(齐射式的攻击),offensive(攻势),counterattack(反攻),crossfire(交叉火力),breakthrough(突围),salvo(火枪齐射),attack(进攻),explosion(爆炸),battle(战役),fight(战斗)等。

　　应该指出的是,这类比喻属于夸张词语,如果夸张失度,便会"使读者在他们的连珠炮的震鸣声里很快感到疲倦"。

V. Analysis of Content

1. The example of Derek (paragraphs 8—10) proves that on the Internet, _____.

　　A. women are more popular than men

　　B. Derek is a man at the highest end of attractiveness

　　C. people tend to become too picky in making their decision

　　D. people don't have a chance to know each other well

2. The word "maximizer" in the text means _____.

　　A. a person who increases sth as much as possible

　　B. a person who makes as much use of sth as possible

　　C. a person who tries to make his/her look as good as possible

D. a person who seeks out the best one as his/her partner
3. Priya deleted her online dating app because _____.
   A. she didn't find it useful
   B. she found it less effective and more stressful
   C. she didn't believe the profiles online
   D. she failed to find a proper date online
4. According to the author, the most important factor in a successful romantic relationship is _____.
   A. looks   B. common likes and dislikes
   C. passionate love   D. commitment
5. The author's view on online dating is _____.
   A. positive   B. unknown
   C. objective   D. critical

VI. Questions on the Article

1. What kind of marriage was the marriage of the author's parents? Why does the author always find it fascinating?
2. What are the biggest changes for the present generation in dating?
3. What is the root cause of those changes?
4. How popular is online dating according to the article?
5. What are the reasons for online-dating's popularity?
6. What does the author want to prove by citing Dan Slater's book *Love in the Time of Algorithms*?
7. Does the author think that the effort put into sorting profiles on dating websites and apps is very useful? Why or why not?
8. What is the similarity between Tinder and traditional arranged dating?
9. What problem did Amarnath Thombre analyze in his research?
10. What are the characteristics of the first stage of a relationship?
11. According to NYU social psychologist Jonathan Haidt, what are the two danger points in every romantic relationship?
12. What lesson did the author draw from the breakup of four couples?

VII. Topics for Discussion

1. Is online dating better than the old way of dating?
2. Do the options offered by modern technology for dating doom love or save it?

Unit 4
第四单元 行为风尚

Lesson 13

Take Your Planet to Work

Businesses find that green offices cut energy costs, attract employees—and help the earth too.

By Lisa Takeuchi Cullen

We can compost and conserve all we want at home. But as soon as we hit the office, we turn into triplicate-printing, paper-cup-squashing, run-our-computers-all-night-so-the-boss-thinks-we're-working earth befoulers.[1] One office worker can use a quarter ton of materials in a year—which includes 10,000 pieces of copier paper. Heating, cooling and powering office space are responsible for almost 40% of carbon dioxide emissions[2] in the U.S. and gobble more than 70% of total electricity usage. Commuters spew 1.3 billion tons of CO_2 a year. Computers in the office burn $1 billion worth of electricity annually—and that's when they're not producing a lick of work.[3]

All our unnecessarily generated company waste adds up to unnecessarily wasted company cash. Goosed by the color of money, companies from global empire to mom-and-pop, from high tech to local government are embracing environmentally friendlier architecture, supplies and attitudes.[4] Wal-Mart is placing solar panels on its stores. Los Angeles County may soon offer its 90,000 commuting employees incentives to buy hybrid vehicles[5]; UCLA already does. The San Francisco Federal Building, Dallas' McKinney Green office building, and New York City's Hearst, Bank of America and Goldman Sachs towers were all designed under green principles.[6] Want a tipping point?[7] Here's one: in May, Rupert Murdoch announced that News Corp. would go carbon neutral.[8]

The business case for going green is increasingly clear, even without Al Gore droning on and on and on about it: where green goes, so goes the bottom line.[9] But employers are beginning to realize it's also about the competition for talent. Several recent surveys show that workers, especially from the generation that grew up separating paper from plastic, don't want to work for big fat polluters[10]. One-third of workers would be more inclined to work for a green company, says staffing firm Adecco USA[11], and more than half wish their employers would be more environmentally friendly.

So what the heck is a green workplace, anyway?[12] Start with the building. If it meets standards for water savings, energy efficiency, materials selection and indoor environmental quality, it can be certified by a nonprofit called the U.S. Green Building Council[13]. The council created its LEED[14] (which stands for leadership in energy and environmental design) certification in 2000 in response to the demand for standardization in the blooming area of green architecture, says Linda Sorrento, director of education and research partnerships. The platinum LEED rating is given to buildings that can minimize their energy dependence by incorporating green principles from the ground up—say, by picking a location near mass transit and using recycled material in construction.[15] Only 41 office buildings in the U.S. are LEED certified at the platinum level, so chances are you don't work in one. You'll know if you do because your employer will have shared the news discreetly on billboards and in full-page newspaper ads.

Which is to say that most businesses are comfortably ensconced in buildings built B.G.[16] (before Gore). What's more, most office space is leased, which means businesses have limited makeover autonomy. To address this, for office interiors, the Green Building Council created a LEED certification rating for making certain modifications. These include installing automatic shutoffs for lighting (which scarfs up 44% of the electricity used in office buildings) and setting computers to power down automatically after 15 minutes of idle time, cutting the machine's energy use 70%.[17] More ambitious retrofits include switching from old toilets that use up to 8 gal. per flush to new ones that use a maximum of 1.6 gal. Don't laugh; toilet flushing is the single biggest water hog in office buildings nationwide, using up to 4.8 billion gal. per day.

Employers' growing demand for green office space is beginning to change the landscape. In the past, commercial builders weren't motivated to, say, install solar panels[18] because paying for electricity is the tenant's problem. But Karl Stumpf, leader of office projects for architects RTKL[19] in Miami, says that has changed over the past two years as renters have begun choosing sites specifically for their green features. "Builders are realizing that if they build green, they can lease faster—and that's cash,"[20] he says. In 1992, when his firm first delved into green architecture with the redesign of the historic Washington headquarters of the Environmental Protection Agency (EPA[21]), few people aside from the EPA's environment nerds had heard of sustainability. Today all Stumpf's clients request it in some form.

Apart from its physical footprint[22], a company has the greatest opportunity to have an environmental impact through green policies that change the behavior and attitudes of its workers. Take commuting. Employers have a major incentive here: congestion created by people getting to and from work costs U.S. employers 3.7 billion hours of lost productivity a year, which adds up to $63.1 billion in wasted time and fuel every year. That's according to the EPA, which recently ranked employers by those that tried hardest to cut down on commuting times. Winners this year included Nike[23], which offers TRAC (Traveling Responsibly? Accept the Challenge), a program that rewards the employees at its headquarters in Portland, Ore., who get to work without guzzling gas. In fiscal 2006, Nike workers saved 719,343 vehicle miles by biking or taking mass transit, thereby not using 35,907 gal. of gasoline. Google provides free buses for commuters, and Sun Microsystems lets workers skip the commute altogether sometimes by clocking in from home[24].

All these employers could learn something from Sun Light & Power of Berkeley, Calif.[25] Its

CEO and founder, Gary Gerber, built his business in 1975 on the environmentalist principles he lives by. Not only does it supply, design and install solar systems, but the company also tries to avoid taking more than it needs from the earth in doing so.[26] That means using no more outside energy than it gives back: its excess solar power is pumped into the electrical grid, crediting the company's account and bringing its bill to zero[27]. It means no fossil fuels[28]: many workers bike to the office, Gerber drives an electric car, and the company's fleet of equipment-carrying truck runs on biodiesel fuel (once produced from restaurant grease but now bought from a local collective). It means no new office furniture: the rug in the conference room is made of recycled soda bottles, and the chairs are secondhand. Green isn't always pristine.

Sun Light & Power's business began heating up, so to speak, during California's energy crisis in 2001. (Thank you, Enron.[29]) Its employees have grown from seven in 2002 to nearly 50. An annex to the original building was added (using wood salvaged from a demolition next door), and the company expects to hit $12 million in sales this year. Inevitably, rapid growth has challenged Gerber's green ways. "We used to have used computers, but now we need the new ones for speed and security," says Gerber in a sad voice. But when it comes to hiring, Gerber says he won't budge from his belief in "green attitude first, skill set second." In interviews, vegetarians and Greenpeace volunteers win points. After all, it is his workers' commitment to the business's core values that drives growth, he says. "It has really paid off." Green, it seems, begets green.[30]

From Time, July 16, 2007

I. New Words

address	[ə'dres]	v.	对付,处理
annex	[ə'neks]	n.	附加物;附层建筑
billboard	['bilbɔ:d]	n.	(户外)广告牌
biodiesel	['baiəuˌdi:zəl]	n.	生物柴油
budge	[bʌdʒ]	v.	to move slightly; to change one's opinion
carbon dioxide	[ˌkɑ:bəndai'ɔksaid]	n.	二氧化碳
certify	['sə:tifai]	v.	证明;证明合格
certification	[ˌsə:tifi'keiʃən]	n.	证明;证书
discreetly	[dis'kri:tli]	adv.	(言行)谨慎地,慎重地
drone	[drəun]	v.	~on to speak in a boring way, usually for a long time
ensconce	[in'skɔns]	v.	to shelter safely; to hide
gobble	['gɔbl]	v.	to eat sth very fast
grease	[gri:s]	n.	油脂
grid	[grid]	n.	电力网
guzzle	['gʌzl]	v.	to consume gas quickly and in large amounts

hog	[hɔg]	n.	贪婪者；过分消耗者
hybrid	[ˈhaibrid]	adj.	混合的
lease	[li:s]	v.	租借，出租
makeover	[ˈmeikəuvə]	n.	整修
nerd	[nə:d]	n.	informal a person who is boring or stupid
pristine	[ˈpristain]	adj.	new or almost new
retrofit	[ˈretrəˌfit]	n.	式样翻新，花样翻新
rug	[rʌg]	n.	（小）地毯，垫子
spew	[spju:]	v.	to make sth flow out in large quantities
sustainability	[səˌsteinəˈbiliti]	n.	可持续性
tenant	[ˈtenənt]	n.	承租人，租户

II. Background Information

节能与环保

　　在人类活动不断扩张，对于物质享受不断追求的同时，所使用的能源也急剧增加，使得人类居住环境遭到严重破坏。当今世界使用的主要能源是煤炭、石油和天然气等化石能源(fossil fuels)。化石能源的使用产生了热排放(heat emission)。大量化石能源的消耗导致了严重的温室效应(greenhouse effect)。温室气体的增加导致了一系列灾难：气温升高、冰川缩小、海平面上升、大片陆地被淹没、降水量分布不均、气象灾害频发等。气候学家警告：21世纪末海平面将上升至少1米。最新研究显示，人为造成的气候变化将使南极洲大块冰盖融化提前10万年，导致海平面升高5米左右。

　　造成温室效应的根源是二氧化碳(carbon dioxide)等温室气体的大量排放。减少温室气体的排放的主要方法是减少能源浪费和采用绿色能源。美国是能源消耗大国，所用主要能源依然是化石能源。据报道，2021年美国所用的石油、天然气和煤炭占其所用能源比例分别是43.4%、23.8%和11.9%。美国人口占世界人口的比例是5%，但所消耗的能源却占全世界消耗能源的25%！美国人均消耗能源量是印度的35倍。最近几年，美国的有识之士意识到节能的紧迫性并积极呼吁社会民众采取有效措施减少能源消耗。为了节省能耗，减少二氧化碳排放，美国不少公司正在采取积极措施，创造环保办公环境，他们对办公人员做出下列要求：

　　1. 节省电脑使用能源。显示器的选择要适当，因为显示器越大，消耗的能源越多。一台17英寸的显示器比14英寸的显示器耗能多35%。关机之后，要将插头拔出，否则电脑会有约4.8瓦的能耗。将打印机联网，办公室内共用一台打印机，可以减少设备闲置，提高效率，节约能源。

　　2. 节省打印复印能源。在打印非正式文稿时，可将标准打印模式改为草稿打印模式。这种方法省墨30%以上，同时可提高打印速度，节约电能。如果长时间不用，应关闭打印机及其服务器的电源，减少能耗，同时将插头拔出。据估计，仅此一项，全国一年可减少二氧化碳排放1474万吨。打印尽量使用小号字。复印、打印纸用双面,单面使用后的复印纸可再利用空白面影印或裁剪为便条纸或草稿纸。

3. 减少使用一次性用品。员工尽量使用自己的水杯,纸杯是给来客准备的。开会时,本单位的与会人员自带水杯。多用手帕擦汗、擦手,可减少卫生纸、面纸的浪费。尽量使用抹布。使用可更换笔芯的圆珠笔、钢笔替换一次性书写笔。减少使用木杆铅笔,多用自动铅笔。公文袋可以多次使用,各部门应将可重复使用的公文袋回收再利用。

还有很多方面,如使用节能型荧光灯,利用自然光取代部分室内照明,制定新的空调能效标准等。

III. Notes to the Text

1. We can compost and conserve all we want at home. But as soon as we hit the office, we... earth befoulers.——在家里我们会尽可能综合利用、节约使用东西。可是一到办公室我们就变成了地球环境污染者:滥印纸张,糟蹋纸杯,电脑彻夜不关,老板还以为我们在通宵工作。(① compost—make a mixture of decayed leaves, food and manure that can be added to soil to help plants grow; ② conserve—to use as little of sth as possible; ③ triplicate—done three times; ④ to squash—to press sth so that it becomes damaged; ⑤ befoul—to make dirty)

2. carbon dioxide emissions——二氧化碳排放

3. Computers in the office burn $1 billion worth of electricity annually—and that's when they're not producing a lick of work.——办公室里的电脑在完全不工作的情况下每年要耗费价值10亿美元的电力。(a lick of—a small amount of)

4. Goosed by the color of money, companies from global empire to mom-and-pop, from high tech to local government are embracing environmentally friendlier architecture, supplies and attitudes.——受金钱的驱使,从跨国大公司到夫妻店,从高技术公司到地方政府,各种机构都乐于采取更加环保的态度,使用更为环保的建筑和用品。(① goose—to make sth work faster; ② mom-and-pop—*AmE* a store owned and run by a family or husband and wife; ③ embrace—to accept sth with enthusiasm)

5. hybrid vehicles——(汽油电力)混合动力车

6. The San Francisco Federal Building, ... and Goldman Sachs towers were all designed under green principles.——旧金山市联邦办公大楼、达拉斯市麦金尼环保能源公司办公楼、纽约市赫斯特大厦、美国银行和高盛公司大楼都是按照环保原则设计的。(McKinney Green—McKinney Green Mountain Energy Company)

7. Want a tipping point?——想要一个引爆点吗? (tipping point—the point at which the number of small changes over a period of time reaches a level where a further small change has a sudden and very great effect on a system)

8. ...Rupert Murdoch announced that News Corp. would go carbon neutral.——鲁伯特·默多克宣

布新闻集团公司将采用碳中和方式。(① Rupert Murdoch—美国传媒业大亨,他所控制的传媒跨国公司2006年营业额为280亿美元。② "碳中和"是现代人为减缓全球变暖所做的努力之一。利用这种环保方式,人们计算自己日常活动直接或间接制造的二氧化碳排放量,并计算抵消这些二氧化碳所需的经济成本,然后个人付款给专门企业或机构,由它们通过植树或其他环保项目抵消大气中相应的二氧化碳量。)

9. The business case for going green... even without Al Gore droning on...: where green goes, so goes the bottom line. —即使没有艾伯特·戈尔喋喋不休地念环经,企业要环保的道理越来越明显:哪里体现环保原则,哪里便会出现经济效益(① Al Gore—艾伯特·戈尔(Albert Arnold Gore Jr.),美国副总统(1993—2001),环保政治家,由于其在气候变化与环境问题上的贡献,曾获2007年度诺贝尔和平奖;② bottom line—the amount of money shown as profit)

10. big fat polluters—污染大户

11. staffing firm Adecco USA—美国艺珂人力资源配备公司(Adecco is a world leader in human resource solutions and a Fortune 500 company.)

12. So what the heck is a green workplace, anyway?—那么到底什么样的工作场所才是绿色的呢?(the heck—on earth)

13. the U.S. Green Building Council—美国绿色建筑委员会(该机构旨在推动工作场所和生活建筑的环保责任意识,简称USGBC。)

14. LEED—leadership in energy and environmental design("能源和环境设计领先地位"是美国绿色建筑委员会主持下进行的一项生态建筑认证计划。)

15. The platinum LEED rating is given to buildings that can minimize their energy dependence by incorporating green principles from the ground up—say, by picking a location near mass transit and using recycled material in construction.—能源和环境设计领先白金级奖只颁发给那些完全体现环保原则,能源依赖降到最低程度的建筑,例如,选择靠近公共交通的地点和在建筑过程中使用回收材料。(① the platinum LEED rating—是LEED绿色建筑评定系统所认定的最高等级;② from the ground up—completely, entirely, thoroughly)

16. B.G.—used in imitation of B.C. It refers to the period before Al Gore, Vice-President of the U.S. (from 1993 to 2000), led the campaign against global warming.

17. These include installing automatic shutoffs for lighting (which scarfs up 44% of the electricity used in office buildings) and setting computers to power down automatically after 15 minutes of idle time, cutting the machine's energy use 70%.—这些整修包括安装照明器具的自动关闭装置(该项节省办公楼用电44%)和设置电脑闲置15分钟以后电源自动关闭的功能(该项设置减少70%的机器耗能)。(① shutoff—the act of stopping electricity supply; ② scarf up— to remove the skin from a whale; to cut off)

18. solar panels—太阳能电池板

19. RTKL—美国RTKL国际建筑事务所(该机构1946年成立,现为世界最大的建筑规划设计公司之一)

20. Builders are realizing that if they build green, they can lease faster—and that's cash—建筑商逐渐认识到如果他们建造的房子符合环保标准,就能更快地租出去——这是经济效益

21. EPA—Environment Protection Agency(美国)环境保护局

22. physical footprint—Here it refers to carbon footprint (碳足迹), the amount of CO_2 and other greenhouse gases emitted by an individual or an organization.
23. Nike—耐克公司（Nike Inc designs, develops and markets footwear, apparel and accessory products worldwide.）
24. Sun Microsystems lets workers skip the commute altogether sometimes by clocking in from home —太阳计算机系统公司有时允许员工在家计时上下班，完全省去来回乘车(clock in—to register on a time clock at the beginning or end of a day's work)
25. Sun Light & Power of Berkeley, Calif.—加州伯克利太阳光电公司
26. Not only does it supply, design and install solar systems, but the company also tries to avoid taking more than it needs from the earth in doing so.—该公司不仅供应、设计和安装太阳能系统，而且在这么做的时候尽量减少对地球资源的消耗。
27. its excess solar power is pumped into the electrical grid, crediting the company's account and bringing its bill to zero —将多余的太阳能输入电网，计入公司的（电量）账目，把公司的（电量）欠账降至零
28. fossil fuels—矿物燃料
29. Thank you, Enron.—这得感谢安然公司的垮台。（① It is a humorous way of saying that the growth and development of Sun Light & Power's business resulted from the energy crisis caused by Enron's bankruptcy. ② Enron—a powerful U.S. energy company which declared bankruptcy in 2001 as a result of financial scandals）
30. Green, it seems, begets green.—看来，环保带来了经济效益。（Note the author's use of metonymy. Here, the word "green" refers to "environment protection" and "economic profits" respectively.）

IV. Language Features

《时代》周刊介绍

现今《时代》周刊共有四个版本，除美国版之外，还有欧洲版(Time Europe, 伦敦印刷)、亚洲版(Time Asia, 香港印刷)和南太平洋版(The South Pacific Edition, 悉尼印刷)。该刊读者主要是受过良好教育的专业人士和高级管理人员、中产阶级。

《时代》周刊创刊于1923年。1989年时代股份有限公司与华纳通讯公司合并，该刊成为时代华纳(Time Warner)公司一部分。

《时代》周刊编辑方针是不仅为读者提供一周的重要消息，而且要提供相关背景解释和评论，使读者不仅能充分理解，而且能从中得到启发。《时代》周刊的写作风格也不同于报纸。它是把新闻事件作为故事来描述。文字力求生动活泼，情节富有趣味。

《时代》周刊在西方新闻界享有很高声誉，其发行量很长时间保持在400万份左右，据称其美国国内读者有2000万，全球读者有2500万，是美国最大的新闻杂志。经过多

年发展,它已形成独特的写作风格。语言学家称之为《时代》周刊风格(Timestyle)。这种风格的特色是:报道夹叙夹议,句式常用倒装,大量使用前置定语,用词力求新颖活泼。尤为值得一提的是其句式倒装。沃尔科特·吉布斯(Wolcott Gibbs)曾在《纽约人》杂志刊登一篇文章以嘲讽语气模仿了《时代》周刊常用的倒装句式:"Backward ran sentences until reeled the mind... Where it all will end, knows God!"

受新媒体的冲击,该刊发行量从1997年开始出现下滑,由原先的420万份跌至302万份(2017)。最近几年《时代》周刊版面出现了较大变化。改版的目的是"为读者提供更清晰、更为睿智、更为前瞻的观点(provide readers with a clearer, smarter and more forward looking take on the world),主要做法是使《时代》周刊传统特色适合21世纪(take the DNA of *Time* and adapt it to the 21st century)"。

新版《时代》周刊主要有四个版面:

一、新闻简报版(The Brief)。该版刊载过去一周重大新闻简要报道,每期均有开篇新闻简报(The Brief Opener)。二、观点版(The View)。该版刊登一些对重要专题的看法、评论和新的见解(ideas, opinions and innovations)的文章。每期都有开篇评论(The View Opener)。三、特稿版(Features)。该版登载有关重要事件和社会问题的解释性报道、精确性报道、调查性报道和新闻特写。四、休闲版(Time Off)。该版提供有关影视、音乐、饮食、保健、旅游等方面有价值的信息。

改版后的《时代》周刊保留和加强了创刊以来的传统特色,提供一周重大事件有深度和力度的特稿。与此同时,新版《时代》周刊还具有以下四个新的特色:

1. 内容方面加强了"商务和旅游服务"报道;面域更广,覆盖政治、经济、科学、军事、社会、文化等方面。

2. 生活栏增设了"饮食"等专题,生活气息更浓,阅读趣味更强。

3. 语言风格更加简洁明快,新闻简报不仅篇幅更加短小,而且语言更加精练。

4. 版面更加活泼。新版内页插图照片增多,图片色泽鲜艳,夺人眼球,增加了文章的吸引力。

《时代》周刊1927年推出年代风云人物版,一直延续至今成为该刊特色品牌,原先称为 The Man of the Year,20世纪60年代后改为 The Person of the Year。这项评选颇受全球关注。1999年12月31日该刊评选出科学家爱因斯坦为"世纪风云人物"(The Person of the Century)。

随着我国世界地位的提高和国际影响的增强,《时代》周刊对我国的报道篇幅也在增加,2018年共有17篇有关我国的新闻报道和评论。其中有一些是正面的,但也有不少是负面的,表现出较深的偏见,甚至敌意。

《时代》周刊的网址是www.time.com。

V. Analysis of Content

1. Which of the following businesses offers rewards to employees who get to work without driving cars?
   A. News Corp.　　　　　　　　B. Nike.
   C. Wal-Mart.　　　　　　　　　D. RTKL.
2. The main reason for companies' efforts to go green is _____.
   A. public pressure　　　　　　B. the environment protection law
   C. concern about profits　　　　D. worry about global warming
3. Which of the following consumes the greatest amount of water in office buildings?
   A. Car washing.　　　　　　　B. Toilet flushing.
   C. Floor mopping.　　　　　　D. Water drinking.
4. The recruiting policy of Sun Light & Power gives preference to those who _____.
   A. have high skill　　　　　　B. have green attitudes
   C. have college degrees　　　　D. are hardworking
5. Which of the following statements is FALSE?
   A. Green companies hold greater attraction for talent.
   B. The idea of going green is getting more and more popular in U.S. companies.
   C. Green office may help the development of business.
   D. Most businesses in the U.S. have now gone green.

VI. Questions on the Article

1. How much carbon dioxide do heating, cooling and powering office space cause in the U.S.? How much electricity do they consume?
2. How popular is the idea of going green becoming in the U.S.? Tell something about the efforts made by the businesses.
3. What are the reasons for the trend to go green?
4. What kind of building can get a certificate from the U.S. Green Building Council?
5. What does LEED stand for? Why was it created?
6. What modifications does a LEED certification rating require for leased office space?
7. According to the EPA, what is the cost of congestion caused by commuting?
8. What efforts does Sun Light & Power make to help improve the environment?

VII. Topics for Discussion

1. Do green ways slow down the development of business?
2. Are green ways cost-effective?

Lesson 14

We Need to Talk about Kids and Smartphones

(Abridged)

By Markham Heid

    Nina Langton had no right to be depressed. She had a great group of friends, lived in a prosperous neighborhood, and was close with her parents. Like most 16-year-olds at her Connecticut high school, Nina spent much of her free time on her smartphone. But unlike many of her classmates, she was never "targeted" on social media—her word for the bullying and criticism that takes place daily on apps like Snapchat. "Part of what made my depression so difficult was that I didn't understand why I was feeling so sad," she says.

    Later, after her attempted suicide and during her stay at a rehabilitation facility[1], Nina and her therapist identified body image insecurity as the foundation of her woe. "I was spending a lot of time stalking models on Instagram[2], and I worried a lot about how I looked," says Nina, who is now 17. She'd stay up late in her bedroom, looking at social media on her phone, and poor sleep—coupled with an eating disorder—gradually snowballed until suicide felt like her only option. "I didn't totally want to be gone," she says. "I just wanted help and didn't know how else to get it."

    Nina's mom, Christine Langton, says she was "completely caught off guard" by her daughter's suicide attempt. "Nina was funny, athletic, smart, personable...depression was just not on my radar[3]," she says. In hindsight, Christine says she wishes she had done more to moderate her daughter's smartphone use. "It didn't occur to me not to let her have the phone in her room at night," she says. "I just wasn't thinking about the impact of the phone on her self-esteem or self-image."

    It seems like every generation of parents has a collective freak-out when it comes to kids and new technologies[4]; television and video games each inspired widespread hand-wringing among grownups[5]. But the inescapability of today's mobile devices—combined with the allure of social media—seems to separate smartphones from older screen-based media. Parents, teenagers and researchers agree that smartphones are having a profound impact on the way adolescents today communicate with one another and spend their free time. And while some experts say it's too soon to ring alarm bells about smartphones, others argue that we understand enough about young people's emotional and developmental vulnerabilities to recommend restricting kids' escalating phone habits.

    The latest statistics on teenage mental health underscore the urgency of this debate. Between 2010 and 2016, the number of adolescents who experienced at least one major depressive episode leaped by 60%, according to a nationwide survey conducted by a branch of the Department of Health and Human Services[6]. The 2016 HHS survey of 17,000 kids found that about 13% of them had at least one major depressive episode the prior year, compared with 8% of the kids surveyed in

2010. Suicide deaths among people age 10 to 19 have also risen sharply; among teenage girls, suicide has reached 40-year highs, according to the Centers for Disease Control and Prevention. All this follows a period during the late 1990s and early 2000s when rates of adolescent depression and suicide mostly held steady or declined.

"These increases are huge—possibly unprecedented," says Jean Twenge, a professor of psychology at San Diego State University and the author of *iGen*[7], which examines how today's super-connected teens may be less happy and less prepared for adulthood than past generations[8]. In a peer-reviewed study that will appear later this year in the journal *Clinical Psychological Science*[9], Twenge shows that, after 2010, teens who spent more time on digital devices were more likely to report mental-health issues than those who spent time on nonscreen activities.

Using data collected between 2010 and 2015 from more than 500,000 adolescents nationwide, Twenge's study found kids who spent three hours a day or more on smartphones or other electronic devices were 34% more likely to suffer at least one suicide-related outcome—including feeling hopeless or seriously considering suicide—than kids who used devices two hours a day or less. Among kids who used electronic devices five or more hours a day, 48% had at least one suicide-related outcome. Overall, kids in the study who spent low amounts of time engaged in real-life social interaction but high amounts of time on social media, were the most likely to be depressed.

Others agree that it's time to approach adolescent device use with greater caution. "What this generation is going through right now with technology is a giant experiment, and we don't know what's going to happen," says Frances Jensen, chair of neurology at the University of Pennsylvania's Perelman School of Medicine[10]. While the science on kids and technology is incomplete, Jensen says that what we know about the minds of tweens and teens suggests that giving a young person all-the-time access to an Internet-connected device "may be playing with fire."

To understand how device use may be affecting a young person's mental health, it's important to recognize the complex changes occurring in an adolescent's still-developing brain. For one thing, that brain is incredibly plastic and able to adapt—that is, physically change—in response to novel activities or environmental cues, says Jensen, who is the author of *The Teenage Brain*.

Some research has already linked media multitasking—texting, using social media and rapidly switching among smartphone-based apps—with lower gray-matter volume in the brain's anterior cingulate cortex (ACC)[11], a region involved in emotion processing and decision making. More research has associated lower ACC volumes with depression and addiction disorders.

"We know for a fact teens have very underdeveloped impulse control and empathy and judgment compared to adults," Jensen says. This may lead them to disturbing online content or encounters[12]—stuff a more mature mind would know to avoid. Teens also have a hyperactive risk-reward system that allows them to learn—but also to become addicted—much more quickly than grownups, she says. Research has linked social media and other phone-based activities with an uptick in feel-good neurochemicals like dopamine[13], which could drive compulsive device use and promote feelings of distraction, fatigue, or irritability when kids are separated from their phones.

Another area of the brain—the prefrontal cortex—is critical for focus and interpreting human emotion, and doesn't fully develop until a person's mid-20s, says Paul Atchley, a professor of psychology at the University of Kansas. "During our teenage years, it's important to train that prefrontal cortex not to be easily distracted," he says. "What we're seeing in our work is that young people are constantly distracted, and also less sensitive to the emotions of others."

As researchers debate appropriate public health messaging, kids are receiving their first smartphone at ever-younger ages—the average is 10, according to one recent estimate—and they're spending more and more time on their devices. "I am probably on my phone 10 hours a day," says Santi Potocnik Senarighi, a 16-year-old 11th grader in Denver. Even when he's not using his phone, it's always with him, and he never considers taking a break. "This is part of my life and part of my work, and [that] means I need to be in constant contact."

Santi's dad, Billy Potocnik, says he worries about his son's phone habit. But every one of Santi's friends has a smartphone and uses it constantly, and so Potocnik says confiscating his son's phone feels oppressive. To complicate matters, many schools and after-school groups now use social media or online platforms to coordinate events or post grades and homework[14]. "It's not as simple as saying, O.K., time to take a break from your phone," Potocnik says.

Colleen Nisbet has been a high school guidance counselor for more than two decades. One of her duties at Connecticut's Granby Memorial High School is to monitor students during their lunch periods. "Lunch was always a very social time when students were interacting and letting out some energy," she says. "Now they sit with their phones out and barely talk to each other."

This scene—of young people gathering in parks or at houses only to sit silently and stare at screens—comes up frequently when talking with parents and kids. "When you're with people you don't know well or there's nothing to talk about, phones are out more because it's awkward," says Shannon Ohannessian, a 17-year-old senior at Farmington High School in Connecticut.

That avoidance of face-to-face interaction worries Brian Primack, director of the University of Pittsburgh's Center for Research on Media, Technology, and Health. "Human beings are social animals," he says. "We evolved over millions of years to respond to eye contact and touch and shared laughter and real things right in front of us." If smartphones are interfering with a teen's facility for these normal human behaviors, that's a big deal[15], he adds.

But while they're not always speaking out loud, kids today are talking to each other—and about each other—on their phones. Not all of it is friendly. "They tell me they're making comments or criticizing each other to friends while they're all sitting together," says Nisbet. Backbiting and gossip are nothing new, of course. But research suggests that, even among adults, the Internet has a disinhibition effect that leads people to speak in coarser, crueler ways than they would offline[16].

Maryellen Pachler, a Yale-trained nurse practitioner who specializes in the treatment of adolescent anxiety disorders[17], says the glamor and gleam of social media is also fueling a rise in teen anxiety. "My patients see their friends' Snapchat[18] or Instagram photos where they look so happy, and they feel like they're the only ones who are faking it," she says, referencing what researchers call the highlight-reel effect of social media.[19] "I want to tell them, listen, this girl you're jealous of—she was in here with me yesterday!"

Teenagers agree social-media whitewashing is the rule, not the exception.[20] "No one's going to post something that makes them look bad," Ohannessian says. "I know that, but it's still hard to separate what you see on social media from real life."

There are doubtless many factors contributing to teen depression. Parents say kids today are busier than ever before—with their lives increasingly crammed with the extracurriculars required to gain admission to a good college. But even researchers who aren't ready to slam smartphones say it's important to restrict an adolescent's device habit. "I don't think these devices are the main cause, but I think they contribute to a lot of the things we worry about," says David Hill, director of the American Academy of Pediatrics Council on Communications and Media[21]. He counsels parents to set more limits—especially when it comes to phones in the bedroom at night."

Educators are also grappling with smartphone-related dilemmas.[22] Most schools allow smartphone use between classes and during free periods, but teachers say keeping students off their phones during class has become a tremendous burden[23]. Now, some schools are fighting back. Starting this fall, a few teamed up with a company called Yondr to restrict smartphone access during school hours. Yondr makes lockable phone pouches that students keep with them but that can't be opened until the end of the day.

Allison Silvestri, the principal at San Lorenzo High School, near Oakland, Calif, says that since the school implemented the restrictions, "the changes have been profound." Kids are more focused and engaged during class[24], and student journals suggest the high schoolers are feeling less stress. Silvestri says fewer fights have broken out this semester—a benefit she attributes to the absence of social media. "They have to look each other in the eye to make conflict happen," she says. "There's so much more joy and interaction, and I can't count the number of parents who have asked me, 'How do I buy this for my home?'"

From *Time*, October 10, 2017

I. New Words

addict	[əˈdikt]	v.	使成瘾
adolescent	[ˌædəˈlesənt]	n.	青少年
allure	[əˈluə(r)]	n.	attraction
app	[æp]	n.	计算机应用程序
athletic	[æθˈletik]	adj.	体格健壮的
backbiting	[ˈbækˌbaitiŋ]	n.	speaking unkindly of an absent person
bully	[ˈbuli]	v.	欺负，威吓
cause-and-effect	[kɔːzəndiˈfekt]	n.	因果关系
coarse	[kɔːs]	adj.	rough in manner
compulsive	[kəmˈpʌlsiv]	adj.	强迫的
confiscate	[ˈkɔnfiskeit]	v.	没收
cortex	[ˈkɔːteks]	n.	[医学]脑皮层，皮质
counsel	[ˈkauns(ə)l]	v.	to advise

cram	[kræm]	v.	to fill sth too full
depression	[dɪˈpreʃ(ə)n]	n.	抑郁症
disorder	[dɪsˈɔːdə]	n.	紊乱
distraction	[dɪsˈtrækʃ(ə)n]	n.	注意力分散
dopamine	[ˈdəupəmiːn]	n.	[生化]多巴胺
empathy	[ˈempəθi]	n.	同感；同情
extracurricular	[ˌekstrəkəˈrikjulə]	n.	课外活动
fatigue	[fəˈtiːg]	n.	extreme tiredness
grapple	[ˈgræp(ə)l]	v.	~(with sth) to work hard to deal with
gray matter		n.	(中枢神经系统)灰质
handwringing	[ˈhændˌriŋiŋ]	n.	扭绞双手(表示绝望、苦恼、焦虑)
hindsight	[ˈhaindsait]	n.	事后的认识
hyperactive	[haipərˈæktiv]	adj.	过分活跃的
impulse	[ˈimpʌls]	n.	a sudden wish to do sth
irritability	[ˌiritəˈbiliti]	n.	易怒，烦躁
multi-tasking	[ˌmʌltiˈtɑːskiŋ]	n.	一心多用，多重任务处理
neurochemicals	[ˌnjuərəuˈkemikəl]	n.	影响神经系统的化学物质
neurology	[njuəˈrɔlədʒi]	n.	神经病学；神经学
overall	[ˌəuvəˈrɔːl]	adv.	on the whole
pouch	[pautʃ]	n.	小袋
prefrontal	[priːˈfrʌnt(ə)l]	adj.	[解剖]前额的；额叶前部的
slam	[slæm]	v.	to shut loudly
snowball	[ˈsnəubɔːl]	v.	to increase in size faster and faster or uncontrolledly
specialize	[ˈspeʃəlaiz]	v.	专门从事
stalk	[stɔːk]	v.	追踪
stigma	[ˈstigmə]	n.	耻辱；污名
therapist	[ˈθerəpist]	n.	(尤指心理疗法的)治疗师
tween	[twiːn]	n.	10—14岁的少年
ubiquitous	[juːˈbikwitəs]	adj.	appearing, happening, done, etc., everywhere
underscore	[ʌndəˈskɔː]	v.	to underline, to emphasize
whitewash	[ˈwaitwɔʃ]	v.	掩饰，粉饰
woe	[wəu]	n.	great sorrow

II. Background Information

智能手机对美国青少年的影响

iGen也被称作"后千禧一代",生于1997年至2012年,成长于一个互联网时代,在智能手机的陪伴下长大。这一代人使用社交媒体成瘾。从出生起,他们就是互联网时代的"原住民",通过社交媒体呼吸。

他们是孤独的一代人,渴望与人交流。有关研究表明,这一代人更希望突破身处的虚拟世界。他们是缺乏安全感的一代人,童年经历了9·11事件、经济危机、校园枪击事件等剧烈冲突使他们对于潜在忧患更为敏感,也变得更加实际和进取。他们总是想要改变世界,极力促使整个社会因为他们而变。

对于这一代人来说,互联网技术的发展让他们能接触各行各业的人,了解各方观点,从指尖上得到想要的一切,而智能手机是实现这一点的重要工具之一。

近年来,智能手机在美国青少年中的普及率持续上升,并潜移默化地影响着他们的日常生活。拥有手机的青少年已经从2012年的41%上升到89%。智能手机现在已经成为青少年生活的必需品。

相关调查显示,越来越多的青少年喜欢远程交流方式,在线交流已成为绝大多数青少年生活的一部分。很多人认为智能手机便于与他人互动、交流,减少孤独感,获取信息,学习新知识,提供自由表达的渠道和娱乐消遣的平台。但是,手机带来的消极影响也不容小觑:减少真实互动,干扰正常社会交往,易于引发网络暴力行为,扭曲现实,影响学业,造成心理问题。许多使用社交媒体的青少年甚至还称在网上遇到过种族歧视、性别歧视或其他仇恨内容。

随着智能手机在青少年中的大量普及,诸多场合都可以看到聚精会神操作手机的年轻"低头族",但是对于他们来说,手机成瘾会严重损害身体和精神健康,一些研究表明,患抑郁症的青少年数量和自杀率的增加都与智能手机密切相关。调查发现,每天在电子设备上花费3小时或更长时间的青少年有自杀风险的可能性要比使用时间较少的青少年高35%。2007年以来,青少年的杀人犯罪率呈下降趋势,但自杀率却有所上升。随着青少年之间相处时间的减少,他们杀害彼此的概率减少,自杀的概率则有所增加。2011年,青少年的自杀率高于青少年的杀人犯罪率,这是24年来首次出现这种情况。

针对iGen一代使用手机的种种问题,美国很多中学采取了应对措施。不少学校制定了严格的要求,规定上课时间不许使用手机。有的寄宿学校还会在晚上宿舍熄灯时,收走学生的手机,保证学生得到充分休息。有的学校会通过设置网络限制来控制学生的手机使用。还有的学校制定了惩罚措施来控制手机使用。与此同时,美国社会和家长也开始正视这一问题。例如,教堂、博物馆、音乐厅等场所禁止使用手机,尤其是接听电话。不少美国家长通过各类应用程序对孩子的手机进行管理,定时关掉家中的无线网或限制无线网络的流量来控制孩子的上网时间。

与此同时,美国的不少"网瘾少年"也正在觉醒。2018年皮尤研究中心的报告显示，青少年正在自觉采取措施限制自己过度使用手机和社交媒体。他们也许认识到，手机和互联网使用不当会成为一个"精神鸦片吸食地"，会毁掉他们的人生。但是仍有一些青少年沉迷其中，无法自拔。

III. Notes to the Text

1. rehabilitation facility——康复机构
2. Instagram——照片墙（一款运行在移动端上的社交应用软件，可让人们分享随时抓拍的照片）
3. ...depression was just not on my radar.——抑郁症全然没有引起我的注意。（① just——completely; ② not on one's radar——used to say that sth did not receive one's attention）
4. It seems like every generation of parents has a collective freak-out, when it comes to kids and new technologies.——看来在对待孩子和新技术的问题上，每一代父母都表现得十分焦虑。(① collective——common; ② freak-out——feeling of great anxiety)
5. television and video games each inspired widespread hand-wringing among grownups.——电视和电子游戏都在成人中引发了普遍的担忧。(handwringing——showing of worry, anxiety)
6. Department of Health and Human Services——卫生与民政服务部
7. iGen——book by Jean M. Twenge, a highly readable and entertaining first look at how today's members of iGen, the children and young adults born in the mid-1990s and later are vastly different from their millennial predecessor and from any other generation.
8. ...which examines how today's super-connected teens may be less happy and less prepared for adulthood than past generations.——文章剖析当今过度使用网络的青少年如何比前几代人更不幸福，更未准备好开始成年人的生活。
9. Clinical Psychological Science——《临床心理学》
10. the University of Pennsylvania's Perelman School of Medicine——宾夕法尼亚大学佩雷尔曼医学院（该学院曾被评为全美排名前五的研究型医学院校）
11. anterior cingulate cortex (ACC)——前扣带脑皮层
12. This may lead them to disturbing online content or encounters...——这可能会导致他们接触令人不安的网上信息或遭遇(encounter——an unexpected and unpleasant experience)
13. Research has linked social media and other phone-based activities with an uptick in feel-good neurochemicals like dopamine...——研究发现，社交媒体和其他使用手机的活动会导致诸如多巴胺一类让人心情愉悦的神经化学物质的增加(① uptick——an increase; ② feel-good——making you feel happy and pleased about life)
14. To complicate matters, many schools and after-school groups now use social media or online platforms to coordinate events or post grades and homework.——许多学校和校外团体现在使用社交媒体或网上平台安排活动，公布成绩和家庭作业，使得问题变得更加复杂。

15. If smartphones are interfering with a teen's facility for these normal human behaviors, that's a big deal.——如果智能手机阻碍了青少年的正常人类行为能力的发展,那问题就严重了。(a big deal——an important and serious situation)

16. ...the Internet has a disinhibition effect that leads people to speak in coarser, crueler ways than they would offline.——互联网起到使人放纵的作用,导致人们在线上说话时会比线下更粗鲁、更冷酷。(disinhibition——the act of helping sb to stop feeling shy so that he/she can relax and show feelings)

17. anxiety disorder——焦虑性障碍(a mental illness characterized by excessive, uncontrollable and irrational worry about events or activities)

18. Snapchat——美国一款"阅后即焚"的照片分享应用程序

19. ...referencing what researchers call the highlight-reel effect of social media.——意指研究人员称之为社交媒体的(视频节目)高能时刻效应。(highlight-reel——由Kotaku网站制作发布的一档集休闲、娱乐和爆笑为一体的游戏视频节目)

20. Teenagers agree social-media whitewashing is the rule, not the exception.——青少年都认为在社交媒体上粉饰自己已经成为一种惯例,屡见不鲜。(whitewashing——covering up a misdemeanor, fault, or error)

21. the American Academy of Pediatrics Council on Communications and Media——美国儿童学会传播与媒体委员会

22. Educators are also grappling with smartphone-related dilemmas.——教育者也在努力解决智能手机使用的相关问题。(① grapple with——to cope with; ② dilemma——state of uncertainty or perplexity especially as requiring a choice between equally unfavorable options)

23. teachers say keeping students off their phones during class has become a tremendous burden.——老师们说,杜绝学生在课上使用手机已成为一种非常沉重的负担。

24. Kids are more focused and engaged during class...——孩子们课堂上更加聚精会神,积极投入。(① focused——showing concentration of mind; ② engaged——actively involved)

IV. Language Features

缩略词

本文多处使用缩略词(shortenings),如ACC,HHS等。

英语的整个发展趋势是逐渐简化,反映在词汇层次上的重叠现象便是大量缩略词的涌现。语言学家埃里克·帕特里奇(Eric Patridge)与西蒙·波特(Simeon Potter)在《变化中的英语》一书中写道:"现实世界中,缩略词大量产生,很难跟踪收集。"出于节约篇幅、精练语言的需要,新闻报道使用缩略词的频率更高,到处皆可见到。

缩略词形式除拼缀词以外,主要还有三种形式。

1. 截短词(clippings)

这是截除原词的某一(或某些)音节所得的缩略词。例如，

doc(doctor)医生　　　　　　　net(Internet)互联网
info(information)信息　　　　 pop(popular)流行的
tech(technology)技术　　　　　semis(semifinals)半决赛
vet(veteran)有经验者,老手　　 con(convict)罪犯
teens(teenagers)青少年　　　　temp(temporary)临时雇员
ex(ex-husband/wife)前夫/前妻　prenups(prenuptial agreement)婚前协议
hood(neighborhood)街坊　　　　COVID(Corona Virus Disease)冠状病毒
dozer(bulldozer)推土机

2. 首字母缩写词(alphabetism)

由词组的每个词的第一字母组成并按字母发音的缩略词。例如，

CD(compact disk)光盘　　　　　　　GM(genetically modified)转基因的
HOV(high occupancy vehicle)多乘员车辆　WFH(Working From Home)在家办公
WTO(World Trade Organization)世贸贸易组织
PPE(Personal Protective Equipment)个人防护设备
AIIB(the Asian Infrastructure Investment Bank)亚洲基础设施投资银行
BPO(business process outsourcing)业务流程外包
UAV(unmanned aerial vehicle)无人驾驶机

3. 首字母缩拼词(acronym)

由词组每个词的第一个字母组成并拼读为一个词的缩略词。例如，

DIMP(double income money problem)双职工困难家庭
ROM(Read Only Memory)只读存储器
UFO(Unidentified Flying Object)不明飞行物
NOW(National Organization for Women)(美)全国妇女组织
BRICS(Brazil, Russia, India, China, South Africa)金砖五国
NEET(not in education, employment or training)尼特族(啃老族)

V. Analysis of Content

1. 1. What caused Nina Langton's suicide attempt was _____.
   A. her school-work pressure
   B. her body-image insecurity
   C. her classmates' online bullying
   D. her lack of parental care and love

2. The average age of American kids receiving the first smartphone is _____.
   A. 10　　　　B. 12　　　　C. 14　　　　D. 16

3. According to the article, the collective reaction of every generation of American parents to their kids' use of new technologies is _____.
   A. neglect   B. encouragement   C. restriction   D. anxiety
4. The effect of social media whitewashing on teenagers is _____.
   A. increasing their sense of well-being
   B. making them fail to see the dark side of the society
   C. fueling a rise in their anxiety
   D. improving teenagers' ties
5. It can be seen from the article that the rule set by most American schools on teenagers' smartphone use is _____.
   A. keeping teenagers off their phones during class
   B. keeping teenagers off their phones at school
   C. keeping teenagers' phones locked until the end of the day
   D. confiscating phones if teenagers use them at school

VI. Questions on the Article

1. What led to Nina Langton's suicide attempt?
2. Why was Christine Langton completely caught off guard by her daughter's suicide attempt?
3. What, do experts think, should be done about young people's use of smartphones?
4. What does Twenge's study show about the overall impact of teenagers' use of digital devices?
5. What is Frances Jensen's view on the effect of young people's overuse of an Internet-connected device?
6. What has some research found about the impact of media multitasking on mental health?
7. What kind of time was the lunch hour? What did students do at this hour in the past? What about now?
8. Why does Brian Primack feel worried about young people's avoidance of face-to-face engagement?
9. What effect does the Internet have on people's ways of speaking according to Nisbet?
10. What does David Hill counsel parents to do about their kids' phone use?
11. What effect have the measures taken by Lorenzo High School produced?

VII. Topics for Discussion

1. Do smartphones do teenagers more harm than good?
2. Should smartphone use be prohibited at school?

Lesson 15

The Beauty Advantage

In today's economy, looking good is no longer something we can dismiss as frivolous or vain. How beauty can affect your job, your career, your life.
(Abridged)

By Jessica Bennett

Most of us have heard the story of Debrahlee Lorenzana, the 33-year-old Queens, N.Y., woman who sued Citibank last month, claiming that, in pencil skirts, turtlenecks, and peep-toe stilettos, she was fired from her desk job for being "too hot."[1] We've also watched Lorenzana's credibility come into question, as vintage clips of her appearance on a reality-TV show about plastic surgery portray a rambling, attention-obsessed twit, stuffed to the brim with implants and collagen.[2] ("I love plastic surgery," she coos. "I think it's the best thing that ever happened.") Creepy, yes. But for all the talk about this woman's motives—and whether or not she was indeed fired for her looks—there's one question nobody seems to want to ask: isn't it possible Lorenzana's looks got her the job in the first place?

Not all employers are that shallow—but it's no secret we are a culture consumed by image.[3] Economists have long recognized what's been dubbed the "beauty premium"—the idea that pretty people, whatever their aspirations, tend to do better in, well, almost everything. Handsome men earn, on average, 5 percent more than their less-attractive counterparts (good-looking women earn 4 percent more); pretty people get more attention from teachers, bosses, and mentors; even babies stare longer at good-looking faces (and we stare longer at good-looking babies). A couple of decades ago, when the economy was thriving—and it was a makeup-less Kate Moss, not a plastic-surgery-plumped Paris Hilton, who was considered the beauty ideal[4]—we might have brushed off those statistics as superficial.[5] But in 2010, when Heidi Montag's[6] bloated lips plaster every magazine in town, when little girls lust after an airbrushed, unattainable body ideal, there's a growing bundle of research to show that our bias against the unattractive—our "beauty bias," as a new book calls it—is more pervasive than ever. And when it comes to the workplace, it's looks, not merit, that all too often rule.

Consider the following: over his career, a good-looking man will make some $250,000 more than his least-attractive counterpart, according to economist Daniel Hamermesh; 13 percent of women, according to the American Society of Plastic Surgeons[7] (and 10 percent of men, according to a new NEWSWEEK survey), say they'd consider cosmetic surgery[8] if it made them more competitive at work. Both points are disturbing, certainly. But in the current economy, when employers have more hiring options than ever, looks, it seems, aren't just important; they're critical. NEWSWEEK surveyed 202 corporate hiring managers, from human-resources staff to senior-level vice presidents, as well as 964 members of the public, only to confirm what no qualified (or unqualified) employee wants to admit: from hiring to office politics to promotions, even, looking good is no longer something we can dismiss as frivolous or vain.[9]

Fifty-seven percent of hiring managers told NEWSWEEK that qualified but unattractive candidates are likely to have a harder time landing a job, while more than half advised spending as much time and money on "making sure they look attractive" as on perfecting a résumé. When it comes to women, apparently, flaunting our assets works: 61 percent of managers (the majority of them men) said it would be an advantage for a woman to wear clothing showing off her figure at work. (Ouch.) Asked to rank employee attributes in order of importance, meanwhile, managers placed looks above education: of nine character traits, it came in third, below experience (No. 1) and confidence (No. 2) but above "where a candidate went to school" (No. 4). Does that mean you should drop out of Harvard and invest in a nose job? Probably not. But a state school might be just as marketable.[10] "This is the new reality of the job market," says one New York recruiter, who asked to have her name withheld because she advises job candidates for a living. "It's better to be average and good-looking than brilliant and unattractive."

Remember the story about the 1960 Nixon-Kennedy debate? It goes to show our beauty bias is nothing novel. At the time, radio listeners thought Nixon had won, but those watching Kennedy's tanned, chiseled face on TV, next to a worn-down, 5 o'clock-shadowed Nixon, were sure it was the junior senator.[11] There are various explanations for some of this. Plato[12] wrote of the "golden proportions[13]," which dubbed the width of an ideal face an exact two thirds its length, a nose no longer than the distance between the eyes. Biologically speaking, humans are attracted to symmetrical faces and curvy women for a reason: it's those shapes that are believed to produce the healthiest offspring. As the thinking goes, symmetrical faces are then deemed beautiful; beauty is linked to confidence; and it's a combination of looks and confidence that we often equate with smarts.[14] Perhaps there's some evidence to that: if handsome kids get more attention from teachers, then, sure, maybe they do better in school and, ultimately, at work. But the more likely scenario is what scientists dub the "halo effect"[15]—that, like a pack of untrained puppies, we are mesmerized by beauty, blindly ascribing intelligent traits to go along with it.

There are various forces to blame for much of this, from an economy that allows pickiness to a plastic-surgery industry that encourages superficial notions of beauty. In reality, it's a confluence of cultural forces that has left us clutching, desperately, to an ever-evolving beauty ideal. Today's young workers were reared on the kind of reality TV and pop culture that screams, again and again, that everything is a candidate for upgrade.[16] We compare ourselves with the airbrushed images in advertisements and magazines, and read surveys—like this one—that confirm our worst fears. We are a culture more sexualized than ever, with technology that's made it easier than ever to "better" ourselves, warping our standards for what's normal. Plastic surgery used to be for the rich and famous; today we've leveled the playing field with cheap boob jobs, tummy tucks, and outpatient procedures you can get on your lunch break.[17] Where that leads us is running to stand still: taught that good looks are no longer a gift but a ceaseless pursuit.

Today's working women have achieved "equality" (or so we're led to believe): they dominate the workforce, they are household breadwinners, and so they balk at having to subvert their sexuality, whether in the boardroom or on the beach. Yet while the outside-work milieu might accept the empowered yet feminine ideal, the workplace surely doesn't.[18] Studies show that unattractive women remain at a disadvantage in low-level positions like secretary, while in upper-level fields that are historically male-dominated, good-looking women can suffer a so-called bimbo effect. They are viewed as too feminine, less intelligent, and, ultimately, less competent—not only by men but also by their female peers.

To add an extra layer of complexity, there's the conundrum of aging in a culture where younger workers are more tech-savvy, cheaper, and, well, nicer on the eyes.[19] Eighty-four percent of managers told NEWSWEEK they believe a qualified but visibly older candidate would make some employers hesitate, and while ageism affects men, too, it's particularly tough for women. As Rhode puts it, silver hair and furrowed brows may make aging men look "distinguished," but aging women risk marginalization or ridicule for their efforts to pass as young.[20] "This double standard," Rhode writes, "leaves women not only perpetually worried about their appearance—but also worried about worrying."

The quest for beauty may be a centuries-old obsession, but in the present day the reality is ugly. Beauty has more influence than ever—not just over who we work with, but whether we work at all.

From *Newsweek*, July 19, 2010

I. New Words

ageism	[ˈeidʒizəm]	n.	(NAmE also agism) unfair treatment of old people
airbrush	[ˈɛəbrʌʃ]	v.	to make a picture or photograph look better
ascribe	[əˈskraib]	v.	~ to to believe sth to be the result of
aspiration	[ˌæspəˈreiʃən]	n.	强烈的愿望,抱负
attribute	[ˈætribjuːt]	n.	a quality or feature of sb/sth
balk	[bɔːk]	v.	~ at especially NAmE 畏缩;回避
bimbo	[ˈbimbəu]	n.	*informal, disapproving* attractive but unintelligent young woman
bloated	[ˈbləutid]	adj.	unpleasantly swollen
breadwinner	[ˈbredwinə]	n.	a person who supports a family with money
clutch	[klʌtʃ]	v.	to hold sb/sth tightly
confluence	[ˈkɔnfluəns]	n.	*formal* (事物的)汇合,汇聚,汇集
coo	[kuː]	v.	to say (sth) in a soft quiet voice, especially to sb you love

credibility	[ˌkrediˈbiliti]	n.	可信性,可靠性
creepy	[ˈkriːpi]	adj.	*informal* causing an unpleasant feeling of fear or slight horror
curvy	[ˈkəːvi]	adj.	*informal*（女性）体型富于曲线美的
dismiss	[disˈmis]	v.	to decide that sb/sth is not important and not worth thinking or talking about
dub	[dʌb]	v.	to give sb/sth a particular name, often in a humorous or critical way
flaunt	[flɔːnt]	v.	*disapproving* to show sth you are proud of in order to impress other people
furrow	[ˈfʌrəu]	v.	使起皱纹
land	[lænd]	v.	*informal* 成功得到,赢得
lust	[lʌst]	v.	~ after sth to feel an extremely strong desire for sth
mesmerize	[ˈmezməraiz]	v.	迷住,吸引
novel	[ˈnɔvl]	adj.	different and unusual
obsession	[əbˈseʃən]	n.	着迷
ouch	[autʃ]		*exclamation* used to express sudden pain
pickiness	[ˈpikinis]	n.	挑剔
plaster	[ˈplɑːstə]	v.	贴满,贴遍
premium	[ˈpriːmiəm]	n.	奖金;<喻>(不公道的)过高价值
quest	[kwest]	n.	a long search (for sth)
rambling	[ˈræmbliŋ]	adj.	(of speech or piece of writing) very long and confused
recruiter	[riˈkruːtə]	n.	招聘人员
savvy	[ˈsævi]	adj.	有见识的;懂实际知识的
scenario	[siˈnɑːriəu]	n.	a description of a possible course of action
sexualize	[ˈsekʃuəlaiz]	v.	to make sb seem sexually attractive
subvert	[sʌbˈvəːt]	v.	*formal* 颠覆
symmetrical	[siˈmetrikəl]	adj.	对称的
trait	[treit]	n.	a particular quality in your personality
unattainable	[ˌʌnəˈteinəbl]	adj.	达不到的
warp	[wɔːp]	v.	歪曲
withhold	[ˈwiðhəud]	v.	*formal* to refuse to give sth to sb

II. Background Information

美容风尚

美国人十分注重自己的形象。据调查,有54%的男子经常考虑自己的外貌,女子经常考虑自己外貌的比例更高,占所有女性的75%。其中40%的女子承认每天要花许多时间来修饰外表。调查还发现有94%的男性和99%的女性希望改变自己身体的某些部位来增强外表美。

男性中有56%的人想改变自己的体重,49%想改变自己的身材,39%想使自己的肌肉更发达,36%想拥有一头秀发。

女性中有78%的人想减轻自己的体重,70%想改善身材,46%想使自己的腿更修长,38%想对自己的臀部进行某些修整,35%想拥有一头迷人的秀发,33%为面部皱纹而烦恼,32%想使自己胸部更丰满。

为了改善自己的形象,许多美国人要做美容手术。据美国美容整形外科协会(American Society of Plastic Surgeons)的年度报告,2018年美国共有1770万例美容整形手术(cosmetic surgical procedures),其中微创美容术(minimal invasive procedures)占90%。

然而,美容是需要付出很高代价的。首先是美容手术的费用。美国2018年美容手术消费总额为165亿美元,数额高居全球榜首。据最近公布的美容价格表,在美国,面部除皱手术(face lift)一般费用为6000—12000美元,隆乳手术(breast enlargement)一般费用为8025美元,曲张静脉切除(vein removal)手术费用为200—500美元,收腹(tummy tuck)外科手术费一般为8275美元,吸脂(liposuction)手术一般费用为6175美元,下巴隆起手术(chin augmentation)一般为4900美元,头发移植(hair transplant)手术费为10000美元,提眉(brow lift)手术费为7225美元,鼻整形术(rhinoplasty)一般费用为7650美元,耳成形术(otoplasty)一般手术费为4350美元。

上述费用仅指支付给外科手术医生的费用。除此之外,病人还得交纳麻醉费和手术设备使用费。这两项费用合在一起数额相当于支付手术医生费用的50%。

美容除需要付出高昂的费用之外,还得承受手术所带来的不适、并发症,甚至生命危险。譬如,面部除皱手术会引起面部神经损伤(nerve injury)、炎症(infection)、伤口愈合差(poor healing)、刀疤(scarring)。不少做过面部除皱手术的人虽然容貌年轻,但出现颜面不对称、表情不自然的情况。又如,女性隆乳手术会导致炎症、植入物硬化(implant hardening)、填物破裂(rupture)、乳房敏感改变(altered breast sensitivity)。再如,收腹手术会造成血液凝块(blood clots)、刀口发炎(inflection)、皮下出血(bleeding under the skin)、疤痕(scarring)和皮肤受损(skin loss)。还如,吸脂手术会引起休克(shock)、疼痛(pain)、红肿(swelling)、出血(bleeding)和器官刺穿(organ perforation)。

每年美容手术引起的官司有很多,如由于隆乳手术造成的乳房不对称、收腹手术引起的肚脐眼错位等索赔案层出不穷。据美国《外科学》(*Surgery*)2022年所刊登的一项研究报告,美国1990—2010年间,每年大约发生近4000起不应该发生的手术事故,医疗系统每年单纯因这类失误要赔偿数百万美元。2021年佛罗里达长达10年的一项研究表明,美容手术的不良事件发生率明显高于其他专科手术,在全部门诊外科手术中所占比例高达45%。

III. Notes to the Text

1. ...the 33-year-old Queens, N.Y., woman who sued Citibank last month, claiming that, in pencil skirts, turtlenecks, and peep-toe stilettos, she was fired from her desk job for being "too hot." ——这位住在纽约市昆斯区的33岁的女士上个月起诉花旗银行,声称她由于身着窄身直筒裙、高翻领套头衫,脚穿露趾细高跟皮鞋而被说成"过于性感"并因此丢掉了原先的白领工作。[① Queens, N.Y.——昆斯区:美国纽约市一独立自治区,位于纽约州东南、长岛西部;② Citibank——花旗银行(纽约分行)(花旗银行是一家世界级金融机构);③ desk job——office job;④ hot——sexy]

2. ...vintage clips of her appearance on a reality-TV show about plastic surgery portray a rambling, attention-obsessed twit, stuffed to the brim with implants and collagen. ——她在整形手术电视真人秀片段中的典型形象是一个说话语无伦次、酷爱个人表现的傻瓜,身体部位填满了植入物和胶原蛋白。[① vintage——having the best characteristics of; ② clip——a short part of a film/movie that is shown separately; ③ obsess——to completely fill your mind so that you cannot think of anything else; ④ twit——a silly person; ⑤ stuffed to the brim——filled up]

3. ...it's no secret we are a culture consumed by image. ——我们的社会对人的形象十分关注,这根本不是秘密。(consume——~ sb with/by sth to fill sb with a strong feeling)

4. A couple of decades ago, when the economy was thriving—and it was a makeup-less Kate Moss, not a plastic-surgery-plumped Paris Hilton, who was considered the beauty ideal... ——20年前经济繁荣时期,人们心目中美的典范是不爱化妆的凯特·莫斯,而不是整形过的帕丽斯·希尔顿(① Kate Moss——凯特·莫斯(英国世界级超级模特,身材单薄娇小,风格简约,20世纪90年代初期走红并开启了模特行业"病态美"时代); ② Paris Hilton——帕丽斯·希尔顿(美国希尔顿集团继承人之一,女商人、模特、时尚设计师、歌手、演员及作家;据报道曾做过鼻部、胸部和臀部整形手术,其发型和着装备受社会关注); ③ plump——to make sth larger or softer, referring to the act of improving through cosmetic surgery)

5. ...we might have brushed off those statistics as superficial. ——我们或许认为这些数据不够真实,未加理会。(brush off——to ignore)

6. Heidi Montag——海迪·蒙塔格(美国真人秀明星,做过多次整形手术)

7. the American Society of Plastic Surgeons——美国整形外科医师协会

8. cosmetic surgery——美容外科

9. ...looking good is no longer something we can dismiss as frivolous or vain. ——我们不再认为相貌好不重要或没价值。(① frivolous——having no useful purpose; ② vain——useless)

10. But a state school might be just as marketable. —但是,州立大学的学历或许同样有助于找工作。(① just as—equally; ② marketable—attractive to employers)

11. At the time, radio listeners thought Nixon had won, but those watching Kennedy's tanned, chiseled face on TV, next to a worn-down, 5 o'clock-shadowed Nixon, were sure it was the junior senator. —当时,收听电台节目的人都认为尼克松赢了,但那些观看电视辩论的人都断定赢者是资历更浅的参议员肯尼迪;屏幕上他的容貌端正、皮肤晒成棕褐色,而旁边的尼克松却是面色憔悴、满脸短髭。[① chiseled—(of a man) having a mouth, nose etc with a strong clear shape; ② tanned—having a brown skin color as a result of being in sunlight; ③ worn-down—looking very tired; ④ five o'clock-shadowed—darkness on the face of a man who has not shaved since the morning]

12. Plato—(古希腊哲学家)柏拉图

13. golden proportions—黄金比例(是一种蕴藏着丰富美学价值的数学比例关系)

14. ...it's a combination of looks and confidence that we often equate with smarts. —我们常把相貌和信心双全等同于才智。(smarts—*informal* intelligence)

15. halo effect—(心理)光环效应

16. Today's young workers were reared on the kind of reality TV and pop culture that screams, again and again, that everything is a candidate for upgrade. —当今的年轻工作者是在不断大肆宣扬一切皆可美化的电视真人秀节目和通俗文化熏陶下长大的。(① rear—to bring up; ② upgrade—improvement; ③ a candidate for sth—suitable for sth)

17. ...today we've leveled the playing field with cheap boob jobs, tummy tucks, and outpatient procedures you can get on your lunch break. —如今隆胸、整腹以及午休时间门诊就可以做的手术收费便宜,人人都能做得起。(① boob—*slang* a woman's breast; ② tummy tuck—a medical procedure used to remove a belly bulge so as to make the stomach tighter and flatter; ③ level the playing field—to give everything the same advantage)

18. Yet while the outside-work milieu might accept the empowered yet feminine ideal, the workplace surely doesn't. —然而,虽然拥有权力但女人味十足的形象在非工作场所或许能被接受,但在工作场所内肯定不能。(① milieu—the social environment that you can work and live in; ② empowered—having power; ③ feminine—having the qualities considered to be typical of women)

19. To add an extra layer of complexity, there's the conundrum of aging in a culture where younger workers are more tech-savvy, cheaper, and, well, nicer on the eyes. —使问题更加复杂的是,由于年轻工作者技术更娴熟、劳力更廉价、容貌更悦目,社会上对老年人存在令人困惑、难以克服的歧视。(conundrum—a confusing problem that is difficult to solve)

20. ...but aging women risk marginalization or ridicule for their efforts to pass as young. —但年长的女性却遭受排斥或由于设法使容颜年轻而被嘲笑(① marginalize—to cause sb to become unimportant and powerless; ② pass as—to be considered and accepted as)

IV. Language Features

拼缀词

　　Brangelina是由一对名人Brad Pitt和Angelina Jolie两人的名字剪裁复合而成的拼缀词。在现代英语中,这类拼缀词日趋增多。由于拼缀法(blending)既可使文字活泼,又可节约用词,它在新闻英语中十分常用。

　　例1. Robodocs and Mousecalls [robodoc—robot + doctor(机器医生,这里指远程运用电脑行医);mousecall是由 mouse + call复合而成的词,意思是"运用鼠标(电脑)出诊"]

　　例2. Holidazed? It's not the happiest time of the year for every one. [holidazed—holiday + dazed(节日忙得头脑发昏)]

　　拼缀词大致可分为以下四类:

1. 前词首部 + 后词尾部,例如:

　　botel(boat + hotel)水上旅馆
　　stagnation(stagnant + inflation)滞胀
　　sharents(share + parents)酷爱在社交媒体上晒娃的父母
　　taikonaut(taikong + astronaut)(中国)太空人,宇航员
　　medicide(medical + suicide)医助安乐死
　　guestimate(guess + estimate)约略估计
　　smog(smoke + fog)雾霾
　　webonomics(web + economics)网络经济

2. 前词全部 + 后词尾部,例如:

　　menterrupt(men + interrupt)男士打断说话
　　fandom(fan + kingdom)粉丝圈
　　finfluencer(finance + influencer)金融网红
　　screenager(screen + teenager)屏幕青少年(从小就看电视、玩电脑的青少年)
　　eyelyzer(eye + analyzer)眼部测醉器
　　workfare(work + welfare)工作福利制
　　filmdom(film + kingdom)电影王国
　　newsgram(news + program)新闻节目
　　staycation(stay + vacation)在家休假

3. 前词首部 + 后词全部,例如:

　　exerhead(exercise + head)运动狂
　　seckill(second + kill)秒杀
　　permacrisis(permanent + crisis)长期危机
　　ecoanxiety(ecology + anxiety)生态焦虑
　　medicare(medical + care)医疗照顾

telescript（television + script）电视广播稿

t-can（trash + can）垃圾箱

ecotourism（ecological + tourism）生态旅游

frenemy（friend + enemy）友敌

Brexit（Britain + exit）英国脱欧

4. 前词首部 + 后词首部，例如：

edtech（education + technology）教育技术

interpol（international + police）国际刑警组织

elint（electronic + intelligence）以电子侦察手段获取情报

comsat（communication + satellite）通信卫星

sitcom（situation comedy）情景喜剧

neocon（neo + conservative）新保守主义者

robodoc（robot + doctor）机器人医生

V. Analysis of Content

1. The meaning of the word "culture" in the sentence "…it's no secret we're a culture consumed by image" (Para. 2) is _____.
   A. way of life   B. literature   C. belief and attitude   D. society
2. The author's impression of Debrahlee Lorenzana is that _____.
   A. she is very hot   B. she is beautiful
   C. she is not trustworthy   D. she is competent
3. Education's ranking on the hiring managers' list of employee attributes is _____.
   A. No. 4   B. No. 1   C. No. 2   D. No. 3
4. Which of the following statements is NOT true?
   A. The American society pays too much attention to image.
   B. Beauty bias is pervasive in America's workplaces.
   C. Older women are treated more favorably than older men.
   D. Good-looking men in the U.S. find it easier to get a job or a promotion.
5. The author's attitude to the beauty advantage is _____.
   A. critical   B. supportive   C. objective   D. unknown

VI. Questions on the Article

1. According to Debrahlee Lorenzana, why was she fired from her desk job?
2. What does Lorenzana think of plastic surgery?

3. What advantage does a good-looking man or woman enjoy at workplaces?
4. What change has taken place in Americans' idea of beauty in the past couple of decades?
5. According to economist Daniel Hamermesh, what advantage does a good-looking man enjoy at workplaces?
6. How important are looks in the current economy according to the article?
7. What's the finding of the *Newsweek* survey of hiring managers about the effects of looks?
8. According to Plato's "golden proportions," what kind of face is ideal?
9. What do studies show about the effects of looks on women's career?
10. What is the effect of aging?

VII. Topics for Discussion

1. Is cosmetic surgery beneficial to the society?
2. Is a person's look a very important factor in his career development?

Unit 5
第五单元 体制观念

Lesson 16

This Corruption in Washington Is Smothering America's Future

How do you regulate banks effectively, if the Senate is owned by Wall Street?

By Johann Hari

This week, a disaster hit the United States, and the after-shocks will be shaking and breaking global politics for years. It did not grab the same press attention as the fall of liberal Kennedy-licking Massachusetts to a pick-up truck Republican, or President Obama's first State of the Union address, or the possible break-up of Brangelina and their United Nations of adopted infants.[1] But it took the single biggest problem dragging American politics towards brutality and dysfunction—and made it much, much worse. Yet it also showed the only path that Obama can now take to salvage his Presidency.

For more than a century, the US has slowly put some limits—too few, too feeble—on how much corporations can bribe, bully or intimidate politicians. On Tuesday, they were burned away in one whoosh. The Supreme Court ruled that corporations can suddenly run political adverts during an election campaign—and there is absolutely no limit on how many, or how much they can spend. So if you anger the investment bankers by supporting legislation to break up the too-big-to-fail banks, you will smack into a wall of 24/7[2] ads exposing your every flaw. If you displease oil companies by supporting legislation to deal with global warming, you will now be hit by a tsunami of advertising saying you are opposed to jobs and the American Way.[3] If you rile the defence contractors by opposing the gargantuan war budget, you will face a smear-campaign calling you Soft on Terror.

Representative Alan Grayson says: "It basically institutionalises and legalises bribery on the largest scale imaginable. Corporations will now be able to reward the politicians that play ball with them—and beat to death the politicians that don't... You won't even hear any more about the Senator from Kansas. It'll be the Senator from General Electric or the Senator from Microsoft."

To understand the impact this will have, you need to grasp how smaller sums of corporate money have already hijacked American democracy. Let's look at a case that is simple and immediate and every American can see in front of them: healthcare. The United States is the only

第五单元 体制观念

major industrialised democracy that doesn't guarantee healthcare for all its citizens. The result is that, according to a detailed study by Harvard University, some 45,000 Americans die needlessly every year. That's equivalent to 15 9/11s every year, or two Haitian earthquakes every decade.

This isn't because the American people like it this way. Gallup has found in polls for a decade now that two-thirds believe the government should guarantee care for every American: they are as good and decent and concerned for each other as any European. No: it is because private insurance companies make a fortune today out of a system that doesn't cover the profit-less poor, and can turn away the sickest people as "uninsurable." So they pay for politicians to keep the system broken. They fund the election campaigns of politicians on both sides of the aisle and employ an army of lobbyists, and for their part those politicians veto any system that doesn't serve their paymasters.

Look for example at Joe Lieberman, the former Democratic candidate for Vice-President. He has taken $448,066 in campaign contributions from private healthcare companies while his wife raked in $2m as one of their chief lobbyists, and he has blocked any attempt in the Senate to break the stranglehold of the health insurance companies and broaden coverage.

The US political system now operates within a corporate cage. If you want to run for office, you have to take corporate cash—and so you have to serve corporate interests. Corporations are often blatant in their corruption: it's not unusual for them to give to both competing candidates in a Senate race, to ensure all sides are indebted to them. It has reached the point that lobbyists now often write the country's laws. Not metaphorically; literally. The former Republican congressman Walter Jones spoke out in disgust in 2006 when he found that drug company lobbyists were actually authoring the words of the Medicare prescription bill, and puppet-politicians were simply nodding it through.

But what happens if politicians are serving the short-term profit-hunger of corporations, and not the public interest? You only have to look at the shuttered shops outside your window for the answer. The banks were rapidly deregulated from the Eighties through the Noughties because their lobbyists paid politicians on all sides, and demanded their payback in rolled-back rules and tossed-away laws.[4] As Senator Dick Durbin says simply: "The banks own the Senate," so they had to obey.

It is this corruption that has prevented Barack Obama from achieving anything substantial in his first year in office. How do you re-regulate the banks, if the Senate is owned by Wall Street? How do you launch a rapid transition away from oil and coal to wind and solar, if the fossil fuel industry owns Congress? How do you break with a grab-the-oil foreign policy if Big Oil provides the invitation that gets you into the party of American politics?[5]

His attempt at healthcare reform is dying because he thought he could only get through the Senate a system that the giant healthcare corporations and drug companies pre-approved. So he promised to keep the ban on bringing cheap drugs down from Canada, he pledged not to bargain over prices, and he dumped the idea of having a public option that would make sure ordinary Americans could actually afford it. The result was a Quasimodo healthcare proposal so feeble and misshapen that even the people of Massachusetts turned away in disgust.[6]

Yet the corporations that caused this crisis are now being given yet more power. Bizarrely, the Supreme Court has decided that corporations are "persons," so they have the "right" to speak during elections. But corporations are not people. Should they have the right to bear arms, or to vote? It would make as much sense. They are a legal fiction, invented by the state—and they can be fairly regulated to stop them devouring their creator. This is the same Supreme Court that ruled that the detainees at Guantanomo Bay are not "persons" under the constitution deserving basic protections. A court that says a living breathing human is less of a "persons" than Lockheed Martin[7] has gone badly awry.

Obama now faces two paths—the Clinton road, or the FDR[8] highway. After he lost his healthcare battle, Clinton decided to serve the corporate interests totally. He is the one who carried out the biggest roll-back of banking laws, and saw the largest explosion of inequality since the 1920s. Some of Obama's advisers are now nudging him down that path: the appalling anti-Keynesian pledge for a spending freeze on social programmes for the next three years[9] to pay down the deficit is one of their triumphs.

But there is another way. Franklin Roosevelt began his Presidency trying to appease corporate interests—but he faced huge uproar and disgust at home when it became clear this left ordinary Americans stranded. He switched course. He turned his anger on "the malefactors of great wealth" and bragged: "I welcome the hatred... of the economic royalists." He put in place tough regulations that prevented economic disaster and spiralling inequality for three generations.

There were rare flashes of what Franklin Delano Obama would look like in his reaction to the Supreme Court decision.[10] He said: "It is a major victory for big oil, Wall Street banks, health insurance companies, and other powerful interests that marshal their power every day in Washington to drown out the voices of everyday Americas." But he has spent far more time coddling those interests than taking them on.[11] The great pressure of strikes and protests put on FDR hasn't yet arisen from a public dissipated into hopelessness by an appalling media that convinces them they are powerless and should wait passively for a Messiah.[12]

Very little positive change can happen in the US until they clear out the temple of American democracy. In the State of the Union, Obama spent one minute on this problem, and proposed restrictions on lobbyists—but that's only the tiniest of baby steps. He evaded the bigger issue. If Americans want a democratic system, they have to pay for it—and that means fair state funding for political candidates. Candidates are essential for the system to work: you may as well begrudge paying for the polling booths, or the lever you pull[13]. At the same time, the Supreme Court needs to be confronted: when the court tried to stymie the new deal[14], FDR tried to pack it with justices on the side of the people. Obama needs to be pressured by Americans to be as radical in democratising the Land of the Fee[15].

None of the crises facing us all—from the global banking system to global warming—can be dealt with if a tiny number of super-rich corporations have a veto over every inch of progress. If Obama funks this challenge, he may as well put the US government on e-Bay[16]—and sell it to the highest bidder. How would we spot the difference?

From *The Independent*, January 29, 2010

I. New Words

advert	[ədˈvə:t]	n.	*BrE informal* 广告
aftershock	[ˈɑ:ftəʃɔk]	n.	余震
aisle	[ail]	n.	（礼堂、课堂等的座席间的）通道
awry	[əˈrai]	adj.	go (run) ~ 背离正道
appease	[əˈpi:z]	v.	姑息，对……做出让步
begrudge	[biˈgrʌdʒ]	v.	to feel very unhappy about having to do sth
bizarrely	[biˈzɑ:li]	adv.	very strangely or unusually
blatant	[ˈbleitənt]	adj.	（恶行）公然的，极明显的
confront	[kənˈfrʌnt]	v.	to deal with a problem or difficult situation
coddle	[ˈkɔdl]	vt.	to treat sb with too much care and attention
devour	[diˈvauə]	v.	to eat all of sth quickly
dump	[dʌmp]	v.	to get rid of sth or sb
dysfunction	[disˈfʌŋkʃən]	n.	机能障碍；社会功能失常
funk	[fʌŋk]	v.	逃避
gargantuan	[gɑ:ˈgæntjuən]	adj.	extremely large
hijack	[ˈhaidʒæk]	v.	抢劫，劫持
indebted	[inˈdetid]	adj.	负债的；受惠的，蒙恩的
lever	[ˈli:və]	n.	（机械装置的）控制杆，操纵杆
malefactor	[ˈmælifæktə]	n.	坏人，作恶者
marshal	[ˈmɑ:ʃəl]	v.	to gather together and organize the people, things, ideas
paymaster	[ˈpeimɑ:stə]	n.	（政府、企业等负责发放薪金的）工薪出纳员
rile	[rail]	v.	to annoy sb or make sb very angry
salvage	[ˈsælvidʒ]	v.	to manage to rescue sth from a difficult situation
smack	[smæk]	v.	~ against sth to hit against sth with a lot of force
smear-campaign	[ˌsmiəkæmˈpein]	n.	（旨在败坏公众人物形象的）造谣中伤运动
smother	[ˈsmʌðə]	v.	to kill sb by covering the face to make sb unable to breathe
spiral	[ˈspaiərəl]	v.	持续急剧上升
stranglehold	[ˈstræŋgəlhəuld]	n.	（摔跤中的）卡脖子；压制，钳制
stymie	[ˈstaimi]	v.	to prevent sb from doing sth
tsunami	[tsu:ˈnɑ:mi]	n.	海啸
uproar	[ˈʌprɔ:]	n.	骚动；吵闹，喧嚣
whoosh	[(h)wuʃ]		*informal, interjection* 嗖；呼

II. Background Information

美国政治的腐败

　　美国最大的腐败就是将腐败合法化。政府部门与私营公司存在一种旋转门（revolving door）关系。许多官员发家致富的主要途径是在政府部门和私营部门几进几出。在政府内，他们积累经验，建立关系，然后就辞职去赚钱，几年后再就职，如此辞职、就职、再辞职、再就职，循环下去。比如，罗斯福总统手下的反托拉斯法干将辞职后在华盛顿办了家很红火的律师事务所，日进斗金，其乐融融。

　　政治献金（political contribution）是美国腐败最突出的表现形式。其中，"软钱"（soft money）是美国全国所关心的腐败问题。在美国，从政离不开钱。按照美国法律，给个人的政治捐款不能超过1000美元，而给政党的捐款则没有限制。给政党的捐款就是所谓的"软钱"，数额不受限制。资本家为政客输血有两条途径：一是政治捐款；二是前政府官员院外游说。华盛顿市K街（K Street）是美国公关公司最为集中的地方，有"说客一条街"之名，游说人也被戏称为"K街一族"。

　　在美国，政客们通常需要花费很多的时间和精力来拉赞助。美国政客如想当官，首先要获得大资本家、大公司和利益集团的支持。有了钱，他们才能去招兵买马，打广告，然后才能取悦于选民。总统候选人需要有一批斗士为其四处奔走，效犬马之劳。总统上台后自然要论功行赏，安插他们到各个部门任职。这种做法被称为"政党分赃制"（spoil system），已经有两百多年历史。美国的许多大使职位都可以供总统还人情用，而且这种情况已经司空见惯，没有人认为这有不妥之处。比如，罗斯福竞选总统时，肯尼迪的父亲帮了大忙，后来当上了美国驻英国大使。2001年小布什就任总统后奖赏给19个在他竞选筹款中有重大贡献者大使职位。在奥巴马任职期间至少有23位捐款大户获得了美国驻外大使的美差。

　　得到政治献金的政客会照顾大资本家和大企业的利益。首先，他们会在政府制定宏观政策或法律时向某些行业倾斜。其次，他们给做过贡献的人提供荣誉。比如，克林顿在好莱坞有许多好友，并得到他们的大量政治献金。这些好友每次前往华盛顿，都要去白宫看望克林顿。克林顿会很热情地招待他们，还请他们在白宫留宿。再次，政客也会在诉讼案件上照顾所谓的"朋友"，但行事方式极为隐蔽。比如，杜勒斯在当上国务卿之前是纽约一家大律师事务所的合伙人。该所的一家客户原本是美国政府反托拉斯诉讼的对象，但当杜勒斯当上国务卿后，此案便不了了之了。一些大公司和大资本家不用上法庭也可应付诉讼案件，而且完全可以在法律允许的范围内摆脱困境。最后，大公司和大资本家政治献金还可能有助于缓解公司财务危机。比如，获得税收减免，在决策失误时获得政府援助，延长债务偿还期，甚至得到豁免债务的好处。

　　2014年美国联邦最高法院通过了一项法案，取消对个人及政党参加竞选活动最高捐款总额的限制（overall campaign contribution limits）。这一法案所产生的效果是使美国本已腐败的政治更加腐败。

III. Notes to the Text

1. It did not grab the same press attention as the fall of liberal Kennedy-licking Massachusetts to a pick-up truck Republican, or President Obama's first State of the Union address, or the possible break-up of Brangelina and their United Nations of adopted infants.—它所引起的报界关注度不如以下事件:民主党人肯尼迪一直轻易取胜的马萨诸塞州的参议院席位落入驾驶皮卡竞选的共和党人手中、奥巴马总统首次发表国情咨文、布拉德·皮特与安吉丽娜·朱莉和其收养的多国儿童的关系可能破裂。(① Kennedy—referring to Edward Moore "Ted" Kennedy who served as US senator from 1964 until his death in 2009; ② a pick-up truck Republican—referring to Scott Brown, who drove his GM pick-up truck during the election campaign in 2010. The pick-up was a symbol of humility, hard work and rugged ideals and helped him to enhance his appeal to the public and become a new US senator from Massachusetts. ③ Brangelina and his United Nations of adopted infants—referring to the celebrity family consisting of Brad Pitt and Angelina Jolie and their adopted infants from Cambodia, Ethiopia and Vietnam; ④ lick—to easily defeat)

2. 24/7—referring to 24/7 Real Media, a technology company headquartered in New York City specializing in digital marketing. It provides digital marketing solutions for publishers, advertisers and agencies globally.

3. ...you will now be hit by a tsunami of advertising saying you are opposed to jobs and the American Way.—你就会遭受广告海啸的袭击,说你反对增加就业机会和美国传统价值观。(the American Way—a set of beliefs or values that many Americans hold but which are not laws written down in any form)

4. The banks were rapidly deregulated from the Eighties through the Noughties because their lobbyists paid politicians on all sides, and demanded their payback in rolled-back rules and tossed-away laws.—从20世纪80年代到21世纪头十年,这些银行很快被解除管控,这是因为他们的说客给所有派别政客都捐了款,要求他们以取消和减少(限制性)法律规章作为回报。(① rolled back—reduced to a lower level; ② tossed away—thrown away; ③ deregulate—to free a business activity from rules or controls; ④ Noughties—the years from 2000 to 2009)

5. How do you break with a grab-the-oil foreign policy if Big Oil provides the invitation that gets you into the party of American politics?—如果大石油公司帮你进入美国政治圈,你又如何会放弃对外抢夺石油的政策?(① break with—to stop continuing; ② Big Oil—referring to major oil companies which control a large share of the market and petroleum products and hold powerful influence on America's politics)

6. The result was a Quasimodo healthcare proposal so feeble and misshapen that even the people of Massachusetts turned away in disgust.—最后出台的是丑八怪卡西莫多式的医改方案,这个方案十分软弱、怪异,就连马萨诸塞州公民也感到厌恶,拒绝接受。[① Quasimodo—the main character (an ugly hunchback) in the book *The Hunchback of Notre Dame*(《巴黎圣母院》) by Victor Hugo; ② Massachusetts—a predominantly Democratic state and a state with

the highest level of healthcare coverage in the US〕

7. Lockheed Martin——洛克希德·马丁（美国一家航空航天业制造商，其前身是Lockheed Corporation洛克希德公司，创建于1912年）

8. FDR——Franklin Delano Roosevelt〔富兰克林·德拉诺·罗斯福（美国第32任总统）〕

9. the appalling anti-Keynesian pledge for a spending freeze on social programmes for the next three years——令人震惊的保证今后三年冻结福利项目开支的反凯恩斯主义的承诺〔Keynesian——凯恩斯主义以凯恩斯（J.M. Keynes）的理论为基础，主张采用国家干预经济的政策，即扩大政府开支、实行财政赤字，从而实现充分就业和经济增长的一个当代经济学流派〕

10. There were rare flashes of what Franklin Delano Obama would look like in his reaction to the Supreme Court decision.——对最高法院的裁决，奥巴马偶尔也表现出类似富兰克林·罗斯福的愤怒情绪。（① Franklin Delano Obama——a blend from Franklin Delano Roosevelt and Barack Obama; ② flash——a sudden emotion of）

11. But he has spent far more time coddling those interests than taking them on.——但是，更多时候他是悉心照顾这些利益集团，而不是跟它们进行斗争。（take sb on——to fight against sb）

12. The great pressure of strikes and protests put on FDR hasn't yet arisen from a public dissipated into hopelessness by an appalling media that convinces them they are powerless and should wait passively for a Messiah.——媒体恐吓民众使其相信自己力量太弱，应该消极等待上帝的救助，从而丧失斗志陷入绝望，不能奋起举行罢工和抗议活动，不能形成对富兰克林·罗斯福那样强大的压力。（① appal——to fill with fear; ② dissipate——to make sb become weak; ③ Messiah——Jesus Christ）

13. the polling booths, or the lever you pull——投票亭或投票机（① polling booth——Br. E voting booth, a small place in a polling station, separated from the surrounding area, where people vote by marking a card; ② the level you pull——referring to voting machines which used to be mechanical devices where voters pull a lever to register his/her vote）

14. the new deal——新政（1933年美国总统罗斯福执政后为挽救当时严重的经济危机而采取的施政纲领）

15. the Land of the Fee——金钱左右一切之国

16. e-Bay——易贝网（电子商务平台，用户遍布150多个国家）

IV. Language Features

新闻评论

　　新闻评论是各种新闻媒介用于阐述对于事件相应立场的体裁。它一直在西方新闻业中占有重要地位。翻开美英报刊便会发现没有一家刊物没有评论版。各种刊物都有撰写社论的主笔、撰写专论的专栏作家、撰写释论的编辑或作家以及撰写各类短评的批评家。

《美国新闻史》一书的作者认为,普利策之所以成功,之所以赢得"最为能干、最可尊敬的美国编辑"的声誉,不在于他是一家现代化报纸的创办人,而在于他"对报纸的作用特别是关于发挥社论的指导作用抱着高尚的想法"。他把社论看作"报纸的心脏"。

美国最负盛名的评论家和专栏作家李普曼(Lippman)不仅在世界各地拥有几千万读者,而且受到美国官方与各国政府政治家和外交家的重视。

新闻评论不同于新闻报道。新闻评论属于议论文范畴,重主观发挥,旨在阐明事件的道理;而新闻报道属于记叙文范畴,重客观反映,旨在报告事实真相。但新闻评论又与新闻报道密切关联。新闻是评论的基础和条件;评论因有新闻提供的事实,可使道理阐述得更具体、更实在。评论是新闻内在思想的引申和提高。

本文是由最高法院所做出的大公司有权在竞选期间资助政治广告的裁决而引发的对美国政治腐败的评论。文章结构如下:

 I. 最高法院的裁决:裁决性质和主要内容
 II. 裁决所造成的影响:增加大公司的影响力
　　　　　　　例证(医疗保险公司通过贿赂政客确保本身利益受到保护)
 III. 美国政治腐败的剖析:大公司给政客提供选金提高政治影响力
　　　　　　　政客当选后为大公司效劳作为回报
　　　　　　　政治腐败所导致的恶果
 IV. 最高法院裁决的荒唐
 V. 奥巴马可以选择的两条道路:克林顿道路:屈服于大公司
　　　　　　　　　　　　　罗斯福道路:与大公司抗争
 VI. 作者的建议:奥巴马应该与大公司对抗

本文主要诉诸说理,逻辑严密,层次清楚,语言十分精练。篇幅虽然不长,但对美国政治的腐败却讲得清清楚楚,使读者心悦诚服。

V. Analysis of Content

1. The term "the American Way" in Paragraph 2 refers to _____.
　A. American life style　　　　　B. Americans' way of doing business
　C. American politicians' way of dealing with corporations　　D. Americans' values
2. Which of the following presidents carried out the biggest roll-back of banking laws?
　A. Roosevelt.　　B. Clinton.　　C. Kennedy.　　D. Obama.
3. The chief means used by corporations to gain political power is _____.
　A. offering political contributions　　B. mobilizing grass movements
　C. organizing political referendum　　D. filing lawsuits against politicians
4. The author's overall attitude towards Obama's presidency is _____.
　A. critical　　B. objective　　C. positive　　D. unknown

5. The article is _____.
   A. a straight news report　　　B. a news comment
   C. an interpretative news report　　D. a news feature

VI. Questions on the Article

1. What disaster hit the US in the week before January 29, 2010?
2. According to Alan Grayson, what effect does the Supreme Court's ruling produce?
3. What has Gallup found about public opinion on health care?
4. Why can't many Americans have health insurance?
5. By what means do the health insurance companies ensure that their interests are best served?
6. What kind of relationship exists between corporations and politicians?
7. Why has Obama failed to achieve anything substantial?
8. What was the Supreme Court's explanation for its decision?
9. What are the two roads faced by Obama now?
10. How did Clinton handle his relationship with corporations after he lost his healthcare battle?
11. How did Roosevelt change his way of dealing with corporate interests?
12. What suggestion does the author make about the democratization of America?

VII. Topics for Discussion

1. Should campaign contribution be protected as freedom of speech?
2. Should campaign contribution be regarded as bribery of politicians?

Lesson 17

East Versus West

A psychology professor dares to compare how Asians and Americans think.

By Hana R. Alberts

Richard Nisbett used to be a universalist. Like many cognitive scientists, the University of Michigan professor held that all people—from the Kung tribe that forages in southern Africa to programmers in Silicon Valley—process sensory information[1] the same way. But after visiting Peking University in 1982 and partnering with an Asian researcher, Nisbett found his beliefs challenged.

He embarked on a project to probe the thought processes of East Asians and European Americans. His experiment presented subjects with a virtual aquarium on a computer screen.[2]

"The Americans would say, 'I saw three big fish swimming off to the left. They had pink fins.' They went for the biggest, brightest moving object and focused on that and on its attributes[3]," Nisbett explains. "The Japanese in that study would start by saying, 'Well, I saw what looked like a stream. The water was green. There were rocks and shells on the bottom. There were three big fish swimming off to the left.'"

In other studies Nisbett discovered that East Asians have an easier time remembering objects when they are presented with the same background against which they were first seen. By contrast, context doesn't seem to affect Western recognition of an object.

"I thought there wasn't going to be any difference, and then we kept coming up with these very large differences," says Nisbett, a stately, white-haired man of 67, as we sit in the Upper East Side headquarters of the Russell Sage Foundation[4]. In lieu of his regular salary, he has a grant from Sage to research the nature of intelligence while on sabbatical from Michigan's psychology department[5], where he has taught since 1971.

Scientists now attach gizmos to people's heads that track eyeball movement; these experiments have confirmed Nisbett's findings, recording that Americans spend more time looking at the featured object in an array while Asians take in the entire scene, darting between background and foreground.[6]

East Asians see things in context, while Westerners focus on the point at hand; the former are dependent, the latter independent; the former are holistic, the latter analytic. There's a social aspect to these differences: Asians are collectivistic, Westerners individualistic.[7]

Even if cognition does differ across cultures, why should we care? For one thing, it might help explain why we're prone to bubbles[8]. In Nisbett's 2003 book *The Geography of Thought*[9] he describes a study in which students were shown a graph with a line snaking upward across it, representing a trend like world deaths from tuberculosis or the GDP of Brazil. Investigators asked subjects to indicate how they thought the trend would continue. Many Americans sketched a line that continued skyward, while most Chinese forecast a peak and then a decline. A colleague of Nisbett's also showed that while Canadians predict a stock whose value is rising will continue to rise, Chinese think what goes up will come down. An intriguing difference, although one wonders if 1998's pancontinental financial crisis in Asia or the real estate and stock market crash in Tokyo affected students; in the U.S. the Nasdaq crash of 2000—02[10] was not as memorable. Nisbett doubts the theory but admits "the Confucian idea that the future will resemble the past is deeply ingrained in the Asian mind."[11]

He reasons that cross-cultural differences can also explain societal phenomena. Nisbett defines a nation's preference for lawyers over engineers as a ratio: the number of the former divided by the number of the latter. When he compared America's ratio to Japan's, he found that the U.S. preferred lawyers over engineers 41-to-1. The American system, he says, prizes win-or-lose judgments, while Japan's preference is for middlemen who draft compromises.[12]

In his most recent book, *Intelligence and How to Get It: Why Schools and Cultures Count*, Nisbett asks why Asian-Americans score higher on the SAT[13] than other Americans and why students in Asian nations do so much better on (**in**) international math and science exams than their U.S. counterparts. The answer is not, Nisbett says, that Asians are smarter. Rather, he writes, "Asian intellectual accomplishment is due more to sweat than to exceptional gray matter."[14] The tests measure proficiency as much as innate skill, and the proficiency comes from cultural forces, such as the Asian sense of obligation to the family. Another factor is that math lessons in Asian schools have a student working out a problem on the board as classmates chime in. That kind of collectivism confirms the commonly held belief that learning by organic induction is more effective than rote memorization.[15]

Why do you find, in a music conservatory, a lot of Asian would-be concert pianists but comparatively few Asian opera-singers-in-training? There's a physical limit to how many hours a day a person can sing, Nisbett says, but not to how many hours one can practice sonatas.

He attributes these differences to history. East Asian agriculture was a communal venture in which tasks like irrigation and crop rotation had citizens acting in concert. In contrast, Western food production led to more lone-operator farmers and herdsmen. Greek democratic philosophy emphasized the individual; the Reformation stressed a personal connection to God[16]; the Industrial Revolution made heroes of entrepreneurs. But in Asia, Confucius said virtue hinged upon appropriate behavior for specific relationships, say, among siblings, neighbors or colleagues.[17]

These tidy generalizations are not without critics.[18] A San Francisco State University professor who edits the *Journal of Cross-Culture Psychology*[19], David Matsumoto, holds that while Nisbett attaches his observations to fascinating raw data, he takes some conclusions too far.[20]

"In cross-cultural work researchers are too quick to come up with some deep, dark, mysterious interpretation of a difference with no data to support it," Matsumoto says. "It's difficult to draw one conclusion [from] a snippet of behavior, and that's what this work tends to do."

Though Nisbett believes our behaviors are shaped by 2,500 years of history, he also thinks they are malleable.

"I got interested in whether you could make people better at reasoning and problem-solving by certain kinds of education, and it turns out you can," he says. If Americans are asked to think about how they are similar to other people they know, they view the aquarium scene more like Asians—

and vice versa. "So these things aren't necessarily locked in.[21]"

When it comes to cross-culture business, Nisbett observes, East Asians want to establish relationships, while Westerners tend to keep their business connections at arm's length. Westerners operate by the exact wording of a contract, while East Asians hold that if circumstances change, so should the agreement. Marketers, of course, are aware of culture differences. For the same phone, Samsung emphasized contrasting messages: In the U.S. the message was "I march to the beat of my own drum," whereas in Korea the ad campaign focused on families staying connected.[22]

But Nisbett noticed shifts within the Asian cohort last year, after he observed a group of Chinese students at a Procter & Gamble focus group.[23]

"My goodness, they were as lively as any group of American graduate students I've ever had. If I said something they didn't agree with, they let me know... I would never, ever feel that way with Japanese or Koreans, who are more concerned with harmony," he says. "I think the Chinese will be more successful than the Japanese have been because they have that sense of obligation to family, but they're also going to get this more Western attitude of wanting to succeed as individuals."

Perhaps, Nisbett speculates, the personal drive one sees in Chinese entrepreneurs is a consequence of China's one-child policy. Because two parents and four grandparents dote on an only child, individualism is emphasized more than it used to be.

In the last half-century Japan has undergone a huge shift toward democracy, but this hasn't been accompanied by an increase in individualism. Nisbett says: "Japan is evidence that nothing changes. China is evidence that things can change like mad."

Why is Nisbett something of a lone wolf in studying the role of geography in cognition?[24] His answer: "A lot of politically correct academics can't stand to hear about differences. They automatically assume that if you're pointing to difference, you're assuming superiority of your own culture. Well, that's just nonsense."

The upshot of Nisbett's research is that differences are real. They might not always be for the better, but they matter. Perhaps Americans should temper their optimism, Asians their reluctance to take center stage. For it seems to Nisbett that those who will be most successful in the 21st century are the ones who grasp what's best about both worldviews.

From *Forbes Magazine*, May 11, 2009

I. New Words

aquarium	[əˈkwɛəriəm]	n.	养鱼缸，水族槽
cognition	[kɔgˈniʃən]	n.	认识，认知
cognitive	[ˈkɔgnitiv]	adj.	认识的，认知的
cohort	[ˈkəuhɔ:t]	n.	a group of people sharing a common feature
conservatory	[kənˈsə:vətəri]	n.	音乐学院

dote	[dəut]	v.	(on sb) to show great love for sb, ignoring his faults
embark	[im'bɑ:k]	v.	(on sth) to start to do sth new or difficult
fin	[fin]	n.	鳍
forage	['fɔridʒ]	v.	to search for food, especially with hands
foreground	['fɔ:graund]	n.	前景
herdsman	['hə:dzmən]	n.	牧主,牧人
holistic	[həu'listik]	adj.	全盘的,全面的;(哲)整体论的
gizmo	['gizməu]	n.	机械装置
Kung	[kuŋ]	n.	布须曼人(非洲纳米比亚、博茨瓦纳、安哥拉等地的居民)
innate	[i'neit]	adj.	(of a quality) that you have when you are born
intriguing	[in'tri:giŋ]	adj.	very interesting because of being unusual
malleable	['mæliəbl]	adj.	easily influenced or changed
obligation	[ˌɔbli'geiʃən]	n.	义务,责任
pancontinental	[pænkɔnti'nentl]	adj.	泛大陆的
proficiency	[prə'fiʃənsi]	n.	熟练,精通
rotation	[rəu'teiʃən]	n.	循环,交替;(农)轮作
sabbatical	[sə'bætik(ə)l]	n.	较长的假期,休假
snippet	['snipit]	n.	a small piece
sonata	[sə'nɑ:tə]	n.	奏鸣曲
stately	['steitli]	adj.	威严的,庄重的
temper	['tempə]	v.	to make sth less severe by adding sth that has the opposite effect
tuberculosis	[tjuˌbə:kju'ləusis]	n.	[医]结核病,肺结核
universalist	[ˌju:ni'və:səlist]	n.	普遍主义者,普遍论者
upshot	['ʌpʃɔt]	n.	conclusion

II. Background Information

东西方观念和思维的差异

　　东西方观念和思维方面存在不少重大差异。首先是价值观的不同。价值观指人们选择的理想、目标、规范和准则,是指导人们生活的是非标准。西方人的核心价值观是个人主义(individualism),东方人的核心价值观是集体主义(collectivism)。西方文化提倡张扬个性、注重个人利益、主张自己抉择、激励个人奋斗。东方文化则强调个人对他人、集体和社会承担的责任和应尽的义务、注重和谐、提倡个人融入社会;在人与自然关系上崇尚天人合一,在人际关系上强调以和为贵、与人为善。这种差异也体现在语言交际方面:西方人表达自己一般开门见山、直截了当;东方人则爱用含蓄婉转的方式表述,其用意在于避免冲突。

观念差异还表现在对人性的假设。西方文化假设人性恶,必须以严格的法制体系加以控制约束,主张权力制衡、权利界定和加强执法。东方儒家文化假设人性善,主张加强个人修养。

东西方文化的价值判断方式也存在不同。西方人注重效果,东方人强调动机。西方人重视达到预想目的所采取的手段、手段使用的效率和产生的效果。东方人侧重办事的良好动机和出发点。

东西方文化在思维方式方面表现出的差异在于:西方文化是分析性思维,其特点在于把整体分解为部分,加以分门别类,把每一部分专门化、专业化,把复杂的现象和事物分解为具体的细节和简单的要素,然后深入考察各部分、各细节、各要素在整体中的性质、地位、作用和联系,从而了解其特殊本质,为了解整体及其要素的因果关系提供依据。为此,必须把各部分、各细节、各要素割裂开来、抽取出来。如若不能把思维上升到全面完整、相对和辩证的层次便会使分析停留在孤立、静止、片面的层次。东方文化是整体性思维,其特点是注重整体的关联性,而不是把整体分解为部分加以逐一分析研究;注重结构、功能,而非实体、元素;注重用辩证的方法去认识多样性的和谐和对立面的统一。

东西方观念和思维差异来源于不同的历史和文化。伴随历史的发展,东西方交流的规模扩大、层次深入,这些观念和思维也会不断发展和改变。

东西方文化各有所长,也各有所短,具有较强的互补性。跨文化交流中我们要注意彼此差异,避免误解,要辩证科学地对待彼此文化,取其所长,避其所短,从而使我们的文化更加健康地发展。

在东西方文化交流中,我们要具备敏锐的鉴别能力。对待先进文化,我们要有海纳百川的宽阔胸襟、借鉴吸收人类一切优秀文明成果的态度,也要有文化自信。中华优秀传统文化源远流长、博大精深,是中华文明的智慧结晶。它植根于中华民族历史文化沃土。对待外国先进文化,我们既不能刻舟求剑、封闭僵化,也不能照抄照搬,食洋不化。要从我国基本国情出发,同中华优秀传统文化相结合。

III. Notes to the Text

1. process sensory information —— 处理感觉信息
2. His experiment presented subjects with a virtual aquarium on a computer screen. ——他的实验是向被测试者在电脑屏幕上展现一个虚拟的水族槽。
3. They went for the biggest, brightest moving object and focused on that and on its attributes...——他们被最大、最亮的物体所吸引,关注这个物体及其特征(① go for sth —to be attracted by sth ② attribute —a quality or feature of sth)

4. the Upper East Side headquarters of the Russell Sage Foundation——拉塞尔·塞奇基金会纽约市上东区总部（the Russell Sage Foundation——an American foundation located in Manhattan, New York City, which funds and publishes research in social sciences）

5. In lieu of his regular salary, he has a grant from Sage to research the nature of intelligence while on sabbatical from Michigan's psychology department...——他用塞奇基金会的拨款而不是自己的固定工资，在密歇根大学心理学系任职休假期间研究智力的性质（①in lieu of sth——instead of sth ②Michigan's psychology department——密歇根大学心理学系，Michigan——referring to University of Michigan）

6. ...Americans spend more time looking at the featured object in an array while Asians take in the entire scene, darting between background and foreground. ——美国人花更多的时间观看一组具有特色的物体，而亚洲人则是关注整个场景，眼光在背景和前景两者之间快速跳动。（① array——a group of things; ② dart——to move suddenly and quickly; ③ featured——including a particular thing as a special feature）

7. There's a social aspect to these differences: Asians are collectivistic, Westerners individualistic. ——这些差异也表现在社会观念方面：亚洲人价值观是集体主义，西方人价值观是个人主义。(individualistic——holding the belief that the rights and freedom of an individual are the most important rights in a society)

8. ...we're prone to bubbles. ——我们（的经济）很容易出现泡沫。(bubble——a good and lucky situation that is unlikely to last long)

9. *The Geography of Thought*——该书全名：*The Geography of Thought: How Asians and Westerners Think Differently*《思维地理：亚洲人和西方人思维有何不同》

10. the Nasdaq crash of 2000—2002——2000年到2002年的纳斯达克股市暴跌[Nasdaq——National Association of Security Dealers Automated Quotations（美国）全国证券交易商协会报价表]

11. ...admits "the Confucian idea that the feature will resemble the past is deeply ingrained in the Asian mind." ——他承认说："孔子看过去知未来的观念深深植根于亚洲人的头脑中。"（本句根据《论语·学而》："告诸往而知来者。"）

12. The American system, he says, prizes win-or-lose judgments, while Japan's preference is for middlemen who draft compromises. ——他说，美国体制看重输赢的裁决，而日本体制则倾向用中间人帮助各方达成妥协。

13. SAT——Scholastic Aptitude Test 美国学业能力（大学入学）考试

14. ...Asian intellectual accomplishment is due more to sweat than to exceptional gray matter. ——亚洲人知识素养的取得更多是因为他们的勤奋而不是他们智力特别好。(gray matter——*informal* brain power)

15. That kind of collectivism confirms the commonly held belief that learning by organic induction is more effective than rote memorization. ——这种集体主义观念证实那种普遍的看法：综合归纳法比死记硬背效果要好。(①organic——consisting of different parts that are connected to each other; ②induction——a method of discovering general rules and principles from particular facts and examples)

16. the Reformation stressed a person's connection to God——宗教改革强调个人与上帝的联系

第五单元 体制观念

（the Reformation—a period of religious changes in the 16th century which led to the start of protestant churches）

17. ...Confucius said virtue hinged upon appropriate behavior for specific relationships, say, among siblings, neighbors or colleagues. —孔子说德行取决于一个人恰当处理好具体人际关系,比如同胞关系、邻里关系和同事关系。(本句根据《论语·里仁》:"德不孤,必有邻。")

18. These tidy generalizations are not without critics. —这些相当宽泛的笼统说法并非赢得一片赞同。(tidy—fairly large)

19. *Journal of Cross-Culture Psychology*—《跨文化心理学杂志》

20. ...while Nisbett attaches his observations to fascinating raw data, he takes some conclusions too far.—虽然尼斯比特的言论是基于十分有趣的素材,但有些结论过于牵强。(go too far —to go beyond what is acceptable)

21. So these things aren't necessarily locked in. —因而这些情况未必是固定不变的。(locked in —fixed)

22. For the same phone, Samsung emphasized contrasting messages: In the U.S. the message was "I march to the beat of my own drum," whereas in Korea the ad campaign focused on families staying connected.—三星公司所做的同样的手机广告所强调的信息却截然不同:美国的广告强调的信息是"我按自己的愿望行事",而韩国的广告强调的信息是与家人保持联系。(Samsung—三星公司,是韩国最大的电子工业公司)

23. Procter & Gamble focus group—宝洁公司焦点小组(① Procter & Gamble—简称P&G,一家美国消费日用品生产商,目前全球最大的日用品公司之一,总部位于美国俄亥俄州辛辛那提;② focus group—a specially selected group who are intended to represent the general public. They have discussions and their opinions are recorded as a form of market research.)

24. Why is Nisbett something of a lone wolf in studying the role of geography in cognition?—为什么尼斯比特在研究地理对认知所起的作用过程中有些孤独无助呢?(lone wolf—someone who remains to himself, especially in opinions)

IV. Language Features

外刊与文化

社会语言学家认为,语言渗透着民族的生活经验,储存了民族的价值观念,蕴含着民族的思维方式。对于第一语言使用者而言,他们在习得这门语言的过程中,由于自身生活在相关文化之中,其思维和行为一直受到该文化的熏陶,因而他们在彼此的交际中基本上不存在文化障碍。然而,对于第二语言习得者而言,情况就大不相同了。他们往往用自己的生活经验、自己所认同的价值观和思维方式去"比附"外国文化,套用到外语交际中去。套用的结果便形成文化干扰和交际障碍。外报外刊涉及英语国家文化诸多方面,不了解这些情况便会造成理解困难。

例1：Violence in language has become almost as casual the possession of handguns. (语言粗鲁几乎就像持枪一样十分随意。)不了解美国的枪支文化就很难理解作者为什么把语言粗鲁看得更为严重。

例2：Busibodies: New Puritans

这是《时代》周刊1991年8月21日一篇文章的标题。不了解清教徒的价值观和美国人对清教主义的看法就无法理解这个标题。

清教主义主张节俭、勤奋(thrift and hard work)。清教牧师强调只有勤劳、节俭，才能得到上帝的拯救。这种勤奋、节俭的价值观在美国发展时期起过积极作用，对今日的美国人也有一定影响。但美国社会中有很多人认为清教主义倡导禁欲苦行。美国知名作家H.L.门肯就曾嘲笑过清教徒，称他们是"不让自己也不让别人过高兴日子的好管闲事的人"。

例3：Early retirement trend to quit working at 65 or sooner: Sterling Phillips, 65, spends 30 hours a month at an on-and-off job... Spurgeon Wilson, 61, is considering a six-week job... George Garrett, 60... prefers playing in local golf tournaments and traveling.

这段文字所举三例，按我国标准，应该属于退休的例子，若说是推迟退休之例(cases of late retirement)那很好理解，说成提早退休(early retirement)就较难接受了。可在美国，退休年龄原为65岁，现为66岁，为了激励更多老人65岁之后继续工作，最近政府还有新的奖励措施：每多工作一年，退休金增加8%。

上述实例说明，外刊阅读过程中确实存在文化干扰。因而，要想增强外刊理解能力，不但要提高语言水平，还要扩充文化背景知识。

V. Analysis of Content

1. The meaning of the word "tidy" in the sentence "These tidy generalizations are not without critics." (Para.13) is _____.
   A. orderly   B. fairly large   C. fairly good   D. quite sound

2. Which of the following is NOT true about Richard Nisbett?
   A. He is a psychology professor.
   B. He is a cognitive scientist.
   C. He is a scholar.
   D. He is a universalist.

3. To Richard Nisbett, Asian students do better in international math and science exams than American counterparts because _____.
   A. they like math and science   B. they have exceptional gray matter
   C. they are more hardworking   D. their parents pay more attention to education

4. According to Richard Nisbett, East Asians _____.
   A. are individualistic   B. are holistic
   C. prize win-or-lose judgments   D. are prone to bubbles
5. Which of the following is NOT on Nisbett's list of reasons for Americans' individualism?
   A. Western food production.   B. Greek philosophy.
   C. The Reformation.   D. The Westward movement.

VI. Questions on the Article

1. What was Richard Nisbett's view on the thought processes of Westerners and Asians?
2. When did Nisbett find his beliefs challenged?
3. What did Nisbett discover in his studies about the effect of background on cognition?
4. What have cognition scientists found through applying gizmos to the heads tracking eyeball movement?
5. How does Nisbett explain the fact that there are a lot of Asian would-be concert pianists but comparatively few Asian opera-singers-in-training?
6. What is Matsumoto's comment on Richard Nisbett's view?
7. What differences exist between Westerners and East Asians in cross-cultural business?
8. What shifts did Nisbett notice within the Asian cohort last year?
9. How does Nisbett explain the personal drive of Chinese entrepreneurs?
10. What is Nisbett's answer to the question why he is something of a lone wolf in studying the role of geography in cognition?
11. What is Nisbett's suggestion to Americans and Asians concerning behavior?

VII. Topics for Discussion

1. Do you accept Richard Nisbett's view on the differences between Westerners and East Asians in cognition?
2. What is the sensible way to treat the differences between foreign culture and Chinese culture?

Unit 6
第六单元 文教体育

Lesson 18

Reining in the Test of Tests[1]

Some say the SAT[2] is destiny. Some say it's meaningless. Should it be scrapped?

By Ben Wildavsky

Richard Atkinson is not typical of those who fret over the SAT, yet there he was last year poring over a stack of prep manuals, filling in the bubbles with his No. 2 pencils[3]. When the esteemed cognitive psychologist, former head of the National Science Foundation[4] and now president of the prestigious nine-campus University of California system[5], decided to investigate his long-standing misgivings about the nation's best known standardized test, he did just what many of the 1.3 million high school seniors who take the SAT do every year. Every night or so for several weeks, the 71-year-old Atkinson pulled out his manuals and sample tests to review and assess the sort of verbal and mathematical questions teenagers are up against.

Atkinson, a testing expert, didn't much like what he saw. There were too many confusing questions and obscure verbal analogies—the kind that require students to figure out that "untruthful" is to "mendaciousness" as "circumspect" is to "caution." Nor was he happy when he visited a Northern California private school last year and saw a class of 12-year-olds practicing for SAT exams—exams that were literally years away. Unlike many SAT critics, however, Atkinson is in a position to do something about the college admission test: In a groundbreaking February 18 speech to the American Council on Education[6], he called for scrapping the SAT I (the formal name for the test) in UC's future undergraduate admissions decisions.

His proposal, which stands a decent chance of approval by the faculty and regents sometime in the next year, is already causing a huge stir on campuses nationwide.[7] Indeed, it has rekindled long-standing arguments about the test that go far beyond California: Is the SAT overrated as a college-admissions tool and predictor of performance? Is it unfair to poor and minority students (critics have long called the test "culturally biased"[8])—especially now that some universities have stopped giving admissions preferences to blacks and Hispanics, whose average SAT scores are much lower than those of whites and Asians? And, perhaps most fundamental, should colleges be picking students based on their acquired knowledge rather than general aptitude? The California system, Atkinson contends, should only use standardized exams directly linked to the material students have studied in school.

Scuttling chances. Esther Walling would be glad to see the SAT go. A college counselor at Jefferson High School in South Central Los Angeles, she says her low-income, Latino students generally do not test well on the SAT, although they are very capable. One of the school's stars, 17-year-old senior Pascual Ramos, has earned straight A's in nine rigorous Advanced Placement courses[9]. But he only managed a combined score of 1080 on the SAT—above the national average of 1019 but well below what elite schools expect. He's applied to several UC schools as well as Cornell[10], Carnegie Mellon[11], and—his dream campus—the Massachusetts Institute of Technology[12]. "I'll get into a couple of them," he predicts. "I only worry about my SAT scores."

It's the nebulous nature of the SAT that bothers many opponents. The test is "a big fuzzball," says testing specialist James Popham, an emeritus professor at UCLA who considers the exam a glorified IQ test. Not so, says the College Board[13], which sponsors the test. But the board hasn't helped clarify matters by executing a couple of rhetorical somersaults in recent years.[14] In 1994 it changed the SAT's name from Scholastic Aptitude Test—the name since it was first developed in 1926—to the Scholastic Assessment Test. These days the official position is that the initials don't stand for anything.

But there's no mystery about what the test does, says College Board President Gaston Caperton. The three-hour exam measures "the sort of higher-order math and literary-reasoning skills that students need to succeed in college and later in life," he argues. The test correlates well with freshman-year college grades, the College Board says, especially when used in combination with high school grades. "Scapegoating the SAT will not provide better teaching and learning in the schools."

The latest assault on the SAT follows the demise of affirmative action in several states, where universities can no longer give special admissions breaks to minority applicants.[15] Continued reliance on test scores makes it hard to sustain previous levels of minority enrollment, so there's been a scramble for race-blind alternatives[16]. Already, the state of Texas and the UC system have adopted college admissions systems based in part on class rank. Regardless of test scores, a student at the top of his or her high school class (the top 10 percent in Texas, the top 4 percent in California) is automatically admitted to state universities. The new policies are politically popular, but critics fret that they rely on the continued segregation of high schools and may lower admissions standards because school quality varies so widely.

In the short term, Atkinson wants UC to continue requiring the subject-specific achievement tests (known collectively as the SAT II), which measure knowledge in such areas as writing, math, history, and foreign languages. Eventually, he'd like to see new tests linked more directly to UC's required college-prep curriculum[17]. There's nothing wrong with "teaching to the test," he says, so long as the test is measuring mastery of the curriculum. UC officials say their research shows that SAT II subject tests are a slightly better predictor of freshman grades than the SAT I. What's more, they note, racial disparities in test results, though still considerable, aren't as dramatic for subject-area tests as they are for the SAT.

But skeptics say that it's only a matter of time before there is pressure to scrap subject-area tests as well. Abigail Thernstrom, an affirmative action critic and author of *America in Black and White*, is especially concerned about the move toward "holistic" criteria that go beyond both test scores and grades[18]. "Getting rid of the SATs is the first step in a wretched direction," Thernstrom says, predicting the move will lower standards.

It's ironic that a test first used as a tool for meritocracy has now come under fire as a barrier to opportunity. As Nicholas Lemann recounts in his 1999 book *The Big Test*, Harvard President James Conant laid the groundwork for the eventual nationalization of the SAT by using the exam in the 1930s to identify talented Mid-western public school scholarship boys who didn't have the advantages of an East Coast prep school education[19]. An objective test, the theory went, could sweep away class advantages. Now the pendulum has swung back[20], and measures of innate aptitude are increasingly under suspicion. But Conant's original concerns aren't going to go away. Right after Atkinson's speech to college officials, Susan Cole, the president of Montclair State University in New Jersey, stood up to warn that moving to curriculum-based tests could worsen inequality for students who didn't have access to good classes and good teachers. Others point out that axing the SAT won't do anything to get rid of racial and socioeconomic gaps in achievement, which show up on a wide variety of tests as well as in high school grades. The SAT debate at UC will be closely watched around the country, but don't expect the testing wars to die down anytime soon.

From *U.S. News & World Report*, March 5, 2001

I. New Words

affirmative	[əˈfɔːmətiv]	adj.	肯定的
analogy	[əˈnælədʒi]	n.	a comparison of one thing with another thing that has similar features
aptitude	[ˈæptitjuːd]	n.	natural ability or skill
assessment	[əˈsesmənt]	n.	evaluation or opinion
cognitive	[ˈkɔgnitiv]	adj.	认知的
disparity	[disˈpæriti]	n.	difference or inequality
emeritus	[iˈmeritəs]	adj.	退休后保留头衔的，名誉的
fret	[fret]	v.	*informal* to feel worried
fuzzball	[ˈfʌzbɔːl]	n.	*informal* 乱糟糟的一团
groundbreaking	[ˈgraundbreikiŋ]	adj.	new and pioneering or innovative
meritocracy	[ˌmeriˈtɔkrəsi]	n.	system based on ability
misgiving	[misˈgiviŋ]	adj.	feeling of doubt or apprehension
nebulous	[ˈnebjuləs]	adj.	not clear, distinct, or definite
obscure	[əbˈskjuə]	adj.	晦涩的，费解的
pendulum	[ˈpendjuləm]	n.	钟摆；摇摆不定的事态

pore	[pɔ:]	v.	~over to examine or study carefully
predictor	[priˈdiktə]	n.	预言者；预测器
scapegoat	[ˈskeipgəut]	v.	to make sb take the blame
scrap	[skræp]	v.	to get rid of sth
scuttle	[ˈskʌtl]	v.	to destroy or bring sth to an end
socioeconomic	[ˈsəuʃiəuˌi:kəˈnɔmik]	adj.	社会经济（学）的
somersault	[ˈsʌməsɔ:lt]	n.	reversal of opinion or decision
wretched	[ˈretʃid]	adj.	very unhappy, extremely bad

II. Background Information

高校招生

美国高校招生与我国相比存在以下四点区别：

1. 考试内容。长期以来，美国各大学所接受的入学考试形式是SAT（Scholastic Assessment Test学习能力评估考试）。SAT分为SAT I（SAT通用考试）和SAT II（SAT单科考试）。美国一般高校只需要提供SAT I的成绩，较少高校要求同时提供SAT II的成绩。考试内容不仅包括对学生所学知识的检查，还包括对学生潜在能力的考查。比较关注学生是否具备继续深造的能力。

2016年SAT经历了一次重要改革。老式SAT由三部分组成，满分是2400分。新式SAT分为两部分：阅读与文法，满分为800分；数学，满分也是800分。考试合计满分是1600分。阅读与文法比较注重考生语言应用、文章分析，词汇部分侧重大学与职业生活中广泛使用的词；数学题偏重实际应用，贴近现实生活。

ACT（American College Testing美国大学入学考试）是另外一种高考形式。ACT既强调学生对学科知识的掌握又注重学生的独立思考和判断能力。相比之下，SAT在美国东北部和西部州流行，而ACT更受中西部和南部州的青睐。

2. 考试次数。美国SAT考试每年举行7次，通常是在1月、3月、5月、6月、10月、11月和12月。学生参加考试次数不限，以成绩最高一次为准。不少学生一考再考，直到考出自己满意的成绩才肯罢休。不少大学要求学生提供几次考试平均成绩（grade-point average，简称GPA）。为了取得较为理想的平均成绩，有的学生预测成绩较差时，在考后5日内通知考试机构予以取消，可以不作计算。美国有些初中生在8年级时就参加SAT考试，目的是想试探自身实力。

3. 录取标准。美国大学录取新生注重学生素质，实行的是全面审核录取方法（holistic admission）。要求学生不仅提供SAT考试成绩，还要提供高中阶段成绩。要想被本科大学录取，不仅要有较好的SAT成绩，而且还得在高中时期各科期评成绩为"良好"（B）以上。美国中学生期评成绩包括三个方面：(1)平时作业，占期评成绩的50%；(2)任务项目评分，占25%；(3)考试成绩，占25%。除此之外，学生还得提供课外活动和社会工作经验。美国比较好的大学还要求学生提供老师或社会团体负责人的推荐信，介绍学生的社会活动能力和成绩。

4. 录取程序。美国高校录取新生是学校与学生双向互动的过程。学生依据自身条件申请多所高等学校,条件好者往往会收到几所高校的录取通知书,然后自己再进行对比做出最后选择,办理登记、注册、缴费等手续。

III. Notes to the Text

1. Reining in the Test of Tests — 严控高考[① rein in—to start to control more strictly;② of —……中(或较)突出的:song of songs 最好的歌;in sb's heart of hearts 在某人的内心深处]

2. SAT—the Scholastic Assessment Test, examination required in the U.S. for admission to undergraduate degree programs

3. filling in the bubbles with his No.2 pencils — 用他的二号铅笔填涂圈圈

4. National Science Foundation — 国家科学基金会

5. nine-campus University of California system— 有九个分校的加州大学 (The California State University is so far-flung and complex in structure and functions that it has been called a "multiversity."

6. American Council on Education — 美国教育委员会

7. His proposal, ... is already causing a huge stir on campuses nationwide. —他的提议很有希望在明年的某个时候被大学院方、校方通过,在全国大学界已经引起了很大的轰动。

8. critics have long called the test "culturally biased"—长期以来批评者称这种考试具有社会歧视 (culturally biased — biased against the poor and minority students)

9. Advanced Placement courses — 预修课程 (classes which give middle school students a chance to earn college credit)

10. Cornell — 康奈尔大学(位于纽约州伊萨卡市,私立)

11. Carnegie Mellon — 卡内基梅隆大学(位于宾夕法尼亚州匹兹堡市的一所私立大学)

12. the Massachusetts Institute of Technology — 麻省理工学院

13. College Board — College Entrance Examination Board 大学入学考试委员会

14. But the board hasn't helped clarify matters by executing a couple of rhetorical somersaults in recent years. — 但是近年来委员会对考试名称的修改未能把问题阐述清楚。

15. The latest assault on the SAT ... give special admissions breaks to minority applicants. — 最近对SAT的抨击发生在几个州结束"肯定行动计划"以后,这几个州的大学不再给少数种族学生提供特殊的入学优惠。(① demise — the end of activity; ② break — informal a lucky chance)

16. so there's been a scramble for race-blind alternatives— 所以(大学)争先恐后地采取无种族歧视的做法(race-blind — treating people from different races equally and fairly)

17. college-prep curriculum — 大学预备课程

18. "holistic" criteria that go beyond both test scores and grades—范畴超出考试分数和等级的全

面标准(holistic—based on the belief that a person is a whole which is more than the small parts added together)
19. prep school education — school education that prepares students for the test
20. Now the pendulum has swung back... — Now the public concern over the test has moved to the other extreme, that is, measuring students with the subject-specific achievements.

IV. Language Features

新闻标题的结构

英语新闻标题,可以按它所占的栏数(column number)分为一栏标题(one-column headline)、两栏标题(two-column headline)等,也可以按标题的内容层次分为一层标题(one-deck headline)、两层标题(two-deck headline)、四层标题(four-deck headline),本文标题是两层标题。英语报刊常用的是一层和两层标题,如:

一层标题:

Republican Wins House Seat in New Mexico

二层标题:

Cultural Earthquake Shakes Marker

Europe's the Casualty as Sellers Head for New York

新闻周刊大部分报道采用双层标题。两个层次,一主一副相互补充和配合,起到概括故事内容、准确反映文章基调、引起注意、激发兴趣的作用。

双层标题之间在功能上是有分工的,其分工情况大致归类为以下三种:

1. 一层引起读者兴趣,二层用以解释说明。

例1. **Farewell to ARMS**

Gun Swaps: Amnesty programs — and outright bribery — are gaining popularity and pulling some of America's 211 million firearms off the street

例2. **BATTLE OF THE BINGE**

A fatal night of boozing at a Louisiana University stirs up the debate over the drinking culture in America's colleges. Are they doing enough to change it?

2. 一层介绍文章核心内容,二层提供重要补充。

例1. **Cops Under Fire**

Their adversaries are more heavily armed and more arrogant than ever. Their allies include an army of second-guessers. Their job can't get much tougher.

例2. **AIDS: A Spreading Scourge**

Incurable and lethal, the disease is taking a mounting toll.

3. 一层介绍文章核心内容,二层激发读者兴趣。

例 1. **The Killing of Carl Stuart**
An implausible story

例 2. **The War Over "Family Values"**
How much effect do middle-class mores have in the ghetto?

V. Analysis of Content

1. From the article we know that Richard Atkinson is NOT _____.
   A. an esteemed cognitive psychologist
   B. the former head of the National Science Foundation
   C. the president of the College Board
   D. the president of the University of California

2. What Atkinson calls for is _____.
   A. stopping the use of SAT I   B. stopping the use of SAT I and SAT II
   C. using a different kind of test   D. basing college admissions on class rank

3. Esther Walling would be glad to see the SAT go because she thinks that SAT _____.
   A. is too difficult for Latino students   B. cannot reflect students' capability
   C. is against the affirmative action   D. is out-of-date

4. To the mind of James Popham, SAT is _____ in nature.
   A. backward   B. culturally-biased
   C. scientific   D. unclear

5. According to the author, SAT was originally used as a tool for _____.
   A. democracy   B. freedom of speech
   C. meritocracy   D. ending cultural bias

VI. Questions on the Article

1. How did Richard Atkinson investigate SAT's problems?
2. What proposal did Atkinson make after the investigation? What impact has the proposal produced?
3. What is the College Board's view on the value of SAT?
4. What change have Texas and the UC system made in college admissions?
5. What is the skeptics' worry?
6. Tell what you know about SAT I and SAT II.
7. What are the prospects of the debate on college admissions test?

VII. Topics for Discussion

1. Should the SAT I be scrapped?
2. Is college entrance examination the most ideal way to select qualified students?

Lesson 19

The COVID-19 pandemic has changed education forever. This is how.

By Cathy Li & Farah Lalani[1]

While countries are at different points in their COVID-19 infection rates, worldwide there are currently more than 1.2 billion children in 186 countries affected by school closures due to the pandemic. In Denmark, children up to the age of 11 are returning to nurseries and schools after initially closing on 12 March, but in Korea students are responding to roll calls from their teachers online.

With this sudden shift away from the classroom in many parts of the globe, some are wondering whether the adoption of online learning will continue to persist post-pandemic, and how such a shift would impact the worldwide education market.

Even before COVID-19, there was already high growth and adoption in education technology, with global edtech investments reaching US$18.66 billion in 2019 and the overall market for online education projected to reach $350 billion by 2025. Whether it is language apps, virtual tutoring, video conferencing tools, or online learning software, there has been a significant surge in usage since COVID-19.

In response to significant demand, many online learning platforms are offering free access to their services, including platforms like BYJU'S, a Bangalore-based educational technology and online tutoring firm founded in 2011, which is now the world's most highly valued edtech company. Since announcing free live classes on its Think and Learn app, BYJU'S has seen a 200% increase in the number of new students using its product, according to Mrinal Mohit, the company's Chief Operating Officer.

Tencent classroom, meanwhile, has been used extensively since mid-February after the Chinese government instructed a quarter of a billion full-time students to resume their studies through online platforms. This resulted in the largest "online movement" in the history of education with approximately 730,000, or 81% of K-12 students, attending classes via the Tencent K-12 Online School in Wuhan.[2]

Other companies are bolstering capabilities to provide a one-stop shop for teachers and students.[3] For example, Lark, a Singapore-based collaboration suite initially developed by ByteDance as an internal tool to meet its own exponential growth, began offering teachers and students unlimited video conferencing time, auto-translation capabilities, real-time co-editing of project work, and smart calendar scheduling, amongst other features.[4] To do so quickly and in a time of crisis, Lark ramped up its global server infrastructure and engineering capabilities to ensure reliable connectivity.

Alibaba's distance learning solution, DingTalk, had to prepare for a similar influx: "To support large-scale remote work, the platform tapped Alibaba Cloud to deploy more than 100,000 new cloud servers in just two hours last month — setting a new record for rapid capacity expansion[5]," according to DingTalk CEO, Chen Hang.

Some school districts are forming unique partnerships, like the one between The Los Angeles Unified School District and PBS SoCal/KCET[6] to offer local educational broadcasts, with separate channels focused on different ages, and a range of digital options. Media organizations such as the BBC are also powering virtual learning; Bitesize Daily, launched on 20 April, is offering 14 weeks of curriculum-based learning for kids across the UK[7] with celebrities like Manchester City footballer Sergio Aguero teaching some of the content.

While some believe that the unplanned and rapid move to online learning — with no training, insufficient bandwidth, and little preparation — will result in a poor user experience that is unconducive to sustained growth, others believe that a new hybrid model of education will emerge, with significant benefits. "I believe that the integration of information technology in education will be further accelerated and that online education will eventually become an integral component of school education," says Wang Tao, Vice President of Tencent Cloud and Vice President of Tencent Education.

There have already been successful transitions amongst many universities. For example, Zhejiang University managed to get more than 5,000 courses online just two weeks into the transition using "DingTalk ZJU". The Imperial College London started offering a course on the science of coronavirus, which is now the most enrolled class launched in 2020 on Coursera[8].

Many are already touting the benefits: Dr Amjad, a Professor at The University of Jordan who has been using Lark to teach his students says, "It has changed the way of teaching. It enables me to reach out to my students more efficiently and effectively through chat groups, video meetings, voting and also document sharing, especially during this pandemic. My students also find it is easier to communicate on Lark. I will stick to Lark even after coronavirus. I believe traditional offline learning and e-learning can go hand in hand.[9]"

There are, however, challenges to overcome. Some students without reliable Internet access and/or technology struggle to participate in digital learning; this gap is seen across countries and between income brackets within countries. For example, whilst 95% of students in Switzerland, Norway, and Austria have a computer to use for their schoolwork, only 34% in Indonesia do, according to OECD[10] data.

In the U.S., there is a significant gap between those from privileged and disadvantaged backgrounds: whilst virtually all 15-year-olds from a privileged background said they had a computer to work on, nearly 25% of those from disadvantaged backgrounds did not. While some schools and governments have been providing digital equipment to students in need, such as in New South Wales, Australia, many are still concerned that the pandemic will widen the digital divide.[11]

For those who do have access to the right technology, there is evidence that learning online can be more effective in a number of ways. Some research shows that on average, students retain 25–60% more material when learning online compared to only 8–10% in a classroom. This is mostly due to the students being able to learn faster online; e-learning requires 40–60% less time to learn than in a traditional classroom setting because students can learn at their own pace, going back and re-reading, skipping, or accelerating through concepts as they choose.[12]

Nevertheless, the effectiveness of online learning varies amongst age groups. The general consensus on children, especially younger ones, is that a structured environment[13] is required, because kids are more easily distracted. To get the full benefit of online learning, there needs to be a concerted effort to provide this structure and go beyond replicating a physical class/lecture through video capabilities, instead, using a range of collaboration tools and engagement methods that promote "inclusion, personalization and intelligence"[14], according to Dowson Tong, Senior Executive Vice President of Tencent and President of its Cloud and Smart Industries Group.

Since studies have shown that children extensively use their senses to learn, making learning fun and effective through use of technology is crucial, according to BYJU'S Mrinal Mohit. "Over a period, we have observed that clever integration of games has demonstrated higher engagement and increased motivation towards learning especially among younger students, making them truly fall in love with learning", he says.

It is clear that this pandemic has utterly disrupted an education system that many assert was already losing its relevance.[15] In his book, *21 Lessons for the 21st Century*, scholar Yuval Noah Harari outlines how schools continue to focus on traditional academic skills and rote learning, rather than on skills such as critical thinking and adaptability, which will be more important for success in the future.[16] Could the move to online learning be the catalyst to create a new, more effective method of educating students? While some worry that the hasty nature of the transition online may have hindered this goal, others plan to make e-learning part of their "new normal" after experiencing the benefits first-hand.[17]

Major world events are often an inflection point for rapid innovation — a clear example is the rise of e-commerce post-SARS.[18] While we have yet to see whether this will apply to e-learning post-COVID-19, it is one of the few sectors where investment has not dried up. What has been made clear through this pandemic is the importance of disseminating knowledge across borders, companies, and all parts of society. If online learning technology can play a role here, it is incumbent upon all of us to explore its full potential.[19]

From *World Economic Forum*, April 29, 2020

I. New Words

access	['ækses]	n.	~ (to sth) 接近；使用
accelerate	[ək'seləreit]	v.	to happen or to make sth happen faster or earlier than expected
assert	[ə'sə:t]	v.	断言，坚称
adoption	[ə'dɔpʃn]	n.	采用，采纳
approximately	[ə'prɔksimətli]	adv.	nearly; about

Bangalore	[ˌbæŋgæˈlɔː(r)]	n.	班加罗尔[印度南部城市]
bandwidth	[ˈbændwidθ]	n.	带宽
bracket	[ˈbrækit]	n.	a group or class fixed according to certain upper and lower limits
catalyst	[ˈkætəlist]	n.	催化剂
closure	[ˈkləuʒə]	n.	关闭
collaboration	[kəˌlæbəˈreiʃn]	n.	合作,协作
concerted	[kənˈsəːtid]	adj.	planned or done together by agreement; combined
consensus	[kənˈsensəs]	n.	一致,共识
disrupt	[disˈrʌpt]	v.	扰乱,打乱
disseminate	[diˈsemineit]	v.	to scatter widely; to spread about
distract	[diˈstrækt]	v.	使分散;使分心
dry	[drai]	v.	~ up (of a supply) to come to an end
extensively	[iksˈtensivli]	adv.	广泛地,广大地
hinder	[ˈhində]	v.	to make it difficult for sb to do sth or sth to happen
hybrid	[ˈhaibrid]	adj.	混合的
inclusion	[inˈkluːʒn]	n.	包括;包容
inflection	[inˈflekʃn]	n.	屈折变化;拐折
influx	[ˈinflʌks]	n.	汇集;涌入
infrastructure	[ˈinfrʌstrʌktʃə]	n.	基础设施
innovation	[ˌinəˈveiʃn]	n.	变革,改革
insufficient	[ˌinsəˈfiʃnt]	adj.	less than is needed; not enough
integral	[ˈintigrəl]	adj.	必要的,基本的
integration	[ˌintiˈgreiʃn]	n.	结合
nursery	[ˈnəːsəri]	n.	托儿所
pandemic	[pænˈdemik]	n.	流行病
persist	[pəˈsist]	v.	to continue to exist
privileged	[ˈprivəlidʒd]	adj.	有特权的;有优势的
project	[prɔˈdʒekt]	v.	to imagine; conceive of; see in one's mind
ramp	[ramp]	v.	~ sth up to make sth increase in amount
replicate	[ˈreplikeit]	v.	to reproduce, copy
retain	[riˈtein]	v.	to keep in one's mind
rote	[rəut]	adj.	死记硬背的;机械的
server	[ˈsəːvə]	n.	[计]服务器
surge	[səːdʒ]	n.	a sudden or abrupt strong increase
suite	[swiːt]	n.	系列;套件
sustained	[səsˈteind]	adj.	持续的
tap	[tæp]	v.	to draw from; to make good use of
transition	[trænˈziʃn]	n.	过度;转变
tout	[taut]	v.	to show off

unconducive	[ˌʌnkənˈdjuːsiv]	adj.	无助的；无益的
utterly	[ˈʌtəli]	adv.	completely; totally; absolutely
virtual	[ˈvəːtʃuəl]	adj.	虚拟的；事实上的

II. Background Information

线上教育的前景

在线学习是一种使用电子设备与学生互动的教育活动。它通过互联网或其他基于计算机的方法，使教学活动打破时间、地点的约束，在任何网络环境下为学生和教师提供远程沟通。这种灵活的教育选择方式，不仅给予学生随时随地学习的途径，还展现出更多的教学方法，并能充分利用互联网的课程资源及学习材料。

在线学习可分为以下三类教学方式：同步学习、异步学习和混合学习。同步学习是实时的在线行为，数百名甚至上千名学生和教师同时在线，交流沟通；异步学习是指学生在非特定时间自行参加课程、讨论、测验等学习活动；混合学习是以上两种方式的结合。

早期的在线教育以视频学习为主，学生在虚拟平台上观看视频讲座。而后，视频平台开始嵌入问题、关键词、指针短语和导航菜单；有些大学也搭建了基于视频的互动学习平台，学生观看教师制作的视频，然后发布答案、提出问题和发表评论。

疫情期间，全球大、中、小学生们不断退出面对面的老式课堂，被迫转向虚拟学习的线上模式。事实上，在线学习在过去的20年一直呈上升趋势，并在2020年成为教育界的中心话题。

得益于智能手机和无处不在的无线网络，在线学习是自助灵活的学习模式。学习被分解成更小的、高度集中的单元。例如，学生可以利用碎片时间，比如搭乘地铁、排队候餐的时间观看一则短视频，听一段简短的播客，或者做一个简单的测验，几分钟内就能完成一个在线学习任务。

随着新兴技术的出现，在线学习呈现出全方位的发展势头。首先是与游戏结合。有学校认为视频游戏对集中注意力有积极影响，能帮助学生提高认知能力。它们已经开始与游戏公司合作开发课程。展望未来，游戏或将成为在线学习不可或缺的一部分。

人工智能正以我们无法想象的方式使教育个性化。佐治亚理工学院在线上安排了一位虚拟助理，回答学生关于学习内容、作业等方面的技术层面的问题。人工智能分析还可以收集学生的学习数据，识别其与理想状态之间的差距，从而及时提醒教师对某些困难学生提高关注度。

虚拟现实技术也是在线学习的发展方向之一。沉浸式的体验缩小理论和实践之间的差距，增加学生的参与度，加快学习过程，并解决在线学习带来的一些社会化问题。学生们可以在虚拟空间与恐龙一起行走，设计3D建筑，练习演讲，参观古罗马，给虚拟病人手术，做大脑可以想象到的任何事情。

III. Notes to the Text

1. Cathy Li & Farah Lalani — ①Cathy Li — the head of Shaping the Future of Media, Entertainment & Sport and is a member of the ExCom, World Economic Forum; ②Farah Lalani — the Community leader of Global Coalition for Digital Safety, World Economic Forum.

2. This resulted in the largest "online movement" in the history of education with approximately 730,000, or 81% of K-12 students, attending classes via the Tencent K-12 Online School in Wuhan. — 这导致了教育史上最大规模的"线上活动",武汉约73万名中小学生(81%的中小学生)通过腾讯K-12网校上课。(K-12 — a short form for kindergarten through twelfth grade)

3. Other companies are bolstering capabilities to provide a one-stop shop for teachers and students. — 其他公司正在增强为教师和学生提供一站式服务的能力。(①bolster — to support and strengthen; ②one-stop shop — a metaphoric expression meaning a comprehensive range of related services)

4. For example, Lark, a Singapore-based collaboration suite initially developed by ByteDance as an internal tool to meet its own exponential growth, began offering teachers and students unlimited video conferencing time, auto-translation capabilities, real-time co-editing of project work, and smart calendar scheduling, amongst other features. — 例如,新加坡的协作套件Lark,起初是由字节跳动公司开发的满足自身快速增长的内部工具,已开始为教师和学生提供无限制的视频会议时间、自动翻译功能、项目工作的实时共同编辑,以及智能日程安排等功能。[①ByteDance — 字节跳动公司,总部在北京,成立于2012年,目前业务范围已覆盖150个国家,在全球推出了包括抖音等多款有影响力的产品;②exponential growth — (of a rate of increase) becoming faster and faster; ③real-time — of or relating to computer systems that update information at the same rate they receive information]

5. Alibaba's distance learning solution, DingTalk, had to prepare for a similar influx: "To support large-scale remote work, the platform tapped Alibaba Cloud to deploy more than 100,000 new cloud servers in just two hours last month — setting a new record for rapid capacity expansion." — 阿里巴巴的远程学习软件"钉钉"也得为类似的大流量做准备:"为了支持大规模的远程工作,该平台上个月使用阿里巴巴云在仅仅两个小时内部署了超过10万台新的云服务器,创下了快速扩容的新纪录。"(①Ding Talk — 阿里巴巴集团为企业打造的免费沟通和协同的多端平台;②Alibaba Cloud — 提供云服务器、云数据库、云存储的全套解决方案)

6. PBS Socal/KCET — (加州)洛杉矶学区和美国公共电视网南加州电视台

7. Media organizations such as the BBC are also powering virtual learning; Bitesize Daily, launched on 20 April, is offering 14 weeks of curriculum-based learning for kids across the UK... — 像英国广播公司一类的媒体机构也在推动虚拟教学;4月20日推出的"一天学一点"课程视频,为英国各地孩子提供14周基于课程的学习内容(Bitesize Daily — launched by BBC, features hundreds of interactive lessons that are all in line with the UK curriculum, aimed at minimising disruption to children's education and providing rhythm and routine

during the coronavirus lockdown)

8. Coursera — a global online learning platform founded in 2012 that offers anyone, anywhere, access to online courses and degrees from leading universities and companies

9. I will stick to Lark even after coronavirus, I believe traditional offline learning and e-learning can go hand in hand. — 即使新冠疫情结束，我依然会使用Lark，我相信传统的线下学习和电子学习可以齐头并进。(hand in hand — happening together and closely connected)

10. OECD — the Organization for Economic Cooperation and Development 经济合作与发展组织

11. ...many are still concerned that the pandemic will widen the digital divide. — ……许多人仍然担心疫情会扩大数字鸿沟。(digital divide — the social and other disparities between those people who have opportunities and skills enabling them to benefit from digital resource and those who do not have these opportunities or skills)

12. This is mostly due to the students being able to learn faster online; e-learning requires 40–60% less time to learn than in a traditional classroom setting because students can learn at their own pace, going back and re-reading, skipping, or accelerating through concepts as they choose. — 这主要是因为学生在网上学得更快；与传统课堂环境相比，在线学习所需的时间减少了40-60%，因为学生可以按照自己的节奏、自己所想的方式学习：回顾、复读、跳读和速读。

13. structured environment — 结构化环境（由实物、图片、数字、文字等可视性强的媒介科学综合组成的环境，这种环境有利于提高学生注意力，改善学习效果）

14. ... using a range of collaboration tools and engagement methods that promote "inclusion, personalization and intelligence"... — 使用一系列能够推动"包容性、个性化和智能化"的协作工具和参与方法

15. It is clear that this pandemic has utterly disrupted an education system that many assert was already losing its relevance. — 很明显，疫情彻底扰乱了教育系统，许多人断言这个系统已失去它的实用性。

16. In his book, 21 Lessons for the 21st Century, scholar Yuval Noah Harari outlines how schools continue to focus on traditional academic skills and rote learning, rather than on skills such as critical thinking and adaptability, which will be more important for success in the future. — 学者尤瓦尔·诺亚·哈拉里在他的著作《21世纪的21课》中概述了学校如何继续专注于传统的学习技能和死记硬背，而不是批判性思维和适应性等技能，而后者对未来的成功更为重要。(①Yuval Noah Harari — 耶路撒冷希伯来大学历史学教授、历史学家、作家；②rote learning — rote (learning is a memorization technique based on repetition))

17. While some worry that the hasty nature of the transition online may have hindered this goal, others plan to make e-learning part of their "new normal" after experiencing the benefits first-hand. — 虽然有些人担心在线学习的转变过于仓促，可能阻碍这一目标的实现，但那些亲身体验过好处的人，打算把在线学习作为他们"新常态"的一部分。

18. Major world events are often an inflection point for rapid innovation — a clear example is the rise of e-commerce post-SARS. — 重大的世界事件往往是快速创新的转折点——"非典"后电子商务的兴起就是一个明显的例子。(SARS — Severe Acute Respiratory Syndrome 重

症急性呼吸道综合征,"非典")

19. If online learning technology can play a role here, it is incumbent upon all of us to explore its full potential. — 如果在线学习的技术能够在这方面发挥作用,我们所有人都有责任探索它的全部潜力。(incumbent upon/on sb — necessary as part of sb's duties)

IV. Language Features

类 比 构 词

本文中有以下一句:
I will stick to Lark even after coronavirus. I believe traditional offline learning and e-learning can go hand in hand.

这一句中,offline(离线)是根据online(在线)类比构成的新词。在英语报刊上有时还会见到根据online learning类比构成的on-ground learning(教室学习)。

英语报刊中常常见到用类比方法构成的新词,了解这些词的构成规律对判读新词、提高外刊理解能力十分有益。类比构词大致有以下五种:

1. 数字类比

英语中原先的the three R's是指reading, writing, arithmetic,这是美国人人皆知的读、写、算三种能力。美国新的童子军手册根据新形势写入新的the three R's,要求童子军对同性恋行为做到"Recognize, Resist and Report",即"识别、抵制、报告",这对孩子们而言既独特新颖,又易于记忆。数字类比构词许多是不变数字只变被修饰语,如:由日语进入英语的the three K's,即kitanai(dirty), kitsai(hard), kiken(dangerous),指脏、累、险的三种工作;the first daughter(第一女儿,总统的女儿),the first cat(第一猫咪,白宫主人的猫)。

数字类比第二种情况是变动数字,但不变修饰语,如the Fourth World(指十分落后的发展中国家)是由the First World, the Second World, the Third World模仿而成的词,再如the Second Lady(第二夫人,副总统夫人)是由the First Lady类比而成的词。

2. 反义类比

这种类比是采用现有词的反义词构成的词,如由baby boomer("婴儿潮代"人)构成baby buster(出生低谷代人);由moonlight(晚上兼职)构成daylight(白天兼职);由high-tech(高技术的)构成low-tech(低技术的)。

3. 近似类比

这是根据相似之处而类比生成的词,如missile gap(导弹差距)类比构成generation gap(代沟)和credibility gap(信用差距);由breathalyzer(呼吸测醉器)类比构成eyelyzer(眼部测醉器)。

4. 地点空间类比

这是通过不同地点空间的词而类比生成的新词,如由landscape生成的moonscape(月面景色),cityscape(城市景色);由ghost town(被废弃的城镇)类比生成ghost site(被废弃的网址)。

5. 色彩类比

这是通过表示不同色彩的词类比所产生的新词。譬如由 blue-collar workers(蓝领工人)或 white-collar workers(白领工人)类比出 grey-collar workers(灰领工人,指维修工),pink-collar workers(粉领工人,指护士、文书等职业妇女)。最近又出现 steel-collar workers(钢领工人,指机器人),open-collar workers(开领工人,指电脑联勤族)。

V. Analysis of Content

1. According to the article, the world's most highly valued edtech company is _____.
   A. Lark
   B. Coursera
   C. Ding Talk
   D. BYJU'S

2. Which of the following is NOT listed as a factor in the differences of online education?
   A. Different age groups.
   B. Different income groups.
   C. Different countries.
   D. Different school districts.

3. Which of the following statements about online education is FALSE?
   A. The unplanned and rapid move to online learning might result in a poor user experience.
   B. Before the COVID pandemic, online education did not receive much attention.
   C. On average, students retain more material when learning online compared with learning in a classroom.
   D. E-learning requires less time to learn than in a traditional classroom setting.

4. Which of the following is NOT the author's view about the effects of the pandemic on education?
   A. It has changed education forever.
   B. It has brought about a significant surge in online education usage.
   C. It has utterly disrupted the education system.
   D. It has made the education system lose its relevance.

5. The article is _____.
   A. a book review
   B. a straight news report
   C. a feature article
   D. a news commentary

VI. Questions on the Article

1. How many children in the world are affected by school closures due to the pandemic?
2. Did technology promote education in some way before the pandemic?
3. How did many online learning platforms respond to the market after the pandemic?

4. What accounts for a 200% increase in the number of new students using the product made by BYJU'S?
5. What did DingTalk do to support large-scale online learning?
6. What is BBC doing for online education?
7. What does the new hybrid model of education in Paragraph 9 refer to?
8. Is online education suitable for universities?
9. What are the benefits of e-learning according to Dr Amjad?
10. How are the prospects of online education?

VII. Topics for Discussion

1. Which is more effective, classroom education or online education?
2. What changes, do you think, the move to online education will bring about?

Lesson 20

Time to Get Moving

Do you have to run an hour a day or is a 30-minute walk enough?
Experts are looking for new ways to help you shape up.

By Claudia Kalb

Karen Mayes, 45, is no marathoner, but she's in excellent shape. Almost every day for the last 10 years, Mayes has walked up and down the hills in her tree-lined neighborhood in Cleveland Heights, Ohio.[1] A few years ago she added a Pilates class to tone her muscles.[2] "My goal is to still be able to do things when I'm 80," she says. Even over the holidays, Mayes trooped through snow and ice for a payoff she knew she could count on.[3] "I feel better, sleep better, eat better and look better," she says. "Exercise is a great thing."

If only the rest of the world felt the same way. Unfortunately, too many of us sit for hours at desk jobs, relying on e-mail, cell phones and, when we finally get home, the TV remote. Technology has fast-forwarded our minds, but slowed our bodies—and dangerously so. One in four adults in America leads a completely sedentary lifestyle and more than 60 percent of the population doesn't do enough physical activity to gain vast health benefits, chief among them a dramatic drop in the risk of dying prematurely[4].

We all know we should exercise. But we're too busy and too tired. And we're also increasingly confused: How much is necessary? Is it 60 minutes (gasp!) most days of the week, as the Institute of Medicine suggested last fall? Or 30 minutes? Three days a week or five? Running or mall walking? Researchers are attacking those questions and they're delving even further into how physical activity affects our bodies at the molecular level.[5] No matter how far the science goes, though, there's one finding that will remain indisputable: any amount of exercise is better than none. "Being active and fit is good for you whether you're young or old, man or woman, tall or short, skinny or fat," says Steven Blair, president of the Cooper Institute in Dallas, a health-research group.

That's not a revelation. Scientists dating back to Hippocrates[6] have known that exercise bolsters health. But it wasn't until the mid-20th century that data about the specific benefits of physical activity began building to what is now a breathtaking list[7]: lower cholesterol and blood pressure; a reduced risk of heart disease, stroke, osteoporosis, diabetes and colon cancer; strengthening of bones, joints and muscle, and an improvement in anxiety and depression.

The population's sedentary habits have led U.S. public-health officials to pursue a dramatic shift in exercise recommendations in the mid-1990s. For years, the emphasis had been on getting the heart revved at least three times a week through vigorous aerobic activity like running, as recommended by the American College of Sports Medicine in 1978.[8] But as it became increasingly clear that only a sliver of the population was actually going to leap up and start sprinting, researchers realized there was an urgent need to scale back expectations. In 1996, the U.S. surgeon general[9] issued a landmark report on physical activity and a bold new directive: at least 30 minutes of moderate-intensity exercise—the kind you can fit into your daily routine, like brisk walking, bicycling and gardening—on all or most days of the week. Rather than get a handful of people superfit, officials theorized, let's get the masses up and moving.

Still, vigorous exercise may offer even greater benefits than moderate-intensity activity. In a study published in *The Journal of the American Medical Association*[10] in October, Harvard researchers found that men who ran for an hour or more each week reduced their risk of heart disease by 42 percent compared with nonrunners. Men who walked briskly for more than half an hour per day had an 18 percent reduction, and the faster their pace, the greater the drop in risk. "The more you do, the less heart disease you're going to have," says study coauthor Dr. Mihaela Tanasescu.

For those who are already active, picking up the pace is a worthy goal. But right now, experts are focused on the positive and growing links between exercising more often at a moderate pace and good health. In a study of 73,743 postmenopausal women published in September, researchers led by Dr. JoAnn Manson, chief of preventative medicine at Harvard's Brigham and Women's Hospital, found that women cut their risk of heart disease by 30 to 40 percent whether they exercised vigorously in sports like jogging, swimming and aerobics or walked briskly for 30 minutes a day. "The important question is, does moderate-intensity exercise provide benefit? And the answer to that is an unqualified yes," says Blair. If everyone walked briskly for 30 minutes a day, he says, "the public-health battle would be won."

So where does the 60-minute recommendation fit in?[11] When it was issued in September, the Institute of Medicine report seemed to fly in the face of the surgeon general's guidelines[12], but the two may not be quite as incompatible as they seem. The 30 minutes is aimed at reducing the risk of chronic disease in the future. The 60 minutes, on the other hand, is paired with dietary recommendations and focuses on weight control in the present. Researchers found that among healthy people with a body mass index[13] (a ratio of weight to height) of less than 25 (within 18.5 to 25 being desirable), 60 minutes of physical activity was necessary to maintain body weight and avoid excess gain. But the finding should not negate what the CDC[14] recommends, says Dr. Ben Caballero, who was a member of the Institute of Medicine panel and is director of the Center for Human Nutrition at Johns Hopkins school of public health. The two guidelines, he says, "are complementary."

If you've made it to even half an hour a day, congratulations. You're near the top of a very small heap. You deserve a big glass of water. The rest of us, however, need a kick. Start by setting realistic goals. Don't focus on weight loss; reducing your dietary intake will help a lot more in that department. Think instead about your health, which will improve no matter how much you weigh and whether or not you lose any pounds. If you're investing in your first pair of athletic shoes, walk for a few minutes a day until you walk up to 30 or more. A brisk pace is critical: to get the full health benefits, you should feel your heart beat faster, your breath quicken, your sweat drip. Consider using a pedometer, which tracks the number of steps you take per day, and aim for 10,000. Make physical activity part of your daily routine (no, you don't have to go to a gym), and make it a priority. And yes, you can accumulate that half hour throughout the day. Studies have shown that exercising in three 10-minute sessions is comparable to a workout in 30 minutes all at once. "Whether it's walking to work, walking a little extra after you park the car or doing planned exercise, everything counts," says the CDC's Dr. Michael Pratt.

Any exercise program should also include resistance training for 20 minutes three times a week, using weights or exercise bands, or doing push-ups or squats.[15] Weight training increase muscles and improves bone density—critical for baby boomers who'd rather bungee-jump than use a walker.[16] "There's no other way you retain muscle mass and strength," says William Haskell, an exercise specialist at the Stanford School of Medicine. Better strength also means fewer falls, which are the leading cause of death from injury in people older than 65.

Even with all the evidence that has accumulated, researchers are continuing to dig deeper into the connection between exercise and the body, and at an even more microscopic level. A study led by Duke University researchers published in November zeroed in on the precise changes in cholesterol after exercise. Researchers found that over-weight, sedentary people who were assigned weekly exercise programs produced more and larger HDL[17] particles (the good kind of cholesterol) and fewer LDL particles (the bad) than those who did no exercise. Other researchers are looking at how cells activated during exercise regulate glucose, a critical link in the onset of diabetes.[18] And scientists like Frank Booth, of the University of Missouri-Columbia, are examining the genetic underpinnings. Booth believes humans were programmed to be physically active: our genes, in other words, expect us to be moving. By becoming sedentary, he says, we've messed with the blueprint and are now suffering the consequences of disease. Rather than study the benefits of doing some exercise, Booth is waging war against the detrimental effects of doing none.

As the science gets more finely tuned[19], doctors may one day be able to prescribe a specific dose of exercise at a specific intensity for a specific condition, says Duke's Dr. Bill Kraus: a 25-year-old who wants to get fit, for example, versus a 55-year-old with high cholesterol or a 70-year-old diabetic. Behavioral researchers are also looking hard at how to get people better motivated, one of the greatest challenges in the field. And others are studying the design of suburbs, cities and schools (are there sidewalks or bike paths?), figuring out how to fit exercise more naturally into our daily lives.

In the meantime, it's up to you. If you're not bounding off the couch by now, consider two more pieces of data: a recent Stanford study of more than 6,000 men found that tolerance for exercise (tested on a treadmill) was a stronger predictor of risk of death than high blood pressure, smoking, disease, high cholesterol and heart disease. And, finally, in the study of 73,743 women, just sitting for longer periods of time predicted an increased risk of cardiovascular disease[20]. Heart disease, by the way, is the nation's No. 1 killer. So, stand up. And get moving.

From *Newsweek*, January 20, 2003

I. New Words

cholesterol	[kəˈlestərəul]	n.	胆固醇
colon	[ˈkəulən]	n.	结肠
complementary	[ˌkɔmpliˈmentəri]	adj.	combining well to form a balanced whole
diabetes	[ˌdaiəˈbi:ti:z]	n.	糖尿病
detrimental	[ˌdetriˈmentəl]	adj.	causing harm or damage
dose	[dəus]	n.	prescribed amount of medication
fast-forward	[ˌfɑ:stˈfɔ:wəd]	v.	to move forward quickly
glucose	[ˈglu:kəus]	n.	[生化]葡萄糖
guideline	[ˈgaidlain]	n.	an official recommendation
incompatible	[ˌinkəmˈpætəbl]	adj.	unable to cooperate or coexist
marathoner	[ˈmærəθɔnə]	n.	马拉松赛跑者
microscopic	[ˌmaikrəˈskɔpik]	adj.	thorough and detailed
molecular	[məuˈlekjulə]	adj.	分子的
osteoporosis	[ˌɔstiəupɔ:ˈrəusis]	n.	骨质疏松症
particle	[ˈpɑ:tikl]	n.	basic unit of matter
payoff	[ˈpeiɔf]	n.	payment or fruit of doing sth
pedometer	[piˈdɔmitə]	n.	计步器
rev	[rev]	v.	to make an engine go faster
revelation	[ˌrevəˈleiʃən]	n.	information that is newly disclosed, especially surprising
sedentary	[ˈsedəntəri]	adj.	involving a lot of sitting and correspondingly little exercise
sliver	[ˈslivə]	n.	a small narrow piece
sprint	[sprint]	v.	to run, swim, or cycle as rapidly as possible
stroke	[strəuk]	n.	中风
treadmill	[ˈtredmil]	n.	跑步机
underpinning	[ˌʌndəˈpiniŋ]	n.	基础；根据
unqualified	[ʌnˈkwɔlifaid]	adj.	total, unlimited or complete

II. Background Information

健康意识

美国人工作、生活条件优越,许多人的工作是坐在办公室操作电脑,出门购物、上班、下班以车代步。回到家中,丢下饭碗,电视迷(couch potatoes)便轻松地往柔软的沙发上一坐,长时间看起电视来,嘴里没完没了吃着爆米花、甜点,喝着啤酒、果汁和可乐。美国人室内、室外要干的许多活由机器代劳，车房开关用遥控，草坪修整用割草机（lawn-mower）、扫雪用扫雪机（snowblower），室内打扫卫生用吸尘器（vacuum cleaner），洗碗刷碟用洗碗机（dishwasher）。

由于饮食过剩，缺乏运动，许多美国人身体肥胖。然而，肥胖不仅使体态臃肿、行动不便、有损体形，而且导致了一系列身体疾病。其中最为突出的是心脏病，它已成为美国人第一死亡因素。

20世纪90年代末美国政府提出新的健康体重标准。根据这一标准，美国成年人有9700万，近55%的成年人体重超标，属于不健康范畴。肥胖问题引起了社会关注，许多医疗保健专家呼吁："美国人，增进健康。"(Shape up, America.)

近些年来，伴随医疗保健知识的普及，美国人的健康意识（health consciousness）不断增强，比较注重食品的选择和健身运动。

调查显示，美国有93%的消费者表示十分关心或比较关心食品成分。为了迎合人们对健康饮食的关切心理，美国联邦食品药物局规定，市场出售的食品必须注明营养成分、所含脂肪和纤维量。不少美国人在选购食品时挑选低脂（low-fat）、低卡（low-calorie）、低钠（low-sodium）、无糖（sugar-free）、高纤维（high-fiber）、清淡（light）的食物。高糖、高热量、高脂食品被人们称作"垃圾食品"（junk food）。比较讲究的美国人减少用糖、用盐量，挑选低卡甜味剂（low-cal sweetener）、盐代用品（salt substitute）、低脂牛奶（low-fat milk）、脱脂牛奶（skimmed milk）、无卡饮料（no-cal drink）。有些美国人喜爱素食式生活（vegetarian mode of life）。

许多美国人加入健身行列。时下最热门的运动是慢跑（jogging）和快走。他们三五成群定时沿着林荫大道而行。一些年长者喜爱在宽阔的超市里行走（mall walking），那里全年温度合宜，又比较安全。经济状况较好者喜欢去健身馆（gym），那里提供各种运动器械，还有专人指导。不少人参加健美运动（body building exercise），既锻炼体质，又健美身姿。周末，美国人纷纷远离喧嚣都市，去往风光秀丽的景区，徒步旅行，呼吸新鲜空气，缓解心理压力。一些人成了背包客（backpackers），他们背着行囊，穿越丛林，登山、攀岩、野营、漂流、划船，经受体力的锻炼、意志的磨炼。假期里，许许多多美国人涌向海边，年轻者喜爱冲浪、潜水、帆船、划船运动，年长者喜爱海边步行和驾艇航行。

III. Notes to the Text

1. Mayes has walked up and down the hills in her tree-lined neighborhood in Cleveland Heights, Ohio.——梅斯每天沿着俄亥俄州的克利夫兰高地居住区的林阴山道来来回回地走。

2. A few years ago she added a Pilates class to tone her muscles.——几年前，她又参加了"普拉提"健身课程锻炼肌肉。(① Pilates class — The Pilates method is a program that improves muscle control, flexibility, coordination, strength and tone through physical and mental conditioning; ② tone — to improve the strength and firmness)

3. Even over the holidays, Mayes trooped through snow and ice for a payoff she knew she could

count on. — 即使是假期,梅斯仍然与其他人结伴在冰雪中步行,她相信这样做有益。(① troop—to walk together as a group; ② payoff — the good result of a series of actions; ③ count on — to be certain of sth)

4. chief among them a dramatic drop in the risk of dying prematurely— 主要好处就是大大降低过早死亡的危险。(① them — referring to vast health benefits; ② prematurely — too early)

5. Researchers are attacking those questions and they're delving even further into how physical activity affects our bodies at the molecular level. — 研究者正在努力攻克那些问题,进一步探讨体育锻炼是怎样影响我们的身体细胞。(delve into—to search deeply and laboriously into)

6. Hippocrates — 希波克拉底(约公元前460 — 前370年,古希腊名医,被称为医学之父)

7. But it wasn't until the mid-20th century that data ... what is now a breathtaking list... — 但是直到20世纪中期才发现有关锻炼身体具体益处的资料多得令人吃惊,可列出以下一大串

8. For years, the emphasis had been on getting the heart revved at least three times a week through vigorous aerobic activity like running, as recommended by the American College of Sports Medicine in 1978.— 几年来,强调的重点是按美国运动医学协会所建议的那样,每周至少三次,通过跑步之类的强劲有氧运动加快心脏的跳动。(rev—to make an engine go faster)

9. the U.S. surgeon general — 美国卫生局局长

10. *The Journal of the American Medical Association* —《美国医疗协会杂志》

11. So where does the 60-minute recommendation fit in? — 这个运动60分钟的建议在哪些方面(与原先的建议)是一致的?(fit in — to be similar)

12. fly in the face of the surgeon general's guidelines — to be contrary to the surgeon general's guidelines

13. body mass index — 体重指数 (a measure which takes into account body weight and height to gauge total body fat in adults. Under the guidelines, people with a BMI of 25 to 29.9 are considered overweight.)

14. CDC — Centers for Disease Control 疾病控制中心

15. Any exercise program should also include resistance training for 20 minutes three times a week, using weights or exercise bands, or doing push-ups or squats. — 任何运动项目都应该包括每星期三次的20分钟抗阻力锻炼,可以负重或使用运动带,或者做俯卧撑或下蹲运动。(exercise band — 运动弹力带。注:由橡胶制成,根据松紧程度分为几种等级,用颜色标示,主要用于锻炼肌肉。)

16. ... critical for baby boomers who'd rather bungee-jump than use a walker. — 这对于婴儿潮代人来说非常重要,他们宁可玩蹦极也不愿走路。(①bungee-jump — dive with a safety rope; ② critical — very important; ③ walker—shoe for walking)

17. HDL — high-density lipoprotein[生化]高密度脂蛋白; LDL — low-density lipoprotein[生化]低密度脂蛋白

18. Other researchers are looking at how cells activated during exercise regulate glucose, a critical link in the onset of diabetes. — 其他研究者正在研究运动过程中激活的细胞如何控制血糖,这是防止糖尿病发作的关键一环。

19. As the science gets more finely tuned... — 随着科学分工越来越精密细微(finely tuned — developed in such a precise way as to take into consideration all the specific conditions)

20. cardiovascular disease — 心血管疾病

IV. Language Features

《新闻周刊》介绍

《新闻周刊》(*Newsweek*)原名为 *News-Week*,是新闻企业家托马斯·马丁(Thomas John Martyn)于1933年创办的。它模仿《时代》周刊,将一周国内外大事分门别类加以综合叙述。1937年,该刊与《今日》(*Today*)杂志合并,取消原名连字符,更名为 *Newsweek*。

1961年,《新闻周刊》转手给华盛顿邮报公司(The Washington Post Company)。易手之后,资金投入增多,编辑队伍充实,竞争力量加强。目前每期发行量为300万份左右,在美国三大新闻周刊中名列第二。

近些年来,在电子媒体的强大冲击下,《新闻周刊》与其他报刊一样,广告收入急剧减少。为了扭亏为盈,该刊裁减了四分之一的员工。除此之外,该刊还采取了几项新的措施。为了迎合网络新闻时新性强的优势,该刊更加突出观点和评论,更多依赖知名度高的记者和专栏作家撰写文章,该刊对其读者群重新定位,缩小了读者订阅规模。2008年初,订阅量从以前的310万减少到260万,2009年7月又进一步缩减到190万。杂志提高了订阅价格,受众定位在中上层。改版后的《新闻周刊》党派倾向性更为明显。为此,杂志又丢失了不少读者。

这些措施均未改变杂志的亏损局面。2008年财务数据显示该年度亏损为1610万美元,2009年亏损额升至2930万美元。2010年8月2日华盛顿邮报公司决定将该刊出售给音响制造商悉尼·哈曼(Sidney Harman)。后又经过3个月的协商,《新闻周刊》于11月份与新闻网站 The Daily Beast 合并。原网站总编 Tina Brocon 兼任该刊主编。

2011年3月《新闻周刊》版面做了新的调整。新版共设5大版块:1.专栏版(Columns)。该版刊登专栏作家、编辑和特邀作者的文章,一般篇幅较短。2.野兽新闻版(NewsBeast)。该版体现美国每日野兽网站(The Daily Beast)特色,刊登可供读者快速阅读的简洁明快的新闻报道、新闻人物访谈和具有网站风格的鲜明图表。3.特写版(Features)。该版所占篇幅较多,刊登体现原《新闻周刊》特色的详细报道、解释性报道和新闻特写。4.杂色新闻版(Omnivore)。该版刊登艺术、音乐、书籍、影视、戏剧、饮食、旅游等专题的报道和评论。5.其他内容版(Plus)。该版刊登读者来信、历史回忆和城市介绍。

从2013年开始该刊停止发行纸质版,只发行电子版,其网址是 www.newsweek.com。

V. Analysis of Content

1. According to the article, _____ of American adults now lead a completely sedentary lifestyle.

   A. 25 percent   B. 60 percent   C. 40 percent   D. half

2. What led the U.S. public-health officials to pursue a dramatic shift in exercise recommendations was _____.

   A. the public pressure

   B. the American government's influence

   C. the doctors' advice

   D. the population's sedentary habits

3. From the article we know that the number one killer in America is _____.

   A. cancer   B. heart disease

   C. kidney trouble   D. violent crime

4. Weight training can help people to _____.

   A. control weight

   B. improve bone density

   C. improve the shape

   D. build up endurance

5. Blair believes that the public-health battle would be won if everyone _____.

   A. ran for 60 minutes a day

   B. walked briskly for half an hour a day

   C. did high-intensity exercise for an hour a day

   D. had resistance training every day

VI. Questions on the Article

1. What kind of lifestyle do many Americans lead today?
2. What is the indisputable finding about physical exercise?
3. What do the data show about the health benefits of physical exercise?
4. According to Dr. Ben Caballero, what kind of relationship exists between the two guidelines for physical exercise?
5. What are the author's suggestions concerning physical exercise?
6. Why do people need resistance training? What kind of exercise provides resistance training?
7. What are the behavioral researchers trying to do?

VII. Topics for Discussion

1. Is obesity the inevitable result of modern life?
2. Are modern conveniences to blame for the health problems in the present-day society?

Unit 7
第七单元　企业经济

Lesson 21

Thinking Outside the Box[1]

(Abridged)
As American shoppers move online, Walmart fights to defend its dominance.

THERE is little outward sign that Walmart's "supercentre" in Rogers[2], Arkansas differs from any other of the giant retailer's outlets. Walmart conquered America with such "big box" stores—vast concrete blocks in an ocean of parking spaces. Inside stretches aisle upon aisle of merchandise. But this particular store, near Walmart's headquarters in Bentonville[3], is different. It is where the world's biggest retailer hones some of the new ideas which, it hopes, will help it keep its crown.

Recently the company has had lots of such brainwaves, from vegetables in plastic bins etched to look like wood, to wands that let customers scan items as they shop, thereby speeding up checkout.[4] They are part of a multibillion-dollar bid to keep thriving as America's retail industry is upended.[5] And for the first time in decades, it is not Walmart that is doing the upending.

Since April share prices for some of America's best-known retailers, including Macy's[6] and Gap[7], have plunged by more than 25%. Some of their problems are fleeting, but one is not. Rather than driving to a big box, many Americans are shopping online instead. American e-commerce accounted for 10.4% of retail sales last year, up from 9.3% in 2014, according to Morgan Stanley[8], a bank. Amazon[9] is the force behind this, with sales in North America rising by nearly 30% in 2015. The choice for bricks-and-mortar retailers is clear: evolve or decline.[10]

Amid this tumult Walmart remains a titan. It is not just the world's biggest retailer but also its largest private employer and company, measured by revenue. Last year it raked in $482 billion. Walmart's empire is global, but America is its particular dominion, accounting for three-quarters of its sales. And on home turf Walmart still towers above Amazon, accounting for 10.6% of America's retail sales, more than twice Amazon's share, according to Cowen[11], a financial-services firm. Yet Amazon is still growing fast, and Walmart may be past its peak. In 2009 Walmart commanded 11.6% of American retail sales. By 2018 Cowen reckons its share will be stuck at 10.6%, whereas Amazon's will have jumped.[12]

Walmart is spending furiously to fight back against Amazon's online onslaught. "We will win with a strategy that only Walmart can execute," Doug McMillon, its chief executive, said in his annual letter to shareholders, shoppers and staff. To that end, Walmart is spending $2.7 billion to raise workers' wages, which should improve service in its shops. It will devote more than $1 billion to e-commerce this year. Last year it poured a staggering $10.5 billion into information technology, more than any other company on the planet, according to an estimate by the International Data Corporation[13], a research firm.

These investments have squeezed profits, but the firm is banking on growth.[14] Walmart's leaders aim to prove that an old-fashioned retailer can continue to dominate in the age of e-commerce. Walmart may show how to merge physical and online retail. It is sure to boast of its progress at its annual meeting on June 3rd: it was one of the few American retailers to post cheering first-quarter results in May. Yet its reign as undisputed retail champion is over.[15]

Since Sam Walton opened his first shop over five decades ago, the firm has thrived with a simple strategy, zealously executed: operate with the lowest costs, sell at the cheapest prices and watch sales grow. The success of this formula has given Walmart a unique place in America's economy as well as its psyche.[16]

Clicks versus bricks[17]

The challenge for Walmart, and for all other retailers in the e-commerce era, is to protect both sales and profits. But these goals nay (**may**) be mutually exclusive. Retailers face pressure to offer both free shipping and competitive prices, which generally makes selling a product online less profitable than doing so in existing stores. To expand sales online, retailers must spend on technology, which squeezes margins further. Making matters even worse, retailers are often not gaining new customers but simply selling the same item to the same person online for less profit. "You pour from one bucket into a less profitable bucket," explains Simeon Gutman of Morgan Stanley.

This makes stores themselves less productive, creating yet another dilemma. America has more retail space per person than any other country and double the amount of Australia, the next-closest market. As e-commerce sales rise, some retailers may need to cut their networks down to size. Yet stores still account for the vast majority of retailers' sales. Closing underperforming shops may end up sending consumers to competitors' shops—or to Amazon.

Walmart itself is bolting some doors for the last time. In January it said it would shut 269 shops worldwide, including 154 in America. That is a small fraction of the total. Most closures were not of supercentres but of "express" shops, an ill-fated try at running small convenience stores. Companies specialising in smaller formats, such as Aldi[18] and Dollar General[19], are growing quickly. Walmart is keeping its medium-sized grocery stores but dumped its express shops this year.

Its plans, to the surprise of some investors, include opening up to 60 supercentres and 95 grocery stores this year. The addition of another 10m square feet of retail space is a slower pace of expansion, but is still almost as much as the combined additions planned by the 23 other big American retailers that Morgan Stanley monitors. Faced with a rapidly changing market, Walmart is trying to do what it has always done best: grow.

It is building more stores because, instead of reinventing itself, it wants to carry on offering more goods at low prices to more consumers, more conveniently. "The best thing you can do is always something that makes what you already do better," explains Neil Ashe, head of Walmart's e-commerce effort. That means making its operations more expansive and efficient by combining Walmart's growing number of physical assets, including its logistics network and more than 5,200 American stores, with a growing e-commerce business and array of new digital and analytical tools.

To that end its e-commerce hub is not in Bentonville but San Bruno[20], California, which has more tech talent. Walmart has built a new technology platform, changing everything from how its website works to how the company manages customer payments and analyses data. The flurry of activity in San Bruno has helped Walmart.com's selection rise from 2m items less than four years ago to over 10m today.

Walmart is scrutinising the minutiae of e-commerce as closely as it monitors every aspect of its business. For example, in the past year Walmart has combed through data to learn how to pack its boxes more efficiently. Using 27 different boxes rather than the 12 they use now, the company has concluded, would lower the total volume of boxes shipped by about one-third. Packing more into each lorry could save fuel and 7.2m cubic feet of space taken up by cardboard boxes, enough to fill about 82 Olympic swimming pools.

Walmart's main differentiator online, however, may be its stores. It is combining sales figures from its shops and data from its website to discern which goods to keep where; its algorithms weigh up billions of variables.[21] Like Amazon before it, the company is building large warehouses to serve its e-commerce business, but it is also shipping products from store distribution centres and from stores themselves. It is letting customers buy online, then collect from stores at no charge.

Some of these strategies are not unique to Walmart, but its scale and logistical skills help the company implement them better than others. For example, Walmart is already expert at the complexities of handling perishable items. It has tried delivering groceries, but is expanding a pickup service instead, betting that this will be both convenient for shoppers and profitable for the company. Such a service may work especially well in America's sprawling suburbs, where delivery would be expensive. In Rogers, online shoppers park in special bays and their Walmart app signals their arrival. Staff roll out crates of groceries, load them briskly into the waiting vehicles and send shoppers on their way.

As for the stores themselves, Walmart is trying to boost sales by making them more attractive, easier places to visit. The company raised its minimum wage to $10 this year, as part of an effort to improve customer service. In Rogers, signs for different departments are easier to read. Customers can use an app to pinpoint this salsa or that pram, view an expanded selection online and, as of this summer, pay for them.

Store operations continue to get better. Staff are armed with hand-held devices with apps to simplify common tasks, like managing inventory. The company fretted that bakers were leaving too much icing at the bottom of tubs, so Walmart gave them new scrapers. The company reckons this will save more than 35 lorryloads of buttercream icing each year.

These efforts are likely to intensify but may not do enough to keep it in the lead.[22] Walmart says that customers who shop both in stores and online spend more than those who shop only in stores. Yet the e-commerce business is not growing as quickly as the company would like. Its sales in the first quarter of this year rose by 7% globally. American online sales were slightly better, but the company will not say by how much. Meanwhile, Amazon's North American e-commerce sales jumped by 27%.

Get serious

Even as Walmart pushes forward, it is in the unfamiliar position of trying to catch up.[23] As Amazon Prime[24] offers more functions, Walmart is still testing a $49 annual fee for free delivery. The shipping costs and technology investments required by e-commerce may make Walmart less profitable in the long term. So would the decline of the mighty supercentre, which is showing signs of age. In the most recent quarter sales at Walmart's medium-sized, less profitable grocery stores rose seven times as fast as the broader American business.

The most troubling change (**question**) would be if the company's virtuous cycle of scale and low prices were to start breaking down.[25] In October Walmart said it would cut its prices, beginning this year. The company is confident that this will propel sales higher—as low prices have for more than 50 years. However, Mr Fassler of Goldman Sachs[26] argues that competitors' low prices and shoppers' preference for convenience may mean that its familiar trick will not boost market share as it once did. Walmart conquered America with its big boxes. It must now contend with millions of small ones, piled high on America's doorsteps.

From *The Economist*, June 4, 2016

I. New Words

array	[əˈrei]	n.	一系列
bet	[bet]	v.	断定, 确信
bid	[bid]	n.	努力, 尝试
briskly	[ˈbriskli]	adv.	轻快地
command	[kəˈmɑːnd]	v.	占据, 拥有
crate	[kreit]	n.	板条箱
differentiator	[difəˈrenʃieitə]	n.	不同之处
dominion	[dəˈminjən]	n.	the land held in complete control by a ruler
dump	[dʌmp]	v.	to get rid of
fleeting	[ˈfliːtiŋ]	adj.	lasting for only a short time
flurry	[ˈflʌri]	n.	a sudden burst of intense activity
fraction	[ˈfrækʃən]	n.	小部分, 微量
fret	[fret]	v.	to be worried about sth
hone	[həun]	v.	磨炼 (技术等)
hub	[hʌb]	n.	the central or main part of sth

ill-fated	[ilˈfeitid]	adj.	注定要遭厄运的
implement	[ˈimpliment]	v.	实行,实施
intensify	[inˈtensifai]	v.	增强,加剧
inventory	[ˈinvəntəri]	n.	(商品等的)目录,存货清单
logistics	[ləˈdʒistiks]	n.	后勤,物流
margin	[ˈmɑ:dʒin]	n.	盈余,利润
merge	[mə:dʒ]	v.	(使)合并
minutiae	[maiˈnju:ʃii:]	n.	very small details
onslaught	[ˈɔnslɔ:t]	n.	a fierce attack
outlet	[ˈautlet]	n.	零售店,经销店
perishable	[ˈperiʃəbəl]	adj.	(食物)易坏的
pinpoint	[ˈpinpɔint]	v.	to locate or identify with precision
plunge	[plʌndʒ]	v.	to (cause to) move suddenly downwards
pram	[præm]	n.	童车,婴儿车
rake	[reik]	v.	~ in to earn a lot of money
reinvent	[ri:inˈvent]	v.	再发明,重新创造
revenue	[ˈrevinju:]	n.	收入,收益
salsa	[ˈsælsə]	n.	(墨西哥烹饪中的辣味)沙司,调味汁
scraper	[ˈskreipə]	n.	刮刀
scrutinise	[ˈskru:tinaiz]	v.	仔细或彻底检查
sprawling	[ˈsprɔ:liŋ]	adj.	(都市、街道等)不规则扩张或延伸的
titan	[ˈtaitn]	n.	*literary* a person who is very large, powerful, intelligent or important
turf	[tə:f]	n.	*AmE slang* an area claimed by a group as its own
zealously	[ˈzeləsli]	adv.	热心地,积极地

II. Background Information

沃尔玛公司当今面临的挑战

　　沃尔玛百货有限公司由山姆·沃尔顿于1962年在阿肯色州创立。经过五十多年的发展,它已成为世界上最大的连锁零售企业,多次荣登《财富》世界500强排行榜榜首。目前,沃尔玛在美国50个州和全球15个国家开设了近8500家商场和门店,雇佣员工人数210多万。

　　沃尔玛的成功之道有以下五点:

　　1. 低价经营策略。从进货渠道、分销方式以及营销费用、行政开支等方面,沃尔玛都想尽一切办法节省资金,提出"天天平价、始终如一"的口号,努力实现价格比其他商店更便宜的承诺。

2. 品牌经营策略。沃尔玛选择了多种零售形式以针对不同层次的目标消费者。正是由于沃尔玛全方位出击,抢占了高、低档市场,才取代了曾经风靡整个美国的西尔斯,成为零售业第一品牌。

3. 细致周到的服务。沃尔玛经营项目繁多,品种齐全,商品包括肉类果蔬、食品干货、家用电器、服装玩具、化妆用品,为消费者提供"一站式"购物(One-Stop Shopping)的便捷。

4. 快速高效的物流配送中心和"无缝"供应链。

5. 先进的信息技术。沃尔玛通过自己完善的通信网络,随时掌握各个商店的销售、上架、库存状况,做到货物及时配送,了解顾客需求,不断改进服务。

然而,随着互联网和智能移动设备的普及,美国电子商务市场迅猛发展,2020年美国电子商务销售额增长率高达32%。电子商务对传统的实体零售业构成了巨大挑战。

在线购物的方便、便宜、随时、随地、随意的优势,吸引了众多的顾客,尤其是消费力强的年轻群体。全球范围的零售业大洗牌正在上演。在这次巨大浪潮中,巨头沃尔玛首当其冲。

为应对亚马逊等新兴销售模式的冲击,沃尔玛也在不断地调整经营策略,应对挑战。在美国,沃尔玛非常重视发展电子商务,向顾客提供线下线上无缝连接的购物体验。

2012年4月,沃尔玛推出了一种名为"现金支付"(Pay with Cash)的新功能,允许用户在线下单购买商品,然后在附近的沃尔玛实体零售店进行支付。

2015年12月,沃尔玛在官方应用中推出了自己的移动支付服务 Walmart Pay,iOS 和 Android 用户均可使用。

2017年10月,沃尔玛宣布计划对网页进行重新设计,新版网页将侧重电子商务以及其他在线商品交易业务。

此外,沃尔玛还采取措施进一步提高顾客的满意度。

2018年3月15日,在国际消费者权益保护日活动现场,沃尔玛承诺线下实体店无理由退货:实体门店除店内公示的特殊商品及例外情况外,消费者可享受普通商品90天无理由退货。通过种种努力,沃尔玛的销售业绩目前得以维持。

但是,面临电子商务市场的巨大挑战和零售业之间的巨大竞争,沃尔玛能否长期保住其"零售业之王"的地位,还是一个未知数。

III. Notes to the Text

1. Thinking Outside the Box —进行创造性思维(It is a metaphor that means: to think differently, unconventionally, creatively, or from a new perspective.)

2. Rogers —罗杰斯市(a city in northwest Arkansas, the location of the first Walmart store)

3. Bentonville —本顿维尔市(a city in Arkansas, the world headquarters of Walmart)

4. Recently the company has had lots of such brainwaves, from vegetables in plastic bins etched to look like wood, to wands that let customers scan items as they shop, thereby speeding up check-out. —沃尔玛最近采用了很多妙招,如:采用蚀刻得像木料的塑料箱装蔬菜,增设条形码识读电子装置,让顾客边选购边扫描商品价格条形码,从而加快结账速度。[①brainwave—a sudden good idea; ② wand — (设置在商场内、固定在一根铁杆上的商品价格条形码)识读电子装置]

5. They are part of a multibillion-dollar bid to keep thriving as America's retail industry is upended. —这些只是沃尔玛的一项投资数十亿美元的举措的一部分,这项举措的意图是在美国的零售业遭遇颠覆时能保持生意兴隆。(① bid — an effort to do sth; ② upend — to turn sth upside down)

6. Macy's —梅西百货公司(美国一家著名连锁百货公司)

7. Gap —盖璞服装公司(美国最大的服装公司之一)

8. Morgan Stanley —摩根士丹利公司(一家成立于美国纽约的国际金融服务公司)

9. Amazon —亚马逊公司(美国最大的网络电子商务公司)

10. The choice for bricks-and-mortar retailers is clear: evolve or decline. —实体零售商面临的选择很明确:要么发展要么衰退。(bricks-and-mortar — relating to or being a traditional business serving customers in a building as contrasted to an online business)

11. Cowen — 科文公司(美国一家资产管理控股公司,总部位于纽约,通过其子公司为客户提供另类投资管理、投资银行、投资研究和交易的服务)

12. By 2018 Cowen reckons its share will be stuck at 10.6%, whereas Amazon's will have jumped. —科文公司认为,到2018年,沃尔玛的市场份额将停滞在10.6%,而亚马逊的市场份额将大幅提高。(reckon — to think)

13. International Data Corporation — 国际数据公司(一家国际数据集团旗下的全资子公司,是信息技术、电信行业和消费科技市场咨询、顾问和活动服务专业提供商)

14. These investments have squeezed profits, but the firm is banking on growth. —这些投资的确减少了利润,但沃尔玛还是寄希望于发展。(① squeeze — to reduce the amount of money that you can use; ② bank on — to rely on)

15. Yet its reign as undisputed retail champion is over. —然而,其作为毋庸置疑的"零售业之王"的时代已经结束了。(reign — the period during which a king rules)

16. The success of this formula has given Walmart a unique place in America's economy as well as its psyche. —这种运营方式的成功使沃尔玛在美国经济上和美国人的心理上都获得了独一无二的地位。(① formula — a particular method of doing sth; ② psyche — the human mind, soul or spirit)

17. Clicks versus bricks — 线上零售业与实体零售业的对决(这里使用了英语中的借代修辞手法,clicks指代电子商务,bricks指代实体门店。)
18. Aldi — 阿尔迪(德国一家以经营食品为主的连锁超市)
19. Dollar General — 多来店(美国一家日用消费品知名连锁零售店,以价格低廉著称)
20. San Bruno — A city in western California, a residential suburb of San Francisco on San Francisco Bay
21. It is combining sales figures from its shops and data from its website to discern which goods to keep where; its algorithms weigh up billions of variables. — 它将来自门店的数字和网站的数据综合起来分析,用以识别物品的最佳存放地点,其算法确定几十亿个变量的值。(① discern — to know, recognize or understand sth, especially sth that is not obvious; ② algorithm — 算法,规则系统; ③ weigh up — to measure; ④ variable — a number that can vary)
22. These efforts are likely to intensify but may not do enough to keep it in the lead. — 这些努力可能会增强竞争力,但却不一定足够令其保持领先地位。
23. Even as Walmart pushes forward, it is in the unfamiliar position of trying to catch up. — 尽管沃尔玛奋力推进,但它所要赶超的领域是其所不熟悉的领域。
24. Amazon Prime — 亚马逊所提供的一种可以享受特权和优惠的收费会员制(目前美国亚马逊Prime会员每年缴上99美元年费便可享受包邮、提前参加闪购、获得会员折扣等增值服务。)
25. The most troubling change (**question**) would be if the company's virtuous cycle of scale and low prices were to start breaking down.—最令人烦恼的问题是沃尔玛公司的规模大与价格低的良性循环会不会开始失效。(virtuous cycle — a situation that once a good thing starts, other good things happen, which causes the first thing to continue happening)
26. Goldman Sachs — 高盛集团(一家国际领先的投资银行,向全球提供广泛的投资、咨询和金融服务)

IV. Language Features

网络新词

本文中e-commerce(电子商务)意指通过网络购买和销售的过程。互联网的出现和应用不仅给商务活动和社会生活造成巨大影响,而且也导致英语发生变化,促使大批相应新词的出现。

英语中net原先表达的是"网"的意思,在因特网出现后,又常做"因特网"之意。本文标题中net是动词,意思是"使用网络"。除此之外,还有些词在因特网的发展过程中衍生出新意。如web用以表达"万维网",site表示"网站"。值得关注的是,因特网的广泛使用产生了一大批新词。

因特网语言中有几个极具组词能力的前缀和组合语素,如:cyber-, E-, hyper-等,由

它们构成的新词汇层出不穷,以下是一些常用派生词:
1. 由前缀 E- 构成的词
   E-paper 电子报   E-business 电子商务
   E-currency 电子货币   E-book 电子图书
2. 由前缀 hyper- 构成的词
   hyperlink 超链接   hyperaccess 超级访问软件
   hypertext 超文本   hypermedia 超媒体
3. 由组合语素 cyber- 构成的词
   cyberculture 电脑化社会   cybercommunity 电脑界,网络界
   cyber-crime 电脑犯罪,网络犯罪 cyber-friend 网友
   cyberspeak 网络用语   cybernaut 网络用户

在因特网语言中,有三个非常活跃的词:web,net 和 virtual,它们同其他词汇结合后生成了大量的复合词:
1. 由 web 生成的复合词
   websurf 网上漫游   webpage 网页
   webcast 网络播放   webhead 网虫
   webzine 网络杂志
2. 由 net 生成的复合词或拼缀词
   netizen 网民   netspeak 网络用语
   netpreneur 网络企业家   netgroup 网络用户组
   netiquette 网上行为规范
3. 由 virtual 生成的复合词
   virtual library 虚拟图书馆   virtual office 虚拟办公室
   virtual community 虚拟社区   virtual university 虚拟大学

V. Analysis of Content

1. The challenge for Walmart, and for all other retailers in the e-commerce era, is _____.
   A. to make new investments   B. to protect both sales and profits
   C. to expand sales online   D. to improve customer service
2. The reason why Walmart sets its e-commerce hub in San Bruno instead of Bentonville is that ____.
   A. San Bruno has a growing number of physical assets
   B. San Bruno has more tech talent
   C. San Bruno has a better logistics network
   D. San Bruno has more stores
3. Walmart's zealously executed simple strategy is _____.
   A. keeping improving customer service
   B. operating with the lowest costs, selling at the lowest prices and watching sales grow

C. continuous expansion of its stores

D. using advanced technology to improve store operation

4. Which of the following is NOT on the list of measures taken by Walmart to deal with dilemmas?

   A. Further expansion of its stores.

   B. Scrutinizing the minutiae of e-commerce closely.

   C. Better implementation of its strategies through its scale and logistical skill.

   D. A careful study of customers' real needs.

5. The author's view on Walmart's ability to keep its position as undisputed retail champion is ____.

   A. optimistic   B. satirical   C. subjective   D. skeptical

VI. Questions on the Article

1. What did Walmart conquer America with?
2. What is the purpose of Walmart's multibillion-dollar bid?
3. How much market share do Walmart and Amazon have respectively?
4. How much market share will Walmart and Amazon have respectively by 2018, according to Cowen?
5. What are the difficult problems for America's retailers in the e-commerce era?
6. What surprised some investors?
7. Why is Walmart building more stores?
8. What effect does Walmart's new technology platform produce?
9. What is Walmart's main differentiator online?
10. Why is Walmart expanding a pickup service instead of delivery service?
11. What effects have Walmart's efforts produced?
12. What would be the most troubling question?

VII. Topics for Discussion

1. Will online retail business replace traditional retail business?
2. Can Walmart's traditional success strategy help it increase its market share?

Lesson 22

The Lessons of the GM Bankruptcy

Everybody knew that it was ridiculous and unsustainable to pay UAW[1] workers not to work.

By Paul Ingrassia[2]

Today is the first anniversary of one of this country's less-than-crowning milestones[3]: the bankruptcy of General Motors, once the largest and richest company in the country, and indeed the world.

Keeping GM alive, albeit in shrunken form, was an expensive undertaking for America's taxpayers: about $65 billion in all, if one counts government aid to the company's former financial arm, formerly GMAC, now renamed Ally Bank.[4] For all that money we, as a country, should take away some lessons from the experience. The following get my vote for the most important[5]:

Problems denied and solutions delayed will result in a painful and costly day of reckoning.

In corporate governance, the right people count more than the right structure.[6]

Appearances can be deceiving.

All three might sound blindingly obvious[7], but it's amazing how frequently they're ignored. That's especially true for the first lesson, about denial and delay.

Everybody knew that it was ridiculous and unsustainable to pay workers indefinitely not to work (in the United Auto Workers Union's Jobs Bank), to keep brands such as Saturn and Saab[8] that hardly ever made money, and to pay gold-plated pension and health-care benefits to employees. But all of these practices, paid for by mounting debt obligations, continued for decades in GM's 30-year, slow-motion crash.

Yet there were plenty of warnings. A dramatic one came in a January 2006 speech by auto-industry veteran Jerome B. York, who represented the company's largest individual shareholder at the time, Kirk Kerkorian. Unless GM undertook drastic reforms "the unthinkable could happen" within 1,000 days, predicted by York (who died recently). As things turned out, he was a mere 30 days off.

The relevant question looking forward is whether the unthinkable—going broke—also could happen to America.

Everybody knows that we are running unsustainable federal deficits. And that Fannie Mae and Freddie Mac[9] created financial sinkholes by helping lenders make mortgages to people who couldn't afford them. And that many states' public-employee[10] pensions funds are hopelessly underfunded for the level of benefits they provide. And that shoveling more money into the public schools without insisting on structural reforms and accountability hasn't produced results and won't do so in the future.[11]

Addressing these issues inevitably means enforcing spending discipline and standing up to public-employee unions in a way that GM failed to do with the UAW. Continued denial and delay will prove ruinous. To put it another way: America bailed out General Motors, but who will bail out America?

The second lesson is as important as the first, even though the term "corporate governance" sounds about as exciting as, well, dental floss.[12] But good governance is critical because it is private enterprise that creates capital and funds government (though few people in Washington seem to recognize this). What happened at GM, in contrast to its crosstown rival Ford[13], is instructive.

On paper, General Motors was a model of good corporate governance, while Ford was (and is) a disaster. The Ford family's super-voting Class B shares[14] give it 40% of the votes with less than 4% of the shareholder equity. Class B shares get about 31 votes for every share of the Class A stock that nonfamily members own. And the Ford family gets veto power over any corporate merger or dissolution.

This structure seems to fly in the face of what is generally understood to be sound principles of good corporate governance.[15] Such "undemocratic" provisions are sure to be lamented this month at two major corporate-governance conferences: the ODX (Outstanding Directors Exchange)[16] in New York, and the annual confab at the Millstein Center for Corporate Governance at Yale[17].

But the Ford board of directors and family came together in 2006 to seek a new CEO from outside the struggling economy, even though that meant family scion Bill Ford Jr. had to relinquish command. He volunteered to do so and remains chairman, but not CEO. Meanwhile, the GM board, consisting of blue-chip outside directors who chose a "lead director[18]" from their ranks, steadfastly backed an ineffective management from one disaster to another and wrung its collective hands while the company ran out of cash. Some GM retirees dubbed the directors the "board of bystanders."

Ford's governance might be undemocratic. But at least it concentrates decision-making power in the hands of a few people with a significant emotional and financial stake in the company, and they proved willing to act. Absolutely no one on the General Motors board had either such stake, which helps explain why the directors did nothing.

GM's current board—appointed by the company's controlling shareholder, the US government— has a handful of holdovers from the prior board. Maybe they aren't bad people, but they surely showed judgment that was beyond bad.[19] As the new GM prepares for an initial public offering of stock[20]—so that the government can recoup the taxpayer investment—it will need credibility at the board level. The holdover directors should resign.

As for appearances versus facts, the GM bailout—along with the similar exercise at Chrysler[21] —offers ample evidence. The understandable objection to bailouts is that they foster moral hazard, the willingness to act recklessly without fear of consequences. Yet the bailouts of these two companies had painful consequences aplenty for the major actors.

Shareholders of both companies got wiped out. Creditors took major hits, including those who held secured debt at Chrysler. (Their loans to the company were reckless, the equivalent of subprime mortgage loans[22], but they did recover more than they would have in a Chrysler liquidation.) Many workers and executives lost their jobs. Many dealers lost franchises.[23] The Jobs Bank was abolished, albeit belatedly. So was no-cost health insurance.

All this seems plenty of pain to discourage future moral hazard. Letting the companies liquidate would have produced far more pain, of course, but much of it would have fallen on innocent bystanders—the ordinary citizens who participate in an economy that was on its knees[24] last spring. The Obama administration, to its credit, tried to walk a fine line: doing enough for Detroit to protect the economy, but not doing so much to foster future irresponsible behavior.[25]

Nobody on any point of America's political spectrum really liked this bailout.[26] But having paid for it, let's hope that we as a nation are willing to learn from it.

From *The Wall Street Journal*, June 1, 2010

I. New Words

accountability	[əˌkauntəˈbiliti]	n.	负有责任
albeit	[ɔːlˈbiːit]	conj.	*formal* although
ample	[ˈæmpl]	adj.	enough or more than enough
aplenty	[əˈplenti]	adj.	丰富的，大量的
bail	[beil]	v.	~ out to rescue sb from a serious situation
bankruptcy	[ˈbæŋkrəp(t)si]	n.	破产
blue-chip	[ˈbluːtʃip]	adj.	*slang* first-rate
broke	[brəuk]	adj.	*informal* having no money; having to stop doing business
confab	[ˈkɔnfæb]	n.	（某一组织的）成员会议
crash	[kræʃ]	n.	collapse
crosstown	[ˈkrɔstaun]	adj.	位于城市另一边的
dissolution	[disəˈljuːʃən]	n.	分解，解散
equity	[ˈekwiti]	n.	（某公司的）股权，股本
foster	[ˈfɔstə]	v.	to help sth to grow or develop
franchise	[ˈfræntʃaiz]	n.	特许经营权
gold-plated	[ˈɡəuldˌpleitid]	adj.	镀金的；待遇优厚的
governance	[ˈɡʌvənəns]	n.	the act of controlling a company
hazard	[ˈhæzəd]	n.	a danger or a risk
holdover	[ˈhəuldˌəuvə(r)]	n.	留任官员
lament	[ləˈment]	v.	哀悼；为……遗憾
liquidation	[ˌlikwiˈdeiʃən]	n.	清偿（债务等），清算（破产公司）
merger	[ˈməːdʒə]	n.	（公司、企业等）合并
obligation	[ˌɔbliˈɡeiʃən]	n.	债务
provision	[prəˈviʒən]	n.	条文，规定
reckoning	[ˈrekəniŋ]	n.	<喻>算账；惩罚

第七单元　企业经济

recoup	[riˈkuːp]	v.	to get back an amount of money that you've lost
relinquish	[riˈliŋkwiʃ]	v.	to stop having sth especially when this happens unwillingly
ruinous	[ˈruːinəs]	adj.	破坏性的,灾难性的
scion	[ˈsaiən]	n.	富家子孙
shareholder	[ˈʃeəhəuldə]	n.	股票持有人,股东
sinkhole	[ˈsiŋkhəul]	n.	污水池,地面排水沟
underfund	[ˌʌndəˈfʌnd]	v.	对……提供资金不足
unsustainable	[ˌʌnsəsˈteinəbl]	adj.	that cannot be continued at the same level
wring	[riŋ]	v.	~ one's hands　为某事苦恼(或悲痛、绝望地)绞扭双手

II. Background Information

通用汽车公司的破产

　　通用汽车公司发展历程有三大阶段:一、兴盛阶段。公司成立后几十年里迅速崛起成为美国汽车制造业的主力军,20世纪60年代达到最高峰。当时美国销售每两辆汽车中就有一辆出自通用汽车公司。二、衰落阶段。20世纪80年代和90年代公司开始衰败,最终于2009年宣布破产。三、复兴阶段。2009年破产重组之后,公司走上了复兴之路,现已恢复生机。

　　1908年9月16日,当时美国最大的马车制造商威廉·杜兰特创建了通用汽车公司。一百多年以来,通用汽车公司先后通过联合或兼并的方式将别克、凯迪拉克、雪佛兰、庞帝亚克等公司纳入自己旗下,并拥有铃木、五十铃和斯巴鲁的股份,形成了丰富的产品线,所生产的汽车具有豪华、宽大、内部舒适、速度快、储备功率大等特点。自1927年以来,通用汽车公司一直是全世界最大的汽车公司之一。从2005年开始通用汽车公司几乎一直亏损,2009年6月1日正式申请破产保护。

　　导致通用公司破产的因素有三点:

　　1. 战略决策失误。20世纪中东地区的战争引发了石油危机,预示着以石油为驱动原料的汽车行业将进入减少对石油依赖的新阶段,但这并未引起通用汽车公司的足够重视。通用汽车公司未能及时把握住所在行业未来的发展趋势,依然把重心放在体积大、油耗高的传统汽车上。后来,油价一路攀升,使得通用汽车公司的产品与小体积的混合动力车相比完全没有竞争力,失去了消费者的青睐。2.劳动成本过高。迫于强势工会的压力,通用公司不得不支付员工明显高于业内平均水平的工资。作为百年老厂,公司有大批退休工人。每年养老金、医疗支出数额高达数百亿。公司财务账目显示:从2007年第二季度开始,公司对退休员工的债务合计为425亿美元,对在岗员工的债务合计为340亿美元。3.金融危机影响。2009年美国金融危机加剧了通用公司的财

207

务及经营危机。金融危机严重影响了美国实体经济,大量企业倒闭导致社会失业率急剧上升,促进市场消费能力不断下降,汽车销售市场也随之萎缩。通用公司在盈利能力不断下降的同时,受信贷政策紧缩的影响,现金流出现了枯竭。在这双重打击之下,公司最终只得申请破产保护。通用汽车公司提出的是"出售式重组模式"。重组后的通用汽车公司,联邦政府将持有61%的股份。新公司将裁掉三成高管。为降低成本,工人工资降至日本丰田公司工人的工资水平。公司将保留"雪佛兰""凯迪拉克""别克"和GMC四个核心品牌,出售"萨博""悍马"等亏损品牌。与破产前相比,新通用汽车公司将减少480亿美元债务和医疗开支,削减40%盈利能力较差的经销商。

经历破产重组后的通用公司焕发了新的活力,2012年通用公司全球汽车销量达930万辆,仅次于丰田汽车集团,该公司所创的"出售式重组模式"已成为经典案例。

III. Notes to the Text

1. UAW—United Automobile Workers（美国）联合汽车工会
2. Paul Ingrassia—a Pulitzer Prize-winner and the author of *Crash Course: the American Automobile Industry's Road from Glory to Disaster*
3. less-than-crowning milestones—不太光彩的里程碑(crowning—glorious)
4. Keeping GM alive, albeit in shrunken form, was an expensive undertaking for America's taxpayers: about $65 billion in all, if one counts government aid to the company's former financial arm, formerly GMAC, now renamed Ally Bank.—对美国纳税人而言,保持规模有所缩小的通用汽车公司的生存要付出很高的代价:如果把政府对其先前所属金融机构"通用金融"(现更名为Ally银行)的援助包括在内,总额大约为650亿美元。(GMAC—the General Motors Acceptance Corporation 通用汽车金融服务公司,简称"通用金融",是通用集团全资子公司,现更名为Ally Financial)
5. The following get my vote for the most important—以下是我认为最重要的(教训)
6. In corporate governance, the right people count more than the right structure.—在公司管理方面,用人正确比机构正确更为重要。(governance—control, management)
7. blindingly obvious—extremely obvious
8. brands such as Saturn and Saab—"土星"和"萨博"这类品牌
9. Fannie Mae and Freddie Mac—房利美与房地美[①Fannie Mae—Federal National Mortgage Association(联邦国民抵押贷款协会),成立于1938年;②Freddie Mac—Federal Home Loan Mortgage Corp(联邦住宅贷款抵押公司),成立于1970年]
10. public-employee—公职人员
11. And that shoveling more money into the public schools without insisting on structural reforms and accountability hasn't produced results and won't do so in the future.—向公立学校投入更多资金而不坚持体制改革,不坚持问责制,现在未能,将来也不会奏效。(shovel sth into—to put a lot of sth into...)

12. The second lesson is as important as the first, even though the term "corporate governance" sounds about as exciting as, well, dental floss.——第二条教训和第一条同样重要,即使"公司管理"这个术语听上去如同洁牙线一样索然无味。(dental floss——a type of thread used for cleaning between teeth)

13. Ford——福特汽车公司(1903年创办,美国三大汽车公司之一)

14. super-voting Class B shares——福特家族拥有超级表决权的B类股(Class B shares——Different share classes typically confer different rights on their owners. For example, a private company may choose to issue Class A shares to its new investors, while the original owners of the company receive Class B shares. In this case, Class B shares would typically have enhanced voting rights.)

15. This structure seems to fly in the face of what is generally understood to be sound principles of good corporate governance.——这一体制似乎公然违背大家普遍认为的良好企业管理的合理原则。(fly in the face of——to intentionally act in opposition to what is usual, reasonable)

16. ODX(Outstanding Directors Exchange)——卓越高管经验交流会

17. Millstein Center for Corporate Governance at Yale——耶鲁大学密尔斯坦公司管理研究中心

18. lead director——首席董事

19. Maybe they aren't bad people, but they surely showed judgment that was beyond bad.——或许他们并非是坏人,但他们所表现出的判断力却是糟透了。(beyond bad——extremely bad)

20. initial public offering of stock——首次公开募股

21. Chrysler——克莱斯勒汽车公司(美国三大汽车公司之一,1922年创建,2009年4月申请破产)

22. subprime mortgage loans——次级抵押贷款(指贷款机构向信用程度较差和收入不高的借款人的贷款)

23. Many dealers lost franchises.——许多汽车商失去了特许经营权。(dealer——a person whose business is buying and selling a particular product)

24. an economy that was on its knees——an economy that could hardly function

25. The Obama administration, to its credit, tried to walk a fine line: doing enough for Detroit to protect the economy, but not doing so much to foster future irresponsible behavior.——值得称赞的是,奥巴马政府设法按正确的路线行事:既尽力保住底特律(汽车)工业,又不提供过多救助去助长将来不负责任的行为。(credit——praise)

26. Nobody on any point of America's political spectrum really liked this bailout.——美国任何政治派别都没有人真正喜欢这个紧急财政救助。(spectrum——a complete range of related qualities, ideas)

IV. Language Features

名词定语

本文多处使用名词定语,如:pensions funds, taxpayer investment, board level, health insurance, mortgage loans 等。

新闻写作中常常使用名词定语,这是因为它是精练句式的有效方式,从下面两例便可看出这一功效:

diet pill (the kind of pill which helps people to reduce weight)

boom generation (the generation born between 1946 and 1964, when many more babies were born than in other periods)

翻开报纸便可发现名词定语到处可见。熟悉这一语言现象并掌握对它的判断能力可以提高对英语报刊的理解水平。例如:

power game 权力游戏　　　　　　turf war 势力范围之争
property tax 财产税　　　　　　　tube strike 地铁工人罢工
perk city 特权城(指国会)　　　　poverty line 贫困线
interest group 利益集团　　　　　minimum wage 法定最低工资
pressure group 压力集团　　　　　convenience food 方便食品
health insurance 医疗保险　　　　stone killer 铁石心肠的杀手
TV violence 电视暴力　　　　　　scare talk 吓人之谈
remarriage rate 再婚率　　　　　　drug dealer 毒品犯
sex worker 妓女　　　　　　　　　emergency shelter (应急)收容所
supervision agency 审批机构　　　refugee law 难民法
breast cancer surgery 乳腺癌手术　race riot 种族骚乱
workplace crime 工作场所犯罪　　job training 职业培训
child abuse 虐待孩子　　　　　　cardboard condos 纸板箱居住区
welfare mother 靠救济生活的母亲　gun control law 限制枪支法
street gang 街头团伙/帮派　　　　abortion advocate 主张堕胎者
teen sex 青少年性行为　　　　　　clothing drive 募集衣物活动
discount store 减价商店　　　　　panic buying 抢购

语言学家对名词定语褒贬不一,有的指责名词定语造成理解困难,读者往往难从表层确定语意,必须联系深层结构理解。有人赞扬名词定语可以浓缩句式、节省篇幅、避免句式拖沓。

语言学家西蒙·波特在他所著的《变化中的英语》(*Changing English*)一书中指出,名词定语是现代英语的发展趋势。同时他也告诫:在名词定语使用方面"为了语意明晰和句式美观不要累积使用超过三个"。

V. Analysis of Content

1. Which of the following is NOT on the author's list of GM's wrong practices?
   A. Paying retired employees gold-plated pensions.
   B. Keeping some brands that hardly ever made money.
   C. Paying many workers indefinitely not to work.
   D. Keeping an undemocratic structure.

2. Which of the following problems existing in the U.S. is NOT mentioned in the article?
   A. Federal deficits.
   B. Widening social gap.
   C. Subprime mortgage loans.
   D. Government financial deficit in many states.

3. The author believes that GM's ineffective governance mainly resulted from _____.
   A. the board members' lack of significant emotional and financial stake in the company
   B. the board members' lack of financial knowledge
   C. the board members' lack of work experience
   D. lack of public supervision on the board

4. Which of the following statements is FALSE?
   A. GM was a model of good corporate governance on paper.
   B. GM's denial and delay produced ruinous effects.
   C. What happened at GM in contrast with Ford is instructive.
   D. Letting GM liquidate would have produced far less destructive effects.

5. The author's attitude to the Obama administration's bailout policy is _____.
   A. supportive
   B. critical
   C. objective
   D. unknown

VI. Questions on the Article

1. When did GM announce its bankruptcy?
2. How much aid did the American federal government provide for the bailout of GM?
3. What are the three most important lessons from the GM bankruptcy?
4. What was the warning sounded by Jerome B. York?
5. To the author's mind, what measures should GM have taken to address its issues?
6. Why is good corporate governance critical?
7. Why does the author say that Ford was a disaster on paper?
8. What positive effect did Ford's governance produce?

9. What is the problem with GM's current board appointed by the U.S. Government?
10. If GM and Chrysler had been allowed to liquidate, what would have happened?

VII. Topics for Discussion

1. Do right people count more than the right structure in corporate governance?
2. Could bankruptcy happen to the U.S. in the future?

Lesson 23

Help Wanted

Five things that are making it more difficult to get advanced economies back to work.

By Byron Auguste, Susan Lund, and James Manyika

Today, 40 million workers across advanced economies are unemployed. Yet businesses can't fill job openings because they can't find qualified workers. This labor market dysfunction is a manifestation of the rapid evolution of the nature of work and the inability of worker skills—and labor market institutions—to keep up with the pace of creative destruction[1] in business. As a result of these changes, many jobs that were lost during the recession may be gone for good—bad news for the workers who held them and perhaps for the economies in which they live, too. To meet the long-range challenge, wealthy nations will need to find new approaches that go beyond simply stimulating growth.

Here are five trends from the McKinsey Global Institute's[2] latest discussion paper, "Help wanted (**Wanted**): The Future of Work in Advanced Economies,"[3] that explore the forces shaping which jobs are created, who fills them, where they are located, and what they pay.

1. Technology is changing the nature of work. Over the past three decades, technology has altered how production and routine transaction work is done—substituting machines for assembly-line workers and ATMs for bank tellers, for example.[4] The next frontier is "interaction work,"[5] the fastest-growing employment category, which includes low-skill jobs that must be done face face-to to-face (**done face-to-face**) (such as day-care work), as well as the managers and professionals who are the costliest corporate resources. One shift underway is for companies to disaggregate these jobs into multiple tasks and reassigning (**reassign**) the routine tasks to lower-skill employees, the way a paralegal takes on the routine work of attorneys.[6] This model applies to other professions and to corporate roles, such as human-resources managers[7], which in many companies has been broken down into subspecialties (benefits administration, compensation, etc.) Jobs today are also becoming more "virtual"—with broadband connections, cloud computing[8], and other technology, many interaction jobs can be conducted "anytime, anywhere," making it possible for employers to engage talent (full-time employees or contract workers) on an as-needed basis.[9]

2. The growing skills mismatch. The divergence between the prospects of highly educated workers with advanced skills and those with less education is growing. In the United States, the unemployment rate for college graduates has *never* topped 5 percent since 2008, while the unemployment rate for high school drop-outs rose to more than 15 percent at its peak in 2009 and 2010. Across OECD countries, the trend is clear: jobs that are being created are increasingly for workers with more education and skills. As a result, many workers are being left behind. By 2020, MGI projects that the United States may be short **(of)** 1.5 million workers with college or graduate degrees—and face a surfeit of nearly 6 million workers who have not completed high school.[10] Similarly, France's employers could be looking for 2.2 million more baccalaureate holders than will be available, while that nation will have an oversupply of 2.3 million workers who do not have their "bacs." If this skill mismatch persists, advanced economies will face a growing pool of permanently unemployed.[11]

3. Geography matters. Exacerbating the skilled vs. unskilled problem are geographic mismatches: workers with desired skills are often in short supply where companies are hiring, while places with the highest unemployment may have little job creation. This geographic imbalance is occurring both across national borders and within them. In the United States, while unemployment stands at more than 12 percent in Nevada (which was badly hurt by a massive real estate bubble[12]), only three states away, Nebraska has only 4 percent of the workforce out of a job. And surprisingly, compared with their parents and grandparents, today's working-age Americans are less likely to relocate to find work. Other advanced economies, such as Britain, France, and even Germany, have similarly stark differences in regional levels of growth and employment. Unemployment in southern Europe is almost twice as high as in northern Europe. Within Britain, for example, the unemployment rate is 6 percent in the southeast and 12 percent in the northeast. Policymakers must find new ways to encourage mobility, for instance through tax incentives, such as generous tax deductions for moving expenses incurred in connection with employment.[13] Some companies are creating virtual jobs that allow them to hire people wherever they are located—gaining access to a broader base of talent and saving on real estate costs in the process.

4. Growing pools of untapped talent.[14] Because of changes in the nature of work and demographics, many advanced economies have growing pools of untapped talent, especially among the young, women, and people approaching retirement age. The growing number of unemployed youth poses a serious long-range challenge.[15] Across the OECD, youth unemployment has risen to nearly 18 percent—and in some countries it is twice that average. Young people who cannot find work suffer life-long handicaps; their earnings never catch up and they are far more likely to rely on government assistance down the road.[16] Unemployment among Spanish youth has continued to rise since the debt crisis and now stands at close to 50 percent, which could lead to many years of joblessness—and diminished career opportunities—for millions of young Spaniards as well as additional costs for a government that is trying to reduce its fiscal deficits[17]. Creating pathways to employment for these young people must be a priority.[18] Raising the labor force participation[19] of women and older workers also presents an opportunity and can help fill the skill gap. Workers older than 55 will be an increasingly important resource in advanced economies. In Europe, where the population is aging rapidly, the potential loss of talent is significant. Advanced economies that can raise the employment rate for older workers—rather than seeing them pensioned off[20]—will have an easier time filling the high-skill jobs that will drive growth and productivity. In many countries, women represent an under-utilized labor pool, too.[21] For instance, if Germany raised the labor participation rate of women (currently 53 percent) to Sweden's level (61 percent) it could cut its anticipated shortage of skilled workers by one-third.

5. Disparity in income growth. Trends in job creation are contributing to growing income polarization across advanced economies.[22] Households at the bottom of the distribution have seen little or no income growth in many countries over the last (**past**) decade, raising questions about aggregate demand, living standards, and social stability.[23] As we have seen, globalization and technology have greatly increased demand for highly skilled workers, pushing up wages for these people and reducing demand for the less-skilled. Other factors are driving growing income disparity as well. One is shifting patterns in family formation: across the OECD, the proportion of single-headed households[24] (single adults with and without children) has risen by 25 percent since the 1980s, limiting the growth of household income. At the same time, marriage rates rise along with educational attainment—and with high earners more frequently marrying one another, it further widens the income gap. As a result, most advanced economies have seen incomes grow faster for the highest earners than for the lowest.

***

As a result of these trends, advanced economies face a long-term jobs (**job**) problem that they will not be able to address adequately with standard solutions. Both policy makers (**policymakers**) and business leaders will need to find new approaches. Of course, governments will need to continue to encourage overall economic growth—using fiscal and monetary policy[25], and removing barriers to business expansion. But restoring aggregate demand alone may not be enough to put all of today's unemployed back to work.

To do so, governments will need to adopt policies and strategies aimed directly at preparing the workforce—making sure there are bodies and skills ready for the jobs of tomorrow. It's of fundamental importance for national competitiveness. Continuing to improve primary and secondary education and overhauling post-secondary and vocational education for young people who are not headed to college and for mid-career workers who need retraining[26] must be a priority. Relatively simple steps like creating a national jobs database—to enable students and workers to see what jobs are in demand and what credentials are needed—would help. In addition, policy makers (**policymakers**) can unlock growth and job creation by promoting entrepreneurship and innovation[27], catalyzing investment in infrastructure, and streamlining regulatory approval processes.

Business also has a critical interest in finding solutions to the jobs challenge. In a global economy, companies will continue to seek talent wherever they can find it and at the most attractive cost. But this formula is becoming more complex and simply finding the best-priced labor is no longer always the optimum solution. Companies have rising concerns about supply chain[28] risk— from natural disasters and other causes—and are seeing wages rise in coastal China and in India's offshoring (**offshore**) capitals.

One strategy is for companies to make talent development a competitive advantage; when the critical resource is talent, companies that can find a steady supply of highly qualified workers and teach them distinctive skills should outperform rivals who can't. This will require stepping up investments in workforce training to levels we have not seen previously. Infosys[29], the Indian IT services giant, has become one of the top training institutions in the world, capable of putting 14,000 new employees at a time through its 23-week program. This capability has given Infosys a competitive advantage and has helped enable its rapid growth. Companies can also tap into new pools of skilled talent by using technology to bridge the geographic divide[30]—offering flexible, remote work arrangements to workers they could not hire otherwise. In the coming years, companies that can build up their own supplies of the best trained and motivated workers will win—and so will the economies in which they operate.

From *Foreignpolicy.com*, March 16, 2012

I. New Words

attorney	[əˈtəːni]	n.	〈美〉律师
catalyze	[ˈkætəlaiz]	v.	to make a chemical reaction happen faster
compensation	[kɔmpənˈseiʃən]	n.	工资
credential	[kriˈdenʃəl]	n.	证明书，证件
database	[ˈdeitəbeis]	n.	数据库
day-care	[ˈdeikeə]	n.	日托
demographic	[deməˈɡræfik]	adj.	人口的，人口统计的
disaggregate	[disˈæɡriɡeit]	v.	分解
disparity	[diˈspæriti]	n.	差异，悬殊
divergence	[daiˈvəːdʒəns]	n.	the state of differing; difference
dropout	[ˈdrɔpaut]	n.	退学；退学生
dysfunction	[disˈfʌŋkʃən]	n.	机能障碍
exacerbate	[iɡˈzæsəbeit]	v.	to make sth worse
infrastructure	[ˈinfrəstrʌktʃə]	n.	基础；基础设施
manifestation	[mænifeˈsteiʃən]	n.	显示，表明
optimum	[ˈɔptiməm]	adj.	the best possible
outperform	[autpəˈfɔːm]	v.	to achieve better results than
paralegal	[pærəˈliːɡəl]	n.	〈主美〉律师助理
polarization	[pəuləraiˈzeiʃən]	n.	两极分化
relocate	[riːˈləukeit]	v.	to move to a new place to work
stark	[staːk]	adj.	明显的
stimulate	[ˈstimjuleit]	v.	刺激，激励
streamline	[ˈstriːmlain]	v.	使现代化，提高……效率
subspecialty	[sʌbˈspeʃəlti]	n.	（专业下细分的）分专业，分科
teller	[ˈtelə]	n.	银行出纳员

II. Background Information

美国就业市场结构变化

美国的结构性失业起始于21世纪初全球化浪潮,加剧于经济大衰退。21世纪初至2007年12月大衰退开始时,美国企业为优化利用全球资源和提高竞争力,加速产业外移和服务外包的步伐。由于缺乏足够规模的新兴产业来吸收那些被裁减下来的美国工人,结构性失业开始出现。

伴随着美国第二、第三产业结构的演变,美国就业结构及其劳动力的配置也发生了非常大的变化。20世纪80年代以来的三十多年间,美国就业人数增长最快的行业,如金融保险地产、商业服务、信息服务、医疗教育等均属服务业,而随着第二产业占GDP的比重由30%以上降到20%左右,美国制造业就业人数一直处于下降状态。制造业所需的非技能劳动力越来越少,对高技能工人的需求越来越大,技能缺口进一步推高了美国失业率。

关于劳动力市场结构变化对就业形势的影响美国存在两种看法:

一般认为,新技术提高了劳动生产率,必将导致就业率的降低;新兴工业和新技术所取代的传统工业和旧技术的就业机会,将大大多于现时能提供的就业机会。例如:微处理机、机器人的应用,在一定时期内对某些企业的工人就业造成很大威胁。美国通用电器公司原有37000多名装配工,据称,如使用机器人进行装配工作,人数可减少一半。阿卢马克思公司在南卡罗来纳州查尔斯顿新建的计算机化的铝加工厂,只雇佣了仅为通常具有同样生产能力工厂的一半工人。美国舆论界和政府曾纷纷预测,由于结构性失业现象,美国的失业率不会很快降下来。

另一些人则认为,从全社会范围来看,一定时期内,科技进步会带来经济增长和社会发展。其结果不是就业率减少,而是更高的职业开发率。美国季刊《经济影响》最近刊载的一篇文章指出:"科学技术进步,只会引起就业结构的变化,不会使就业总人数减少。"美国一些高新技术发达的州的失业率相对较少的情况,似乎可为这一论点做证。在佛罗里达州,25%的劳动者受雇于高新技术工业。1982年1月美国全国失业率为9.8%,但这个州只有7.7%。1984年1月,在电子业发达的马萨诸塞州失业率为6.5%,全国失业率为8%。恰恰相反,以传统工业为主的密歇根州的失业率高达11.5%。

在失业群体中,无可置疑的现象是"蓝领"多于"白领",非熟练工人多于熟练工人。据1983年12月的统计资料,美国全部失业者中有50%的人是属于"蓝领"行业的。美国伊利诺伊州对两万名由于采用自动化技术而失业的工人进行调查后了解到:在被解雇后一年,80%的熟练工人重新获得了工作,而半熟练工人只有59%。

在美国,有一些人认为,结构性失业现象在社会变革过程中不可避免,它是促使人们学习的一种推动力;另一些人则认为,结构性失业将使社会上的一部分人面临严酷现实,即他们在失业后可能很难再就业或难以找到适合自己能力和兴趣的职业,促使他们起来反对导致就业市场结构变化的各种社会变革。

III. Notes to the Text

1. creative destruction——创造性破坏（Please refer to Note 18 of Lesson 6）
2. McKinsey Global Institute——麦肯锡全球研究院
3. "Help wanted (**Wanted**): The Future of Work in Advanced Economies"——"招工：发达经济体的就业前景"（Help Wanted——used in advertisements for recruiting workers）
4. Over the past three decades, technology has altered how production and routine transaction work is done—substituting machines for assembly-line workers and ATMs for bank tellers, for example.——在过去的30年中，技术改变了生产和日常交易的作业模式——譬如机器代替了流水线工人，自动提款机代替了银行出纳员。（① substitute——to take the place of sth；② ATM——automatic teller machine）
5. The next frontier is "interaction work,"... ——下一个新领域是"互动性工作"（frontier——referring to an undeveloped field）
6. One shift underway is for companies to disaggregate these jobs into multiple tasks and reassigning (**reassign**) the routine tasks to lower-skill employees, the way a paralegal takes on the routine work of attorneys. ——公司正在进行的一项改革是把这些工作分解成许多项任务，把常规任务再分配给技术水平较低的雇员，就像律师助理承担律师的日常工作那样。（disaggregate——to break down into small parts）
7. human-resources managers——人力资源部门的经理
8. broadband connections, cloud computing——宽带连接，云计算（云计算是一种新兴的商业计算模型。它将计算任务分布在大量计算机构成的资源池中，使各种应用系统能够根据需要获取计算力、存储空间和各种软件服务。）
9. ...making it possible for employers to engage talent (full-time employees or contract workers) on an as-needed basis. ——使雇主能根据需要聘用人才（全职或合同工）（engage——to employ sb to do a particular job）
10. By 2020, MGI projects that the United States may be short 1.5 million workers with college or graduate degrees—and face a surfeit of nearly 6 million workers who have not completed high school.——麦肯锡全球研究院预测：到2020年，美国将出现150万本科和研究生学历人才的缺口，而未完成高中学业工人的过剩数量接近600万。（surfeit——an amount that is too large）
11. If this skill mismatch persists, advanced economies will face a growing pool of permanently unemployed.——如果这种技能匹配不当的情况持续下去，发达经济体中永久失业群体的人数将不断增加。
12. real estate bubble——房地产泡沫
13. Policymakers must find new ways to encourage mobility, for instance through tax incentives, such as generous tax deductions for moving expenses incurred in connection with employment.——决策者必须采取税收优惠之类的新措施鼓励人员流动，比如对就业所带来的搬家开支提供大幅减税奖励。（incur——to experience sth usually unpleasant as a result of actions you have taken）

14. Growing pools of untapped talent.——无业人才群体扩大。(untapped—available but not yet used)

15. The growing number of unemployed youth poses a serious long-range challenge. ——失业青年数量不断增长构成严重而长期的问题。

16. ...they are far more likely to rely on government assistance down the road. ——他们将来更有可能依赖政府帮助。(down the road— at some time in the future)

17. fiscal deficits——财政赤字

18. Creating pathways to employment for these young people must be a priority. ——当务之急是为这些失业青年开辟就业门路。

19. labor force participation——劳动力参与

20. seeing them pensioned off——发放养老金让他们退休(pension sb off—to allow or force sb to retire and pay him/her a pension)

21. In many countries, women represent an under-utilized labor pool, too.——在许多国家,妇女也是一个未能充分利用的劳力群体。(① under-utilized—not used as much as it should be; ②pool—a group of people)

22. Trends in job creation are contributing to growing income polarization across advanced economies. ——这些就业趋势造成所有发达经济体收入两极分化的扩大。(contribute—to be one of the causes of sth)

23. ...raising questions about aggregate demand, living standards, and social stability. ——给国民总需求、生活水平和社会稳定造成问题。(aggregate—total)

24. single-headed households——单身/亲户

25. fiscal and monetary policy——财政金融政策

26. ...overhauling post-secondary and vocational education for young people who are not headed to college and for mid-career workers who need retraining——全面改革不读大学的年轻人和需要重新培训的在职工人的中学后教育和职业教育(overhaul—to examine thoroughly and repair if necessary)

27. ...policy makers (**policymakers**) can unlock growth and job creation by promoting entrepreneurship and innovation——决策者可以通过倡导创业和创新精神为经济发展和创造就业机会松绑(entrepreneurship—the state of being an entrepreneur)

28. supply chain——供给链

29. Infosys——Infosys Limited Technologies (印孚瑟斯公司,一家总部在印度班加罗尔的全球信息技术和商务咨询服务公司)

30. Companies can also tap into new pools of skilled talent by using technology to bridge the geographic divide... ——公司还可以通过采用技术手段弥合地理距离的办法利用新的技术人才(tap into—to make use of a source of energy)

IV. Language Features

标题句式

本文标题"Help Wanted"是个省略句,句中省去了 is,这是招工广告常见形式,本文作者也采用了这一形式。英语报刊标题语言高度凝练,经常采用省略手段。初读外刊的人由于不了解标题省略方式,往往感到理解困难。

新闻标题常常省略下列成分:

1. 冠词

例1. Actor in Crash (An Actor in a Crash)

例2. U.S. set for missile attack on Iraq (The U.S. is set for a missile attack on Iraq)

2. 人称代词

例1. Man quizzed after wife is knifed in sports store (A man is quizzed after his wife is knifed in a sports store)

例2. Anne and Baby Are Well (Anne and Her Baby Are Well)

3. 连系动词

例1. Cops under Fire (Cops Are under Fire)

例2. Bankers Silent (Bankers Keep Silent)

4. 被动语态或进行时的助动词

例1. Pensioner raped, criminal jailed (A pensioner was raped, the criminal is jailed)

例2. Bulls closing in on sixth title, lead 3-1 (Bulls is closing in on the sixth title, lead 3-1)

标题除采用省略手段精练句式,还运用下列手段:

1. 使用名词定语,省去前置词

例1. Bread Price Rise (A Rise in the Price of Bread)

例2. Nuke Protesters Convicted (Protesters Against Nuclear Weapons Are Convicted)

2. 使用标点符号替代词

(1) 运用逗号替代连接词"and"

例1. Rubin, Greenspan at odds (Rubin and Greenspan are at odds)

例2. U.A.W. faces cloudy future, dwindling membership (U.A.W. faces cloudy future and dwindling membership)

(2) 使用冒号替代说意动词

例1. Owen: Watch Me Get Better

例2. Emerson: Robson Neigh Can Do!

(3) 使用冒号代替连系动词,甚至其他动词

例1. Koreans: Grumpy Toward America (Koreans Are Grumpy Toward America)

例2. Tests: Akiwande has hepatitis B (Tests show Akiwande has hepatitis B)

V. Analysis of Content

1. According to the article, the kind of work that will be next affected by technology is _____.
   A. manufacturing
   B. routine transaction
   C. house construction
   D. interaction work
2. Which of the following groups of people is NOT underutilized in advanced economies?
   A. Middle-aged men.
   B. Women.
   C. Young people.
   D. People over 55.
3. The author's list of factors contributing to the growth of income disparity does NOT include ____.
   A. globalization
   B. technology
   C. increase of single-headed households
   D. racial discrimination
4. Which kind of companies will win in the future?
   A. Companies which make best use of advanced technology.
   B. Companies that build up their own supplies of the best trained and motivated workers.
   C. Companies that keep seeking talent.
   D. Companies that are well-financed.
5. Which of the following statements is FALSE?
   A. Technology has changed the job market in the way of substituting machines for assembly-line workers.
   B. The unemployment rate of college graduates is much lower than that of high school dropouts.
   C. Many people are unemployed because they don't want to move to find work.
   D. The participation of older workers will decrease in advanced economies.

VI. Questions on the Article

1. What does the labor market dysfunction show?
2. What does the article "Help Wanted: The Future of Work in Advanced Economies" discuss?
3. How has technology changed the labor market over the past three decades?
4. What effects is technology producing on interaction jobs?
5. How is the divergence between the prospects of highly educated workers and those of less-educated workers changing in the U.S.?

6. In what way does geography affect the U.S. labor market?

7. What problem does the growing number of unemployed youth pose?

8. How is wealth distributed in advanced economies?

9. What approach does the author suggest governments should adopt?

10. What is the strategy suggested for companies?

VII. Topics for Discussion

1. Will technology change all kinds of interaction work?

2. Is income polarization unavoidable?

Unit 8
第八单元 社会问题

Lesson 24

Text A

Social Media March on Wall Street[1]

Twitter alone does not make a revolution.

It must have seemed the perfect time for a social media-meets-political-protest moment[2]. Earlier this month, New York City Mayor Mike Bloomberg said, "You have a lot of kids graduating college who can't find jobs. That's what happened in Cairo. That's what happened in Madrid. You don't want those kinds of riots here."

Some do. Editors at Adbusters, a Vancouver-based magazine (mission: "topple existing power structures") wanted to see if they could spark demonstrations just by posting the idea using social media. It created a Twitter topic with the hashtag #OccupyWallStreet, asking people to come to New York's Financial District to join what they said would be tens of thousands in a "leaderless resistance movement" objecting to banks, capitalism and other perceived evils. Egypt's Tahrir Square[3] was cited as precedent.

The protests last week were a bust, but perhaps the young protesters learned a lesson: Just because it's on social media doesn't make it true.

A few hundred self-described "over-educated and under-employed" young people turned up for several days to camp out and carry cardboard signs. They occupied Zuccotti Park[4], a few blocks from Wall Street. This dislodged recent immigrants from their lunchtime chess matches and local teenagers from their evening skateboarding.[5] New Yorkers mostly rolled their eyes[6], or as comedian Stephen Colbert put it, "If there's one thing New Yorkers never ignore, it's people sleeping in a park."

Some protesters were wryly self-aware[7], such as the one with the sign, "College Taught Me Nothing (But They Got My Money)." Most were typical left-wing critics of markets, Zionism and people who wear fur[8]—perhaps with an exemption for the fellow demonstrator who along with a fur cap wore a long burlap vest and goggles. A woman drew attention by going topless with "Free Bradley Manning" written on her chest, referring to the Army private accused of leaking intelligence reports to WikiLeaks[9].

A tabloid's headline, "Violence Erupts at Wall St. Protest," proved overstated. There were arrests for erecting tents (protesters said they were trying to keep their laptops dry) and wearing masks (violating a century-old statute against masked gatherings).

Liberal bloggers were briefly scandalized when Yahoo! blocked emails that included "OccupyWallStreet," until it turned out this wasn't censorship: The email service had blocked the messages assuming they must be advertising spam. *Adbusters* editors probably weren't pleased when Livestream, the online video service protesters used to air their activities, featured advertising for Natural Instincts, part of megacorporation Procter & Gamble's Clairol line.[10]

New York police closed off several of the area's narrow streets and sidewalks to keep protesters from reaching landmarks such as the New York Stock Exchange[11]. This worked, but it is inconveniencing hundreds of thousands of locals who live and work in the area.

When a father tried to explain to his 5-year-old son that the detours on the way to his school on Broad Street were to stop people who didn't like Wall Street, the youngster complained loudly about the barricades, "Why, why, why?" Local residents and office workers joined the "Why?" chant for a brief counter-demonstration. (By the way, those of us who live in the Financial District[12] would like to point out that most banks have moved to midtown, which has lovely wide boulevards suitable for future protests.)

Comparing the U.S. to Egypt can't withstand scrutiny even of a 140-character Twitter protest announcement. Hadear Kandil, a New York college student whose family came from Egypt, used her blog, TahririNYC, to reject comparisons to Tahrir Square.

"It is not acceptable for a bunch of young anarchist hippies to call this Zuccotti sleepover, reminiscent of '69 Woodstock scenes, the 'spark of a revolution[13],'" she wrote after spending time with the protesters. "It's insulting. And it's disrespectful to the thousands who were brutally murdered and tortured and raped all across the Middle East and North Africa in their actual fights for freedom from their chains."

The antics on Wall Street weren't the only recent social-media misfire.[14] President Obama's campaign team, which brilliantly leveraged Facebook and Twitter in the 2008 race, decided to launch a Web campaign they call "Attack Watch." Supporters were invited to report alleged falsehoods about the president.

A funny thing happened. The Twitter hashtag #AttackWatch was hijacked by conservative humorists, turning the effort into a subject of ridicule[15]. One wag posted, "I want to report someone at home on the range who said a discouraging word." Another posted, "Of course Obama is for a Palestinian state. He'd carry it in '012 for sure." Embarrassed, the Obama campaign hasn't used its @AttackWatch Twitter account since Sept. 14, two days after its launch.

Wall Street has survived much worse than some ragged protesters trying to occupy it. As for demonstrators lured by a Twitter post, maybe they learned something on their disappointing field trip to Wall Street, for instance that some ideas deserve to be sold short.[16]

From *The Wall Street Journal*, September 26, 2011

第八单元 社会问题

I. New Words

barricade	[ˈbærikeid]	n.	路障
boulevard	[ˈbuːlivɑːd]	n.	a broad street in the town
bunch	[bʌntʃ]	n.	a group
burlap	[ˈbəːlæp]	n.	(制衣物用的)细麻布
bust	[bʌst]	n.	a complete failure
cardboard	[ˈkɑːdbɔːd]	n.	薄纸板
censorship	[ˈsensəʃip]	n.	审查
chant	[tʃɑːnt]	n.	单调而有节奏的喊叫声
detour	[ˈdiːtuə(r)]	n.	绕行的路
erect	[iˈrekt]	v.	to put sth in position and make it stand vertical
exemption	[igˈzempʃən]	n.	official permission not to do
goggle	[ˈgɔgl]	n.	护目镜,风镜
inconvenience	[ˌinkənˈviːnjəns]	v.	to cause trouble or difficulties
landmark	[ˈlændmɑːk]	n.	有历史意义的建筑物
laptop	[ˈlæptɔp]	n.	便携式电脑
Madrid	[məˈdrid]	n.	马德里(西班牙首都)
overstate	[ˌəuvəˈsteit]	v.	把……说得过分,夸大
private	[ˈpraivit]	n.	(陆军或海军陆战队)二等兵
ragged	[ˈrægid]	adj.	informal very tired
range	[reindʒ]	n.	<美>牧场
scandalize	[ˈskændəlaiz]	v.	to offend or horrify by doing sth thought to be wrong
spam	[spæm]	n.	[计] 垃圾邮件
self-aware	[ˌselfəˈweə]	adj.	自知的,自我意识的
statute	[ˈstætjuːt]	n.	成文法,法令
tabloid	[ˈtæblɔid]	n.	小报
topless	[ˈtɔplis]	adj.	(of a woman) not wearing any clothes on the upper part of the body
wag	[wæg]	n.	a person who enjoys making jokes
withstand	[wiðˈstænd]	v.	经受,承受
wry	[rai]	adj.	露出怪相的
Zionism	[ˈzaiənizəm]	n.	犹太复国主义

II. Background Information

占领华尔街运动

2008年美国次贷危机引发了金融危机。在这场危机中,对于危机发生负有重大责任的华尔街金融业虽然受到重击,但却得到联邦政府的巨额资金的救助。然而,其他企业享受不到如此优厚的待遇。金融危机促使经济衰退形势进一步恶化,许多公司宣布破产或是缩小规模,大批工人丢掉工作。2011年8月美国共有30个州就业人数进一步下降,其中纽约降幅最大,当月裁员人数多达2.2万。美国民众终于看清美国是金权天下,华尔街寡头操纵美国政坛。他们对此形势极度不满,对美国金融业充满仇恨。

2011年9月17日5000名示威者聚集在纽约市曼哈顿,其中不少人带了帐篷,试图占领华尔街。由于警方采取街道封锁措施,示威者最终扎营在离华尔街几个街区的布鲁克菲尔德房地产公司所拥有的祖科蒂公园。

游行是由网络杂志《广告克星》(Adbusters)组织发起的。示威者的意图是反对美国政治权钱交易、要把华尔街变成埃及的解放广场。他们高喊"我们代表美国99%的人,我们不再忍受1%的人的贪婪和腐败!""我们要工作!""亿万富翁(Billionaires)的日子到头了!"等口号。示威者对记者说,要通过这次示威迫使华尔街吐出侵吞人民的财产。他们打出了引人注目的口号:"大银行出卖了我们,民主党和共和党出卖了我们,现在是我们起来捍卫自己利益的时候了!"

这场运动迅速升级。10月5日纽约参加抗议活动人数增至近万人。运动还得到许多城市的响应,三周之后扩展到美国近千个城镇和全世界110多个国家。

游行队伍成分多样,既有失业工人,也有大学生、越战老兵和家庭主妇。其诉求很多,从社会就业到反战,从反金融大亨到免费医疗。但是对社会现状的不满和对金融界的愤怒把这个反叛群体凝聚起来,把示威斗争推向全社会。

这场斗争持续了两个多月。11月15日凌晨纽约警局发起行动,对运动大本营祖科蒂公园实施强行清场。此后其他国家和美国其他城市相继采取类似行动,运动结束。

这次运动是继20世纪60年代反战运动之后规模最大的抗议活动,有人称此为"一场神圣抗争","是一次美国民众意识的大觉醒"。从表面上看,这次运动是对金融界发起的抗争活动,但实际上它却反映了美国社会酝酿已久的思潮。它向社会发出强大的警示:金融界监管必须加强;贫富巨大差距必须遏制。

III. Notes to the Text

1. Social Media March on Wall Street ——社交媒体发起的抗议华尔街运动(march —a demonstration or protest)
2. a social media-meets-political-protest moment ——社交媒体用以发起政治抗议活动的时刻(meet—satisfactory or good enough to fulfil a task)

3. Tahrir Square —（埃及）塔利尔广场（The square was a focal point for the 2011 Egyptian movement against former president Hosni Mubarak. Over 50,000 protesters first occupied the square on January 25th.The number of protesters grew to 300,000 on January 31st.）

4. Zuccotti Park —祖科蒂公园［目前归属布鲁克菲尔德房地产公司（Broookfield Properties Corporation），该公园坐落在纽约曼哈顿下城，面积有3100平方米。］

5. This dislodged recent immigrants from their lunchtime chess matches and local teenagers from their evening skateboarding. —这项行动使得新近移民不能在午餐时间举办棋局，当地孩子不能晚上做滑板运动。（dislodge sb from sth—to force sb to leave a place or an activity）

6. New Yorkers mostly rolled their eyes... —大多数纽约人都冷眼相看
（roll one's eyes —to show surprise or disapproval）

7. Some protesters were wryly self-aware... —一些抗议者表现出十分可笑的自我意识
（wryly —amusingly）

8. Most were typical left-wing critics of markets, Zionism and people who wear fur... —大多数是典型的左翼人士，反对市场经济、犹太复国主义和穿皮草（① markets —referring to market economy, a system of producing wealth based on the free operation of business and trade without government controls; ② critics of people who wear fur—referring to the animal rights group who hold the idea that people should treat animals well, and especially not use them in tests to develop medicine or other products.）

9. WikiLeaks —维基解密网站

10. *Adbusters* editors probably weren't pleased when Livestream, the online video service protesters used to air their activities, featured advertising for Natural Instincts, part of megacorporation Procter & Gamble's Clairol line.—当抗议者用来宣传他们活动的Livestream视频服务网站播放特大企业宝洁公司伊卡璐系列产品中的"天然本质"牌染发水广告时，《广告克星》杂志编辑很可能不高兴。（① *Adbusters* —加拿大一家非营利、为保护环境而反对消费主义组织机构出版的双月刊；② Clairol —a personal-care product division of Procter & Gamble that began in 1931 and by 1959 became known as the leading company in the U.S. hair-coloring industry. Natural Instincts is one of its famous brands. ③ Procter & Gamble —a large U.S. company whose products include washing powder, soap, shampoo and baby nappies）

11. the New York Stock Exchange —纽约证券交易所（It is the largest stock exchange in the U.S. It is known as the Big Board, and its building is on Wall Street.）

12. the Financial District —纽约市金融区（It is a neighborhood on the southernmost section of Manhattan which comprises the offices and headquarters of many of the city's major financial institutions.）

13. It is not acceptable for a bunch of young anarchist hippies to call this Zuccotti sleepover, reminiscent of '69 Woodstock scenes, the (spark of a revolution)... —祖科蒂公园的露营使人联想到1969年伍迪斯托克摇滚音乐节的场景，一批无政府主义的嬉皮士称此为"革命的火花"是不能被接受的（①reminiscent—reminding you of sb or sth;②Woodstock —a music festival held over 3 days in 1969 near the town of Woodstock in New York State, where about 500,000 young people went to see rock, pop and folk singers and bands. It is

remembered especially for the hippies who attended it and is seen as a very typical example of the hippie culture.)

14. The antics on Wall Street weren't the only recent social-media misfire. ——社交媒体最近的失败不只是占领华尔街的愚蠢行动。(①antics ——behavior which is silly and funny; ②misfire——failure)

15. turning the effort into a subject of ridicule ——使这次行动成了人们的笑柄(ridicule——laughter in mockery)

16. ...they learned something on their disappointing field trip to Wall Street, for instance that some ideas deserve to be sold short. ——他们从这次令人失望的华尔街学习考察之行中学到了一些东西，比如对有些看法应该不屑一顾。(① field trip ——a journey made by a group of students to study sth in its natural environment; ② sell short ——to have a low opinion of)

IV. Language Features

外报外刊中的意识形态

新闻话语也是意识形态的话语。西方主要报刊基本都是资本主义垄断集团手中的媒体。它们向读者灌输的是这些特权集团的意识形态和观念。《华尔街日报》是美国金融界最具权威的专业报纸，读者对象是金融业资本家、企业家和企业高管。无疑，其报道内容和风格得迎合这些人的口味。

外报外刊的意识形态和观念反映在主题结构、句式、用词和配置的图片和说明文字上。因此，通过对这些方面的分析可以透视出文章所隐含的意识形态和观念。

本课两篇文章充分显示该报对占领华尔街运动的敌对态度。文章作者站在运动的对立面，镜头对准负面，对运动横加指责、肆意嘲讽。A篇针对运动的发起者，讲的是社交媒体所发起的抗议活动是失败的，说明社交媒体本身并不能发动一场革命。B篇针对运动参与者扎营场所(祖科蒂公园)，提出该公园是权贵资本主义(crony capitalism)的产物，抗议者扎营之所以成功是因为该公园的准公共性质(quasipublic)；警方难以直接管控，政府和财产主双方推卸责任。作者呼吁抗议者把矛头从华尔街金融巨头转向权贵资本主义，具体行动就是撤离这个公园。

文章作者在以下四个方面表现出对运动的仇视、敌对情绪：

1. 贬低运动价值。文章称抗议活动为"愚蠢行动"(antics)、"令人失望的学习考察"(disappointing field trip)、"土地霸占"(land grab)，几处提及运动是失败(failure, bust, misfire)的，无法与"阿拉伯之春"(Arab Spring)相提并论。

2. 丑化参与者形象。报道称活动参与者为"无政府主义的嬉皮士"(anarchist hippies)，描述他们"淫荡、抚摸、酗酒、吸毒"(lewd, groping, drinking, drugging)、"好斗"(aggressive)、"服毒后精神恍惚"(drugged out)。

3. 强调运动负面效应。文章称占领活动"使得新近移民不能在午餐时间下棋"，"当地孩子不能晚上做滑板运动"，大多数纽约人对此"冷眼相看"；当地居民对绕道而

第八单元　社会问题

行十分反感,高喊"为什么?"表现出"反对示威"(counter-demonstration)情绪。作者着重提到占领活动给当地带来"噪音、污物和恶臭"(noise, filth and stink),"深夜击鼓、喊叫、吹喇叭",造成当地工人和居民"疲惫"。

　　4. 只引用反对派的话。两篇文章没有一处引用运动同情者或支持者的话,引言全都出自运动的反对派。如引用 Hankdear Kandil 的话:"一批年轻捣乱的嬉皮士称祖科蒂公园露宿为'革命火花'是不可接受的。"

　　引语使新闻报道"具有强烈的真实感和直接感"。记者通常选择与自己观点类似的引言,这样既可以表达出自己的意识形态,还可以显得客观、真实、可信。因此,它具有较大的欺骗性。

V. Analysis of Content

1. The meaning of the word "march" in the headline is _____.
   A. a journey made by soldiers
   B. music meant for marching
   C. distance covered by marching
   D. a demonstration

2. Which group of people were absent from the march?
   A. Left-wing group.
   B. Critics of Zionism.
   C. Market supporters.
   D. Unemployed young people.

3. According to the article, New Yorkers' attitude to the protesters' sleepout was _____.
   A. supportive
   B. negative
   C. unknown
   D. tolerant

4. Yahoo! blocked emails including "occupy Wall Street" because _____.
   A. those messages were assumed to be advertising spam
   B. those messages were considered antisocial
   C. the email service did not like the movement
   D. the government had ordered Yahoo! to do so

5. Which of the following statements is in agreement with the author's view on the function of social media?
   A. Social media are highly effective in making a revolution.
   B. The march on Wall Street was a big success for social media.
   C. Ideas on social media should have full attention from the public.
   D. Social media's function in making a revolution is limited.

VI. Questions on the Article

1. According to Mayor Bloomberg, what difference exists between Cairo and New York?
2. Who organized the Occupy Wall Street movement? What mission did the organizers have in their minds?
3. Which place did the protesters occupy? According to the article, what effect did the occupation produce on the local residents?
4. What accounted for the arrests of some protesters?
5. What measure did New York police take to keep protesters from reaching landmarks? What effect did it produce?
6. What was Hadear Kandil's impression of the occupation?
7. What was "Attack Watch"? What was its aim?
8. What was the result of the Twitter hashtag # Attack Watch?

VII. Topics for Discussion

1. Does the idea of occupying Wall Street deserve to be sold short?
2. Is the Occupy Wall Street Movement a failure?

Text B

Occupy Wall Street's Crony Capitalism[1]

Political extortion created Zuccotti Park, and it allows protesters to remain despite the noise, filth and stink.

The Occupy Wall Street movement, now in its fourth week, has plenty to brag about. Its occasionally published newspaper, the Occupied Wall Street Journal, proclaims: "In the great cathedral of capitalism, the dispossessed have liberated territory from the financial overlords and their police army."

How did protesters manage to take over Zuccotti Park, a half-acre plot a few blocks from Wall Street? It turns out that this land grab is not due to the power of social media. Instead, the main force letting protesters stay in the park is old-fashioned crony capitalism.

The Occupy Wall Street organizers were clever in selecting their protest site. Zuccotti is not a city park, where sleeping overnight is prohibited. Instead, it is one of some 500 "privately owned public spaces" that New York City officials created as part of zoning deals with real estate developers.²

In the case of Zuccotti Park, the crony capitalism goes back to the 1970s, when U.S. Steel³ built the One Liberty Plaza office tower. In exchange for adding nine stories, city officials extracted an agreement that U.S. Steel would fund a 24-hour-a-day park across the street.

These quasipublic spaces are notorious for leaving unclear who's responsible for what. When protesters first moved in to Zuccotti Park, the current owner, Brookfield Properties⁴, and the city pointed fingers at each other. Brookfield cited its rules against sleeping out, excessive noise and illegal activity. City authorities—no doubt happy to have a place for the demonstrators several blocks away from landmarks such as the New York Stock Exchange—passed the buck back by saying this was Brookfield's responsibility.⁵

"Kids have come from all over the country for a big party in our park, and Mayor [Mike] Bloomberg has given them diplomatic immunity⁶," half-joked Ro Sheffe, a member of the city's Community Board⁷ 1, representing lower Manhattan.

Brookfield rules prohibit sleeping bags, tarps and sleeping on the ground. Even if this were a public park, Supreme Court cases on the "time, place and manner" for demonstrations would clearly allow officials to stop a month-long sleepover.⁸

Occupy Wall Street leadership and lawyers picked Zuccotti Park knowing the split responsibility for privately owned public spaces would give them a better chance to stay than in a public park. The absence of quasipublic parks explains why similar Occupy efforts failed in Washington, Chicago and Trenton, N.J., where police quickly removed protesters camping out in parks.

Last week, Brookfield finally asked the New York police commissioner⁹ for help. "The manner in which the protesters are occupying the park violates the law, violates the rules of the park, deprives the community of its rights of quiet enjoyment to the park, and creates health and public safety issues that need to be addressed immediately," its letter to the police reads.

"Complaints range from outrage over numerous laws being broken including but not limited to lewdness, groping, drinking and drug use to the lack of safe access to and usage of the park, to the ongoing noise at all hours, to unsanitary conditions and to offensive odors."

The Brookfield letter also notes that its security team isn't able to screen the many deliveries of large packages to the park: "The park's location in the financial district makes this activity particularly concerning." This is a good point, considering that police have conducted random vehicle searches for terrorists every day since 9/11 on Broadway, diagonally across from the park.¹⁰

The city agreed to Brookfield's requests, starting with a cleaning of the park scheduled for early last Friday. But then liberal City Council¹¹ members and other politicians sympathetic to the protesters strong-armed Brookfield into withdrawing its request to enforce the law.

"Brookfield got lots of calls from many elected officials threatening them and saying, 'If you don't stop this, we'll make your life more difficult,'" Mayor Bloomberg said on his radio show on Friday.

No real estate developer can get on the wrong side of the city pols and zoning regulators, who review thousands of requests every year.¹² Crony capitalism such as zoning deals are all about regulators making sure they can get their way.¹³

Before being shut up by politicians, Brookfield spoke for hundreds of thousands of weary area workers and residents. This columnist, who lives a block from the park, can attest to the impact on the neighborhood, though I suppose I should be grateful that my newborn son is now mostly trained to sleep through late-night drumming, chanting and vuvuzela horns. Anyone tempted to idealize this movement should visit and contrast the aggressive, often drugged-out crew around the campsite with a family community still gamely rebuilding after 9/11.

Occupy Wall Street promised an Arab Spring of regime change.[14] Protesters should know that the street bordering the park now called Liberty Street was called Crown Street from the 1600s until just after the Revolutionary War. The protesters are a couple of centuries late to our democratic revolution, but there's still time to make a statement against crony capitalism. All they have to do is leave.

From *The Wall Street Journal*, October 17, 2011

I. New Words

attest	[əˈtest]	v.	to show or prove that sth is true
cathedral	[kəˈθi:drəl]	n.	大教堂
dispossessed	[ˌdispəˈzest]	n.	the ~ （总称）被剥夺权利的一族
excessive	[ikˈsesiv]	adj.	过多的，过分的
extortion	[iksˈtɔ:ʃən]	n.	敲诈，勒索
extract	[iksˈtrækt]	v.	to obtain sth from sb who is unwilling to give
filth	[filθ]	n.	肮脏，污物
gamely	[ˈgeimli]	adv.	bravely
grab	[græb]	v.	抓，夺取
groping	[ˈgrəupiŋ]	n.	the act of touching sb sexually, esp when they don't want you to
idealize	[aiˈdiəlaiz]	v.	to consider sth as being perfect
lewdness	[ˈlu:dnis]	n.	淫荡，猥亵
notorious	[nəuˈtɔ:riəs]	adj.	well-known for being bad
odor	[ˈəudə]	n.	smell, especially one that is unpleasant
old-fashioned	[ˈəuldˈfæʃənd]	adj.	老式的，过期的
outrage	[ˈautreidʒ]	n.	a strong feeling of shock and anger
overlord	[ˈəuvəlɔ:d]	n.	霸主，巨头
plaza	[ˈplɑ:zə]	n.	（城市中的）广场
quasipublic	[ˈkweizaiˈpʌblik]	adj.	准公共性的（指属公共性质但归私人所有的）
screen	[skri:n]	v.	to check to see if it is suitable
stink	[stiŋk]	n.	恶臭，异味

第八单元　社会问题

strong-arm	[ˈstrɔŋɑːm]	v.	to use threats or violence in order to make sb do what you want
tarp	[tɑːp]	n.	*AmE informal* (防水)油布
unsanitary	[ʌnˈsænitəri]	adj.	不卫生的
vuvuzela	[ˈvuvuzilə]	n.	呜呜祖拉(一种颜色鲜艳的塑料喇叭，声调单一，音量极高)

II. Notes to the Text

1. crony capitalism — 权贵资本主义(指权势阶级靠拉关系借以自肥的做法)
2. ..."privately owned public spaces" that New York City officials created as part of zoning deals with real estate developers.—纽约市官员作为与房地产开发商区域规划交易的一部分而创设的"私人拥有的公共场地"。(①real estate — property in the form of land or buildings; ②zoning—the choosing of areas to be developed for different purposes when planning a town)
3. U. S. Steel—United States Steel Corporation 美国钢铁公司(该公司成立于1901年，是美国最大的垄断跨国公司)
4. Brookfield Properties—a commercial real estate corporation that owns, develops and operates premier assets in the downtown cores of high-growth North American cities
5. City authorities—no doubt happy to have a place for the demonstrators several blocks away from landmarks such as the New York Stock Exchange—passed the buck back by saying this was Brookfield's responsibility.—与纽约证券交易所之类标志性建筑相隔几个街区能有一个容纳游行者的地方，纽约市当局无疑感到庆幸，声称此地归属布鲁克菲尔德房地产公司，把责任一推了之。(pass the buck—to make sb else responsible)
6. Mayor [Mike] Bloomberg has given them diplomatic immunity. —布隆伯格市长给他们提供外交豁免权。(diplomatic immunity—protection against particular laws that is given to diplomats. The term is used sarcastically in the sense of special protection.)
7. Community Board—社区委员会(A community board is made up of a group of volunteers who live, work or have other interests in the area. It often holds public meetings where interested citizens discuss community issues, monitor government performances and advise city agencies on neighborhood matters.)
8. ...Supreme Court cases on the "time, place and manner" for demonstrations would clearly allow officials to stop a month-long sleepover. —最高法院关于游行时间、地点和形式的案例裁决明确容许(执法)官员制止长达一个月的露宿。[美国遵循的是习惯法(Common Law)，最高法院的裁决往往具有法律效应。]
9. police commissioner — 警察局局长
10. This is a good point, considering that police have conducted random vehicle searches for terrorists every day since 9/11 on Broadway, diagonally across from the park. — 考虑到9·11事件之后警方每天都针对公园斜对面的百老汇大街车辆随意搜查恐怖分子，这一点提得有道理。(a good point—an idea that is sensible, logical)

233

11. City Council —市议会

12. No real estate developer can get on the wrong side of the city pols and zoing regulators, who review thousands of requests every year. —没有一个真正的房地产开发商能够得罪城市政客和区域规划管理人员，因为他们每年要审核数千项申请。(①get on the wrong side of sb — to lose sb's favor; ②pol—politician)

13. Crony capitalism such as zoning deals are all about regulators making sure they can get their way. —诸如分区交易之类的权贵资本主义全都是管理者设法确保他们能够为所欲为。(get one's way — to get or do what you want, especially when sb has tried to stop you)

14. Occupy Wall Street promised an Arab Spring of regime change. —占领华尔街运动断言将会带来更迭政权的"阿拉伯之春"。(①Arab Spring —"阿拉伯之春"，指2010年年底在北非和西亚的阿拉伯国家和其他一些国家发生的一系列以"民主"和"经济"为主题的反政府社会运动，先后波及突尼斯、埃及、利比亚、也门、叙利亚等国，导致多名领导人先后下台；②regime change — the term has been popularized by recent U.S. presidents in reference to Saddam Hussein's regime in Iraq and Muammar Gaddafi's regime in Lybia)

Lesson 25

Business Affairs, Bedroom Affairs

Executive recruiters sense that philanderers often move on to corporate shenanigans.[1]
One expert suggests that job candidates be interviewed with spouses.
(Abridged)

By Jayne O'Donnell and Greg Farrell

When Nathan Chapman was sentenced to $7^{1}/_{2}$ years in prison this week for defrauding Maryland's state pension fund system and looting his three publicly traded companies, he could thank testimony from three former mistresses for helping put him behind bars.[2] Chapman is but the latest example of common thread running through some of the recent scandal-prone companies: Many top executives accused of betraying the trust of shareholders also betrayed the trust of their wives.[3]

Tyco's[4] Dennis Kozlowski had at least two affairs with subordinates before he divorced his first wife and married his mistress, according to trial testimony. WorldCom's[5] Bernie Ebbers openly courted a company sales executive while married to his first wife. Enron's[6] Jeff Skilling, who said he left the company in 2001 to tend to "family matters," had divorced his wife four years earlier and taken up with a coworker nicknamed "Va Voom" around the office.[7] Meanwhile, two other top Enron officials were openly dating women—one a stripper and the other a co-worker—outside of their marriages, according to former colleagues and news accounts.

As criminal trials for Kozlowski and Ebbers approach in January—with Skilling's not far behind —many companies are recognizing there may be a lesson here. In a quest for more ethical leaders, recruiters are increasingly looking into executives' personal lives for evidence of womanizing and other behavior that raises questions about their integrity.[8] While there's no scientific proof that a philanderer is more—or less—likely to be involved in financial fraud, many executives implicated in recent corporate scandals exhibited other forms of loose moral behavior along the way.[9]

Thomas DiBiagio, the U.S. Attorney for Maryland[10], says prosecutors investigate cases using "instincts and common sense" and recognize the traits philanderers and white-collar criminals may share. "If their life is a lie, it's not confined to their personal life," says DiBiagio, whose office prosecuted Chapman. "If they are lying to their wife, there's huge potential they are also lying to their colleagues, their board of directors and potentially their auditors."

Recruitment consultants say companies are increasingly asking for more in-depth background checks and research that goes beyond traditional references to help find executives with the highest professional and personal ethics.

More are taking information about morals and ethics into consideration when deciding to hire or promote an executive.

Some experts believe strongly there is a connection between cheating on and off the job—which is one reason for businesses to frown on extramarital affairs.[11]

"Fish rot from the head," says Robert Hogan, a psychologist and management consultant who is an expert in "dark side" traits.

Hogan says it can be difficult for people to make honest choices when they are leading double lives.

"Some of my colleagues in psychology think there's a distinction between embezzling, compulsive lying, substance abuse, and philandering, but it's all of a piece[12]," says Hogan, who owns Hogan Assessment Systems in Tulsa[13].

Of course cheating and ugly divorces occur in the upper ranks of companies that appear squeaky clean[14] as well. Despite his legendary reputation as a CEO, General Electric's[15] Jack Welch endured considerable public humiliation after his retirement in 2001. In 2002, Jane Beasley Welch sought a divorce from her husband after learning of his affair with an editor of the *Harvard Business Review*.

Author and corporate strategist Dave Stein says he recommends that candidates be interviewed at least once with their spouses to help get a more complete picture of the person. It doesn't rule out the possibility the candidate has cheated[16], but "if you expect them to be part of a team, it's helpful to see that person in action and observe how they behave with their significant others," says Stein.

Along with affecting corporate culture, affairs can cause legal problems—not to mention embarrassment—when executives find themselves in hot water.[17] Former federal prosecutor Samuel Seymour says, when he is representing someone at the center of a legal scandal, he tries to learn everything he can about their personal life, including any extramarital affairs.

"Personal problems and legal problems cannot always be kept separate," says Seymour, a white-collar defense lawyer at Sullivan & Cromwell[18]. "If a client's personal difficulties get attention in the press, that can affect the outcome of the case because those potentially embarrassing facts may find their way into the courtroom as well."

Sherron Watkins, who became Enron's internal whistle-blower after alerting former CEO Kenneth Lay of accounting problems, also became an expert on the company's dysfunctional corporate culture.[19] Several top Enron executives cheated on spouses or left them for younger women at the office.

"There are plenty of executives who will not cross those lines," Watkins says of philandering. "But it does set you up for potentially reciprocal behavior, where someone says he might as well cheat on his expense report.[20]"

Watkins says the rapid ascent of Skilling's now-wife Rebecca Carter, the woman once known by coworkers as "Va Voom," raised eyebrows at Enron. Carter moved from her position in corporate relations to a $600,000-a-year job as secretary to the board of directors.

"That was the only problem, she was getting these jobs and promotions," says Watkins.

Ken Rice, former head of Enron Broadband, carried on an open affair with a top female executive, Amanda Martin, according to Watkins and the book, *The Smartest Guys in the Room*[21]. Rice pleaded guilty to participating in the Enron fraud and has agreed to cooperate with prosecutors.[22] "The Ken Rice-Amanda Martin thing was flagrant," says Watkins. "It was widely known and widely talked about. Amanda would be talking in the elevator about how she was on the back of a jet ski with Ken Rice at a retreat. She was almost bragging."

Rice's lawyer did not respond to requests for comment; Martin could not be reached.

Extramarital affairs can help create an "anything goes" atmosphere[23], says Hogan.

Former WorldCom CEO Ebbers, a Baptist Sunday school teacher, would be at his desk most mornings by 8 and often reading the Bible, no matter how late he was out drinking the night before, say former associates. The married Ebbers could often be spotted at Tico's steakhouse in Jackson, Miss.[24], with his then-girlfriend—and current wife—Kristie or at other bars. Kristie Ebbers is a former top sales representative at WorldCom. Before Kristie, the former president of customer service, Diana Day, inspired fear among colleagues because of her close relationship with Ebbers. Some would joke that the company's former name, LDDS, stood for "Listen to what Diana Day Says," say former employees.

Executive suite philandering can easily become fodder for courtroom proceedings[25], as Chapman learned the hard way. On-the-job girlfriends can be implicated as accomplices—or turned into government witnesses.

Chapman managed $100 million of Maryland's $29 billion state pension system until he was fired by trustees in 2002. And his crimes cost the state's funds $5 million. A jury convicted him in August of 23 counts of fraud, including writing "business development" check on his companies' accounts for cash and gifts to girlfriends. Chapman was found innocent of corrupting a pension trustee, Debra Humphries, who was one of the mistresses who received a Hawaiian vacation along with money and gifts.

Chapman's lawyer, William Martin, asked jurors to disregard the evidence of Chapman's affairs: "I hope you will not allow the government to put sex into this case."

But how could prosecutors resist? DiBiagio says because the case involved allegations Chapman looted his companies, having a money trail that led to his girlfriends helped explain Chapman's motive to jurors.

Besides, once Chapman's mistresses learned they were not the only girlfriends, DiBiagio says they made "hard decisions about their loyalty to the defendant."[26]

During the trial of former Tyco CEO Dennis Kozlowski and former CFO[27] Mark Swartz, prosecutors in Manhattan called a variety of former Tyco staffers to the stand as witnesses. Two of these witnesses admitted to affairs with Kozlowski. Barbara Jacques testified about her relationship with Kozlowski in the 1980s, and how she planned an exotic birthday party for his second wife, Karen Mayo, in 2001 using company funds.

There are no statistics on interoffice affairs involving top executives and many corporate crimes are never discovered, so the connection between philandering and fraud is largely anecdotal. But Janis Abrahams Spring, a Westport, Conn.[28], psychologist and author says there are some common personality traits between those who cheat in and outside the office.

"Some people lie a lot and break the rules a lot —it's a way of being," says Spring, author of *How Can I Forgive You*? "They see themselves as entitled to get their needs met, so you may see these behaviors across the board[29]."

From *USA Today*, November 5, 2004

I. New Words

accomplice	[əˈkɔmplis]	n.	a person helping another to commit a crime
allegation	[ˌæliˈgeiʃən]	n.	断言,陈述,辩解
anecdotal	[ˌænikˈdəutəl]	adj.	逸事的,趣闻的
auditor	[ˈɔːditə]	n.	审计员
consultant	[kənˈsʌltənt]	n.	one that gives expert or professional advice
defendant	[diˈfendənt]	n.	被告
defraud	[diˈfrɔːd]	v.	to deceive so as to get sth
disregard	[ˌdisriˈgaːd]	v.	to ignore
embezzle	[imˈbezl]	v.	盗用,挪用
entitle	[inˈtaitl]	v.	to give sb the right to have or do sth
flagrant	[ˈfleigrənt]	adj.	shocking because of being so obvious
fodder	[ˈfɔdə]	n.	饲料;素材
fraud	[frɔːd]	n.	the crime of cheating to get money illegally
implicate	[ˈimplikeit]	v.	to involve or connect intimately
in-depth	[ˌinˈdepθ]	adj.	very thorough and detailed
interoffice	[ˌintəˈɔfis]	adj.	各办公室间的
juror	[ˈdʒuərə]	n.	one who serves as a member of a jury
philander	[fiˈlændə]	v.	玩弄女性,调情
prosecute	[ˈprɔsikjuːt]	v.	起诉,检举
shenanigan	[ʃəˈnænigən]	n.	*informal* a secret or dishonest activity
staffer	[ˈstaːfə]	n.	a member of a staff
steakhouse	[ˈsteikhaus]	n.	牛排餐厅
stripper	[ˈstripə]	n.	脱衣舞表演者
subordinate	[səˈbɔːdinət]	n.	属下
recruitment	[riˈkruːtmənt]	n.	招聘
trait	[treit]	n.	a particular quality in personality
trustee	[trʌsˈtiː]	n.	(董事会)成员

II. Background Information

工作关系与恋情关系

　　工作场所的恋情关系(workplace romance)是美国公司较为普遍的现象。据美国人力资源管理协会(Society of Human Resource Management)2005年所公布的调查数据,大约有40%的人有过工作场所的恋爱经历。社会学者斯普拉金斯(Spragins)估计美国公司里目前有1000万对男女存在爱情关系。无怪乎美国社会中许多人认为:"未来伴侣的最大来源不是网络,也不是酒吧,而是工作场所。"美国有一些公司对这种现象的看法是:工作场所的爱情关系会导致干活分心,影响工作效率,有可能导致性骚扰起诉,给公司带来不必要的麻烦。为此,美国大约有30%的公司明确告诫员工:"不要工作之时偷欢"(Don't mix business with pleasure);"不得在公司内物色对象"(Don't fish off the company pier)。

　　工作场所的恋情关系有相当一部分发生在上下级之间,这些关系有一些结局美好,最终发展成夫妻关系,如通用汽车公司董事长约翰·F.史密斯与其秘书莉迪亚最终步入婚姻的殿堂。然而,管理人员与员工的恋情关系大部分的结局是分手。在这些关系中有一部分是婚外情关系,女方仅是被玩弄的对象。通常关系结束之日也是女方被解雇之时。多数情况下女方自认倒霉,忍气吞声离开。但也有不少女方会诉诸法律,状告男方性骚扰(file a sexual harassment suit)。

　　管理人员与下属的恋情关系对公司可能造成的危害远远超过一般员工之间的爱情关系。管理人员对其所爱对象会过分关爱,在工作分配、职务晋升、工资提级方面给予特殊照顾。这就会严重损害其他员工的工作积极性,同时也会影响公司的风气,其他人会加以仿效。更重要的是,关系破裂引起的官司会破坏公司的形象。

　　美国前总统克林顿与白宫实习生莱温斯基的性丑闻公之于世后,美国许多公司经理变得谨慎起来,一些想继续偷欢又要避免吃官司的经理在发生性关系之前通过法律机构与女方签订"爱情契约"(Cupid or love contract)或"自愿协议"(consensual agreement)。

　　安然公司执行总裁杰弗里·斯基林的财务丑闻、和公司会计的性丑闻败露之后,美国很多公司看清了财务丑闻与性丑闻的内在关联。为防止此类问题发生,越来越多的公司对管理人员与员工的恋情关系采取了相应对策,主要措施有以下两条:

　　1. 禁止(ban)。制定管理人员不得与员工有亲密关系的准则(non-fraternization guidelines)。

　　2. 控制(containment)。规定管理人员如果与员工存在恋爱关系,必须汇报(date-and-tell policies),并接受公司的监督和调动安排。

III. Notes to the Text

1. Executive recruiters sense that philanderers often move on to corporate shenanigans — 经理招聘者感到喜欢调情的男人也常常会在公司里搞欺骗。

2. When Nathan Chapman was sentenced to 7$\frac{1}{2}$ years in prison this week for defrauding Maryland's state pension fund system and looting his three publicly traded companies, he could thank testimony from three former mistresses for helping put him behind bars. — 本周，内森·查普曼因诈骗马里兰州养老基金系统，并且洗劫了他所管理的三家股票公开上市的公司而被判处七年六个月有期徒刑，他可得感谢先前的三个情妇，是她们的证词帮他进入铁牢。

3. Chapman is but the latest example of common thread running through some of the recent scandal-prone companies: Many top executives accused of betraying the trust of shareholders also betrayed the trust of their wives. — 查普曼只不过是显示近来一些常出丑闻的公司所共有问题的一个最新案例，这个问题便是：许多被指控辜负股东们信任的高层管理人员同时也辜负了他们妻子的信任。(scandal-prone — likely to suffer scandals)

4. Tyco — 泰科国际有限公司(《财富》世界500强企业，是一家总部位于美国的全球性的多元化跨国企业，经营消防安全、医疗保健、电子、工程产品与服务行业。)

5. WorldCom — 世通公司(美国的一家电讯公司，为客户提供互联网接入、长途电话、本地电话、数据传输等电讯业务。该公司2002年6月被查出存在重大假账欺诈行为。)

6. Enron — 安然公司(世界上最大的综合性天然气和电力公司之一，成立于1958年，总部设在美国休斯敦。2001年该公司暴露了虚报利润、掩盖巨额债务的财务丑闻。事发后，该公司名称便成了"欺骗"的代名词。)

7. ... taken up with a coworker nicknamed "Va Voom" around the office. — (他)开始与一位在办公室里绰号为"狐狸精"的同事亲密交往(① take up with — *informal* to begin to be friendly with sb, especially sb with a bad reputation; ② Va Voom — *informal* the quality of being sexually attractive)

8. In a quest for more ethical leaders, recruiters are increasingly looking into executives' personal lives for evidence of womanizing and other behavior that raises questions about their integrity. — 为了寻找更有道德的领导，招聘人员正越来越多地考察管理人员们的私生活，看是否存在玩弄女性的情况以及其他人品问题。(womanize — to habitually pay attention to many women for sexual purposes)

9. While there's no scientific proof that a philanderer is more—or less—likely to be involved in financial fraud, many executives implicated in recent corporate scandals exhibited other forms of loose moral behavior along the way. — 虽然没有科学证据证明喜欢调情的男人是更可能或是更不可能参与经济诈骗，但是近来公司丑闻所牵涉的许多管理人员表现出了其他形式的道德放任行为。

10. the U.S. Attorney for Maryland — 美国联邦政府派驻马里兰州检察官

11. Some experts believe strongly there is a connection between cheating on and off the job — which is one reason for businesses to frown on extramarital affairs. — 一些专家坚信工作上

的欺骗和工作外的欺骗是相关的——这也是企业对婚外恋反感的原因之一。(frown on — to disapprove of sth)

12. Some of my colleagues in psychology think there's a distinction between embezzling, compulsive lying, substance abuse, and philandering, but it's all of a piece... — 我的一些心理学同行认为挪用公款、惯于说谎、滥用毒品与玩弄女人之间是有区别的,但这些完全是一回事。(① compulsive—very difficult to stop or control; ② substance—referring to drugs; ③ all of a piece—all the same)

13. Tulsa — 塔尔萨(美国俄克拉何马州东北部一城市)

14. squeaky clean — *informal* completely clean; morally correct in every way

15. General Electric — 美国通用电气公司(美国最大的电器和电子设备制造及提供技术和服务业务的跨国公司)

16. It doesn't rule out the possibility the candidate has cheated... — 这不排除候选人撒谎的可能性(to rule out — to state that sth is not possible)

17. Along with affecting corporate culture, affairs can cause legal problems—not to mention embarrassment—when executives find themselves in hot water. — 婚外情不仅会影响公司的风气,还会带来法律问题,更不用说管理人员陷入困境所造成的难堪局面。(in hot water—in trouble or difficulty)

18. Sullivan & Cromwell — 苏利文与克伦威尔律师事务所(美国纽约著名律师事务所,该所在世界许多大城市设有办事处)

19. Sherron Watkins, who became Enron's internal whistle-blower after alerting former CEO Kenneth Lay of accounting problems, also became an expert on the company's dysfunctional corporate culture. — 由告诫前任执行总裁肯尼思·莱当心账目问题,转而成为安然公司内部丑闻揭发者的谢伦·沃特金斯,也成了处理公司中不正常人事关系的专家。(① whistle-blower—sb who tells people in authority or the public about dishonest or illegal practices in business; ② dysfunctional—not working normally)

20. But it does set you up for potentially reciprocal behavior, where someone says he might as well cheat on his expense report. — 但是玩弄女性确实给可能发生的类似行为创造了条件,使有的人认为他同样也可以在报账方面玩欺骗。(① set sb up for — to provide the conditions sb needs for some activity; ② reciprocal — existing on both sides)

21. *The Smartest Guys in the Room* —《屋内聪明人》(作者Bethany McLean,该书揭露安然公司丑恶的内幕)

22. Rice pleaded guilty to participating in the Enron fraud and has agreed to cooperate with prosecutors. — 赖斯承认参与了安然公司欺骗案,已同意与检察官合作。(plead guilty — to admit in a court of law that one is guilty)

23. Extramarital affairs can help create an "anything goes" atmosphere... — 婚外关系会促使产生"干什么都行"的气氛(anything goes—anything that sb says or does is acceptable or allowed, however shocking or unusual it may be)

24. Jackson, Miss. — 密西西比州杰克逊市

25. Executive suite philandering can easily become fodder for courtroom proceedings... — 经理套房里的调情很容易成为法律诉讼的资料

26. Besides, once Chapman's mistresses learned they were not the only girlfriends, DiBiagio says they made "hard decisions about their loyalty to the defendant." —— 此外，迪比亚吉欧说："一旦查普曼的情妇知道她们并非是唯一的情人，她们便对是否忠实于原告做出无情的决定。"

27. CFO —— Chief Finance Officer 首席财务官

28. Westport, Conn. —— 康涅狄格州韦斯特波特市

29. so you may see these behaviors across the board —— 因此你可以全面来看这些行为。(across the board—involving everyone or everything in an activity)

IV. Language Features

委 婉 语

本文标题中的"bedroom affairs"是委婉语，表达的是"bedroom sexual affairs"之意。

委婉语是用来替代被认为过于露骨、过于伤人或不太悦耳的词或短语，主要有两种：缩小性委婉语和夸张性委婉语。

缩小性委婉语是用较含蓄、性质较轻的词语来表达不便直言的事情。主要表现在以下几个方面：

1. 生、老、病、死

英语中常说：She is expecting 而不直说 She is pregnant（怀孕）；常用 pass away, depart 替代 die; 用 elderly people, senior citizens 替代 old people。

2. 贫穷

英语中 poor 常被 needy, underprivileged, disadvantaged 替代。

3. 犯罪

burglary（夜盗）被说成是 surreptitious entry（秘密进入），prison（监狱）被称为 "correctional center"（教养中心）。

4. 性或性器官

英语中 have sex（发生性行为）常被婉称为 make love（做爱）；illegitimate child（私生子）被称作 love child（爱情生下的孩子）；pornographical movie（黄色电影）被称为 adult film（成人电影）；sexual organs（生殖器官）被说成是 private parts（阴部）。

夸张性委婉语就是将原词语替换成意思更雅致、更体面、更重要的词语。主要有下列几种：

1. 机构

把 college（学院）称作 university（大学）；把一些实力不雄厚的公司称作 industry（企业），如 hotel industry（旅馆业），garage industry（垃圾清理业）。

2. 职业

把 hairdresser（理发员）说成是 beautician（美容师）；floorsweeper（清洁工）被称作 custodian engineer（房屋管理师）；gardener（园丁）被称为 landscaper（园林师）；janitor

（看门的）被说成 superintendant（监管人）

3. 政治、军事

用一些温和词语来掩饰社会问题,美化政府形象。如：把 economic crisis（经济危机）说成 recession（衰退）；strike（罢工）被说成 industrial action（工业行动），industrial dispute（工业纠纷）；slum（贫民窟）被说成 substandard housing（不够标准的住房）；relief（救济）说成 welfare（福利）；ghetto（贫民区）被说成 inner city（内城区）；ground war（地面战争）说成 ground operation（地面行动）；neutron bomb（中子弹）说成 clean bomb（清洁弹）；aggression（侵略）被说成 invasion（进入）或 involvement（介入）；attack（进攻）被说成 pacify the area（绥靖）。

上述美化性词语(cosmetic words)在西方报刊中较为常见,在阅读中应予以注意。

V. Analysis of Content

1. The phrase "business affairs" in the headline of the article refers to _____.
   A. cheating on the job   B. business matters
   C. activities connected with executives   D. extramarital affairs of executives

2. The author's list of problems caused by executives' extramarital affairs does NOT include _____.
   A. legal problems   B. embarrassment to the executives
   C. love children   D. dysfunctional corporate culture

3. The word "hard" in the sentence "they made hard decisions about their loyalty to the defendant (Para. 27) means _____.
   A. difficult   B. unfair
   C. showing no sympathy   D. likely to hurt

4. The connection between philandering and fraud in the article is based on _____.
   A. sound reasoning   B. statistics
   C. hearsays   D. anecdotes

5. It can be inferred from the article that Chapman's mistresses gave testimony and helped put him behind bars because _____.
   A. they were forced to do so   B. they felt that they had been cheated
   C. they wanted to atone from their mistake   D. they had a sense of justice

VI. Questions on the Article

1. Why was Nathan Chapman sentenced to $7\frac{1}{2}$ years in prison? Who helped put him in prison?
2. What was the common problem shared by some of the recent scandal-prone companies?
3. What are recruiters doing to find more ethical leaders?

4. Who is Thomas DiBiagio? What does he think of the relationship between philandering and white-collar crimes?
5. What is Hogan's view on the relationship between cheating on the job and off the job?
6. What does Dave Stein recommend?
7. What does Seymour think of the effects of personal problems on legal problems?
8. What role did Sherron Watkins play in the exposure of the Enron scandal?
9. What effects can extramarital affairs create according to Hogan?
10. Who is Diana Day? Why did she inspire fear among colleagues?
11. Why did prosecutors refuse to disregard the evidence of Chapman's extramarital affairs as his lawyer requested?

VII. Topics for Discussion

1. Is there a connection between cheating on and off the job?
2. Can an executive recruiter get a more complete picture of candidates if they are interviewed with their spouses?

Lesson 26

A Heartbroken Nation

  The United States seems to be failing to protect its people by the week. With the gun massacre in East Buffalo followed by the school shooting in Uvalde, Texas, many Americans have spent the past few days gripped by overwhelming incredulity and grief, exhaustion and fury over the loss of life. What can be done beyond living with heartbreak?

  There is incredulity at the inaction of the police in Uvalde.[1] Seventy-eight minutes elapsed after the gunman walked inside before police, believing "there were no kids at risk," finally confronted him[2], according to Steven C. McCraw, the director of the Texas Department of Public Safety. Meanwhile, 911 dispatchers[3] received several calls from inside the classroom, including repeated calls from a child begging them to send the police. By the end of his rampage, the gunman had killed 19 children and two teachers at Robb Elementary School.

  Mr. McCraw acknowledged the multiple failures of judgment. In response to a question about whether the commander at the scene should offer an apology to the victims' families, he said, "If I thought it would help, I would apologize."

  Police held back a group of horrified parents who gathered even as shots continued to ring out inside the school and begged officers to move in and try to rescue their children. At least one mother was put in handcuffs, only to spring over a fence and sprint into the school to scoop up her child when the opportunity presented itself. The police, she said, were "doing nothing."

  Those officers had been training for years for just such an attack. Yet when the moment came, all that preparation did nothing to stop a gunman wielding an assault rifle in a school full of children.

  There is unspeakable grief over the deaths of children like Layla Salazar, who liked to make TikTok videos, wear denim jackets and sing "Sweet Child o' Mine" on the way to school each morning.

  "They took her away from us," Layla's grandfather Vincent Salazar told *The Times*. "How do you mend a broken heart from a family as close as we had?[4]"

  Irma Garcia, a teacher at Robb Elementary, liked classic rock. Her body was found with children still in her embrace, according to her nephew. A fourth grader who survived the attack said that Ms. Garcia and another teacher, Eva Mireles, had saved his and other students' lives. "They were in front of my classmates to help," he said. "To save them."

  There is also a profound sense of national exhaustion that comes when tragedy is layered upon tragedy.[5] In Buffalo, three funerals were held on Friday for victims of the mass shooting that took place at a supermarket on May 14. Ten people were killed, and three others were wounded.

  "It's like Groundhog's Day.[6] We've seen this over and over again," Mark Talley, the son of one of the victims, Geraldine Talley, said at a news conference on Thursday.

  In Buffalo, a white gunman targeted a predominantly Black neighborhood with his AR-15-style assault rifle; he was an adherent of the racist conspiracy theory known as replacement theory[7], which posits that white Americans are being displaced by immigrants and people of color. Nearly half of Republicans told pollsters recently that they agree with the general thesis that a cabal of powerful people is encouraging immigrants to come here to sway politics.

The combination of paranoia and firearms has led to tragedy again and again.[8] "Why are we willing to live with this carnage?" President Biden asked the nation on Tuesday.

The report of each gunshot in a mass killing echoes long after the next killing eclipses it.[9] According to his family, Joe Garcia, Ms. Garcia's husband, died on Thursday of a heart attack. Mr. Garcia, 50, had just gotten home from the memorial for his wife on Thursday morning when he collapsed.

It is entirely reasonable to ask how much more of this a nation can be expected to bear. The answer is infuriating: There have been 213 mass shootings in the United States in the first 21 weeks of 2022. An average of 321 Americans are shot every single day. And every day, there are roughly more than 50,000 gun sales recorded. Properly maintained, those guns will fire like new for decades.

There was some hope after the massacre at the Sandy Hook Elementary School in Newtown, Conn., in 2012, which left 20 children and six teachers dead, that America had finally reached the limit of tragedy it could withstand and that, perhaps, the gun lobby had reached the high-water mark of its power.[10]

A decade later, neither of those holds true. On Friday, the former president Donald Trump, Senator Ted Cruz of Texas, Gov. Kristi Noem of South Dakota and Lt. Gov.[11] Mark Robinson of North Carolina all spoke at the annual convention of the National Rifle Association[12] in Houston, a few hours' drive from Uvalde. There is no better manifestation of the gun lobby's total capture of so much of the G.O.P.[13]

States around the country have made halting but commendable progress in passing sensible gun safety measures — red flag laws[14], background checks[15] and age of purchase requirements. They face stiff headwinds. A federal court this month struck down a California law that set the age limit for purchasingsemiautomatic weapons at 21.[16] But the legislature is now considering other promising bills that would limit the advertising of certain guns to children and allow Californians to sue gun makers. Anything that introduces friction into the system of gun acquisition is to the good.[17]

In New York this week, a federal judge tossed out a challenge from gun groups to a law that allows civil lawsuits against companies that have endangered public safety.[18] And Gov. Kathy Hochul called on the legislature to raise the age limit to purchase some assault weapons to 21. The shooter in Texas waited until his 18th birthday to buy a pair of assault weapons and hundreds of rounds of ammunition.

In Washington, D.C., there is talk that Republican and Democratic lawmakers might make a deal on some type of national red flag law, which would allow the police to take guns away from people judged to be an imminent danger to themselves or others.

Senator Chris Murphy, Democrat of Connecticut, has been leading a bipartisan group of senators that is considering establishing a more comprehensive federal background check system, a reform supported by 88 percent of Americans.

We have seen these bipartisan efforts on gun safety measures come and go without results. Still, in the face of Republican intransigence, Democrats — Mr. Biden, in particular — should do whatever they can. Senator Murphy, who has led the charge for tougher gun regulations since Sandy Hook, put it well on the floor of the Senate this past week.[19]

"What are we doing?" he asked his colleagues. "Why do you go through all the hassle of getting this job, of putting yourself in a position of authority," he wondered, if the answer is to do nothing "as the slaughter increases, as our kids run for their lives?"[20]

It's a question that speaks to the Senate directly and the entire system of American government more broadly. Yes, the country's democratic system represents the diversity of views in this country on guns. But as currently structured, Congress is fundamentally unresponsive to the needs of its most vulnerable citizens and has been corrupted by powerful interest groups, allowing those groups to block even modest changes that the vast majority of Americans support.

We Americans all share this vast country and need to figure out how to make it better and keep one another alive and thriving. Right now, we're failing at that primary responsibility. There are glimmers of hope, especially at the state level, that things are changing. But even there, progress is agonizingly slow and won't be enough for the hundreds of Americans who will be shot today and tomorrow and every day until action is taken.

From *New York Times*, May 28, 2022

I. New Words

agonizingly	[ˈægənaizɪŋli]	adv.	used meaning "extremely" to emphasize sth negative
ammunition	[ˌæmjuəˈnɪʃ(ə)n]	n.	a supply of bullets
bipartisan	[ˌbaɪˈpɑːrtɪzn]	adj.	involving two political parties
cabal	[kəˈbæl]	n.	阴谋小集团
carnage	[ˈkɑrnɪdʒ]	n.	killing, bloodshed
commendable	[kəˈmendəb(ə)l]	adj.	deserving praise and approval
denim	[ˈdenɪm]	n.	粗纹棉布；~ jacket 牛仔夹克
exhaustion	[ɪgˈzɔstʃ(ə)n]	n.	the state of being very tired
imminent	[ˈɪmɪnənt]	adj.	close in time
incredulity	[ˌɪnkrəˈdjuːləti]	n.	disbelief
infuriating	[ɪnˈfjurieɪtɪŋ]	adj.	making you extremely angry
intransigence	[ɪnˈtrænzɪdʒəns]	n.	an unreasonable refusal to change ideas
massacre	[ˈmæsəkər]	n.	slaughter
paranoia	[ˌpærəˈnɔɪə]	n.	fear or suspicion of other people
pollster	[ˈpoʊlstər]	n.	民意测验员
rampage	[ˈræmpeɪdʒ]	n.	a sudden period of wild and violent behavior

ring	[riŋ]	v.	~ out to be heard loudly and clearly (声音)响亮，嘹亮；
scoop	[sku:p]	v.	~ sb/sth up to lift sb/sth with a quick continuous movement
sway	[swei]	v.	to cause sth to change
toss	[tɔ:s]	v.	~ out 扔掉；抛弃
wield	[wi:ld]	v.	to hold sth, ready to use it as a weapon or tool

II. Background Information

美国枪支问题

美国拥有全球最多的民用枪支。根据瑞士日内瓦研究机构"小武器调查"2018年的一份报告，美国人口不到世界人口的5%，但拥有民用枪支的数量却占全球的46%，平均每100名居民拥有120.5支枪支。无论是全国私人持有枪支的总数还是人均持有枪支的数量，美国都高居世界第一。2017年美国私人拥有枪支约3.93亿支，但登记注册的私人拥枪数却只有107万左右，绝大多数枪支未经登记而分散在民间。此外，美国有些人在家用从互联网廉价购得的各种枪支配件组装枪。美国警方认为，如果把这些自己组装成的"幽灵枪（ghost guns）"包括在内，美国人所拥有的枪支数量高达5亿支左右。社会矛盾激化和种族关系恶化导致人们缺乏安全感，也促使购枪数量增加。2020年新冠疫情以来，用于防身的半自动手枪的购买数量持续增加。2020年，美国的枪支销量飙升至从未有过的高度，较2019年增长近64%。2021年美国的枪支销售量为1850万支，仅次于2020年的2100万支。

枪支泛滥，枪祸不断。据《今日美国报》2020年12月18日报道，美国持枪杀人率是其他发达国家的25倍。2019年，美国死于枪击的人数为39596人；2020年为41500人，平均每天110多人；2021年为45079人；2022年为47286人，呈明显上升趋势。枪杀频发，死伤惨重，令人惊心。数据显示，2019年美国发生417起大规模枪击案，2020年611起，2021年692起，2022年又进一步升到647起。多年来的校园枪击事件给社会带来巨大伤痛。过去十年，美国共发生27起大规模校园枪击案。2022年5月24日罗伯小学枪击案总死亡人数高达21人，其中19人为小学生，2人为教师。这是继2012年12月14日桑迪胡克小学校园枪击案以来最严重的校园枪击案。

美国有关持枪和控枪的争论由来已久。美国宪法第二修正案规定了个人持枪权。持枪派和控枪派就该修正案释法问题展开激烈辩论。持枪派主张个人权利不得随意修改，枪支管控非法。而控枪派认为修正案所确立的是集体权利，政府有权对私人持有的枪支进行管控。围绕枪支管制立法，美国政治舞台上形成了以全国步枪协会为首的持枪派和以布雷迪运动为首的控枪派两派政治势力。在美国，控枪的声音通常只会在大规模枪击案后才被听到。每次重大枪击事件发生后，美国社会有关"持枪"和"控枪"的争论热度都会升高。在新闻热点降温以及政治争论价值减弱后,要求控枪的声音几乎也会以惊人的速度消失,直到下一起枪击案再次发生。美国的控枪问题已从政治、经济、文化等多个层面与美国社会深刻"绑定",牵一发而动全身。

枪支暴力导致悲剧不断出现,但枪支问题却顽疾难除,这与美国人的核心价值观——个人主义密切关联。个人主义强调个人权利至高无上,崇尚个人独立自由。持枪派人士认为持枪是公民自己的权利,他人不得过问。美国全国步枪协会(NRA)是美国最大的枪械拥有组织和强大的利益集团,受军火企业商支持。步枪协会手握雄厚资金,对受金钱左右的美国政治影响很大。有不少政府官员和国会议员获得过他们的资助。该协会在2016年总统选举中捐出竞选资金高达5440万美元,其中为特朗普砸下了3000万美元。该协会与政界关系十分密切,每次年会都有政界显赫人物参会讲话。美国两党枪支管控立场相左。总体而言,美国民主党主张控枪,而共和党则一直持相反态度。数据显示,91%的民主党人支持更严格的枪支法,而共和党人只有24%的人支持。美国枪祸频发与美国买枪标准有很大关系。在美国只需通过犯罪背景调查而无须登记就能买到枪支。枪支暴力问题凸显美国治理能力衰败。相互掣肘的政治体制、日益分化的政治生态、无孔不入的利益集团、难以根除的种族歧视,使美国枪支管控举步维艰。

III. Notes to the Text

1. There is incredulity at the inaction of the police in Uvalde. —人们对尤瓦尔迪市警方的不作为感到难以置信。(incredulity—disbelief)

2. Seventy-eight minutes elapsed after the gunman walked inside before police, believing "there were no kids at risk," finally confronted him... —从枪手进入学校到警察最终与他对峙,时间流失了78分钟,警方一直认为"孩子们没有危险"。(①elapse — (of time) to pass by; ② confront — to be faced with)

3. 911 dispatchers—911报警电话中心调度员(911—the telephone number used in the U.S. calling the police, fire or ambulance services in an emergency)

4. How do you mend a broken heart from a family as close as we had?—你们如何愈合我们关系这么亲密的家庭成员的破碎的心?

5. ...when tragedy is layered upon tragedy.—当悲剧接踵而至。(layer — to form in layers)

6. It's like Groundhog's Day. —就像土拨鼠日。(Groundhog's Day — a popular North American tradition observed in the United States and Canada on February)

7. ...he was an adherent of the racist conspiracy theory known as replacement theory... — 他是名为"替换理论"的种族主义阴谋论的信徒。(replacement theory—also known as the Great Replacement, is a white nationalist far-right conspiracy theory disseminated by French author Renaud Camus. The original theory states that, with the complicity or cooperation of "replacist" elites, the ethnic French and white European populations at large are being demographically and culturally replaced with non-white peoples—especially from Muslim-majority coun-

tries—through mass migration, demographic growth and a drop in the birth rate of white Europeans. Since then, similar claims have been advanced in other national contexts, notably in the United States. Mainstream scholars have dismissed these claims as rooted in a misunderstanding of demographic statistics and premised upon an unscientific, racist worldview.)

8. The combination of paranoia and firearms has led to tragedy again and again.—偏执病态心理加上枪支泛滥,导致悲剧一次次发生。

9. The report of each gunshot in a mass killing echoes long after the next killing eclipses it.—每一次大规模枪杀案的报道都会引起长时间的共鸣,直至下一次杀戮令其相形见绌。(eclipse—to cause to seem less important)

10. ...the gun lobby had reached the high-water mark of its power.—枪支游说组织已经到达权力的巅峰。(high-water mark—the highest point)

11. Lt. Gov.—副州长

12. the National Rifle Association(NRA)—美国全国步枪协会

13. There is no better manifestation of the gun lobby's total capture of so much of the G.O.P.—没有什么能比这次年会更好地体现枪支游说集团对共和党这么多大人物的完全掌控。(the G.O.P.—the Grand Old Party; the Republican Party)

14. red flag laws—"红旗法案"(In the United States, a red flag law is a gun control law that permits police to petition a state court to order the temporary removal of firearms from a person who they believe may present a danger to others or themselves.)

15. background checks—背景审查(Background checks are a system that is used to screen individuals who wish to purchase firearms. The process involves submitting personal information, such as name and address, to a government database. This information is then used to check for any criminal history that would make an individual ineligible to purchase a gun.)

16. A federal court this month struck down a California law that set the age limit for purchasing-semiautomatic weapons at 21.—联邦法院本月推翻了加利福尼亚州的一项将购买半自动武器最低年龄限制在21岁的法律。(strike down—to say that a law is illegal and should not be obeyed)

17. Anything that introduces friction into the system of gun acquisition is to the good. —任何能够阻挠枪支获取的做法都不失为一件好事。

18. In New York this week, a federal judge tossed out a challenge from gun groups to a law that allows civil lawsuits against companies that have endangered public safety. —本周在纽约,联邦法官驳回枪支集团所提出的针对一项允许对危害公共安全的公司提出民事诉讼法律的质疑。

19. Senator Murphy, who has led the charge for tougher gun regulations since Sandy Hook, put it well on the floor of the Senate this past week. —自桑迪胡克枪击案以来,一直最积极地设法颁布更加严格的枪支管控法律的墨菲参议员在过去一周的参议院会上说得好。(put well — to express well)

20. "Why do you go through all the hassle of getting this job, of putting yourself in a position of authority," he wondered, if the answer is to do nothing "as the slaughter increases, as our kids

run for their lives?" ——"枪杀的数量在增多,我们的孩子在逃命。如果答案是什么都不干,"他诧异地说,"那你们为什么要奋力拼搏获得这份工作,使自己手中掌权?"(①hassle—struggle; ②authority—power)

IV. Language Features

"说"意动词

本文"说"意动词较为丰富,除say之外,还使用了tell(告诉,讲),ask(问道)和wonder(诧异地说)。

新闻报道经常转述、援引新闻相关人物的谈话,因而频频出现"说"意动词。报刊上所出现的"说"意动词数量很多。这些动词虽然在表示"说"这个总的概念方面是相同的,但是同中有异,在语义、情感、文体上存在不同程度的区别,这些词如果使用妥帖,就会产生以下效果:

1. 有助于语言准确

例1."We're not making any progress,"concludes Dallas officer Nabors.(conclude 推断说)

例2."I need my creative space behind closed doors,"she explains.(explain 解释说)

2. 有助于语言简洁

例1."And mine, too!"hastened Little Lucas.(hasten—say in a hurry 急急忙忙地说)

例2. Addressing foreign journalists here, he emphasized the ANC would not revert to violence...(emphasize—say in an emphatic manner 强调说)

3. 有助于态度鲜明

例1."We're tennis fanatics: we love it,"cheers Christie Ann's aunt...(cheer 喝彩说)

例2."One of the finest speeches I've ever heard,"praised Ford speaking of the brief, touching text drafted by Reagan.(praise 赞扬说)

4. 有助于语言生动

例1."The next guy who hollers 'Headache!', I'm gonna kick his ass," sputters a winded James.(sputter—因激动而愤怒唾沫飞溅地说)

例2. Shrugged a Defense Department official:"They are the ones who walked out of the arms limitation talks."(shrug—耸了耸肩不满地说)

常见的"说"意动词有:

acknowledge 承认	admit 承认	add 又说
affirm 肯定	allege 断言	agree 同意
announce 宣布	argue 争辩	ask 询问
assert 宣称	boast 夸口说	claim 声称
complain 抱怨	challenge 提出异议	conclude 断定
contend 争论	declare 宣称	elaborate 详述

emphasize 强调	explain 解释	imply 暗示说
enquire 询问	insist 坚持说	joke 开玩笑说
maintain 断言	object 反对说	observe 评述
promise 许愿	pledge 保证	reply 回答
refute 反驳	retort 反诘	reveal 透露
state 说,声称	stress 强调	suggest 建议

相比之下,纯新闻报道由于强调客观公正,含有情感意思的"说"意动词一般少用或不用,而解释性报道(interpretative reporting)、特写(features)和新新闻(new journalism)类写作中含有情感意思的"说"意动词使用较多。

V. Analysis of Content

1. The list of gun shootings mentioned in the article does NOT include _____.
   A. gun massacre in East Buffalo   B. school shooting in Uvalde
   C. Sandy Hook shooting   D. Las Vegas Strip shooting
2. The following words share the same meaning with "mass killing" EXCEPT _____.
   A. rampage   B. massacre   C. slaughter   D. carnage
3. How many people were killed at Robb Elementary School shooting?
   A. 22.   B. 21.   C. 20.   D. 19.
4. The list of gun control measures mentioned in the article does NOT include _____.
   A. red flag laws   B. background checks
   C. ghost gun   D. age of purchase requirements
5. The author's attitude towards the gun control is _____.
   A. unknown   B. supportive   C. ambiguous   D. critical

VI. Questions on the Article

1. What charges did police face in the case of Robb Elementary School shooting?
2. Why was one mother put in handcuffs?
3. Who is Layla Salazar?
4. What does "replacement theory" refer to? What effect has the theory produced?
5. Why was there some hope after the Sandy Hook Elementary School Gun Massacre that the gun lobby had finally reached the high water mark of its power?
6. According to the article, what is the red flag law?
7. What efforts have states around the country made at gun control?
8. What kind of attitude does the American Congress take toward gun regulations?

VII. Topics for Discussion

1. Can gun control solve the problem of violence in America?
2. Is it possible to ban guns in the United States?

Lesson 27

Rags to Rags, Riches to Riches[1]

Maybe it's time to stop calling America the "land of opportunity."

By Clive Crook

Opportunity is the crux of the American idea. Opportunity is what the New World has always represented[2]: struggle, risk, self-determination, and the hope of spiritual and material progress. Even now, to new immigrants, that or something like it is the pull—and for them at least, it is no false promise.[3] If you move to America, you move up, and this is true whether you are rafting across the Rio Grande or negotiating the hazards of the H1B visa program.[4] British emigrants (I am one) are fond of Spain and the United States. They go to Spain to retire; they come here to rise to new challenges. This lure, barely diminished after more than three centuries, has ever been an incalculable source of national strength.

But is America any longer a land of opportunity for the people born here? The evidence, such as it is, points to a surprising and dispiriting answer: no, not especially.

The idea that America is exceptional in its material opportunities is deeply lodged in the culture.[5] For as long as the country had a western frontier with territory beyond, internal migration was just as bold a venture as crossing the ocean had been for the first settlers, and just as promising for the ambitious and self-reliant.[6] The late-19th and early-20th centuries brought extraordinarily rapid industrial development, which nourished the American idea in a new way. Rising incomes made each succeeding generation more prosperous—and they rose so fast that people even felt more prosperous. But that phase, too, has ended. Incomes are now rising more slowly from generation to generation (and for a variety of reasons, the flattening feels worse than it is[7]). Fewer adults today, it seems, expect their children to do better than they did. Pessimism vies with vitality for command of the national consciousness.[8]

Much of this, no doubt, is a natural consequence of growing old. New immigrants notwithstanding, America is a middle-aged country, and striving is not a trait of the middle-aged. Still, an accumulating body of research suggests that the stiffening of America's socioeconomic sinews is more advanced than the culture, even now, seems willing to admit[9]; worse than the scholars who monitor it had hitherto understood; and—how shaming is this? —worse than in many older, wearier countries.

The American model has been regarded as proposing a kind of bargain.[10] This is not Europe: Here, idleness and incompetence are sternly punished—but merit gets rewarded. Much more than elsewhere, your class background will neither prop you up nor hold you back.[11] If you deserve to succeed, you will.

It is an inspiring, energizing offer—and still a profoundly influential one. It colors the national debate about taxes, health care, and other aspects of economic policy.[12] But it is false advertising.

Most researchers now give America much lower marks than they used to for intergenerational economic mobility—the ease with which successive generations move up or down relative to their parents. As flaws in early postwar studies have been addressed, estimates of mobility have fallen. Before the 1990s, researchers tended to put the correlation between parents' incomes and their children's at around 20 percent, implying a high degree of mobility between generations. (Zero would imply no connection at all; a correlation of 100 percent would imply that parents' incomes entirely determined the incomes of their children.) In the 1990s, using better data and techniques, experts tended to put that figure at about 40 percent. Recent estimates run as high as 60 percent. The finding is not that mobility has fallen since World War II—the studies point to no clear trend. It is that as methods of measuring mobility have improved, the result, across a span of recent decades, has gotten worse. The earlier view that postwar America was an economically mobile society is less and less borne out.[13] Perhaps it was once (before data became available to track such things accurately); but it isn't now.

More telling, maybe, is the international comparison. America stands lower in the ranking of income mobility than most of the countries whose data allow the comparison, scoring worse than Canada, all of the Scandinavian countries, and possibly even Germany and Britain (the data are imperfect, and different studies give slightly different results).

Strikingly, the research suggests that mobility within America's middle-income bands is similar to that in many other countries. The stickiness is at the top and the bottom. According to one much-cited study, for instance, more than 40 percent of American boys born into the poorest fifth of the population stay there; the figure for Britain is 30 percent, for Denmark just 25 percent. In America, more than in other advanced economies, poor children stay poor. Other data show that in America, more than in, say, Britain, rich children stay rich as well.

The findings are still tentative, and the causes complicated—hardly a firm basis for prescription.[14] Still, if the government needed another reason to retain the estate tax (aside from the fact that it is one of the most economically efficient taxes), this might serve. In general, a little less tolerance of inherited privilege would not seem amiss (hard for Americans to hear from a Brit, I understand, but look at the facts). Would it hurt, for instance, if the admissions preferences granted by America's most prestigious universities to the children of benefactors and alumni aroused more disgust, or maybe just some mild disapproval?[15] Or if the richest Americans bequeathed less of their wealth to universities that patently have no need of it (Harvard's endowment is more than $30 billion), and more to those that do?

Cleansing as such gestures might be, however, aiming to go further, and improve economic mobility with an all-fronts assault on income inequality, would be misconceived[16], even if it could command political support (which, for now at least, it could not). The sad truth is that such inequality serves a purpose. It spurs effort and ambition—provided, of course, that poor people, through their own skill and industry, can reach the higher tiers.[17]

The real focus of any effort to restore social and economic opportunity in America ought to be ladders out of poverty. An especially good one already exists: the Earned Income Tax Credit[18]. Its coverage should be wider and its terms more generous, but the principle is exactly right: Supplement the wages of the low-paid to reward work, discourage idleness, and relieve poverty. More fundamentally, America needs to improve its worst and poorest schools, which sharply delimit the prospects of many poor children. Education cannot do everything. But dismal school performance is the biggest problem that policy makers concerned with opportunity in America can fix.[19] So far, it ranks low—or not at all—on the list of issues being addressed by the 2008 presidential candidates.[20]

America has no roots in feudalism, no notion of inherited orders of society, no instinct for deference or regard for nobility.[21] And yet the economic mobility that is thought to follow from such freedom, and indeed ought to follow from it, appears to be a myth. Myths that defy the common experience can persist for only so long.[22] Perhaps in the future the country will try harder to foster the opportunity it thinks it already provides. Or perhaps the culture will simply come to accept this un-American reality: a society of rigid economic orders, maintained by inheritance, blessed by its elites, and impotently endured by its underclass.[23]

From *The Atlantic,* June, 2007

I. New Words

alumni	[əˈlʌmnai]	n.	[复]校友
amiss	[əˈmis]	adj.	not quite right; out of place
band	[bænd]	n.	a group of people who have the same feature
benefactor	[ˈbenifæktə]	n.	恩人, 赠送者, 赞助人
bequeath	[biˈkwi:ð]	v.	to leave (property) to a person by a will
crux	[krʌks]	n.	关键
deference	[ˈdefərəns]	n.	polite submission and respect
delimit	[di:ˈlimit]	v.	to determine the limits or boundaries of
dispirit	[disˈpirit]	v.	to cause one to lose enthusiasm or hope
elite	[eiˈli:t]	n.	精英
emigrant	[ˈemigrənt]	n.	a person who leaves his/her country to live in another
endowment	[inˈdaumənt]	n.	捐赠, 捐赠的基金(或财产)
foster	[ˈfɔstə]	v.	to encourage the development of sth
hitherto	[ˌhiðəˈtu:]	adv.	*formal* until now
idleness	[ˈaidlnis]	n.	闲散, 懒惰
incalculable	[inˈkælkjuləbl]	adj.	too great to be calculated or estimated
incompetence	[inˈkɔmpitəns]	n.	the lack of skill or ability to do your job

intergenerational	[ˌintəˌdʒenəˈreiʃənl]	adj.	两代间的
lure	[ljuə]	v.	引诱,诱惑
notwithstanding	[ˌnɔtwiθˈstændiŋ]	prep.	虽然,尽管
patently	[ˈpeitəntli]	adv.	obviously
prop	[prɔp]	v.	to support or keep in position
Scandinavian	[ˌskændiˈneivjən]	adj.	斯堪的纳维亚的
sinew	[ˈsinju:]	n.	肌腱;筋
tentative	[ˈtentətiv]	adj.	not certain or fixed; provisional
tier	[tiə]	n.	等级
underclass	[ˈʌndəˌklɑ:s]	n.	下层社会
visa	[ˈvi:zə]	n.	签证
vie	[vai]	v.	to compete eagerly with someone
weary	[ˈwiəri]	adj.	feeling or showing extreme tiredness

II. Background Information

美国阶级状况

每当谈到阶级问题时,多半美国人会声称美国社会是一个没有阶级的社会(a classless society)。之所以如此,主要是因为美国独特的历史。

美国没有经历过封建社会和世袭的贵族体制。它是一个迅速发展的开拓型国家。来自欧洲的新居民对贵族特权深恶痛绝。此外,美国开创初期,无限的空间和宽松的政治气氛为社会均等和个人奋斗设置了一个大舞台。美国革命打碎了贵族统治的标准。尽管在革命后的美国,人们在财富、地位和生活方式等方面还存在明显的差异,但是总的来说人们对这些差异感受不深。大多数美国人认为,只要勤奋,便有无限的机会。

美国声称其社会是一个具有社会地位流动性(social mobility)、精英治理的社会(meritocracy)。大多数人相信人人机会均等,通过努力都可以获得成功,实现"美国梦"(the American Dream)。美国作家霍拉肖·阿尔杰(Horatio Algier)所著的109部小说,内容都是"穷小子变富翁"的成功故事(rags-to-riches success stories)。这些故事脍炙人口,影响很大。美国历史也不乏其例。美国人常提林肯总统的成功之路。他出身贫苦家庭,然而自强不息,自学成才,后来成为出色的律师,最终登上总统宝座。

然而,在美国并非所有人都能靠自我奋斗就取得个人成功。对于许多少数种族和贫困家庭的孩子而言,他们前进的道路困难重重,地位攀升是终身无法实现的梦想。近几十年来,美国社会贫富差距进一步拉大。主要原因有三点:一是政治和经济体制。美国是公司掌控的国家,大公司通过说客给政客施加影响,政府屈服于这些利益集团,处处保护公司富豪们的利益。过去的几十年富人越来越富,穷人越来越穷。据统计,30年前大公司高管的收入是普通员工的39倍,如今差距已扩大到1000倍。据英国《卫报》2017年的一篇报道,当时美国最富有的三个人(比尔·盖茨、杰夫·贝索斯和沃伦·巴菲特)的财富相当于按财富程度划分的后半部分(1.6亿)美国人财富的总和。二是就业市场结构改变。许多制造业大公司缩减规模,导致不少收入较好的工作岗位消失。与此同时,服务业规模不断扩大,而服务业的工作大多数薪金较低,这就导致很多人的收入下降。三是教育价值日趋显著。随着科技发展,美国财富从物质资源拥有者手中转移到高智能资源拥有者手中,教育越来越成为地位攀升的阶梯。然而,昂贵的学费将那些有才华的贫穷孩子排斥在质量好的学校之外,使他们处于竞争劣势。

对于贫富差距的扩大,社会所存在的不公平现象,美国民众的怒气在不断上升。越来越多的美国人称"美国政府是富人所有、富人所治、富人所享的政府。"(The U.S. Government is a government of the rich, by the rich, and for the rich.)一些社会学者担心这种怨气会发展到难以容忍的地步,影响社会的稳定。

III. Notes to the Text

1. Rags to Rags, Riches to Riches——穷者更穷,富者更富(本文标题源于习语 from rags to riches "从赤贫到巨富")

2. Opportunity is what the New World has always represented...——新大陆一直象征着发展的机会。(the New World——originally referring to North, Central, and South America collectively in relation to Europe, here referring to the U.S.)

3. Even now, to new immigrants, that or something like it is the pull—and for them at least, it is no false promise.——甚至现在对新移民来说,发展机会或者类似的东西仍然吸引着他们——至少对他们来说,这不是虚假的许诺。(pull——sth exerting an influence or attraction)

4. If you move to America, you move up, and this is true whether you are rafting across the Rio Grande or negotiating the hazards of the H1B visa program.——如果移民到美国,你就能地位攀升。无论是从里奥格兰德河上乘木筏过来还是通过克服困难办理H1B类签证而来,你都能做到这一点。(① Rio Grande——里奥格兰德河,北出落基山脉,东南流入墨西哥湾,长约3000千米,其中作为美国同墨西哥界河约2000千米;② H1B visa program —— Specialty Occupations/Temporary Worker Visa program,即特殊专业人员/短期工作签证,是美国发放给公司雇佣的外国籍有专业技能的员工的非移民签证的一种。此类签证持有者可在美国工作三年,到期还可再延三年;③ negotiate——to successfully get over a difficult part)

5. ...is deeply lodged in the culture.——这种观念……深深植根于(美国)文化。(lodge——to fix sth firmly in)

6. ...promising for the ambitious and self-reliant.——在那些雄心勃勃、自力更生的人看来充满希望(promising——likely to develop in a desirable manner)

7. the flattening feels worse than it is——增长渐停给人的感觉比实际情况更糟(① feel——to give you a particular feeling or impression; ② flattening——stopping growing or going up)

8. Pessimism vies with vitality for command of the national consciousness.——悲观情绪总是和乐观情绪争着控制国民的意识。

9. an accumulating body of research suggests that the stiffening of America's socioeconomic sinews is more advanced than the culture, even now, seems willing to admit——越来越多的研究表明，美国社会经济结构的僵化程度，要比现在社会愿意承认的程度更为严重。(advanced——at a late stage of development)

10. The American model has been regarded as proposing a kind of bargain.——美国模式一直被认为是提出一种协议。(bargain——an agreement between two or more people or groups as to what each will do for the other)

11. Much more than elsewhere, your class background will neither prop you up nor hold you back.——阶级出身对个人发展既不会是动力也不会是障碍，与其他国家相比，美国更是如此。(① prop up——to help or give support to; ② hold back——to prevent or restrict the progress or development of someone or sth)

12. It colors the national debate about taxes, health care, and other aspects of economic policy.——它影响美国关于税收、医疗保健以及其他经济政策的讨论。(color——to influence, especially in a negative way; to distort)

13. The earlier view that postwar America was an economically mobile society is less and less borne out.——早期那种认为第二次世界大战后美国社会有很大经济流动性的观点越来越难以被证实。(bear out——to prove)

14. The findings are tentative, and the causes complicated——hardly a firm basis for prescription.——产生该问题的因素很复杂，调查的结论只是初步的，很难作为制定对策的可靠依据。

15. Would it hurt, for instance, if the admissions preferences granted by America's most prestigious universities to the children of benefactors and alumni aroused more disgust, or maybe just some mild disapproval?——譬如美国最有名的大学对赞助人或者校友子女所给予优先录取的照顾激起了社会的愤慨，或是仅仅几分温和的反对，这对社会有害吗？

16. Cleansing as such gestures might be, however, aiming to go further, and improve economic mobility with an all-fronts assault on income inequality, would be misconceived...——虽然此类姿态或许会使道德净化，然而力图更进一步通过全面攻击收入不平等现象来改进经济地位的流动性的设想是错误的(① cleansing——making sb or sth morally clean; ② misconceived——badly planned, not carefully thought about)

17. It spurs effort and ambition——provided, of course, that poor people, through their own skill and industry, can reach the higher tiers.——它也能激发出干劲和雄心——当然，前提必须是穷人通过自身技能和勤奋也能攀升到更高的阶层。(① spur——to give an incentive or encouragement to someone; ② tier——a rank or class)

18. the Earned Income Tax Credit——劳动所得税收抵免(这是美国政府为低收入工作家庭提供的额外救助措施)

19. But dismal school performance is the biggest problem that policy makers concerned with opportunity in America can fix.——但是，教学质量很糟是与美国机会均等之事相关的政策制定者能够解决的最重要的问题。(① dismal——pitifully or disgracefully bad; ② fix——to solve)

20. So far, it ranks low——or not at all——on the list of issues being addressed by the 2008 presidential candidates.——迄今，它在2008年总统候选人的竞选议题中的位置很靠后，或者根本就没有

被列入。(address—to think about and begin to deal with an issue or a problem)

21. America has no roots in feudalism, no notion of inherited orders of society, no instinct for deference or regard for nobility.—美国没有封建主义的思想根基,没有世袭社会等级的观念,没有遵从或尊重贵族的天性。(orders of society—social classes)

22. Myths that defy the common experience can persist for only so long.—违背社会普遍感受的神话只能存在如此长时间。(defy—to be too extreme or very strange and therefore impossible to believe)

23. Or perhaps the culture will simply come to accept this un-American reality: a society of rigid economic orders, maintained by inheritance, blessed by its elites, and impotently endured by its underclass.—或者社会可能全然开始接受这个不合美国传统观念的现实:一个世袭维系、精英庇佑、下层无能为力地忍受的经济等级森严的社会。(① impotent—unable to take effective action; helpless or powerless;② un-American—against American values)

IV. Language Features

习语活用

本文标题"Rags to Rags, Riches to Riches"是习语"from rags to riches"(from being extremely poor to being very rich)的活用,表示"穷者永远穷,富者永远富"的意思。

英语习语浩如烟海。这些习语中有相当一部分由于被过度使用而苍白无力,或因时间过长而腐气浓厚。在现代英美报刊中,作者为了摈弃因袭、刻意求新,或者为了简洁明快、节约篇幅,或是为了形象幽默、增强效果,常常用习语活用的方式。

英语习语活用后的形式从字典中很难找到释义,但它们并非变幻莫测,毫无规则。了解其活用形式对提高外刊阅读能力十分有益。

一般说来,报刊英语中习语活用形式可以归纳为四种:节缩、扩展、套用、拆用。下面分别举例加以说明。

1. 节缩

这是把原习语缩短使用,报刊常常借助前置定语来节缩。例如:

Employees foster nose-to-the-grindstone strategies.

这里,"nose-to-the-grindstone"是习语"keep one's nose to the grindstone"(使某人埋头从事辛苦劳动)的节缩形式。

2. 扩展

在习语中夹字,使其增加新意。例如:

Inside Rosalyn's velvet glove is a stainless steel hand.

这一句中,作者不仅在原习语"the iron hand in the velvet glove"上加上"stainless",而且把"iron"改为"steel",使整个句子语气强烈,趣味盎然。(美国前总统)卡特夫人罗莎琳外柔内刚的本性便活脱脱地刻画出来。

3. 套用

套用是通过改变习语中的个别词来表达新意和加强语意。例如：

Salaries did increase. But so did the race to keep up with the Wangs.

这一句摘自《新闻周刊》一篇关于中国改革开放之后人民生活状况的报道，作者用 Wangs 替代原习语中的 Joneses，染上鲜明的民族色彩，产生活泼风趣的效果。

4. 拆用

拆用就是将原习语的成分拆开加以活用。这样既可避免照搬陈旧形式，又可生出新意。例如：

They have a mountain of high-resounding resolve and a molehill of results.

本句是原习语"make a mountain out of a molehill"的拆用形式，整句意思是：他们的决心很大，调子很高，但收效甚微。

V. Analysis of Content

1. The word "culture" in the sentence "... the stiffening of America's socioeconomic sinews is more advanced than the culture, even now, seems willing to admit"(Para. 4) means _____.
   A. literature   B. way of life   C. artists   D. society
2. "The American model" in the article refers to America's _____.
   A. democracy   B. education   C. mobility   D. freedom
3. Which of the following measures for improving mobility is most highly recommended in the article?
   A. Enlarging the coverage of the Earned Income Tax Credit.
   B. Removing college admission preference.
   C. Retaining the estate tax.
   D. Avoiding income inequality.
4. It can be seen from Para. 10 that America's famous universities grant admission preferences to the children of _____.
   A. minorities   B. poor families
   C. all rich families   D. benefactors and alumni
5. The author's view on the change of America's mobility situation is _____.
   A. radical   B. conservative   C. neutral   D. moderate

VI. Questions on the Article

1. What has the New World always represented?

2. What has given rise to Americans' idea of mobility?

3. What role does America's lure for immigrants perform?

4. What does an accumulating body of research suggest about America's socioeconomic sinews?

5. What has the American model been regarded as? And what is its influence?

6. How does America compare with other countries in the ranking of income mobility?

7. What does the author think of the estate tax?

8. What is the author's view on income inequality?

9. What should be the focus of the efforts to restore social and economic opportunity?

10. What does the author think of the prospects of America's mobility situation?

VII. Topics for Discussion

1. Is America a land of opportunity?

2. Is income inequality beneficial to the society?

Unit 9
第九单元 科技军事

Lesson 28

Power Revolution

Thanks to Silicon Valley's money and ideas, solar and other alternative technologies may finally pay off.[1]
(Abridged)

By Clive Crook

The high-rolling risk takers who brought you personal computing, the telecommunications revolution, the commercialization of the Internet, and, of course, Google now aim to do nothing less than save planet Earth—and make billions while doing it.[2] If the venture capital industry is successful, it might be the ultimate act of "angel investing[3]," and perhaps no one is more emblematic of this new wave of high-minded technology entrepreneurship than Vinod Khosla[4], who, after a failed soy milk start-up in his native India, went on to become one of the driving forces of Silicon Valley[5] as cofounder of Sun Microsystems[6] and later as a venture capitalist. Khosla views climate change as the gravest threat the world has ever faced, and he knows others see America's foreign oil dependence as an urgent crisis. But in his calculus, we've been pitching pebbles at these Goliath problems.[7] "Building a biofuels plant here and a solar plant there is not enough," he says, "unless we can replace 50 percent and hopefully 100 percent of the fossil energy sources."

This grand goal is not remotely in sight, even with wind and solar energy and ethanol growing at a breakneck clip.[8] These renewables now provide just 3.6 percent of the nation's energy, and the government predicts their share will grow to a grand total of 4.2 percent by 2030. By those calculations, it sure looks like a fossil fuel future for America.

But Khosla, through his own Khosla Ventures[9] and often working alongside the legendary VC[10] firm Kleiner Perkins Caufield & Byers[11], where he maintains an affiliation, is in the vanguard of entrepreneurs and financiers who believe their Silicon Valley success stories can be repeated in green energy. They are pouring money and ideas into a new generation of alternatives to fossil fuel— "technologies that scale," in their words.[12] That is, options that can ramp up[13] to serve a large share of the nation's energy needs because they'll cost less than coal or oil. One estimate is that venture capital funds nearly tripled their investment on (in) green energy last year, putting $2.4 billion to work.

Of course, that may not seem like much dough given that some next-generation technologies are massive undertakings, like placing 3-mile-square fields of mirrors in the desert to focus the sun's rays or shooting high-pressure water into the hot rock 3 miles underground to create a man-made geothermal reservoir.[14] And skeptics say that these approaches may not be cost competitive[15] for years. The economic equation might change if Washington puts a limit on carbon dioxide emissions or institutes carbon taxes that make coal power and gasoline more expensive, though that's far from a sure thing.[16] Dan Reicher, a former Clinton administration energy official who heads up a major investment effort on climate change underway at Google, says stronger federal policy, more availability of Wall Street financing, and technological innovation are all equally important in taking green energy to the next level. "If we're going to get to a sustainable energy future, we have to be working hard at all three," he says.

But Khosla believes government policy will move once entrepreneurs take the first step. "Change has to come from somewhere, and our business is about change," he says, recalling the early skepticism that the first microprocessor and telecommunications revolutionaries faced. "All the innovation came from little companies that had breakthrough technologies. The chances of any one experiment failing may be high, but the chances of all of the experiments failing is (**are**) very, very low. You should have a thousand points of innovation, and for sure you'll get a breakthrough."

Just the sort of optimism that's helped make Silicon Valley the world's leading center of innovation. And just the sort of attitude that seems to be finally cracking the tough technological puzzles whose solutions will change the way we power the global economy and our lives.

Solar concentration

Solar energy may be poised to make the leap from the rooftop down to the floor of the desert—where some advocates say it needs to be if it's going to take its rightful place as a member of Big Energy.[17] The nation's largest utility in customers served, investor-owned Pacific Gas & Electric[18], this fall announced a bold plan to install nearly five times the amount of solar power that is now operating across the United States and do it cheaper, bigger, and faster than has ever been tried before. Instead of using semiconducting material to convert light to energy—those familiar black photovoltaic panels—PG&E and its technology partners, like the Israeli firm Solel[19], will use nothing more complicated than mirrors, lots of them, to concentrate some of the highest-intensity sunlight[20] in the world. The arrays will heat water to drive turbines just as in an old-fashioned power plant.

Although solar PV arrays[21] have been crowning more and more American buildings—the 1.6-megawatt project opened this year at Google's headquarters in Mountain View, Calif., is the largest—they're expensive. Developments are underway to bring down the price by reducing the silicon from its usual wafer form to an ultrathin film deposited on glass. But at this point, PV cost estimates span from an uncompetitive 23 to 32 cents per kilowatt-hour, while residential electricity prices in this country range from 5.8 to 16.7 cents.

With current technology, "concentrating solar power" would cost about 40 percent less than PV—tantalizingly close to competitive in areas like California with high energy prices.[22] Exactly how the mirrors will be configured could bring the cost down more. Rows of curved reflectors work well; since the 1980s, a dazzling "parabolic trough[23]" display has provided reliable power to California, the only operating concentrating solar power project in the country. But Spanish firm Abengoa this summer aimed for greater efficiency by focusing circles of mirrors onto a central "power tower" near Seville for the first commercial European Union CSP plant. [24]

Deep geothermal

One of the most promising renewable-energy wellsprings is underground.

Geothermal is lower profile than a range of other alternative energy technologies[25], even though many homes—including President Bush's Crawford ranch—have heat pumps that tap into the Earth's steady, reliable warmth. But few realize that the United States is the world's biggest mass producer of geothermal power, with long-running plants in western hot springs and geyser areas that generate more electricity than all U.S. wind and solar energy combined. It was long thought that big-scale geothermal had reached its natural limit. Few locales are graced with steamy water reservoirs close enough to the surface (less than 2 miles under) to be easily tapped to run electric turbines on the ground above. [26] And many hot spots happen to be beneath scenic treasures like Yellowstone National Park[27] or on American Indian reservations.

But recent study shows deep-drilling and seismic-exploration techniques[28] developed in the oil industry could be exploited to draw out the geothermal energy found 3 or more miles underground, locked in dry rock that's more than 300 degrees Fahrenheit. A developer could drill a well and use high-pressure water to open fractures in the rock. Then, injection wells would be drilled to circulate the water in the man-made reservoir and extract steam to the surface to run electric turbines. This year, a government-sponsored study led by Massachusetts Institute of Technology concluded that these "heat mining" methods could offer access to a staggering amount of energy.[29] Just 2 percent of the U.S. geothermal resource base could yield nearly 2,000 times the power that the nation now consumes each year.

High-pressure ethanol

In alternative transportation fuels, the holy grail quest is the search for the next ethanol. [30] Sure, the business of fuel alcohol distilled from corn is booming, with production having tripled since 2002 and up 33 percent this year to 6.5 billion gallons. Historically, ethanol has been more expensive than gasoline, but crude oil prices are now so high that ethanol would be cheaper even without its 51-cent-per-gallon subsidy. Indeed, one reason pump prices[31] have not skyrocketed along with the price of crude oil is that so much fuel is blended with 10 percent ethanol. Politicians would like to mandate that refiners use still more. But even if you don't agree that diverting corn to energy has strained the food industry or environment—and the ethanol industry most assuredly does not—there is a practical limit to squeezing fuel from the cob.[32]

Hence, the pursuit of "cellulosic ethanol," the same fuel made by breaking down the tough starches found in hardier plant matter—from cornstalks to fast-growing switch grass[33] to paper-mill waste. Ideally, the feedstock would be abundant and wouldn't require a lot of water, fertilizer, or tending. Cellulosic works in the laboratory but at great cost. So dozens of companies are trying to hit on the formula to make it economic, mainly through bioengineering of enzymes that would convert grass, husks, or wood to sugar that could be fermented into fuel. The government predicts the first cellulosic plant will cost five times more than a corn refinery and will come on line no sooner than 2010.

But Range Fuels, a Broomfield, Colo., firm founded by Khosla, aims to beat that projection by two years. One of six companies that received Department of Energy grants to accelerate the new technology, Range will be the first to break ground on a commercial plant on November 6 near Georgia forestland, where it plans to refine abundant timber-industry waste wood.[34] Instead of relying on expensive enzymes, Range will use heat and pressure to turn wood chips to gas, then extract ethanol with a catalyst.

New efficiency

Congress is dithering over a proposal to force American cars to average miles per gallon by 2020, a seemingly modest goal with smaller cars and more-efficient diesel engines helping the European Union near 44.2 MPG[35] and Japan attain more than 45 MPG. But a race is on for the technology that could blow all those numbers away.[36] "You see the difficulty Congress has in setting a new standard, and we know the best way to help is to have some cars that get 100 miles per gallon and to make them gorgeous and affordable," says Larry Brilliant, executive director of Google's philanthropic arm[37]. That would mean more than 70 percent oil savings, since the current fuel-efficiency standard is just 27.5 MPG goal set in 1975 and reached by the late 1980s.

Google is putting its considerable muscle behind the drive for the "plug-in hybrid" technology to take the hybrid gas-electric engine system already found in the Toyota Prius to a new level.[38] Add a larger battery that can store electricity longer and can be charged with an ordinary household outlet, and the car could run on home electricity instead of gasoline most of the time. Last week, Google closed bidding on its request for plug-in or hybrid technology proposals it plans to fund to the tune of $10 million[39]. The goal is to make renewable energy more attractive to utilities through the use of green vehicles. One problem those companies have with wind and solar is that they are intermittent. Some days, the skies are cloudy and the air still. "But if you had a large number of plug-ins with significant battery capacity plugged into the grid, we'd have a very compelling storage opportunity," says Google.org's Reicher.[40] "If we can crack the code on plug-in vehicles, I think it will be transformative.[41]" Now that's thinking big.

From *US News & World Report,* November 5, 2007

I. New Words

affiliation	[əˌfiliˈeiʃən]	n.	联系;从属关系
biofuel	[ˌbaiəuˈfjuːəl]	n.	生物燃料

cellulosic	[ˌseljuˈləusik]	adj.	有纤维质的
configure	[kənˈfigə]	v.	to arrange sth for a particular purpose
cornstalk	[ˈkɔːnstɔːk]	n	玉米秆；麦秆
crack	[kræk]	v.	to solve (a problem, etc.)
distill	[diˈstil]	v.	to turn liquid to vapor by heating
dither	[ˈdiðə]	v.	to hesitate about what to do
emblematic	[ˌembliˈmætik]	adj.	seeming to represent sth
enzyme	[ˈenzaim]	n.	[生化]酶
ethanol	[ˈeθənɔl]	n.	乙醇
feedstock	[ˈfiːdstɔk]	n.	给料（送入机器或加工厂的原料）
ferment	[ˈfə(ː)mənt]	v.	使发酵
fracture	[ˈfræktʃə]	n.	破裂；裂口
geothermal	[ˌdʒi(ː)əuˈθəːməl]	adj.	地热的, 地温的
geyser	[ˈgiːzə]	n.	间歇喷泉
gorgeous	[ˈgɔːdʒəs]	adj.	*informal* very attractive
grid	[grid]	n.	电网
high-minded	[ˈhaimaindid]	adj.	having strong moral principles
husk	[hʌsk]	n.	（果类或谷物的）外壳
intermittent	[ˌintəˈmitənt]	adj.	断断续续的
mandate	[ˈmændeit]	v.	to order sb to do sth
megawatt	[ˈmegəwɔt]	n.	兆瓦特
photovoltaic	[ˌfəutəuvɔlˈteiik]	n.	光生伏打电池, 太阳电池
plummet	[ˈplʌmit]	v.	to fall steadily or rapidly
pricey	[ˈpraisi]	adj.	expensive
reflector	[riˈflektə]	n.	反射体, 反射镜
retrofit	[ˈretrəufit]	v.	式样翻新
seismic	[ˈsaizmik]	adj.	[地]地震的
semiconducting	[ˌsemikənˈdʌktiŋ]	adj.	半导体的, 有半导体特性的
skyrocket	[ˈskaiˌrɔkit]	v.	to rise quickly to a high level
sustainable	[səˈsteinəbl]	adj.	能持续的
tackle	[tækl]	v.	to deal with (a difficult problem)
tantalize	[ˈtæntəlaiz]	v.	to make a person want sth he can't have
trough	[ˈtrɔːf]	n.	槽, 水槽
turbine	[ˈtəːbain]	n.	涡轮
undertaking	[ˌʌndəˈteikiŋ]	n.	enterprise or task
wafer	[ˈweifə]	n.	[电子]薄片, 晶片（如硅片）

II. Background Information

再生能源

　　再生能源(renewable energy)是消耗后可以恢复补充,循环再生的能源。这类能源数量无限,不会耗尽,使用时极少或根本不会产生环境污染,故也被称为清洁能源(clean energy)。我国也提出了"绿水青山就是金山银山"的理念,积极稳妥推进碳达峰碳中和,一方面推动能源清洁低碳高效利用,另一方面加快规划建设新型能源体系,确保能源安全。

　　早在20世纪70年代,随着能源危机的爆发,西方国家便意识到不可再生能源的有限性和能源结构多元化的必要性。近些年来,越来越多的人意识到化石燃料(fossil fuels)造成了严重的环境污染。以太阳能、风能、生物能、水能和地热能等为代表的可再生能源和地热等环保能源便在此背景下得以开发利用。

　　太阳能(solar energy)是各种再生能源(renewable energies)中最重要的基本能源。太阳能可以转换成电能、热能和化学能。太阳能的优点是取之不尽、用之不竭、清洁环保。但目前有关太阳能开发的技术水平亟待提高。从规模效益上看,目前太阳能热电系统根本无法与大型常规电力系统相提并论。太阳能是一种间歇性能源,因昼夜变化和天气影响,其开发成本较高。但从总体上来看,太阳能是一种有着广阔前景的新能源。

　　风能(wind energy)是由空气运动所产生的能量,具有极大的发电潜力。风电的优点是蕴藏量大、可再生、无污染、占地少、建设周期短、投资灵活、自动控制水平高、运行管理人员少等。风能的利用受地理条件的限制,风速较大,风向稳定,变幅较小的风才宜于风力发电。

　　生物质能(biomass energy)是自然界中有生命的植物提供的能量,一直是人类赖以生存的重要能源之一。就其总量而言,它是仅次于石油、煤炭、天然气列于第四位的能源,占世界能源消耗总量的15%左右。生物质能具有成本低、分布广、污染小等优势。生物质能的开发和利用有助于减轻温室效应、促进生态良性循环。但值得注意的是,开发生物质能应避免过度消耗而引发的生态环境恶化。

　　水能(hydroenergy)指水体的动能、势能和压力能等能量资源。水力发电将水的势能和动能转化成电能。水能是非常重要且前景广阔的替代能源。

　　地热能(geothermal energy)是从地壳抽取的天然热能,分为地热发电和直接利用。地热能储量丰富,潜力巨大。地热发电具有投资少、污染小等优势。在矿物能源日益枯竭、生态日趋恶化、人类生存面临威胁的今天,地热能将成为又一潜在的新能源。

　　人类在利用再生能源方面所做出的努力正在产生喜人的成效。据国际可再生能源署的研究,2030年可再生能源在全球能源构成比例可达到36%以上。

　　再生能源资源丰富,数量惊人。据专家估计,只要开发全球风能和太阳能的5%就可以满足2050年世界能源消费总需求(total enegy consumption need)。如果全球充分开发利用太阳能、风能、生物质能、地热能、水能和其他可再生能源,人类所面临的能源问题将会得到根本解决,生活环境将变得更加美好。

III. Notes to the Text

1. pay off—*informal* (of a plan or an action, esp. one involving risk) to be successful and bring good results
2. The high-rolling risk takers who brought you personal computing, the telecommunications revolution, the commercialization of the Internet, and, of course, Google now aim to do nothing less than save planet Earth—and make billions while doing it.—给人们带来个人电脑、电信革命、互联网商业化,当然还有谷歌搜索引擎的高风险投资商们现在试图干的事业如同拯救地球,他们还要在做这项事业的同时赚得数十亿美元的利润。(① high-rolling—spending money in a risky way; ② nothing less than—used to emphasize how great sth is)
3. angel investing—天使投资(一种将高科技与金融相结合,把资金投入风险很大的创新项目的研究和开发中,与传统的投资理念截然不同的新型投资方式)
4. Vinod Khosla—维诺德·科斯拉(美籍印度裔风险投资商,是硅谷最具影响力的风险投资商之一)
5. Silicon Valley—硅谷(旧金山东南圣克拉拉谷的别称,美国主要微电子工业公司集中于此。因为电子工业材料主要是硅片,故名。)
6. Sun Microsystems—太阳计算机系统公司(创建于1982年,1986年成为纳斯达克上市公司。)
7. But in his calculus, we've been pitching pebbles at these Goliath problems.—但是在他看来,我们所做的只是杯水车薪。(① calculus—analysis; ② pitch—to throw; ③ Goliath—sth that is very large and powerful)
8. This grand goal is not remotely in sight, even with wind and solar energy and ethanol growing at a breakneck clip.—即使风能、太阳能和乙醇的开发在极快地增长,离这个宏伟目标还相距甚远。(at a breakneck clip—very quickly)
9. Khosla Ventures—a venture capital firm seeking to invest in computing, alternative energy, semiconductors, silicon technologies and clean technology areas such as bio-refineries for energy and bio-plastics, solar battery and other environmentally friendly technologies
10. VC—全称 venture capital,风险资本(一种由职业金融家投入新兴的、迅速发展并且具有巨大竞争潜力的企业中的一种权益资本)
11. Kleiner Perkins Caufield & Byers—KPCB公司(美国风险投资公司,主要承担各大名校的校产投资业务)
12. They are pouring money and ideas into a new generation of alternatives to fossil fuel— "technologies that scale," in their words.—他们把大量资金和技术投入新一代矿物燃料的替代性能源,也就是他们所说的"使用越来越广的能源技术"。(scale—to expand in scale)
13. ramp up—to increase in amount
14. Of course, that may not seem like much dough given that some next-generation technologies are massive undertakings, like placing 3-mile-square fields of mirrors in the desert to focus the sun's rays or shooting high-pressure water into the hot rock 3 miles underground to create a man-made geothermal reservoir.—当然,考虑到下一代的一些技术项目都是诸如在沙漠

地区3英里见方场地安置镜子搜集阳光束,或是向地下3英里深处的热岩喷射高压水柱开凿人工地热库等浩大的工程,这笔投资并不算大。(dough—*slang* money)

15. cost competitive—具有成本竞争性
16. The economic equation might change if Washington puts a limit on carbon dioxide emissions or institutes carbon taxes that make coal power and gasoline more expensive, though that's far from a sure thing. —如果美国政府对二氧化碳排放进行限制或对碳排放进行征税使得火力发电或汽油价格增高,这种经济平衡关系也许会改变,但这种情况还很难实现。(carbon taxes—taxes levied on carbon dioxide emissions)
17. Solar energy may be poised to make the leap from the rooftop down to the floor of the desert—where some advocates say it needs to be if it's going to take its rightful place as a member of Big Energy. —太阳能的开发利用可能已做好跳跃式发展的准备,范畴从屋顶扩展到沙漠,一些主张开发太阳能者以为,太阳能要取得应有的重要能源地位必须如此。
18. Pacific Gas & Electric—美国太平洋天然气电力公司
19. Solel—以色列太阳能系统有限公司(该公司为世界最大的太阳能技术公司之一)
20. highest-intensity sunlight—最高强度阳光
21. PV arrays— 一排排光伏发电板(① PV—photovoltaic; ② array—a group of things, often one that is large)
22. With current technology, "concentrating solar power" would cost about 40 percent less than PV—tantalizingly close to competitive in areas like California with high energy prices. —采用目前的技术"集中太阳能发电"比利用光伏发电节约成本大概40%,这个价格在能源价格居高不下的加州这类地区颇有诱惑力,已接近具有竞争力的价格。
23. parabolic trough —碗状水槽式收集器(Parabolic systems use parabolic trough-shaped mirrors to focus sunlight on thermally efficient receiver tubes that contain a heat transfer fluid. This fluid is heated to 390℃ and pumped through a series of heat exchangers to produce superheated steam which powers a conventional turbine generator to produce electricity.)
24. But Spanish firm Abengoa this summer aimed for greater efficiency by focusing circles of mirrors onto a central "power tower" near Seville for the first commercial European Union CSP plant. —西班牙Abengoa公司今年夏天力图提高位于塞维利亚附近的欧盟第一座商业性的集中太阳能发电厂的功效,其方式是将一圈圈镜子聚焦于发电塔。[① CSP—concentrating solar power,这里指塔式太阳能发电站(solar tower plant),镜面将太阳能反射到塔顶,将水加热到1000℃以上,其中产生的蒸汽驱动涡轮机发电;② Seville—西班牙南部城市,塞维利亚省省会]
25. Geothermal is lower profile than a range of other alternative energy technologies... —与其他一系列替代性能源相比,地热引起的关注较少(low-profile—receiving very little attention)
26. Few locales are graced with steamy water reservoirs close enough to the surface (less than 2 miles under) to be easily tapped to run electric turbines on the ground above. —很少有地点条件理想,具有离地面很近(不到2英里深)的充满热气的水库,能够很容易驱动电力涡轮机。(① locale—a place where sth happens; ② grace sb with—to favor sb with; ③ tap—to make use of)

27. Yellowstone National Park —黄石国家公园(美国著名风景区,位于落基山)
28. deep-drilling and seismic-exploration techniques —深度钻井和地震勘探技术
29. This year, a government-sponsored study led by Massachusetts Institute of Technology concluded that these "heat mining" methods could offer access to a staggering amount of energy. —今年,由政府资助的、麻省理工学院领导的一项研究结论是,"热能开采"方法可以提供数量惊人的能源。(Massachusetts Institute of Technology—麻省理工学院,始建于1861年,是美国最重要的科技研发基地之一)
30. In alternative transportation fuels, the holy grail quest is the search for the next ethanol. —在交通车辆替代性燃料方面,人们长期寻求的是下一代乙醇。(holy grail—the cup believed to have been used by Jesus at the Last Supper just before his death. Now it is often used in the sense of sth that people try very hard to find.)
31. pump prices —出泵价格,零售价格
32. But even if you don't agree that diverting corn to energy has strained the food industry or environment—and the ethanol industry most assuredly does not—there is a practical limit to squeezing fuel from the cob. —但是,即使你认为将玉米转化为能源不会给食品工业和环境造成压力——乙醇工业绝对不会带来这样的问题——从玉米棒中提取燃料实际也是有限的。
33. switch grass—柳枝稷(一种制造乙醇的可行燃料)
34. One of six companies that received Department of Energy grants to accelerate the new technology, Range will be the first to break ground on a commercial plant on November 6 near Georgia forestland, where it plans to refine abundant timber-industry waste wood. —Range公司是6家获能源部拨款、加速新能源技术开发的公司之一,它将于11月6日在佐治亚州林地附近首先动工创建商业性电厂,打算用大量木材企业的废料提炼乙醇。
35. 44.2 MPG—每加仑燃料可行驶44.2英里 (MPG—miles per gallon)
36. But a race is on for the technology that could blow all those numbers away. —但是一场旨在超越所有这些记录的技术上的角逐正在展开。(blow away—to surpass and defeat)
37. executive director of Google's philanthropic arm—谷歌基金会慈善项目行政主管
38. Google is putting its considerable muscle behind the drive for the "plug-in hybrid," technology to take the hybrid gas-electric engine system already found in the Toyota Prius to a new level. —谷歌公司在推动"可外接充电式混合动力"技术使用方面正在发挥很大的作用,这项技术将把丰田普锐斯汽车所采用的油电混合动力发动机系统提高到新的水平。
39. fund to the tune of $10 million —出资达1000万美元之多(to the tune of—*informal* used to emphasize how much money sth has cost)
40. "But if you had a large number of plug-ins with significant battery capacity plugged into the grid, we'd have a very compelling storage opportunity," says Google.org's Reicher.—谷歌公司的赖克说:"如果能有一大批可以插入输电线路、具有很大储电容量的外接式充电装置,那就会使我们不得不采用这种充电装置。"(compelling—very exciting and interesting and making you want to have)

41. If we can crack the code on plug-in vehicles, I think it will be transformative. ——我认为,如果我们能解决外接充电装置的难题,那种情况就会完全改变。(① crack the code—to manage to understand a secret message; ② transformative—serving to change completely in form or function)

IV. Language Features

词义变化

　　本文所用的"green energy"中的"green"这个词并非表示色彩,而是表示"不会造成环境破坏的"(not causing harm to the environment)。最近一些年,"green"成为颇为时髦的词,常表示"主张环境保护的""不污染环境的",如 green politics, green policies, green products。这种词义变化现象被称为词义升格。

　　词义扩大指词义从特定的意义扩大为普通的意义,主要有以下四种形式:

　　1. 词义由特指转到泛指,如:economy(家庭料理 → 经济),orientation(向东 → 方向)。

　　2. 词义由具体到抽象,如:arrive(靠岸 → 到达),place(广场 → 地方)。

　　3. 术语用作一般词语,如:introvert(性格内向的人 → 不爱交际的人),bottom-line(账本底线 → 基本意思),allergic(对……过敏的 → 对……反感的)。

　　4. 专有名词成为普通名词,如:watt(瓦特),volt(伏特),xerox(静电复印)。

　　词义变化除词义扩大现象外,常见的还有词义缩小(Specialization)、词义降格(Degeneration)和词义升格(Elevation)。

　　词义缩小有以下四种形式:

　　1. 词义由一般到特指,如 exploitation(利用→商业色情利用),the pill(药片→避孕药片)。

　　2. 普通名词用作专有名词,如:the Hill(国会山), the City(伦敦商业区)。

　　3. 一般词语用作术语,如:web(电脑网络),virus(电脑病毒),page(网页),server(服务器),memory(存储器)。

　　4. 抽象名词用作具体名词,如:youth(青年人),counsel(律师),failure(不及格的学生),terror(令人厌烦的人)。

　　词义降格指词从原先表示中性意义或褒义转为表示贬义,如:peasant(农民 → 粗野无知的人),vulgar(普通人的 → 庸俗的),propaganda(宣传 →宣传伎俩),gay(高兴的→ 男同性恋的),hussy(家庭妇女 → 轻佻的女人),villain(村民 → 坏人)。

　　词义升格指词从原先表示中性意义或贬义转为表示褒义,如:nimble(偷东西手脚敏捷的 → 灵巧的、敏捷的),shrewd(邪恶的 → 机灵的),craftsman(骗术高明的人 → 名匠),paradise(花园→天堂)。最近一些年随着人们健康意识、环保意识的增强,natural(天然的),green(绿色的)的词义也就升格了,分别产生了"无污染的、有益健康的"和"有益环境保护的"的意思。

V. Analysis of Content

1. The word "scale" in the sentence "They are pouring money and ideas into a new generation of alternatives of fossil fuel—'technologies that scale,' in their words." (Para. 3) means _____.
   A. climb up   B. become better
   C. become green   D. increase in its share of use
2. In Khosla's opinion, all the innovations come from _____.
   A. big companies with enough funds   B. small companies with breakthrough technologies
   C. research institutions   D. universities with a lot of grants
3. It can be inferred from the article that the most important factor in the success of green technologies is _____.
   A. government's support   B. public consciousness of their importance
   C. their cost competitiveness   D. Wall Street financing
4. The world's biggest mass producer of geothermal power is _____.
   A. the U.S.   B. Canada
   C. Spain   D. European Union
5. Of the following alternative energy technologies, which one is the most low-profile in the U.S.?
   A. Ethanol.   B. Solar energy.
   C. Wind energy.   D. Geothermal.

VI. Questions on the Article

1. Why do venture capitalists like Khosla display so much enthusiasm over developing alternative energy technologies?
2. Why does the author say that it sure looks like a fossil fuel future for America?
3. According to Dan Reicher, what are needed to take green energy to the next level?
4. What was the bold plan announced by Pacific Gas & Electric this fall?
5. By what means does Abengoa plan to achieve greater efficiency?
6. According to the recent study, what techniques could be used to draw all the geothermal energy found three or more miles underground?
7. What is the potential of geothermal energy according to the study led by MIT?
8. How is cellulosic ethanol produced?
9. By what means will Range produce ethanol?
10. What is Google doing about the "plug-in hybrid" technology?

VII. Topics for Discussion

1. Should the technology of converting corn to energy be popularized?
2. Can renewable energies solve the grave problem of climate change?

Lesson 29

The Robots Are Coming

By Daniela Rus[1]

Robots have the potential to greatly improve the quality of our lives at home, at work, and at play. Customized robots working alongside people will create new jobs, improve the quality of existing jobs, and give people more time to focus on what they find interesting, important, and exciting. Commuting to work in driverless cars[2] will allow people to read, reply to e-mails, watch videos, and even nap. After dropping off one passenger, a driverless car will pick up its next rider, coordinating with the other self-driving cars in a system designed to minimize traffic and wait times[3]—and all the while driving more safely and efficiently than humans.

Yet the objective of robotics is not to replace humans by mechanizing and automating tasks; it is to find ways for machines to assist and collaborate with humans more effectively. Robots are better than humans at crunching numbers, lifting heavy objects, and, in certain contexts, moving with precision. Humans are better than robots at abstraction, generalization, and creative thinking, thanks to their ability to reason, draw from prior experience, and imagine. By working together, robots and humans can augment and complement each other's skills.

Still, there are significant gaps between where robots are today and the promise of a future era of "pervasive robotics,"[4] when robots will be integrated into the fabric of daily life, becoming as common as computers and smartphones are today, performing many specialized tasks, and often operating side by side with humans. Current research aims to improve the way robots are made, how they move themselves and manipulate objects, how they reason, how they perceive their environments, and how they cooperate with one another and with humans.

Creating a world of pervasive, customized robots is a major challenge, but its scope is not unlike that of the problem computer scientists faced nearly three decades ago[5], when they dreamed of a world where computers would become integral parts of human societies. In the words of Mark Weiser[6], a chief scientist at Xerox's Palo Alto Research Center[7] in the 1990s, who is considered the father of so-called ubiquitous computing[8]: "The most profound technologies are those that disappear. They weave themselves into the fabric of everyday life until they are indistinguishable from it.[9]" Computers have already achieved that kind of ubiquity. In the future, robots will, too.

A robot's capabilities are defined by what its body can do and what its brain can compute and control. Today's robots can perform basic locomotion on the ground, in the air, and in the water. They can recognize objects, map new environments, perform "pick-and-place"[10] operations on an assembly line, imitate simple human motions, acquire simple skills, and even act in coordination with other robots and human partners. One place where these skills are on display is at the annual RoboCup[11], a robot soccer World Cup, during which teams of robots coordinate to dribble, pass, shoot, and score goals.

This range of functionality has been made possible by innovations in robot design and advances in the algorithms that guide robot perception, reasoning, control, and coordination.[12] Robotics has benefited enormously from progress in many areas: computation, data storage, the scale and performance of the Internet, wireless communication, electronics, and design and manufacturing tools. The costs of hardware have dropped even as the electromechanical components used in robotic devices have become more reliable and the knowledge base available to intelligent machines has grown thanks to the Internet.[13] It has become possible to imagine the leap from the personal computer to the personal robot.

In recent years, the promise of robotics has been particularly visible in the transportation sector.[14] Many major car manufacturers have announced plans to build self-driving cars and predict that they will be able to sell them to consumers by 2020. Google's self-driving cars have now driven close to two million miles with only 11 minor accidents, most of them caused by human error; the company will begin testing the cars on public roads this summer. Several universities around the world have also launched self-driving-car projects. Meanwhile, California, Florida, Michigan, and Nevada have all passed legislation to allow autonomous cars on their roads, and many other state legislatures in the United States are considering such measures. Recently, an annual report by Singapore's Land Transportation Authority[15] predicted that "shared autonomous driving"[16] — fleets of self-driving cars providing customized transportation—could reduce the number of cars on the road by around 80 percent, decreasing travel times and pollution.

Self-driving cars would not merely represent a private luxury: as the cost of producing and maintaining them falls, their spread could greatly improve public transportation. Imagine a mass transit system with two layers: a network of large vehicles, such as trains and buses, that would handle long-distance trips and complementary fleets of small self-driving cars that would offer short, customized rides, picking up passengers at major hubs and also responding to individual requests for rides from almost anywhere. In 2014, the Future Urban Mobility project[17], which is part of the Singapore-MIT Alliance for Research and Technology[18], invited the public to ride on self-driving buggies that resembled golf carts[19] at the Chinese Garden in Singapore, a park with winding alleys surrounded by trees, benches, and strolling people. More than 500 people took part. The robotic vehicles stayed on the paths, avoided pedestrians, and brought their passengers to their selected destinations.

So far, that level of autonomous-driving performance has been possible only in low-speed, low-complexity environments. Robotic vehicles cannot yet handle all the complexities of driving "in the wild," such as inclement weather and complex traffic situations. These issues are the focus of ongoing research.

The broad adoption of robots will require a natural integration of intelligent machines into the human world rather than an integration of humans into the machines' world. Despite recent significant progress toward that goal, problems remain in three important areas. It still takes too much time to make new robots, today's robots are still quite limited in their ability to perceive and reason about their surroundings, and robotic communication is still quite brittle.

Many different types of robots are available today, but they all take a great deal of time to produce. Today's robot bodies are difficult to adapt or extend, and thus robots still have limited capabilities and limited applications. Rapidly fabricating new robots, add-on modules[20], fixtures, and specialized tools is not a real option, as the process of design, assembly, and programming is long and cumbersome. What's needed are design and fabrication tools that will speed up the customized manufacturing of robots.

Better-customized robots would help automate a wide range of tasks. Consider manufacturing. Currently, the use of automation in factories is not uniform across all industries. The car industry automates approximately 80 percent of its assembly processes, which consist of many repeatable actions. In contrast, only around ten percent of the assembly processes for electronics, such as cell phones, are automated, because such products change frequently and are highly customized. Tailor-made robots could help close this gap by reducing setup times for automation in industries that rely on customization and whose products have short life cycles.[21] Specialized robots would know where things are stored, how to put things together, how to interact with people, how to transport parts from one place to another, how to pack things, and how to reconfigure an assembly line. In a factory equipped with such robots, human workers would still be in control, and robots would assist them.

A second challenge involved in integrating robots into everyday life is the need to increase their reasoning abilities. Today's robots can perform only limited reasoning due to the fact that their computations are carefully specified. Everything a robot does is spelled out with simple instructions[22], and the scope of the robot's reasoning is entirely contained in its program. Furthermore, a robot's perception of its environment through its sensors is quite limited. Tasks that humans take for granted—for example, answering the question, "Have I been here before?"—are extremely difficult for robots. Robots use sensors such as cameras and scanners to record the features of the places they visit. But it is hard for a machine to differentiate between features that belong to a scene it has already observed and features of a new scene that happens to contain some of the same objects. In general, robots collect too much low-level data. Current research on machine learning is focused on developing algorithms that can help extract the information that will be useful to a robot from large data sets.[23] Such algorithms will help a robot summarize its history and thus significantly reduce, for example, the number of images it requires to answer that question, "Have I been here before?"

Robots also cannot cope with unexpected situations. If a robot encounters circumstances that it has not been programmed to handle or that fall outside the scope of its capabilities, it enters an "error" state and stops operating. Often, the robot cannot communicate the cause of the error. Robots need to learn how to adjust their programs so as to adapt to their surroundings and interact more easily with people, their environments, and other machines.

Today, everyone with Internet access—including robots—can easily obtain incredible amounts of information. Robots could take advantage of this information to make better decisions. For example, a dog-walking robot could find weather reports online and then consult its own stored data to determine the ideal length of a walk and the optimal route: perhaps a short walk if it's hot or raining, or a long walk to a nearby park where other dog walkers tend to congregate if it's pleasant out.

The integration of robots into everyday life will also require more reliable communication between robots and between robots and humans. Despite advances in wireless technology, impediments still hamper robot-to-robot communication. It remains difficult to model or predict how well robots will be able to communicate in any given environment. Moreover, methods of controlling robots that rely on current communications technologies are hindered by noise—extraneous signals and data that make it hard to send and receive commands. Robots need more reliable approaches to communication that would guarantee the bandwidth they need, when they need it. One promising new approach to this problem involves measuring the quality of communication around a robot locally instead of trying to predict it using models.

Communication between robots and people is also currently quite limited. Although audio sensors and speech-recognition software[24] allow robots to understand and respond to basic spoken commands ("Move to the door"), such interactions are both narrow and shallow in terms of scope and vocabulary. More extensive human-robot communication would enable robots to ask humans for help. It turns out that when a robot is performing a task, even a tiny amount of human intervention completely changes the way the robot deals with a problem and greatly empowers the machine to do more.

In a robot-rich world[25], people may wake up in the morning and send personal-shopping robots to the supermarket to bring back fruit and milk for breakfast. Once there, the robots may encounter people who are there to do their own shopping but who traveled to the store in self-driving cars and who are using self-driving shopping carts that take them directly to the items they want and then provide information on the freshness, provenance, and nutritional value of the goods—and that can also help visually impaired shoppers navigate the store safely.[26] In a retail environment shaped by pervasive robotics, people will supervise and support robots while offering customers advice and service with a human touch. In turn, robots will support people by automating some physically difficult or tedious jobs: stocking shelves, cleaning windows, sweeping sidewalks, delivering orders to customers.

Personal computers, wireless technology, smartphones, and easy-to-download apps have already democratized access to information and computation and transformed the way people live and work. In the years to come, robots will extend this digital revolution further into the physical realm[27] and deeper into everyday life, with consequences that will be equally profound.

From *Foreign Affairs*, July/August 2015

I. New Words

algorithm	[ˈælgəriðəm]	n.	（电脑程序中的）算法
augment	[ɔːgˈment]	v.	to increase the amount, value, size, etc. of sth
autonomous	[ɔːˈtɔnəməs]	adj.	able to do things and make decisions without help from anyone else
bandwidth	[ˈbændwidθ]	n.	带宽
brittle	[ˈbritl]	adj.	脆弱的；靠不住的
buggy	[ˈbʌgi]	n.	（无顶无门的）专用小汽车
congregate	[ˈkɑːŋgrigeit]	v.	to come together in a group
crunch	[krʌntʃ]	v.	to deal with large amounts of data very quickly
cumbersome	[ˈkʌmbərsəm]	adj.	slow and complicated
customize	[ˈkʌstəmaiz]	v.	to make or change sth to suit the needs of the owner
democratize	[diˈmɔkrətaiz]	v.	to make sth available to all people
dribble	[ˈdribəl]	v.	（足球及其他某些体育运动）运球，带球
electromechanical	[iˈlektrəumiˈkænikəl]	adj.	电动机械的，电机的
extraneous	[ikˈstreiniəs]	adj.	not directly connected; coming from outside
fabricate	[ˈfæbrikeit]	v.	to make or produce goods, equipment, etc. from various different materials
fixture	[ˈfikstʃə]	n.	固定装置，固定设施
hamper	[ˈhæmpə(r)]	v.	to prevent sb from easily doing or achieving sth
hardware	[ˈhɑːdweər]	n.	the machinery and electronic parts of a computer system
hub	[hʌb]	n.	the central and most important part of a particular place or activity
impair	[imˈpeə]	v.	to damage sth or make sth worse
impediment	[imˈpedimənt]	n.	妨碍，阻碍，障碍
inclement	[inˈklemənt]	adj.	formal (of weather) bad, especially cold or stormy
indistinguishable	[indiˈstiŋgwiʃəbl]	adj.	无法分辨的，无法区分的
integral	[ˈintigrəl]	adj.	being an essential part of sth
locomotion	[ləukəˈməuʃn]	n.	movement or the ability to move
manipulate	[məˈnipjuleit]	v.	to control or use sth in a skilful way
mechanize	[ˈmekənaiz]	v.	to change a process, so that the work is done by machines rather than people
optimal	[ˈɔptiməl]	adj.	最佳的，最优的

perception	[pəˈsepʃn]	n.	the way you notice things, especially with the senses
provenance	[ˈprɒvənəns]	n.	发源地，来源
reconfigure	[riːkənˈfɪɡə(r)]	v.	[计]重新配置，重新设置
robotics	[rəʊˈbɒtɪks]	n.	the science of designing and operating robots
scanner	[ˈskænər]	n.	扫描仪
sensor	[ˈsensər]	n.	（探测光、热、压力等的）传感器
storage	[ˈstɔːrɪdʒ]	n.	the process of keeping information on a computer
synergistic	[sɪnəˈdʒɪstɪk]	adj.	协同的，协作的
transit	[ˈtrænzɪt]	n.	the activity or process of moving sth or sb from one place to another
ubiquitous	[juːˈbɪkwɪtəs]	adj.	无所不在的，十分普遍的

II. Background Information

机器人的发展与前景

　　机器人是一种集机械、电子、控制、传感、人工智能等多学科先进技术于一体的自动化装备。它既可以接受人类指挥，又可以运行预先编排的程序，也可以根据以人工智能技术制定的原则纲领行动。

　　自1954年机器人产业诞生后，经过六十多年发展，机器人已经被广泛应用于装备制造、新材料、生物医药、智慧新能源等高新产业。机器人与人工智能技术、先进制造技术和移动互联网技术的融合发展，推动了人类社会生活方式的变革。全球机器人的发展可以大致分为四个阶段：

　　第一阶段，发展萌芽期。1954年，第一台可编程的机器人在美国诞生。1958年，美国发明家恩格尔伯格建立了Unimation公司，并于1959年研制出了世界上第一台工业机器人。

　　第二阶段，产业孕育期。1962年，美国AMF公司生产出第一台圆柱坐标型机器人。1969年，日本研发出第一台以双臂走路的机器人。随着计算机技术、现代控制技术、传感技术、人工智能技术的发展，机器人也得到了迅速的发展。这一时期的机器人只具有记忆、存储能力，按相应程序重复作业，对周围环境基本没有感知与反馈控制能力。

　　第三阶段，快速发展期。随着传感技术以及信息处理技术的发展，出现了有感觉的机器人。2002年，丹麦iRobot公司推出了吸尘器机器人，是目前世界上销量最大的家用机器人。2006年起，机器人模块化、平台统一化的趋势越来越明显。与此同时，服务机器人发展迅速，应用范围日趋广泛，以手术机器人为代表的医疗康复机器人形成

第九单元 科技军事

了较大产业规模,空间机器人、仿生机器人和反恐防暴机器人等特种作业机器人实现了应用价值。

第四阶段,智能应用期。这一阶段,随着感知、计算、控制等技术的不断升级和图像识别、自然语音处理、深度认知学习等人工智能技术在机器人领域的深入应用,机器人领域的服务化趋势日益明显,逐渐渗透到社会生产、生活的每一个角落。

今天,新一代的机器人已经渗透到人类生活的各个领域。机器人的发展不再是某一个国家的问题,而成了一个国际问题。全球许多国家都将机器人产业的发展作为一种国家战略,这说明机器人将是未来发展的一种趋势。这是一场新工业革命,成本、技术进步、用户个性化定制、生产方式、生产工具等方面都要进行大的变革。可以说,机器人正在改变人类的生产、生活方式。

未来,随着资本和技术力量的聚集,机器人的开发应用将会迎来行业发展的黄金期,并可能呈现以下几种趋势:

第一,机器人与信息技术深入融合。第二,机器人产品易用性与稳定性提升。第三,机器人向模块化、智能化和系统化方向发展。

机器人的广泛使用也引起了一些人的担忧,他们认为未来机器人会对劳动力市场产生巨大冲击,甚至会取代人。诚然,在未来十到二十年,很多传统工种确实会被机器人取代或者优化,这是非常明显的趋势。但从历史角度看,更多、更具效率的机器的使用,不仅极大地释放了生产力,同时也会产生一些新的工作岗位。此外,机器人的使用会引起就业结构的变化。机器人的引入将使就业结构高端化。从长远看,未来智能机器人还将对人才提出更高的要求。不管技术怎么发展,都会存在只有人类才能胜任的工作。

III. Notes to the Text

1. Daniela Rus — a professor of Electrical Engineering and Computer Science and Director of the Computer Science and Artificial Intelligence Laboratory at the Massachusetts Institute of Technology
2. driverless cars —无人驾驶汽车
3. After dropping off one passenger, a driverless car will pick up its next rider, coordinating with the other self-driving cars in a system designed to minimize traffic and wait times...—在一名乘客下车后,无人驾驶汽车将接载下一名乘客,与其他自动驾驶汽车协同组合为一个能够把汽车流量和等车时间减到最低程度的系统(① drop off — leave or unload ② minimize — to reduce sth, especially sth bad, to the lowest possible level)
4. era of "pervasive robotics" — "机器人普及"的时代(pervasive — existing in all parts of a place or thing)
5. Creating a world of pervasive, customized robots is a major challenge, but its scope is not

unlike that of the problem computer scientists faced nearly three decades ago... — 创建一个遍布定制的机器人的世界是一个巨大的挑战,但其难度与大约三十年前计算机科学家所面临的问题的难度并非不同。

6. Mark Weiser — a chief scientist at Xerox PARC in the United States. (Weiser is widely considered to be the father of ubiquitous computing, a term he coined in 1988.)

7. Xerox's Palo Alto Research Center — 施乐公司帕洛阿尔托研究中心(a research and development company in Palo Alto, California, with a distinguished reputation for its contributions to information technology and hardware systems)

8. ubiquitous computing — 普适计算(a concept in software engineering and computer science where computing is made to appear anytime and everywhere. In contrast to desktop computing, ubiquitous computing can occur using any device, in any location, and in any format.)

9. They weave themselves into the fabric of everyday life until they are indistinguishable from it. — 这些科技融入了日常生活的各个方面,已经无法察觉。(① weave sth into sth — to put facts, events, details, etc. together to make a closely connected whole; ②fabric — the basic structure of a society, an organization, etc. that enables it to function successfully)

10. pick-and-place — 拾取和放置

11. RoboCup —机器人世界杯赛(RoboCup is an annual international robotics competition proposed and founded in 1996 by a group of university professors. The aim is to promote robotics and AI research. The competition's full name is "Robot World Cup.")

12. This range of functionality has been made possible by innovations in robot design and advances in the algorithms that guide robot perception, reasoning, control, and coordination. — 机器人设计的创新以及在引导机器人认知、推理、控制和协调方面的算法进步使得如今的机器人拥有如此多的功能。

13. ...the knowledge base available to intelligent machines has grown thanks to the Internet. — 由于有互联网,智能机器可用的知识库得到了拓展。[knowledge base (KB) — a technology used to store complex information used by a computer system.]

14. In recent years, the promise of robotics has been particularly visible in the transportation sector. — 近年来,机器人技术的光明前景在交通领域表现得特别明显。(promise — an indication of future success)

15. Singapore's Land Transportation Authority — 新加坡陆路交通管理局(It is a statutory board under the Ministry of Transport in Singapore, responsible for planning, designing, building and maintaining Singapore's land transport infrastructure and systems.)

16. shared autonomous driving — (汽车)共享自动驾驶

17. Future Urban Mobility project — 未来城市交通项目(The project was started in 2010 with support from the Singapore National Research Foundation, and aims to develop, in and beyond Singapore, a new paradigm for the planning, design and operation of future urban mobility systems.)

18. Singapore-MIT Alliance for Research and Technology—新加坡—麻省理工学院科研中心(The Singapore-MIT Alliance for Research and Technology (SMART) is a major research

enterprise established by the Massachusetts Institute of Technology in partnership with the National Research Foundation of Singapore in 2007. SMART is MIT's first, and to-date only, research centre outside the United States. It is also MIT's largest international research programme.）

19. golf cart — 高尔夫球车（a small motor vehicle in which golfers can ride between shots）

20. add-on module — 附加模块

21. Tailor-made robots could help close this gap by reducing setup times for automation in industries that rely on customization and whose products have short life cycles. — 特别定制的机器人能够填补这一空白，帮助这些依赖定制化生产、产品拥有较短寿命周期的制造产业缩短自动化生产所需的组装时间。

22. Everything a robot does is spelled out with simple instructions... — 机器人所做的一切都是由简单的指令清楚地交代的（spell out — explain in detail or in a very clear way）

23. Current research on machine learning is focused on developing algorithms that can help extract the information that will be useful to a robot from large data sets. — 目前有关机器学习的研究集中在开发可以从大型数据集提取对机器人有用信息的算法上。（① extract — to choose information, etc. from a book, a computer, etc. to be used for a particular purpose; ② data set — a collection of data which is treated as a single unit by a computer; ③ machine learning — 一门多领域交叉学科，专门研究计算机怎样模拟或实现人类的学习行为，获取新的知识或技能，重新组织已有的知识结构使之不断完善自身性能。）

24. audio sensors and speech-recognition software — 音频传感器和语音识别软件

25. robot-rich world — 机器人普及的世界

26. That can also help visually impaired shoppers navigate the store safely. — 这也可以帮助那些视障的购物者安全地在商店中穿行。（visually impaired — having greatly reduced vision）

27. physical realm — 物质领域

IV. Language Features

科技新闻报道语言特色

科技新闻在英语报刊中占有较大比重。科技新闻具有新闻报道的共性，即新鲜性、及时性和真实性。然而，科技新闻报道的是科技内容，所以更强调真实性。从新闻写作的角度分析，科技新闻报道具有五大特点：

一是准确。新闻的生命在于真实。科学恰恰是最讲究实事求是的，对于事实，既不容许扩大，也不允许缩小，因此科技新闻不但要真实，而且要求高度准确。二是新颖。科技新闻要突出反映新成果、新技术，多在"新"字上着眼，关注高科技、新成果、学术前沿动态。三是通俗。科技新闻一般是写给广大普通读者看的，而非特供行家阅读,因此,科技新闻的报道必须在准确的前提之下尽可能做到通俗易懂,尽量避免使用只有专家才懂的专有术语,非用不可时,就力争选用准确、简短、通俗的语言加以解释。四是精练。科技新闻不同于科研报告或学术讲座,一般无须反映研究过程或细节,只需酌情报道最重要、最精华的事实,即科技成果及其成功的意义和关键。五是生动。科技新闻虽然反映的是严肃精准的科技信息,但同时也应是有趣味的、吸引人的。记者在写作时需立意新颖,用有趣的方式提出严肃的科技问题,吸引读者去思考,增加新闻的可读性,从而将知识性与趣味性有机地融合在一起。

　　英语科技新闻与一般英语新闻既有共同之处,又有其自身特点。科技新闻具有准确、新颖的特点,因此报道中通常会采用新词或专门领域的词汇来介绍新的科学成果和重要的科技事件。但是科技新闻的受众大多数是没有专业知识的一般大众,科技新闻还需做到用词通俗,在传播科技知识的时候,必须考虑到受众的接受能力,选用通俗词汇来代替专业术语词汇。因此,英语科技新闻通常会用通俗易懂的词汇代替晦涩的专业词汇,消除受众的阅读障碍,取得良好的传播效果。其次,英语科技新闻中格外注意用词的科学性。科技新闻中的用词讲究准确,恰如其分,既不夸大,也不缩小。在报道数据及科技成果时,往往还会涉及数字信息。记者在采写英语科技新闻的时候,通常会对数字进行灵活的处理,让抽象、枯燥的数字生动起来,成为能被受众接受的、有意义的信息。常见的处理手法之一是运用对比手法,对数字进行换算,以"比例""倍数"等形式对数字加以解释。

　　在句法上,英语科技新闻侧重叙事逻辑,强调客观准确。在新闻中,第三人称的使用较为普遍,因为第一、第二人称使用过多会给读者造成主观臆断的印象。第三人称的角度更适合叙述新闻事实。这样不仅可以合理地体现报道的客观准确性,而且可以充分地体现句子表达的层次性和逻辑性,同时也符合英语新闻报道ABC原则(即Accuracy, Brevity and Clarity Principles)中的"清晰"(Clarity)原则。此外,英语科技新闻在遣词造句时广泛使用被动语态,通常将主要信息前置放在主语部分。这一句法特点主要也是为了更好凸显科技新闻的客观准确性。科技新闻中,还经常会使用一些修辞手法,如比喻法、转换法、拟人法,使文章显得生动形象且有趣。目前在英语科技新闻报道中,直接或间接引语所占比重日益增大,表达方式自然生动的口语倾向已越来越明显。

　　读者可以结合文章中的具体词句,更深刻直观地感受英语科技新闻的特点。

V. Analysis of Content

1. Compared with humans, robots are better at _____.
　　A. learning lessons from history　　　　B. creative thinking
　　C. logical reasoning　　　　　　　　　D. data processing
2. Which of the following is NOT related to the application of robotics in the transportation sector?
　　A. Testing of Google's self-driving cars.　　B. Passing of legislation in Nevada.
　　C. Future Urban Mobility project in Singapore.　D. Holding of the annual RoboCup.

3. What is the purpose of involving customized robots in the field of manufacturing?

   A. To store and put things together.

   B. To bridge the gap between car industry and electronic industry.

   C. To speed up the manufacturing of highly-customized industries.

   D. To cooperate with human workers.

4. Which of the following is NOT listed among the problems with the robotics?

   A. It still takes too much time to make new robots.

   B. Robots are not much better than humans at moving with precision.

   C. Today's robots are still quite limited in their ability to perceive and reason about their surroundings.

   D. Robotic communication is quite brittle.

5. What will life be like in the future robot-rich world?

   A. Robots can help people buy necessities from the supermarket.

   B. Self-driving shopping carts also provide information on the goods.

   C. Blind people can navigate the store safely with the help of robots.

   D. All of the above.

VI. Questions on the Article

1. What are the advantages of driverless cars compared with manned cars?
2. What is the objective of robotics?
3. What does the era of "pervasive robotics" mean?
4. What have contributed to the fast development of robotics today?
5. How can self-driving cars improve public transportation?
6. What are the main challenges robotics now face?
7. What factors lead to the limited reasoning abilities of today's robots?
8. What will happen when a robot encounters unexpected situations?
9. How can we provide reliable approaches to robots' communication?
10. What will the retail environment be like in the future world of pervasive robotics?

VII. Topics for Discussion

1. Should self-driving cars be allowed in all kinds of environments?
2. Will robots replace human workers in the future?

Lesson 30

A Third Industrial Revolution

As manufacturing goes digital, it will change out of all recognition[1], says Paul Markillie[2]. And some of the business of making things will return to rich countries.

By Paul Markillie

Outside the sprawling Frankfurt Messe, home of innumerable German trade fairs[3], stands the "Hammering Man," a 21-metre kinetic statue[4] that steadily raises and lowers its arm to bash a piece of metal with a hammer. Jonathan Borofsky, the artist who built it, says it is a celebration of the worker using his mind and hands to create the world we live in. That is a familiar story. But now the tools are changing in a number of remarkable ways that will transform the future of manufacturing.

One of those big trade fairs held in Frankfurt is EuroMold[5], which shows machines for making prototypes of products, the tools needed to put those things into production and all manner of other manufacturing kit[6]. Old-school engineers worked with lathes, drills, stamping presses and moulding machines[7]. These still exist, but EuroMold exhibits no oily machinery tended by men in overalls. Hall after hall is full of squeaky-clean American, Asian and European machine tools, all highly automated. Most of their operators, men and women, sit in front of computer screens. Nowhere will you find a hammer.

And at the most recent EuroMold fair, last November, another group of machines was on display: three-dimensional (3D) printers[8]. Instead of bashing, bending and cutting material the way it always has been, 3D printers build things by depositing material, layer by layer. That is why the process is more properly described as additive manufacturing[9]. An American firm, 3D Systems, used one of its 3D printers to print a hammer for its correspondent, complete with a natty wood-effect handle and a metallised head.[10]

This is what manufacturing will be like in the future. Ask a factory today to make you a single hammer to your own design and you will be presented with a bill for thousands of dollars. The makers would have to produce a mould, cast the head, machine it to a suitable finish, turn a wooden handle and then assemble the parts. To do that for one hammer would be prohibitively expensive. If you are producing thousands of hammers, each one of them will be much cheaper, thanks to economies of scale[11]. For a 3D printer, though, economies of scale matter much less. Its software can be endlessly tweaked and it can make just about anything. The cost of setting up the machine is the same whether it makes one thing or as many things as can fit inside the machine; like a two-dimensional office printer that pushes out one letter or many different ones until the ink cartridge and paper need replacing, it will keep going, at about the same cost for each item.

Additive manufacturing is not yet good enough to make a car or an iPhone, but it is already being used to make specialist parts for cars and customised covers for iPhones[12]. Although it is still a relatively young technology, most people probably already own something that was made with the help of a 3D printer. It might be a pair of shoes, printed in solid form as a design prototype before being produced in bulk[13]. It could be a hearing aid, individually tailored to the shape of the user's ear. Or it could be a piece of jewellery, cast from a mould made by a 3D printer or produced directly using a growing number of printable materials.

But additive manufacturing is only one of a number of breakthroughs leading to the factory of the future, and conventional production equipment is becoming smarter and more flexible, too. Volkswagen[14] has a new production strategy called Modularer Querbaukasten[15], or MQB. By standardising the parameters of certain components, such as the mounting points of engines, the German carmaker hopes to be able to produce all its models on the same production line.[16] The process is being introduced this year, but will gather pace as new models are launched over the next decade. Eventually it should allow its factories in America, Europe and China to produce locally whatever vehicle each market requires.

They don't make them like that any more

Factories are becoming vastly more efficient, thanks to automated milling machines[17] that can swap their own tools, cut in multiple directions and "feel" if something is going wrong, together with robots equipped with vision and other sensing systems. Nissan's British factory in Sunderland[18], opened in 1986, is now one of the most productive in Europe. In 1999 it built 271,157 cars with 4,594 people. Last year it made 480,485 vehicles—more than any other car factory in Britain, ever—with just 5,462 people.

"You can't make some of this modern stuff using old manual tools," says Colin Smith, director of engineering and technology for Rolls-Royce[19], a British company that makes jet engines and other power systems. "The days of huge factories full of lots of people are not there any more."

As the number of people directly employed in making things declines, the cost of labour as a proportion of the total cost of production will diminish too. This will encourage makers to move some of the work back to rich countries, not least because new manufacturing techniques make it cheaper and faster to respond to changing local tastes.[20]

The materials being used to make things are changing as well. Carbon-fibre composites[21], for instance, are replacing steel and aluminium in products ranging from mountain bikes to airliners. And sometimes it will not be machines doing the making, but micro-organisms that have been genetically engineered for the task.[22]

Everything in the factories of the future will be run by smarter software. Digitisation in manufacturing will have a disruptive effect every bit as big as in other industries that have gone digital[23], such as office equipment, telecoms, photography, music, publishing and films. And the effects will not be confined to large manufacturers; indeed, they will need to watch out because much of what is coming will empower small and medium-sized firms and individual entrepreneurs. Launching novel products will become easier and cheaper. Communities offering 3D printing and other production services that are a bit like Facebook are already forming online—a new phenomenon which might be called social manufacturing[24].

The consequences of all these changes, this report will argue, amount to a third industrial revolution. The first began in Britain in the late 18th century with the mechanisation of the textile industry. In the following decades the use of machines to make things, instead of crafting them by hand, spread around the world. The second industrial revolution began in America in the early 20th century with the assembly line, which ushered in the era of mass production.

As manufacturing goes digital, a third great change is now gathering pace. It will allow things to be made economically in much smaller numbers, more flexibly and with a much lower input of labour, thanks to new materials, completely new processes such as 3D printing, easy-to-use robots and new collaborative manufacturing services available online.[25] The wheel is almost coming full circle[26], turning away from mass manufacturing and towards much more individualised production. And that in turn could bring some of the jobs back to rich countries that long ago lost them to the emerging world.

From *The Economist*, April 21, 2012

I. New Words

aluminium	[ˌæljuˈminjəm]	n.	铝
bash	[bæʃ]	v.	to strike very hard
cartridge	[ˈkɑːtridʒ]	n.	色带盒,墨盒
cast	[kɑːst]	v.	浇铸,铸造
craft	[ˈkrɑːft]	v.	精心制作
deposit	[diˈpɔzit]	v.	to leave a layer of a substance on the surface of sth
drill	[dril]	n.	钻床
empower	[imˈpauə]	v.	to give sb the power to do sth
kit	[kit]	n.	a set of tools
finish	[ˈfiniʃ]	n.	成品
lathe	[leið]	n.	车床
micro-organism	[ˈmaikrəuˈɔːgənizəm]	n.	微生物
mould	[məuld]	v. & n.	使软材料成型,模子,铸模
natty	[ˈnæti]	adj.	neat and fashionable in appearance
novel	[ˈnɔvəl]	adj.	新奇的,新颖的
oily	[ˈɔili]	adj.	covered or soaked with oil
old-school	[ˈəuldskuːl]	adj.	old-fashioned, or traditional
overalls	[ˈəuvərɔːlz]	n.	工装裤,工作服
prohibitively	[prəˈhibitivli]	adv.	过高地,过分地
prototype	[ˈprəutətaip]	n.	原型,模型
robot	[ˈrəubɔt]	n.	机器人

sprawling	[ˈsprɔːlɪŋ]	adj.	spreading over a wide area in an untidy or unattractive way
squeaky-clean	[ˌskwiːkiːˈkliːn]	adj.	completely clean
swap	[swɔp]	v.	to exchange
tailor	[ˈteɪlə]	v.	to make or adapt sth for a special purpose
telecom	[ˈtelɪkɔm]	n.	telecommunication 电信
transform	[trænsˈfɔːm]	v.	to change the form of sth
tweak	[twiːk]	v.	to make slight changes to a machine

II. Background Information

数字化制造技术

数字化制造技术（digital manufacturing technology）是指在数字化技术和制造技术融合的背景下，并在虚拟现实（virtual reality）、计算机网络（computer network）、快速原型（rapid prototyping）、数据库（data bank）和多媒体（multi-media）等支撑技术的支持下，根据用户的需求，迅速收集资源信息，对产品信息、工艺信息和资源信息进行分析、规划和重组，实现对产品设计和功能的仿真以及原型制造，进而快速生产出达到用户要求的产品的整个制造过程。

通俗地说，数字化就是将许多复杂多变的信息转变为可以度量的数字、数据，再以这些数字、数据建立起适当的数字化模型，把它们转变为一系列二进制代码（binary code），引入计算机内部，进行统一处理，这就是数字化的基本过程。

英国《经济学人》杂志负责创新与科技报道的编辑保罗·麦基里坚信，制造业数字化将引领第三次工业革命。他认为，制造业的数字化进程正从五个方面向前推进：

一是更智能的计算机软件（computer software）。目前，大多数物品都能通过软件在电脑上转化为一个三维模型，用户可以在电脑上检测产品并开发新功能。数字化模型大大提高了生产速度并降低了成本。

二是新材料的出现。碳纤维（carbon-fiber）是一种典型的新材料，它和钢材一样结实，却比后者轻一半，目前已被广泛应用于制造山地自行车、钓鱼竿、航空器和汽车等。其他新材料，如纳米，能赋予产品一些新的特性，比如利用纳米颗粒制造的玻璃可以实现自动除尘。总之，新材料比旧材料更轻、更坚固、更耐用。

三是更灵巧的机器人。麦基里认为，下一代机器人将适用于中小型企业。它们会抓取、装运、暂存、拾取零部件以及进行清理打扫等，这些技能让它们可以应用于更广泛的领域。

四是基于网络的制造业服务商。在互联网上，这些服务商促成了完整的产业链。在线制造业服务商能够撮合全球大大小小的企业展开合作并相互购买产品和服务。而诸如shapeways.com之类的网站则向任何一个可以拿着笔记本上网的人，提供加入制造业及使用3D打印(three-dimensional printing)技术的一条有效路径。

五是新的制造方法。3D打印技术(也称立体印刷或添加式制造)是其中翘楚,通过这种技术可以一层一层地"堆砌"出与样品完全相同的产品。3D打印机能够制作许多对传统工厂来说太复杂而做不了的东西。

3D打印技术和数字化制造虽有诸多益处,但在这场变革之中,我们必然也会遇到各种各样的法律和道德问题,例如,知识产权可能彻底失效,盗版会更加容易,不法分子可能利用这一尖端技术制造枪支或其他杀伤性武器。技术的革新永无止境,如何使法律更新适应技术的快速发展,如何确保数字化制造的伦理和安全,这些问题值得思考。在数字化制造技术不断迭代的背景下,建立现代化产业体系,推动制造业高端化、智能化、绿色化发展,也成为建设数字中国的必经之路。

III. Notes to the Text

1. As manufacturing goes digital, it will change out of all recognition...—数字化进程将使制造业彻底改变

2. Paul Markillie—保罗·麦基里(英国《经济学人》杂志负责创新与科技报道的编辑、《第三次工业革命》系列报道撰稿人)

3. Frankfurt Messe, home of innumerable German trade fairs...—法兰克福国际展览中心,这里举办过无数次德国商品展销会(这是世界第三大展览中心,每年春秋两季此地举行的法兰克福消费品展是世界上影响最大、规模最大的高品质消费品博览会。)

4. kinetic statue—a statue that depends for its effect on the movement of some of its parts 动态雕像

5. EuroMold—欧洲模具博览会(此展每年举办一次,只对专业观众开放,是目前世界上规模最大、水平最高、最具专业代表性的模具盛展。)

6. all manner of other manufacturing kit—各种各样的其他制造工具

7. stamping presses and moulding machines—冲压机和铸造机

8. three-dimensional (3D) printer—3D打印机(一种以数字模型文件为基础,运用粉末状金属或塑料等可粘合材料,通过逐层打印的方式来构造物体的技术。许多专家认为,这种技术代表制造业发展新趋势。)

9. additive manufacturing—增材制造(数字化增材制造技术是一种三维、实体、快速、自由成形的制造新技术,它综合了计算机的图形处理、数字化信息和控制、激光技术、机电技术和材料技术等多项高技术的优势。)

10. An American firm, 3D Systems, used one of its 3D printers to print a hammer for its correspondent, complete with a natty wood-effect handle and a metallised head.—美国3D Systems公司使用一台3D打印机给远地客户打印了一个有木质感精巧把手和金属锤头的完整锤子(① wood-effect—giving the sense or feel of wood; ② correspondent—a person or a company who has regular business with another in a distant place; ③ 3D Systems—成立于

1986年,主要生产三维立体打印机)

11. economies of scale—规模经济[又称"规模利益"(scale merit),指在一定科技水平下生产能力扩大,使长期平均成本下降的趋势,即长期费用曲线呈下降趋势。]

12. customised covers for iPhones—按客户要求定制的iPhone外壳(customize—to make or change sth to suit the needs of the owner)

13. in bulk—in large quantities

14. Volkswagen—大众汽车公司(德国主要的汽车制造公司,德文VolksWagenwerk意为大众使用的汽车,1937年创立,公司总部设在沃尔夫斯堡。)

15. Modularer Querbaukasten—MQB,英文表达法为modular transverse matrix,即横置发动机模块化平台(MQB将大量的汽车零部件实现标准化,令它们可以在不同品牌和不同级别的车型中实现共享,可以极大降低车型开发费用、周期以及生产环节的制造成本。)

16. By standardising the parameters of certain components, such as the mounting points of engines, the German carmaker hopes to be able to produce all its models on the same production line.—这家德国汽车制造商希望通过将具体部件参数(如发动机悬置点)标准化的方法在同一条生产线生产所有车型的汽车。

17. milling machines—铣床

18. Nissan's British factory in Sunderland—日产汽车公司在英国桑德兰市的工厂(①Nissan—日产汽车株式会社,创立于1933年,是日本三大汽车制造商之一;②Sunderland—桑德兰市,英格兰东北部重要港口城市)

19. Rolls-Royce—劳斯莱斯[世界顶级豪华轿车厂商,1906年成立于英国,公司创始人为Frederick Henry Royce和Charles Stewart Rolls。劳斯莱斯公司除制造汽车外还涉足飞机发动机制造领域,2003年劳斯莱斯汽车公司被宝马(BMW)收购。]

20. This will encourage makers to move some of the work back to rich countries, not least because new manufacturing techniques make it cheaper and faster to respond to changing local tastes.—这将激励制造商将一些工作转回到富裕国家,其重要原因是新的制造技术使得产品适应当地不断变化的品位的速度更快,代价更低。(not least—especially)

21. Carbon-fibre composites—碳纤维复合材料(碳纤维是由碳元素构成的无机纤维,不仅具有碳材料的固有特性,还兼具纺织纤维的柔软可加工性,是新一代增强纤维。)

22. And sometimes it will not be machines doing the making, but micro-organisms that have been genetically engineered for the task.—有时不会是机器制造产品,而是用转基因的微生物来做这件事。(目前科学界正在考虑根据微生物特性,通过转基因方法使其长成所需要的产品。美国加州大学旧金山分校等机构正在研究bacteria 3D printing项目。)

23. Digitisation in manufacturing will have a disruptive effect every bit as big as in other industries that have gone digital... —制造业数字化将产生大乱,乱的程度与其他企业数字化后完全一样 (①disruptive—causing problems so that sth cannot continue normally; ②every bit as big as—just as big as)

24. social manufacturing—社会制造(社会制造是利用3D打印、网络技术和社会媒体,通过众包等方式让社会民众充分参与产品的全生命制造过程,实现个性化、实时化、经济化的生产和消费模式。)

25. ...such as 3D printing, easy-to-use robots and new collaborative manufacturing services available

online. —诸如3D打印,易于使用的机器人和网络所提供的新式协同制造[collaborative manufacturing—协同制造(不同地方、分散作业情况下的合作性制造,其条件是具有互操作性的合作平台,如网络)]

26. The wheel is almost coming full circle...—历史的车轮几乎转了一整圈 (come full circle—to be in the same situation in which it began, even though there have been changes during the time in between)

IV. Language Features

借 词

本文使用德语借词Modularer Querbaukasten, Frankfurt Messe。

语言学家的研究表明,英语词汇数量已逾百万,在西方语言中雄居榜首。而这些词汇大部分是来自其他语言。据统计,英语中外来词的比例高达80%。纵观英语发展史,我们不难发现英语"具有吸收外来语的特异功能"。长时期的兼收并蓄使英语形成了词汇国际性的特色。

借词分早期借词和近期借词。早期借词的拼写和发音都已英语化(Anglicized)。人们使用这些词时根本感觉不到它们是异国之物。

现代英语仍然源源不断地从其他语言中吸收新词,这些近期借词依然保留自己的拼写和发音,因而易于识别。

外刊上时而可见外来词,这些借词的使用主要有以下两个目的。

1. 无对等词表达新概念

例 American bars—and living rooms—may never be the same, now that a Japanese singalong fad known as Karaoke has begun to infiltrate American popular culture.

Karaoke(卡拉OK)发源于日本,英文中无对等词表达这一概念。

2. 营造特定文化气氛

例 1. Perched on the steep cliffs overlooking a wide expanse of the St. Lawrence River, the walled city of Quebec resembles nothing so much as a tranquil 18th-century French provincial town. Stone houses with green copper roofs line narrow streets, bright posts of geraniums decorate their fronts and crocheted lace curtains hang in casement windows. The boulangeries sell croissants and brioches; the bookstores, the latest Parisian titles.

这段文字描述加拿大魁北克市所具有的鲜明的法国文化特色,法语借词的使用使这种文化气氛更为浓厚。(boulangeries—面包店;croissants—月牙形小面包;brioches—奶油鸡蛋卷)

例 2. Mr. Peter Broke was yesterday morning recovering from a press of work and steeling himself for the task of instilling a little perestroika into Conservative Central Office in his new role as party chairman.

本段文字摘自报道苏联经济改革的文章，俄语词 perestroika(改革)的使用增添了异国情调。

应该指出的是，借词的使用虽然有助于增强表达效果，但也带来一定的阅读困难。一般来讲，新闻报道由于强调文字通俗易懂，因此尽量少用或不用新的借词，这些词较多出现在新闻周刊所刊载的解释性报道或评论之中。

V. Analysis of Content

1. The word "correspondent" in the sentence "An American firm, 3D Systems, used one of its 3D printers to print a hammer for its correspondent, complete with a natty wood-effect handle and a metallised head." means _____.

   A. a person who has regular business with another
   B. a person who writes letters to another person
   C. a person who reports news for a news publication
   D. a thing similar to something else

2. Which of the following statements is NOT true about 3D printing?

   A. It builds things by depositing layer by layer.
   B. It is more properly described as additive manufacturing.
   C. It is digital manufacturing.
   D. It is a kind of advanced mass production.

3. It can be seen from the article that 3D printing at present cannot produce _____.

   A. specialist parts of cars
   B. iPhones
   C. hammers
   D. moulds for casting a piece of jewellery

4. The author's list of effects produced by 3D manufacturing does NOT include _____.

   A. reducing waste of raw materials
   B. reducing labor cost
   C. increasing job chances in rich countries
   D. increasing efficiency

5. According to the author, the second industrial revolution began with _____.

   A. the mechanization of the textile industry
   B. the assembly line
   C. the use of locomotives
   D. the use of cars

VI. Questions on the Article

1. What kind of machines does EuroMold usually show?
2. What kind of machines were on display at the most recent EuroMold fair?
3. Why is the process of 3D printing described as additive manufacturing?
4. How do 3D printers manufacture things?
5. What is the new production strategy Volkswagen plans to use?
6. Why will the use of new manufacturing techniques encourage makers to move some of the work back to rich countries?
7. What are the effects produced by digitisation on small and medium sized firms and individual entrepreneurs?
8. How important are the changes brought about by new manufacturing techniques?

VII. Topics for Discussion

1. Will 3D printing start a third industrial revolution?
2. What effects will manufacturing digitisation produce on the job market?

Lesson 31

The Dark Side of Recruiting

Persuading young Americans to join a wartime Army is never easy. But the pressures on recruiters in one Texas battalion have been deadly.
(Abridged)

By Mark Thompson

When Army Staff Sergeant[1] Amanda Henderson ran into Staff Sergeant Larry Flores in their Texas recruiting station last August, she was shocked by the dark circles under his eyes and his ragged appearance. "Are you O.K.?" she asked the normally squared-away[2] soldier. "Sergeant Henderson, I am just really tired," he replied. "I had such a bad, long week, it was ridiculous." The previous Saturday, Flores' commanders had berated him for poor performance.[3] He had worked every day since from 6:30 a.m. to 10 p.m., trying to persuade the youth of Nacogdoches to wear Army green. "But I'm O.K.," he told her.

No, he wasn't. Later that night, Flores hanged himself in his garage with an extension cord[4]. Henderson and her husband Patrick, both Army recruiters, were stunned. "I'll never forget sitting there at Sergeant Flores' memorial service with my husband and seeing his wife crying," Amanda recalls. "I remember looking over at Patrick and going, 'Why did he do this to her? Why did he do this to his children?'" Patrick didn't say anything, and Amanda now says Flores' suicide "triggered" something in her husband. Six weeks later, Patrick hanged himself with a dog chain in their backyard shed.

The wars in Iraq and Afghanistan are now the longest waged by an all-volunteer force in U.S. history. Even as soldiers rotate back into the field for multiple and extended tours, the Army requires a constant supply of new recruits.[5] But the patriotic fervor that led so many to sign up after 9/11 is now eight years past. That leaves recruiters with perhaps the toughest, if not the most dangerous, job in the Army. Last year alone, the number of recruiters who killed themselves was triple the overall Army rate. Like posttraumatic stress disorder and traumatic brain injury, recruiter suicides are a hidden cost of the nation's wars.

Behind the neat desks and patriotic posters in 1,650 Army recruiting stations on Main Streets and in strip malls is a work environment as stressful in its own way as combat.[6] The hours are long, time off is rare, and the demand to sign up at least two recruits a month is unrelenting.[7] Soldiers who have returned from tours in Iraq and Afghanistan now constitute 73% of recruiters, up from 38% in 2005. And for many of them, the pressure is just too much. "These kids are coming back from Iraq with problems," says a former Army officer who recently worked in the Houston Recruiting Battalion[8].

The responsibility for providing troop replacements falls to the senior noncommissioned officers who have chosen to make recruiting their career in the U.S. Army Recruiting Command (USAREC).⁹ They in turn put pressure on their local recruiters to "make mission" and generate the recruits — sometimes by any means necessary. Lawrence Kagawa retired last July after more than 20 years in uniform; he spent the latter half as a highly decorated recruiter¹⁰, and his tenure included a stint in the Houston battalion from 2002 to 2005. "There's one set of values for the Army, and when you go to Recruiting Command, you're basically forced to do things outside of what would normally be considered to be moral or ethical," he says.

Because station commanders and their bosses are rated on how well their subordinates recruit, there is a strong incentive to cut corners to bring in enlistees.¹¹ If recruiters can't make mission legitimately, their superiors will tell them to push the envelope.¹² "You'll be told to call Johnny or Susan and tell them to lie and say they've never had asthma like they told you, that they don't have a juvenile criminal history," Kagawa says. "That recruiter is going to bend the rules and get the lies told and process the fraudulent paperwork." And if the recruiter refuses? The commander, says Kagawa, is "going to tell you point-blank that 'we have a loyalty issue here, and if I give you a "no" for loyalty on your annual report, your career is over.'"

It's not surprising, then, that some recruiters ignore red flags to enlist marginal candidates.¹³ "I've seen [recruiters] make kids drink gallons of water trying to flush marijuana out of their system before they take their physicals¹⁴," one Houston recruiter says privately. "I've seen them forge signatures." Sign up a pair of enlistees in a month and a recruiter is hailed; sign up none and he can be ordered to monthly Saturday sessions, where he is verbally pounded for his failure.¹⁵

The military isn't known for treating underperformers with kid gloves.¹⁶ But the discipline can be harder for recruiters to take because they are, in most cases, physically and socially isolated. Unlike most soldiers, who are assigned to posts where they and their families receive the Army's full roster of benefits, 70% of Army recruiters live more than 50 miles (80 km) from the nearest military installation. Lacking local support, recruiters and their spouses turn to Internet message boards. "I hate to say it, but all the horror stories are true!" a veteran Army recruiter advised a rookie online. "It will be three years of hell on you and your family." One wife wrote that instead of coming home at the end of a long workday, her husband was headed "to Super Wal-Mart to find prospects because they're open for 24 hours."

Today's active-duty Army recruiting force is 7,600-strong.¹⁷ Soldiers attend school at Fort Jackson, S.C., for seven weeks before being sent to one of the 38 recruiting battalions across the nation. There they spend their days calling lists of high school seniors and other prospects and visiting schools and malls. At night, they visit the homes of potential recruits to sell them on one of the Army's 150 different jobs and seal the deal with hefty enlistment bonuses: up to $40,000 in cash and as much as $65,000 for college. The manual issued to recruiting commanders warns that, unlike war, in recruiting there will be no victory "until such time when the United States no longer requires an Army." Recruiting must "continue virtually nonstop" and is "aggressive, persistent and unrelenting."

Nowhere has the pace been more punishing than inside the Houston Recruiting Battalion. One of every 10 of the Army's recruits last year came from Texas—the highest share of any state—and recruiters in Harris County enlisted 1,104, just 37 shy of first-place Phoenix's Maricopa County[18]. The Houston unit's nearly 300 recruiters are spread among 49 stations across southeast Texas. Since 2005, four members recently back from Iraq or Afghanistan have committed suicide while struggling, as recruiters say, to "put 'em in boots[19]." TIME has obtained a copy of the Army's recently completed 2-inch-thick (50 mm) report of the investigation into the Houston suicides. Its bottom line: recruiters there have toiled under a "poor command climate" and an "unhealthy and singular focus on production at the expense of soldier and family considerations."[20] Most names have been deleted; the Army said those who were blamed by recruiters for the poor work environment didn't want to comment. While some recruiters were willing to talk to TIME, most declined to be named for fear of risking their careers.

Captain Rico Robinson, 32, the Houston battalion's personnel officer[21], was the first suicide, shooting himself in January 2005. But one of his predecessors, Christina Montalvo, had tried to kill herself a few years earlier, gulping a handful of prescription sleeping pills in a suicide attempt that was thwarted when a co-worker found her. Montalvo says a boss bullied her about her weight. And she was shocked by the abuse that senior sergeants routinely levied on subordinates. "I'd never been in a unit before where soldiers publicly humiliated other soldiers," says Montalvo, who left the Army in 2002 after 16 years. "If they don't make mission, they're humiliated and embarrassed."

The way things rolled in Houston, it turns out, was especially harsh. Until recently, the Army told prospective recruiters they'd be expected to sign up two recruits a month. "All of your training is geared toward prospecting for and processing at least two enlistments monthly[22]," the Army said on its Recruit the Recruiter website until TIME called to ask about the requirement. Major General Thomas Bostick, USAREC's top general, sent out a 2006 letter declaring that each recruiter "Must Do Two." But if each recruiter did that, the Army would be flooded with more than 180,000 recruits a year instead of the 80,000 it needs. In fact, the real target per recruiter is closer to one a month. Yet the constant drumbeat for two continued.

The Houston battalion's punishing work hours were also beyond what was expected. In June 2007, Bostick issued a written order to the 5th Recruiting Brigade and its Houston battalion requiring commanders to clarify the battalion's fuzzy work-hour policy, which could be read as requiring 13-hour workdays. He demanded a new policy "consistent with law and regulation." The brigade and battalion commanders ignored the order.

By mid-2008, a Houston battalion commander complained to subordinates of "getting numerous calls on recruiters being called 'dirtbags' or 'useless' when they do not accomplish mission each month." He'd heard that recruiters who had been promised birthdays or anniversaries off were being "called back to work on the day of the anniversary and during the birthday and/or anniversary party when they already had family and friends at their homes."

It wasn't until reports in the Houston *Chronicle*[23] provoked Republican Senator John Cornyn of Texas to demand answers that the Army launched an investigation into the string of suicides. "It's tragic that it took four deaths to bring this to the attention of a U.S. Senator and to ask for a formal investigation," Cornyn says. After Cornyn began asking questions, the Army ordered Brigadier General[24] F.D. Turner to investigate. Recruiters told him that their task is a "stressful, challenging job that is driven wholly by production, that is, the numbers of people put into the Army each month," Turner disclosed Dec. 23 after a two-month probe.

The report found that morale was particularly low in the Houston battalion. After Turner's report, Lieut. General Benjamin Freakley, head of the Army Accessions Command[25] that oversees USAREC, asked the Army inspector general to conduct a nationwide survey of the mood among Army recruiters. The Army also ordered a one-day stand-down for all recruiters in February so it could focus on proper leadership and suicide prevention. The worsening economy is already easing some of the recruiters' burden, as is the raising of the maximum enlistment age, from 35 to 42. But with only 3 in 10 young Americans meeting the mental, moral and physical requirements to serve, recruiting challenges will continue.

From *Time*, April 20, 2009

I. New Words

asthma	[ˈæsmə]	n.	[医]气喘,哮喘
bonus	[ˈbəunəs]	n.	奖金
bully	[ˈbuli]	v.	to frighten or hurt a weaker person
delete	[diˈli:t]	v.	to remove sth that has been written
enlistment	[inˈlistmənt]	n.	征募,入伍
dirtbag	[ˈdə:tbæg]	n.	邋遢鬼;可鄙的家伙
drumbeat	[ˈdrʌmbi:t]	n.	鼓声;鼓动
fervor	[ˈfə:və]	n.	very strong feelings about sth
fuzzy	[ˈfʌzi]	adj.	confused, not expressed clearly
gulp	[gʌlp]	v.	to swallow
hefty	[ˈhefti]	adj.	(of an amount of money) large
levy	[ˈlevi]	v.	to use official authority to demand a payment
marijuana	[ˌmæriˈwɑ:nə]	n.	大麻毒品
pound	[paund]	v.	to attack with words
replacement	[riˈpleismənt]	n.	补充兵员
rookie	[ˈruki]	n.	新兵
roster	[ˈrɔstə]	n.	a list
shed	[ʃed]	n.	工作棚,车棚
spouse	[spaus]	n.	*formal or law* husband or wife
stand-down	[ˈstænˌdaun]	n.	a period when soldiers relax after a period of duty
stint	[stint]	n.	a period of time that one spends working somewhere
stressful	[ˈstresful]	adj.	充满压力的
stun	[stʌn]	v.	to surprise or shock sb so much that he/she cannot speak

| thwart | [θwɔːt] | v. | to prevent sb from doing what he/she wants to do |
| trigger | [ˈtrɪɡə] | v. | to make sth happen suddenly |

II. Background Information

美国征兵

　　第二次世界大战之后较长时期，美军兵源主要依赖征兵制（military draft）。1973年美国废除了征兵制，实行了"全志愿兵"（all volunteer force）制度（募兵制）。这是美国兵役制度的一大改革。

　　这一变化的主要原因有以下三条：1. 政治原因。20世纪60年代，美国国内反战情绪高涨。美国政客认为，只有缓解这种情绪，才能争取民心、稳定形势。2. 经济原因。征兵制实施时期，实际征兵人数较少。募兵制提供较高待遇，可以吸引较多青年参军。3. 技术原因。随着高科技武器的发展和应用，对兵员的文化水平要求也相应提高。征兵制兵员服役期短，无法适应这种要求。

　　征兵制对于服现役（on active duty）兵员提供的物质奖励有：入伍奖金、教育补助金、民用技能奖金、教育贷款偿还、退伍就业照顾和住房/创业补助金等。美国军方认为，"全志愿兵"制是成功的。1983年，前美国国防部长温伯格（Weinberger）宣称："组建一支由志愿者组成的军队（an all-volunteer force）是可行的。"

　　9·11事件点燃了美国广大青年的爱国情绪，许多受过良好教育的学生踊跃报名参军，一度出现了供大于求的局面。

　　然而，长期以来，美国民众中除了厌恶强行征兵情绪外，还存在反对军队规模庞大的情绪和痛恨旷日持久的战争的情绪。近些年来，美国深陷两次长期战争（阿富汗战争和伊拉克战争）之中。战争不仅使美国耗费了巨大物力，也带来了惨重的人员伤亡。据统计，伊拉克战争中美军死亡人数为4260人，受伤人数为3.1万。阿富汗战争中美军死亡2442人，受伤两万多人。伴随对伊拉克战争和阿富汗战争的历史真相的披露，美国人的厌战情绪不断升高。

　　上述因素导致最近几年招兵困难，连续几年出现较大缺额。为了确保兵力的不断供应，美军采取了种种措施降低征兵缺额，其中主要措施如下：1. 增加参军奖励力度。美军根据不同技术的具体情况，提高相应入伍奖金数额。2. 适度放宽征兵条件。例如，对于体检中查出毒品阳性者提供一段时间戒毒，再次检查合格者依然可以被接纳入伍。3. 扩大征兵人选范畴。过去是美国公民或绿卡持有者才有资格申请参军。现在美军对于具有特殊技能（如外语或医学）持临时签证或寻求避难的外国人也积极接收。作为回报，政府为被接受的应征者尽快办理入籍手续。4. 加大征兵人员压力。许多征兵站对征兵数额未完成的征兵人员施加种种压力，强行要求他们加班，对他们严厉训斥、公开奚落、威胁恐吓，甚至人身攻击。一些承受不了繁重的工作压力和沉重的心理压力的征兵人员患上了抑郁症，有的甚至选择自杀。

　　目前美国征兵难度达到历史新高；有资格参军的人数继续减少。因肥胖、吸毒或犯罪记录而不合标准的年轻人比以往任何时候都多。据报道,在17—24岁的美国人中,只有23%有资格在无须豁免的情况下服役。此外,符合条件的美国年轻人大部分不想参军。

征兵困难已经导致美国军队兵力缺员。据报道,2021年年底,美国空军缺少1650名飞行员,2022年陆军新兵缺员25%。征兵危机导致美国军界质疑"全志愿兵制"的呼声越来越高。

III. Notes to the Text

1. staff sergeant —(美国)参谋军士,文书军士
2. normally squared-away —通常穿戴整洁的(squared-away—in good order; tidy and neat)
3. The previous Saturday, Flores' commanders had berated him for poor performance. —上周六,弗罗里斯的长官指责他的工作成绩差。(berate—to criticize)
4. extension cord —(一端有插头另一端有插座的)延长线
5. Even as soldiers rotate back into the field for multiple and extended tours, the Army requires a constant supply of new recruits. —即使士兵多次轮换上战场,延长驻期,陆军仍需不断补充新兵。(rotate—to take turns to do a particular job)
6. Behind the neat desks and patriotic posters in 1,650 Army recruiting stations on Main Streets and in strip malls is a work environment as stressful in its own way as combat. —美国陆军1650个征兵站坐落在各地的主街和公路旁的商业街。在这些整洁的办公桌和爱国征兵广告之后的工作环境与作战一样充满着压力。(① Main Street—the most important street in many small towns of the US; ② strip mall—a line of shops and restaurants beside a main road)
7. The hours are long, time off is rare, and the demand to sign up at least two recruits a month is unrelenting. —工作时间长,休息时间少,工作要求苛刻,每月至少要征到两个兵。(① unrelenting —not giving way to feelings of kindness or compassion, not relaxing in severity; ② sign sb up —to make sb sign a form or contract that he/she agrees to become a soldier)
8. the Houston Recruiting Battalion —休斯敦征兵站
9. The responsibility for providing troop replacements falls to the senior noncommissioned officers who have chosen to make recruiting their career in the U. S. Army Recruiting Command (USAREC). —负责提供部队补充兵源的任务落在那些选择美国陆军征兵司令部领导下的以征兵工作为职业的资历较老的军士肩上。
10. a highly decorated recruiter —受过多次表彰的征兵者(decorate—to give sb a medal as a sign of respect for sth he/she has done)
11. Because station commanders and their bosses are rated on how well their subordinates recruit, there is a strong incentive to cut corners to bring in enlistees. —由于征兵站站长和他们的上司是依据其下属征兵情况而评定业绩,于是就存在采用讨巧办法招募新兵的强烈动机。(cut corners —to do sth in the easiest, cheapest or quickest way)

第九单元 科技军事

12. If recruiters can't make mission legitimately, their superiors will tell them to push the envelope. ——如果征兵人员以正当方式无法完成任务,他们的上级会告诉他们要挑战极限去干。(push the envelope——to do one's utmost)

13. It's not surprising, then, that some recruiters ignore red flags to enlist marginal candidates. ——一些征兵人员铤而走险,把条件十分勉强的人招入军队,这种情况不足为怪。(① red flag —— a flag used as a signal of danger; ② marginal ——barely qualified)

14. before they take their physicals ——before they take their physical tests

15. ... sign up none and he can be ordered to monthly Saturday sessions, where he is verbally pounded for his failure. ——如果他一个兵也没有招到,就会被命令参加每月一次的周六会议,会上对他的失败会进行严厉批评。(pound ——to attack)

16. The military isn't known for treating underperformers with kid gloves. ——从没听说军队对待工作成绩差者心慈手软。(treat sb with kid gloves——to deal with sb in a very careful way so as not to offend him/her)

17. Today's active-duty Army recruiting force is 7,600-strong. ——目前,陆军现役征兵人员共有7600名。(active-duty ——full time duty/service in the armed force)

18. just 37 shy of first-place Phoenix's Maricopa County——比(征兵人数)第一的亚利桑那州菲尼克斯市下属马里科帕县的数量仅少37名(① shy——less than the number mentioned; ② Phoenix ——the capital and largest city of Arizona)

19. put 'em in boots——enlist them

20. Its bottom line: recruiters there have toiled under a "poor command climate" and an "unhealthy and singular focus on production at the expense of soldier and family considerations." ——(这份报告的)主要内容是那里的"领导作风很差","表现很不正常,一味关注征兵人数,不考虑征兵人员和其家庭利益",征兵人员(工作)十分劳累。(bottom line——the essential point)

21. personnel officer ——人事军官

22. All of your training is geared toward prospecting for and processing at least two enlistments monthly... ——所有训练工作都是为了完成每月找到和办理至少两名应征入伍者的任务。(① gear ——to prepare a person for a particular type of activity; ② prospect for——to search for)

23. the Houston *Chronicle*——休斯敦市《记事报》

24. Brigadier General——陆军准将

25. the Army Accessions Command ——陆军招募司令部

IV. Language Features

借　代

本文中有这么一句:But the patriotic fervor that led so many to sign up after 9/11 is now eight years past. 该句中9/11并非表示日期而是表示:2001年9月11日美国纽约所

301

发生的恐怖分子劫持的民航飞机对世贸中心大楼进行的袭击事件。这里作者使用了"借代"修辞手法。

借代是新闻写作中所常用的修辞手法,它可以节省篇幅,避免重复,增加语言的形象性和表达效果。

在报刊上常见的借代形式有以下几种:

1. 借地名代机构。例如:

  Capitol (Hill)/ Hill ——国会山;美国国会
  White House ——白宫;美国政府
  Whitehall ——白厅;英国政府
  Scotland Yard ——苏格兰场;伦敦警察厅
  Elysee ——爱丽舍宫;法国政府

2. 借地名代行业、社会阶层:

  Wall Street ——华尔街;美国金融市场
  Hollywood ——好莱坞;美国电影业
  Beverly Hills ——贝弗利山;美国明星阶层
  Madison Avenue ——麦迪逊大街;美国广告业

3. 借商标、品牌、店名代相关物:

  Cadillac ——凯迪拉克品牌;凯迪拉克汽车 McDonald's ——麦当劳快餐;快餐

4. 借所具特色代某国、某机构:

  Big Apple ——大苹果城;纽约市 Dice City ——赌城;拉斯维加斯市
  Motor City ——汽车城;底特律市

5. 借典型姓氏代某人或某国:

  Ivan ——伊凡;俄罗斯人 Wang ——王;中国人
  John Bull ——约翰牛;英国人 John Doe ——约翰·多伊;美国人

6. 借人名、地名、国名代相关事件:

  Hello, <u>Kuwait</u>. Goodbye, <u>Vietnam</u>. (*Time*, March 11, 1991)
  欢迎你呀,海湾战争胜利的捷报! 见鬼去吧,越战失败的耻辱!
  The court drills a crack in the foundation of Roe. (*Newsweek*, July 17, 1989)
  最高法院将罗诉威德案决定的基础石钻出了裂缝。[这一句中 Roe 指 1973 年美国最高法院对罗诉威德案(Roe v. Wade)的裁决,判定罗可以堕胎,从而使妇女堕胎合法化。而 1989 年最高法院的裁决又修正和削弱了 1973 年的裁决。]

V. Analysis of Content

1. Which of the following states produced the highest number of recruits according to the article?
  A. New York. B. Texas. C. North Carolina. D. Massachusetts.

2. The word "go" in the sentence, "I remember looking over Patrick and going, ..." (Para. 2) means _____.

    A. moving from one place to another   B. leaving one place

    C. starting an activity   D. saying

3. The direct cause of the four Houston recruiters' suicides was _____.

    A. lack of psychological counseling

    B. work pressure exerted by the recruiting command

    C. post-traumatic stress disorder

    D. fear of being sent to the battlefield

4. From the article we know that if a recruiter refuses to do recruiting by bending rules, getting lies told, the commander would punish him by _____.

    A. reducing his pay

    B. discharging him from the Army

    C. sending him to the battlefield

    D. giving him a no for loyalty on the annual report

5. It can be inferred from the context that the phrase "put 'em in boots" in the sentence "Since 2005, four members recently back from Iraq or Afghanistan have committed suicide while struggling, as recruiters say, to 'put 'em in boots.'" (Para. 10) means _____.

    A. give them a hard kick   B. enlist them

    C. criticize them   D. give them training

VI. Questions on the Article

1. Why did Larry Flores look ragged?
2. What impact did Flores' suicide have on Patrick?
3. What effects did 9/11 have on the Army's recruiting?
4. How stressful is the job of recruiting?
5. Why is there a strong incentive to cut corners to bring in enlistees?
6. Why does the author say that the discipline can be harder for underperforming recruiters?
7. How do recruiters usually do their job?
8. Tell something about the pressure on recruiters of the Houston Recruiting Battalion.
9. What led to the investigation into the recruiters' suicides? What was the finding?
10. What is the impact of the worsening economy on the Army's recruiting?

VII. Topics for Discussion

1. Should all youth have the experience of army service?
2. Which is better, compulsory military service or voluntary military service?

Unit 10
第十单元 世界风云

Lesson 32

Warming Arctic Opens Way to Competition for Resources

By Joby Warrick and Juliet Eilperin

NUUK[1], Greenland—Here, just south of the Arctic Circle, where the sea ice is vanishing like dew on a July morning, the temperature isn't the only thing that's heating up.

Across the region, a warming Arctic is opening up new competition for resources that until recently were out of reach, protected under a thick layer of ice[2]. As glaciers defrost and ice floes diminish, the North is being viewed as a source of not only great wealth but also conflict, diplomats and policy experts say.

In recent months, oil companies have begun lining up for exploration rights to Baffin Bay[3], a hydrocarbon-rich region on Greenland's western coast that until recently was too ice-choked for drilling. U.S. and Canadian diplomats have reopened a spat over navigation rights to a sea route through the Canadian Arctic that could cut shipping time and costs for long-haul tankers.

Even ownership of the North Pole has come into dispute, as Russia and Denmark pursue rival claims to the underlying seabed in hopes of locking up access to everything from fisheries to natural gas deposits.[4]

The intense rivalry over Arctic development was highlighted in diplomatic cables released last week by the anti-secrecy Web site Wikileaks. Messages between U.S. diplomats revealed how northern nations, including the United States and Russia, have been maneuvering to ensure access to shipping lanes as well as undersea oil and gas deposits that are estimated to contain up to 25 percent of the world's untapped reserves.

In the cables, U.S. officials worried that bickering over resources might even lead to an arming of the Arctic.

"While in the Arctic there is peace and stability, however, one cannot exclude that in the future there will be a redistribution of power, up to armed intervention," a 2009 State Department cable quoted a Russian ambassador as saying.

Concern over competition in the Arctic was partly behind an extraordinary diplomatic gathering last week in Greenland's tiny capital Nuuk.[5] This year's meeting of the eight-nation

Arctic Council drew seven foreign ministers, including Russia's Sergey Lavrov and Secretary of State Hillary Rodham Clinton[6], the highest-ranking U. S. diplomat to attend an Arctic Council session. Accompanying Clinton was a second U.S. Cabinet member, Interior Secretary Ken Salazar[7].

Clinton and her aides sought to call attention to climate change during the visit, highlighting new studies that show Arctic ice melting far more rapidly than scientists had believed. But Clinton also promoted a message of international cooperation in the Arctic.

"The challenges in the region are not just environmental," Clinton said in Nuuk following talks with her Danish counterpart, Lene Espersen. "The melting of sea ice, for example, will result in more shipping, fishing and tourism, and the possibility to develop newly accessible oil and gas reserves. We seek to pursue these opportunities in a smart, sustainable way that preserves the Arctic environment and ecosystem."

Clinton's presence at the Nuuk meeting was intended to show U. S. support for the Arctic Council as a critical forum for cooperation and to resolve conflicts. With strong backing from the Obama administration, the Council on Thursday approved the first legally binding treaty in its history, a pact that sets the rules for maritime search and rescue in the region. Although modest in scope, the treaty, authored mainly by Russia and the United States, was hailed as a template for future agreements on issues ranging from oil-spill cleanup to territorial disputes.[8]

Significantly, the eight member nations voted to establish a permanent secretariat to the council, to be located in Tronso (**Tromso**)[9], Norway. Clinton asserted that the region's powers must recognize the council as the "preeminent intergovernmental body, where we can solve shared problems and pursue shared opportunities."

"The opportunities for economic development in the Arctic must be weighed against the need to protect its environment and ecosystems.[10] And governments will not always see eye to eye on how to achieve this balance[11]," Clinton said. "That's why this Council is so important."

In the diplomatic cables obtained by Wikileaks, there was no dispute about rapid warming underway. The predominant questions revolved around how the region's newly accessible resources would be carved up.[12]

Several cables showed U.S. officials and others seeking to curry favor with Greenlanders and other indigenous groups amid speculation that oil wealth would soon bring independence to the ice-covered island and its 60,000 inhabitants.[13]

One cable authored Nov. 17, 2007, by the U.S. ambassador to Denmark, James P. Cain, detailed how Americans have sought to establish closer links to Greenland's leaders in an effort to shore up[14] what Cain described as the U.S.'s "real security and growing economic interests in Greenland."

"A recent study of hydrocarbon potential, led by the U. S. Geological Survey[15], concluded the continental shelf off northeast Greenland alone could harbor oil and gas reserves to rival Alaska's North Slope[16]" Cain wrote. "Whether because of man-made climate change or a massive, cyclical shift in weather patterns, Greenland's carbon riches are more easily accessible now than ever."

Cain not only proposed establishing a diplomatic post in Greenland, but worked to promote drilling plans that would benefit companies such as Chevron[17] and Exxon-Mobil, part of a four-company consortium that had won oil and gas licenses off the western coast of Greenland.

"To help Greenlanders secure the investments needed for such exploitation, I recently introduced Home Rule Premier [Hans] Enoksen and Minister of Finance and Foreign Affairs Aleqa Hammond[18] to some of our top U.S. financial institutions in New York," he wrote in the cable.

In some instances the cables reveal American diplomats' unease with the competition in the Arctic, even among close allies. One missive sent July 31, 2006, from the U.S. Embassy in Ottawa includes the simple summary: "The GOC [Government of Canada] is taking steps to secure sovereign rights over seabed resources that extend to the edge of the continental shelf."

Kert Davies, research director for Greenpeace[19] USA, said the leaked cables show that when it comes to nations with a claim on the Arctic, "the tensions are higher than we thought."

"The Arctic Council is woefully unprepared to regulate the corporate interests that strive to get in there," Davies said, adding that comments like Cain's show how individual governments will push to provide an advantage to their domestic companies. "When the corporate interests and the government interests align, the government does the corporate interests' bidding.[20]"

But in an interview, Sweden's Ambassador to the Arctic Gustaf Lind said there were broad misconceptions about the region. "This is not the unregulated Wild West, but a well-regulated place," he said.

From *The Washington Post*, May 16, 2011

I. New Words

bickering	[ˈbikəriŋ]	n.	arguing or quarrelling about unimportant things
choke	[tʃəuk]	v.	to fill
consortium	[kənˈsɔːtjəm]	n.	an association of companies for some definite purpose
defrost	[di(ː)ˈfrɔst]	v.	解冻
deposit	[diˈpɔzit]	n.	沉积物
ecosystem	[ˈiːkəˌsistəm]	n.	[生]生态系统
floe	[fləu]	n.	浮冰块
glacier	[ˈglæsiə]	n.	冰川
highlight	[ˈhailait]	v.	to emphasize sth, esp. so that people give more attention
hydrocarbon	[ˌhaidrəuˈkɑːbən]	n.	烃,碳氢化合物
intergovernmental	[ˌintəgʌvənˈmentəl]	adj.	政府间的
long-haul	[ˈlɔŋhɔːl]	adj.	长途货运的
maneuver	[məˈnuːvə]	v.	耍花招;用策略
maritime	[ˈmæritaim]	adj.	海的;海上的
misconception	[ˌmiskənˈsepʃən]	n.	误解

missive	[ˈmisiv]	n.	*formal* a letter, esp. a long or an official one
preeminent	[priˈeminənt]	adj.	greatest in importance or degree or achievement
promote	[prəˈməut]	v.	to contribute to the progress or growth of
reserve	[riˈzə:v]	n.	a supply of sth that is available for use when it is needed
rival	[ˈraivəl]	v.	be in competition with
secretariat	[ˌsekrəˈteəriət]	n.	秘书处
spat	[spæt]	n.	a quarrel about petty points
sustainable	[səˈsteinəbl]	adj.	可持续的
tanker	[ˈtæŋkə]	n.	a cargo ship designed to carry crude oil in bulk
template	[ˈtemplit]	n.	a model or standard for making comparisons
underlying	[ˌʌndəˈlaiiŋ]	adj.	existing under the surface of sth else
underway	[ˌʌndəˈwei]	adj.	currently in progress
unease	[ʌnˈi:z]	n.	the feeling of being worried or unhappy about sth
unregulated	[ʌnˈregjuleitid]	adj.	未受管理（控制）的
vanish	[ˈvæniʃ]	v.	to disappear suddenly or in a way that cannot be explained
woefully	[ˈwəufuli]	adv.	in an unfortunate or deplorable manner

II. Background Information

北极之争

北极地区指以北极点（North Pole）为中心的地区，总面积2100万平方千米，约占地球总面积的二十五分之一。陆地近800万平方千米，全归属于8个环北极国家，但北冰洋仍属国际公共海域，该地区有居民700多万人。北冰洋沿岸国家有俄罗斯、加拿大、美国、丹麦和挪威，通常被称为北极5国。国土进入北极圈的国家还有瑞典、芬兰和冰岛。这8个国家通常被称为北极8国。

北极地区蕴藏着丰富的资源。据报道，该地区石油储量为1000亿—2000亿桶；天然气储量为50万亿—80万亿立方米；煤炭储量高达1万亿吨，占全世界煤炭储量的四分之一。除此之外，北极地区还有富饶的渔业资源、林业资源以及镍、铅、锌、铜、钴、金、银、金刚石等矿产资源。

北极领土纷争始于20世纪50年代。当时加拿大率先宣布对北极享有领土主权。

1983年,美国总统里根签署了美国的北极政策议案,强调"美国在北极地区有着独特的关键性利益"。丹麦提出北极海底山脉是格陵兰岛海脊的延伸,丹麦对该区域拥有开发权。俄罗斯则一再重申:包括北极在内的半个北冰洋都是其西伯利亚大陆架的延伸。

随着全球气候变暖以及冰川消融,北极资源之争迅速加剧,2007年形成了小高潮:当年8月2日,俄罗斯科考队乘坐深海潜水器,在北冰洋北极点下4261米深海海床底部插上一面一米高的特制俄罗斯国旗;加拿大宣布将在北极地区建立两个军事基地。4天后,美国在西雅图港起锚一艘重型破冰船,开赴北冰洋"科考";8月12日,丹麦同样派出一支科考队前往北冰洋。

为了提升美国在北极的地位,2020年7月美国特朗普政府曾任命一名职业外交官担任北极地区事务协理员。2022年8月美国拜登政府提名一名负责北极地区事务的"无所任大使"(roving ambassador)。

在北极争夺中,北极国家在地理上享有很大优势。由于相关国际法的缺失,这些国家采取各种手段圈地,试图控制更多的北极领土和海域。他们利用自己所处的地理优势,既不愿意制造新的国际条约来约束自己在北极的行动,也不希望区域外的国家介入,企图将北极变为它们独享的"领地"。

环境保护人士对北极资源开发所造成的环境破坏感到担忧。一些研究成果显示:北极地区石油开采已经对环境产生了不利影响。公路通常建在较厚沙砾层的滩沿上,这将引发洪水泛滥以及灰尘的产生,并且改变动物的栖息地;石油勘探的地震研究对冻土层造成了长期破坏。使北极居民更加担心的是那些突发的重大污染事件,例如,石油泄漏导致海洋生态环境广泛遭破坏;油田中的垃圾吸引了熊、狐狸和渡鸦,导致一些鸟类数量下降;出于对海岸附近地震勘探的噪音做出的反应,北极露脊鲸开始向海洋深处迁徙等。油田虽然改善了当地居民的生活条件,但也增加了不少社会问题,如大量传统文化的丧失。

不少专家建议采用破坏性较小的方法,譬如通过实施新技术以及用冰而不是沙砾层修建公路。尽管如此,已建好的公路和其他基础设施不大可能被拆除,被破坏的栖息地只有1%会恢复,而且自然恢复的进程十分缓慢。有鉴于此,提出"没有破坏的发展"作为人类在北极实施的一种可持续发展方式是科学和合理的。这不仅有利于北极区域,也有利于全球的环境。

III. Notes to the Text

1. Nuuk——努克(格陵兰首府,一座港口城市)
2. a warming Arctic is opening up new competition for resources that until recently were out of reach, protected under a thick layer of ice——北极变暖正在造成一场新的资源争夺,而此前这些资源被封存在厚厚的冰层下,还无法利用(open up——to cause sth to start)
3. In recent months, oil companies have begun lining up for exploration rights to Baffin Bay...——最近几个月,石油公司开始努力争先获得对巴芬湾的勘探权(① line up——to form a

line; ② Baffin Bay—巴芬湾,位于北美洲东北部巴芬岛、埃尔斯米尔岛与格陵兰岛之间。)

4. Even ownership of the North Pole has come into dispute, as Russia and Denmark pursue rival claims to the underlying seabed in hopes of locking up access to everything from fisheries to natural gas deposits.—甚至连北极的归属都成为争论之点:俄罗斯和丹麦对北极的海床所有权都争相提出要求,期望确保从渔业到天然气的所有资源的开发权。(lock up access to sth—secure the right to sth)

5. Concern over competition in the Arctic was partly behind an extraordinary diplomatic gathering last week in Greenland's tiny capital Nuuk.—上周在格陵兰首府努克小城召开异乎寻常的外交官员会议,部分原因是对北极地区之争的担忧。(behind—responsible for starting or developing sth)

6. This year's meeting of the eight-nation Arctic Council drew seven foreign ministers, including Russia's Sergey Lavrov and Secretary of State Hillary Rodham Clinton...—今年八国北极理事会会议共有七名外交部长参加,包括俄罗斯外长谢尔盖·拉夫罗夫和美国国务卿希拉里·罗德姆·克林顿(Arctic Council—北极理事会,是一个高层次国际论坛,1996年9月在加拿大渥太华成立,成员包括芬兰、瑞典、挪威、丹麦、冰岛、加拿大、美国和俄罗斯。北极理事会成员国外长会议每两年举行一次。)

7. Interior Secretary Ken Salazar—内政部长肯·萨拉查

8. Although modest in scope, the treaty, authored mainly by Russia and the United States, was hailed as a template for future agreements on issues ranging from oil-spill cleanup to territorial disputes.—主要由俄罗斯和美国执笔的会议协定虽然涉及范畴不太广,但被称赞为将来起草有关溢油清除和领土争端等问题协议的样板。(hail as—to describe sth as very good or special)

9. Tronso (**Tromso**)—特罗姆瑟(挪威北部北极圈内重要城市、海港)

10. The opportunities for economic development in the Arctic must be weighed against the need to protect its environment and ecosystems.—在北极地区寻求经济发展机遇时必须认真考虑当地环境和生态系统保护的需要。(weigh—to consider or compare carefully in order to form a judgement)

11. And governments will not always see eye to eye on how to achieve this balance...—各国政府对于如何取得这种平衡不会永远看法一致(see eye to eye—to be in agreement)

12. The predominant questions revolved around how the region's newly accessible resources would be carved up.—最突出的问题围绕如何分配该地区新近可开发利用的资源展开。(① predominant—most obvious or noticeable; ② revolve around—to center around; ③ carve up—to divide; ④ accessible—easy to reach and use)

13. Several cables showed U.S. officials and others seeking to curry favor with Greenlanders and other indigenous groups amid speculation that oil wealth would soon bring independence to the ice-covered island and its 60,000 inhabitants.—好几份电文显示,美国官员和一些其他人由于推测石油财富将很快使这个冰所覆盖的格陵兰岛及其6万居民独立,便努力讨好格陵兰人和其他当地群体。(① curry favor with—to try to get sb to like you by praising or offering help; ② indigenous—belonging to a place rather than coming from somewhere else; ③ speculation—the act of forming opinions about what might happen without knowing all

the facts; ④ Greenland—a large island belonging to Denmark, but having its own government)

14. shore up—to protect

15. U.S. Geological Survey—美国地质调查局(缩称 USGS,隶属美国内政部)

16. North Slope—阿拉斯加北坡(美国石油、天然气产区)

17. Chevron—雪佛龙石油公司(美国第二大石油公司,创始于1879年,主要业务为提炼石油,总部设在加州旧金山)

18. Home Rule Premier [Hans] Enoksen and Minister of Finance and Foreign Affairs Aleqa Hammond—格陵兰总理汉斯·埃诺克森和丹麦财政与外交大臣阿勒卡·哈蒙德

19. Greenpeace—绿色和平(是一个国际性非政府组织,从事环保工作,1971年在加拿大成立,总部位于荷兰的阿姆斯特丹。它开始时以使用非暴力方式阻止大气和地下核试验以及公海捕鲸著称,后来转为关注其他的环境问题,包括捕鲸、捕杀海豹、水底拖网捕鱼、全球变暖和基因工程等。)

20. When the corporate interests and the government interests align, the government does the corporate interests' bidding.—当公司与政府的利益一致时,政府便会保护公司的利益。(① do sb's bidding—to obey sb; ② align—to bring oneself or come into agreement)

IV. Language Features

"说"意句式

本文表达"说"的句式较为丰富,主要有下列两种:
1. "说"意动词置于引语之前,主语之后

Sweden's Ambassador to the Arctic Gustaf Lind said there were broad misconceptions about the region.

2. "说"意动词置于两个引语之间

"The challenges in the region are not just environmental," Clinton said ... "The melting of sea ice..."

新闻报道为了提高所述内容的客观性,常常转述或援引提供消息和发表意见人士所说的话,因而表示"说"的句子往往多次出现。为了避免句式单调刻板,用笔娴熟的新闻写作人员总是注意变化句式,使其不拘一格,机动灵活,从而使语言生动活泼。

报刊上所出现的"说"意句式大致可归纳为以下六种:

1. SVO(主语+谓语+宾语)

例:The court added, "If it is the will of the people in this country to amend the United States Constitution to protect our nation's symbol, it must be done through our normal political channels."

2. VSO(谓语动词+主语+宾语)

例：Said a CNN staffer: "I think we're relieved. CNN did the right thing, but embarrassed by the fact that this appears to be a monumental failure of journalism."

3. OVS(宾语 + 谓语动词 + 主语)

例："Today marks the day when TV Guide is no longer just a magazine," says News America Publishing Group CEO Anthea Disney.

4. OSV(宾语 + 主语 + 谓语动词)

例："We basically destroyed everything there," Hagen said.

5. O_1SVO_2(宾语1 + 主语 + 谓语动词 + 宾语2)

例："We were all concerned ... about the breakdown of the family," Tipper Gore says, "we thought 'What can we do to be part of the solution? What can we do to start strengthening families?'"

6. O_1VSO_2(宾语1 + 谓语动词 + 主语 + 宾语2)

例："Our focus," says Guard Steve Kerr, one of the best three-point shooters in the NBA, "is to play it out and see what happens. That's what we can do."

V. Analysis of Content

1. The meaning of the word "behind" in the sentence "Concern over competition in the Arctic was partly behind an extraordinary diplomatic gathering last week in Greenland's tiny capital Nuuk." is _____.

    A. in support of

    B. at the back of

    C. concealed by

    D. responsible for starting

2. Which two countries pursue rival claims to the underlying seabed of the North Pole?

    A. Russia and Denmark.

    B. U.S. and Canada.

    C. Denmark and Sweden.

    D. Finland and Iceland.

3. What was extraordinary about the diplomatic gathering held at Nuuk?

    A. The time of the gathering.

    B. The place of the gathering.

    C. The attendance of 7 foreign ministers.

    D. The approval of the first legally binding treaty.

4. It can be inferred from the cables sent by U.S. diplomatic officials to Greenland's leaders that _____.

    A. the U.S. government wants to ensure peace in the region

B. the U.S. government is really concerned about environmental protection in the region

C. the U.S. government wants to help Greenland to gain independence

D. the U.S. government wants to protect the interests of American companies in the region

5. The message which Sweden's ambassador to the Arctic intends to convey is that _____.

A. there exist peace and harmony in the Arctic region

B. the northern countries have close ties

C. Sweden does not like other countries' interference with its development plans

D. the Arctic region is a place with sound management and good order

VI. Questions on the Article

1. What is happening in the Arctic region as a result of climate warming?
2. What are U.S. and Canadian diplomats disputing over?
3. What did the diplomatic cables released by Wikileaks highlight?
4. According to the cables, what did U.S. officials worry about?
5. What treaty did the Arctic Council approve? What was the significance of the pact?
6. What did Clinton stress at the gathering?
7. What did the cables reveal about American diplomats' worry?
8. According to Kert Davies, what do the cables show?

VII. Topics for Discussion

1. Should the Arctic's energy resources be fully exploited?
2. Is the Arctic a well-regulated place?

Lesson 33

Tough Terrain Ahead on Road Map[1]

Israeli settlement issue is one among many details to be resolved.

By Barbara Slavin

With his meeting Wednesday with the Palestinian and Israeli prime ministers, President Bush put his personal prestige behind the first real US attempt[2] to mediate a Middle East peace agreement in three years.

But beyond the photo opportunity of smiling men shaking hands and the upbeat statement they released, real progress will depend on fulfilling a tradeoff first set forth by the United Nations Security Council 36 years ago: Israeli withdrawal from much of the West Bank and Gaza[3] in return for Palestinians ending attacks on Israelis.

Disputes about the extent of this tradeoff remain intense and were reflected in statements issued on the windy shore at Aqaba[4], Jordan. Bush praised Israeli Prime Minister Ariel Sharon's pledges to permit creation of an eventual Palestinian state.

Sharon said he understood "the importance of territorial contiguity in the West Bank for a viable Palestinian state[5]" and promised to begin removing "unauthorized outposts[6]" set up by Israeli settlers in the West Bank since he took office two years ago. But Israel Radio reported that all but 10 of 102 outposts are in various stages of becoming "legal."

Skeptical of success

Palestinians, Israelis and others question whether Sharon, the historic architect of a policy that has put 200,000 Israelis deep into the West Bank and Gaza and an additional 200,000 in East Jerusalem, will ever agree to the kind of pull-backs **(that)** Palestinians say are the minimum required to create a viable Palestinian state.[7]

And as Sharon made eminently clear, Palestinian failure to end attacks on Israelis will immediately jeopardize the entire effort.[8]

Although Palestinian Prime Minister Mahmoud Abbas pledged to do his utmost to end the armed intifada[9], or uprising, that began in September 2000, Palestinian militant groups vowed Wednesday to continue resistance until the end of Israeli "occupation." Hamas[10], responsible for most of the suicide attacks of the past 32 months, said it would not allow itself to be disarmed.

Palestinians who have watched US presidents come and go say they appreciate Bush's new-found interest in their plight but remain extremely skeptical of Israeli intentions and US resolve.[11] At Aqaba, says Khalil Shikaki, a prominent Palestinian pollster, Sharon once again refrained from endorsing in full a US-backed road map for peace and instead spoke only of taking "steps" in the plan.[12]

Details are everything in the Middle East and will bedevil the peacemakers at every step.[13] U.N Security Council resolution 242[14], passed after a war in 1967 gave Israel control over the West Bank, Gaza, Syria's Golan Heights[15] and Egypt's Sinai[16] desert, calls for Israeli withdrawal from "territories occupied in the recent conflict." Israel, which gave back all of Sinai in return for peace with Egypt in 1982, has interpreted the resolution to mean that it does not have to concede all of the rest; Arabs insist on a return to the boundaries that existed before the war in 1967.

The Clinton administration came the closest to drawing new borders for Israel and Palestine that would have allowed Israel to retain key settlements and swapped parts of pre-1967 Israel for the settlements.[17] But Clinton and Israel Prime Minister Ehud Barak left office before a deal could be clinched[18].

The Bush administration's road map leaves all the toughest issues to the end of the process: settlements, final borders, the status of Jerusalem and the fate of more than 3.5 million Palestinian refugees. The goal is a Palestinian state in 2005, when the Bush administration may no longer be in power.

"Contiguous" state

Tuesday, meeting with Arab leaders in Sharm el-Sheik, Egypt, Bush seemed to give a bigger nod toward Palestinian territorial aspirations.[19]

"Israel must deal with the settlements," he said. "Israel must make sure there's a continuous territory that the Palestinians can call home."

The White House clarified later that Bush meant to use the word "contiguous."

Secretary of State Collin Powell elaborated. "Contiguous means that if you are going to have a state that people will recognize as a state, it has to be connected," Powell told reporters . "So that it can't be chopped up in so many ways in some form of *bantustan*"[20] as small, autonomous black African enclaves in white-ruled South Africa were called.

Palestinians are circulating maps showing a state with provisional borders, called for as early as this year in the road map. Meeting with Powell in Jericho[21] on May 11, Shikaki gave him a map of a provisional state that would require the evacuation of 34 settlements with a total population of 14,000. Most of the settlements are small, but several have populations of around 1,000 and were created shortly after Sharon's Likud Party[22] first came to power in 1977.

Israeli acceptance of such a proposal is sure to provoke civil strife between Jewish settlers and Israeli troops. It would also probably bring down Sharon's center-right coalition, which includes parties that are adamantly opposed to territorial withdrawal.[23]

Yossi Alpher, a former director of the Jaffee Center for Strategic Studies in Tel Aviv and adviser to Israel Prime Minister Ehud Barak, doubts a crunch will come. Sharon, Alpher says, "will do everything possible to avoid dismantling real, veteran settlements" and seeks only a more peaceful version of the status quo.[24]

Some Palestinians were encouraged by Bush's new language on settlements.

"This is the first time Bush has spoken of a contiguous state," says Hassan Abdel Rahman, the Palestinian representative in Washington. "Bush was very unambiguous and forceful, and that was noted by everyone present."

But according to Alpher, Sharon's definition of "contiguous" means linking Palestinian towns and villages with tunnels and bridges but retaining the land in between.

Sharon's vision of a Palestinian state is one of "bits and pieces," says Edward Walker, a former US ambassador to Israel. "What we need is more precision and elaboration."

From *USA Today*, July, 2003

I. New Words

architect	[ˈɑːkitekt]	n.	the person who created or invented sth
clarify	[ˈklærifai]	v.	to make sth clearer by explaining
contiguous	[kənˈtiguəs]	adj.	in actual contact
crunch	[krʌntʃ]	n.	a critical time or situation; a turning point
dismantle	[disˈmæntl]	v.	to put an end to sth
elaborate	[iˈlæbərit]	v.	to give more details about sth
enclave	[ˈenkleiv]	n.	孤立的小国或地区
endorse	[inˈdɔːs]	v.	to support
eventual	[iˈventjuəl]	adj.	happening in the course of time or events, usually much later
mediate	[ˈmiːdieit]	v.	to achieve agreement between disputing groups
plight	[plait]	n.	a bad or unfortunate situation
pollster	[ˈpəulstə]	n.	sb who conducts public opinion polls
provisional	[prəˈviʒənəl]	adj.	temporary
strife	[straif]	n.	bitter and sometimes violent conflict, struggle, or rivalry
tradeoff	[ˈtreidɔːf]	n.	exchange involving compromise
unambiguous	[ˌʌnæmˈbigjuəs]	adj.	completely clear in meaning or intention
upbeat	[ˈʌpbiːt]	adj.	optimistic
unauthorized	[ʌnˈɔːθəraizd]	adj.	未经许可的,未经批准的
viable	[ˈvaiəbl]	adj.	able to survive

II. Background Information

巴以冲突

巴勒斯坦位于西亚,面积约2.7万平方千米,位于地中海与死海、约旦河之间,地处亚、非、欧三洲交通枢纽,具有重要战略地位和经济意义。

历史上,巴勒斯坦是阿拉伯人和犹太人的共同居住地。公元7世纪,阿拉伯帝国兴起,巴勒斯坦成为其一部分。阿拉伯人不断移入,在这里世代定居。从19世纪开始,犹太复国主义运动兴起,大量的犹太人从世界各地移居到这里。阿犹民族矛盾也由此产生。

1947年11月29日,联合国大会通过了181号决议。该决议将约2.7万平方千米的巴勒斯坦一分为二:1.52万平方千米用于建立犹太国,1.15万平方千米用于建立阿拉伯国家。三大教圣地耶路撒冷管理权由联合国控制。以色列宣布建国后,中东地区爆发了5次战争。通过这些战争,以色列实际上吞并了整个巴勒斯坦78%的土地。残余的22%则是以1967年战争停火线为界的加沙地带、约旦河西岸和东耶路撒冷。这些土地被联合国安理会决议确定为以色列应该退出的范围,也成为国际社会和多数阿拉伯国家默认的巴勒斯坦未来民族的基本国土。为了重返家园,恢复民族权利,巴勒斯坦人进行了长期的斗争。多年来,巴以流血冲突一直不断。

巴以和平路线图是根据布什总统2002年6月提出的建议,此后,联合国、欧盟、俄罗斯和美国四方几经磋商,最终于当年年底基本达成协议,确定为三步解决巴以冲突的和平方案。此方案也被称为和平路线图计划(Roadmap Peace Plan)。但由于以色列的阻挠,美国没有及时公布方案的具体内容。2003年4月30日中东问题四方代表分别向巴以双方递交了路线图计划文本,并公布了路线图计划内容。

该计划三个阶段主要内容如下:

第一阶段(计划公布之日—2003.5):结束恐怖与暴力,巴勒斯坦民众恢复正常生活,组织机构进行改革建立新的政治体制。以色列则应撤离2009年9月28日以后占领的巴方领土,拆除2001年3月以后建立的定居点。

第二阶段(2003.6—2003.12):为过渡期,重点是在2003年年底建立一个有临时边界和主权象征的巴勒斯坦国。

第三阶段(2004—2005):达成最终地位协议,实现和平,建立巴勒斯坦国。

路线图得以实现的前提是双方停止流血冲突。然而,几年来的实际情况是冲突一直未止。以色列在2004年相继杀害了哈马斯组织领导人亚辛和巴哈默德·扎哈尔,激化了巴勒斯坦反以情绪,使得路线图的实施更加艰难。

2009年以色列总理内塔尼亚胡首次同意巴勒斯坦建国,但提出了苛刻的条件:未来的巴勒斯坦国必须彻底实现非军事化,不得拥有导弹、火箭等重武器和制空权;不能和伊朗、真主党等国家或组织结盟;耶路撒冷是统一和不可分割的以色列首都;约旦河西岸的犹太定居点可以停止建设,但不能阻止其"自然增长"。在巴方看来,这意味着国家主权和管辖权的残缺,以色列对巴勒斯坦土地的继续蚕食和分割。

几十年来在国际社会的调解下巴以曾签订了不少和平协议,但总是因为耶路撒冷的归属、犹太人的定居点、巴勒斯坦的难民回归、巴以边界等关键问题分歧太大,未能达成永久性的和平协定。

值得一提的是,美国在巴以冲突中一直偏袒以色列。造成这种倾向的主要因素有两点:其一是美国犹太人利益集团政治势力很大,迫使政府采取保护以色列利益的立场;其二是美国出于自身利益考虑。以色列是美国在中东地区最可靠的盟友,美国需要借助以色列控制中东,保住其重要战略资源石油的供应。阿拉伯世界的动荡有利于美国军火制造商的武器销售。正因为如此,美国对于巴以冲突的解决往往起着"绊脚石"的作用。

III. Notes to the Text

1. Tough Terrain Ahead on Road Map—路线图前途坎坷(road map—a plan presented by America after the Iraqi War in 2003 to solve the long-term conflict between Israel and Arab countries)
2. President Bush put his personal prestige behind the first real US attempt—President Bush used his personal influence to help make the first real US attempt a success.
3. West Bank and Gaza —(约旦河)西岸以及加沙地带(① West Bank—territory in southwestern Asia, bounded on the north, west, and south by Israel, and on the east by Jordan. It is located on the western bank of the Jordan River in the northeast, and on a portion of the Dead Sea in the southeast. Once part of Palestine, the West Bank was annexed by Jordan in 1950, then occupied by Israel in 1967. Israel continues to maintain control over the West Bank, which today is populated by a large Palestinian majority and Israeli minority. ② Gaza — the Gaza Strip, a coastal area in the Middle East, between Egypt and Israel, which came under Israeli occupation in 1967.)
4. Aqaba—阿克巴(a seaport in the south west of Jordan)
5. the importance of territorial contiguity in the West Bank for a viable Palestinian state—西岸领土毗连对于巴勒斯坦国的独立生存十分重要(①contiguity—closeness or contact; ②viable—able to continue to exist)
6. unauthorized outposts—未经批准的边远定居点
7. Palestinian, Israelis and others question whether Sharon, the historic architect of a policy that..., will ever agree to the kind of pullbacks **(that)** Palestinians say are the minimum required to create a viable Palestinian state. — 沙龙是历史上将20万以色列人迁往西岸和加沙腹地,并将另外20万人迁往东耶路撒冷定居的策划者。因而,巴勒斯坦人、以色列人和其他人都怀疑他是否会同意把以色列人从定居点撤离,达到巴勒斯坦人所认为建立一个独立的巴勒斯坦国家的最起码条件。(East Jerusalem—Jerusalem is a city lying at the intersection of Israel and the West Bank. Jews Christians, and Muslims consider it a holy city, and it contains sites sacred to all three religions. It is composed of two distinct sections: West Jerusalem and East Jerusalem. East Jerusalem was first controlled by Arabs, then it was seized by Israel in the war which was started on June 5, 1967.)
8. And as Sharon made eminently clear, Palestinian failure to end attacks on Israelis will immediately jeopardize the entire effort.—沙龙十分清楚地表示,巴勒斯坦如果不能停止对以色列人的袭击,便会直接危及整个努力的成果。(jeopardize—to put sb or sth at risk of being harmed or lost)

9. intifada—meaning "shaking off" in Arabic. It refers to a rebellion by Palestinian Arabs to protest against Israel's occupation of the West Bank and Gaza strip.

10. Hamas—a Palestinian radical resistance group which was founded in 1988

11. Palestinians who have watched US presidents come and go say they appreciate Bush's newfound interest in their plight but remain extremely skeptical of Israel intentions and US resolve.—关注过美国几届总统如何处理巴以问题的巴勒斯坦人说他们感谢布什新近表现出来的对他们所处困境的关切,但他们仍然对以色列的意图和美国的决心持十分怀疑的态度。(① newfound — recently discovered or met;② plight— serious and difficult situation)

12. Sharon once again refrained from endorsing in full a US-backed road map for peace and instead spoke only of taking "steps"in the plan.—沙龙对美国支持的和平路线图又一次没有完全赞同,而只是谈到采取计划中所列入的"步骤"。

13. Details are everything in the Middle East and will bedevil the peacemakers at every step. — 在中东地区,细节问题至关重要,每一步都会使调停者感到困难。(① everything— used to emphasize that sb or sth is the most important person or thing; ②bedevil— to trouble sb or sth greatly)

14. U.N Security Council resolution 242— 联合国安理会242号决议(Resolution 242 is one of the most commonly referenced UN resolutions to end the Arab-Israeli conflict, and basis of later negotiations. It includes the application of the principle of Israel's withdrawal of armed forces from occupied territories.)

15. Golan Heights—戈兰高地 (a region in southwestern Syria, occupied by Israel since 1967)

16. Sinai— 西奈半岛 (a peninsula in northeastern Egypt. Israel invaded the peninsula and captured the entire territory from Egypt in the Six-Day War. In 1982, Israel completely withdrew from this peninsula.)

17. The Clinton administration came the closest to drawing new borders for Israel and Palestine that would have allowed Israel to retain key settlements and swapped parts of pre-1967 Israel for the settlements.—克林顿政府差一点儿就办成划定新的巴以边界之事,新的疆界允许以色列保留重要的居民点,代价是以部分1967年之前的以色列国土做交换。(swap— to trade or exchange one thing or person for another)

18. a deal could be clinched— a deal could be won (clinch— to succeed in getting)

19. Bush seemed to give a bigger nod toward Palestinian territorial aspirations.— 布什看来更加赞同巴勒斯坦人的领土要求。(give a nod toward—to show agreement or recognition)

20. "So that it can't be chopped up in so many ways in some form of *bantustan*" — "这样它就不会被切割成类似班图斯坦的许许多多部分"(*bantustan*—指前南非当局实行种族隔离期间控制的黑人自治区)

21. Jericho— 杰里科 (a town in the West Bank, located in the Jordan Valley)

22. Likud Party — 利库德集团 (a right-wing political party in Israel which was established in 1973)

23. It would also probably bring down Sharon's center-right coalition, which includes parties that are adamantly opposed to territorial withdrawal.—沙龙的中间派与右翼的联盟将很可能由此倒台,这个联盟包括那些坚决反对从所占领地撤离的政党。(adamantly— in a very

determined way）

24. Yossi Alpher, ... doubts a crunch will come. Sharon, Alpher says, "will do everything possible to avoid dismantling real, veteran settlements" and seeks only a more peaceful version of the status quo.——特拉维夫"雅法战略研究中心"前主任、前总理伊哈德·巴拉克的顾问亚瑟·阿尔法不相信形势会出现转折。他说沙龙只是寻求保持现状的一种更加和平的解决方式，"将会尽其所能避免拆除那些真正的老定居点"。（① veteran—old and experienced；② status quo— the condition or state of affairs that currently exists）

IV. Language Features

新闻报道引语

本文作者大量使用引语，使整个事件的报道增强了真实感、客观性和生动性。

值得注意的是，新闻报道在引语使用方面形式多种多样，显得十分活泼。据笔者观察，主要形式如下：

1. 借助"说"意动词，这是最常见的形式。例如：

"Make no mistake—the U.S. will hunt down and punish those responsible for these cowardly acts," Bush said.

2. 借助"说"意名词。例如：

State Department Spokesman John Hughes issued a polite but justified scolding: "The tradition has been not to criticize the U. S. from foreign platforms— particularly from countries hostile to the U.S."

3. 借助表示说话态度的形容词。例如：

Post Executive Editor Ben Bradles was more upbeat: "We are delighted our reporting was vindicated. It is a great day for newspapers."

4. 借助介词短语"according to"。例如：

But according to a top White House official, "Until Jim Baker and his legislative strategic group took the thing over, we didn't have a very good idea of whether or how we could win."

5. 借助上下文。例如：

A young woman (said) at a rally: "Ferraro is wonderful....We'll get millions who might otherwise have stayed at home."

6. 与间接引语结构混合使用。例如：

Mr. Hintor said the arrest of opposition leader was "one of the unfortunate aspects of the election."

引语的使用使语言具有强烈的真实感和直接感，同时还可增加结构变化和趣味性。由于这种功能，报刊英语中常出现含糊引语(Inexplicit Quotation)。本文含糊引语

使用较多,例如:

> Sharon ... promised to begin remvoing "unauthorized outposts" set up by Israeli settlers in the West Bank....

V. Analysis of Content

1. From the article, we know that the architect of the policy of settling Israelis in the West Bank, Gaza and East Jerusalem was _____.
   A. the United Nations   B. Sharon   C. Bush   D. Arafat
2. According to the article, the road map is _____.
   A. a geographic map
   B. an economic plan to aid Palestine
   C. the U.S. plan for a settlement of the Middle East problem
   D. the U.N. plan for a Middle East peace agreement
3. The idea of the territory-for-peace trade-off was first set forth by _____.
   A. Palestine   B. Israel
   C. the U.N. Security Council   D. the U.S.
4. According to the "road map", in return for Palestinians ending attacks on Israelis, Israel will have to pull back from much of _____.
   A. the West Bank and Gaza   B. the Golan Heights
   C. the Sinai desert   D. Jericho
5. The author believes that the road map places the toughest issues _____.
   A. at the beginning of the process   B. in the middle stage of the process
   C. at the end of the process   D. off the process

VI. Questions on the Article

1. According to the article, what will real progress of the road map depend on?
2. What did Sharon say about the trade-off? What did his statement imply?
3. What did Palestinian militant groups vow to do?
4. What are Palestinians still extremely skeptical of?
5. What does U.N. Security Council resolution call for?
6. What are the toughest issues in the solution to the conflicts between Palestine and Israel?
7. According to Yossi Alpher, what will Sharon do?
8. What is Sharon's definition of "contiguous"? And what is his vision of a Palestinian state?

VII. Topics for Discussion

1. Can the road map ensure peace in the Middle East?
2. Has the U.S. been impartial in handling the conflict between Israel and Palestine?

Lesson 34

Age Invaders

(Abridged)

A generation of old people is about to change the global economy. They will not all do so in the same way.

IN THE 20th century the planet's population doubled twice. It will not double even once in the current century, because birth rates in much of the world have declined steeply. But the number of people over 65 is set to double within just 25 years. This shift in the structure of the population is not as momentous as the expansion that came before. But it is more than enough to reshape the world economy.

According to the UN's population projections, the standard source for demographic estimates, there are around 600m people aged 65 or older alive today. That is in itself remarkable; the author Fred Pearce claims it is possible that half of all the humans who have ever been over 65 are alive today. But as a share of the total population, at 8%, it is not that different to what it was a few decades ago.

By 2035, however, more than 1.1 billion people—13% of the population—will be above the age of 65. This is a natural corollary of the dropping birth rates that are slowing overall population growth; they mean there are proportionally fewer young people around.[1] The "old-age dependency ratio"[2]—the ratio of old people to those of working age—will grow even faster. In 2010 the world had 16 people aged 65 and over for every 100 adults between the ages of 25 and 64, almost the same ratio it had in 1980. By 2035 the UN expects that number to have risen to 26.

In rich countries it will be much higher. Japan will have 69 old people for every 100 of working age by 2035 (up from 43 in 2010), Germany 66 (from 38). Even America, which has a relatively high fertility rate, will see its old-age dependency rate rise by more than 70%, to 44. Developing countries, where today's ratio is much lower, will not see absolute levels rise that high; but the proportional growth will be higher. Over the same time period the old-age dependency rate in China will more than double from 15 to 36. Latin America will see a shift from 14 to 27.

The big exceptions to this general greying are south Asia and Africa, where fertility is still high. Since these places are home to almost 3 billion people, rising to 5 billion by mid-century, their youth could be a powerful counter to the greying elsewhere. But they will slow the change, not reverse it. The emerging world as a whole will see its collective old-age dependency rate almost double, to 22 per 100, by 2035.

The received wisdom is that a larger proportion of old people means slower growth and, because the old need to draw down their wealth to live, less saving; that leads to higher interest rates and falling asset prices.[3] Some economists are more sanguine, arguing that people will adapt and work longer. A third group harks back to the work of Alvin Hansen who argued in 1938 that a shrinking population in America would bring with it diminished incentives for companies to invest —a smaller workforce needs less investment—and hence persistent stagnation.

Who is right? The answer depends on examining the three main channels through which demography influences the economy: changes in the size of the workforce; changes in the rate of productivity growth; and changes in the pattern of savings.[4]

Amlan Roy, an economist at Credit Suisse[5], has calculated that the shrinking working-age population dragged down Japan's GDP growth by an average of just over 0.6 percentage points a year between 2000 and 2013, and that over the next four years that will increase to 1 percentage point a year. Germany's shrinking workforce could reduce GDP growth by almost half a point. In America, under the same assumptions, the retirement of the baby-boomers would be expected to reduce the economy's potential growth rate by 0.7 percentage points.

The real size of the workforce, though, depends on more than the age structure of the population; it depends on who else works (women who currently do not, perhaps, or immigrants) and how long people work. In the late 20th century that last factor changed little. An analysis of 43 mostly rich countries by David Bloom, David Canning and Günther Fink, all of Harvard University, found that between 1965 and 2005 the average legal retirement age rose by less than six months. During that time male life expectancy[6] rose by nine years.

Since the turn of the century that trend has reversed. Almost 20% of Americans aged over 65 are now in the labour force, compared with 13% in 2000. Nearly half of all Germans in their early 60s are employed today, compared with a quarter a decade ago.

This is in part due to policy. Debt-laden governments in Europe have cut back their pension promises and raised the retirement age. Half a dozen European countries, including Italy, Spain and the Netherlands, have linked the statutory retirement age[7] to life expectancy. Personal financial circumstances have played a part, too. In most countries the shift was strongest in the wake of the 2008 financial crisis[8], which hit the savings of many near-retirees. The move away from corporate pension plans that provided a fraction of the recipient's final salary in perpetuity will also have kept some people working longer.[9]

But an even more important factor is education. Better-educated older people are far more likely to work for longer. Gary Burtless of the Brookings Institution[10] has calculated that, in America, only 32% of male high-school graduates with no further formal education are in the workforce between the ages of 62 and 74. For men with a professional degree the figure is 65% (though the overall number of such men is obviously smaller). For women the ratios are one-quarter versus one-half, with the share of highly educated women working into their 60s soaring. In Europe, where workers of all sorts are soldiering on into their 60s more than they used to, the effect is not quite as marked, but still striking.[11] Only a quarter of the least-educated Europeans aged 60-64 still work; half of those with a degree do.

It is not a hard pattern to explain. Less-skilled workers often have manual jobs that get harder as you get older. The relative pay of the less-skilled has fallen, making retirement on a public pension[12] more attractive; for the unemployed, who are also likely to be less skilled, retirement is a terrific option. Research by Clemens Hetschko, Andreas Knabe and Ronnie Schöb shows that people who go straight from unemployment to retirement experience a startling increase in their sense of well-being.[13]

Higher-skilled workers, on the other hand, tend to be paid more, which gives them an incentive to keep working. They are also on average healthier and longer-lived, so they can work and earn past 65 and still expect to enjoy the fruits of that extra labour later on.

This does not mean the workforce will grow. Overall work rates among the over-60s will still be lower than they were for the same cohort when it was younger. And even as more educated old folk are working, fewer less-skilled young people are. In Europe, jobless rates are highest among the least-educated young. In America, where the labour participation rate (at 63%) is close to a three-decade low, employment has dropped most sharply for less-skilled men. With no surge in employment among women, and little appetite for mass immigration, in most of the rich world the workforce looks likely to shrink even if skilled oldies stay employed.[14]

A smaller workforce need not dampen growth, though, if productivity surges. This is not something most would expect to come about as a result of an ageing population. Plenty of studies and bitter experience show that most physical and many cognitive capacities decline with age. A new analysis by a trio of Canadian academics based on the video game "Star Craft II"[15], for instance, suggests that raw brainpower peaks at 24.[16] And ageing societies may ossify. Alfred Sauvy, the French thinker who coined the term "third world", was prone to worry that the first world would become "a society of old people, living in old houses, ruminating about old ideas". Japan's productivity growth slowed sharply in the 1990s when its working-age population began to shrink; Germany's productivity performance has become lacklustre as its population ages.

But Japan's slowed productivity growth can also be ascribed to its burst asset bubble, and Germany's to reforms meant to reduce unemployment;[17] both countries, ageing as they are, score better in the World Economic Forum's[18] ranking for innovation than America. A dearth of workers might prompt the invention of labour-saving capital-intensive technology[19], just as Japanese firms are pioneering the use of robots to look after old people. And a wealth of job experience can counter slower cognitive speed. In an age of ever-smarter machines, the attributes that enhance productivity may have less to do with pure cognitive oomph than motivation, people skills and managerial experience.[20]

Perhaps most important, better education leads to higher productivity at any age. For all these reasons, a growing group of highly educated older folk could increase productivity, offsetting much of the effect of a smaller workforce.

Evidence on both sides of the Atlantic bears this out. A clutch of recent studies suggests that older workers are disproportionately more productive—as you would expect if they are disproportionately better educated. Laura Romeu Gordo of the German Centre of Gerontology and VegardSkirbekk, of the International Institute for Applied Systems Analysis[21] in Austria, have shown that in Germany older workers who stayed in the labour force have tended to move into jobs which demanded more cognitive skill. Perhaps because of such effects, the earnings of those over 50 have risen relative to younger workers.

Demographic trends will shape the future, but they do not render particular outcomes inevitable.²² The evolution of the economy will depend on the way policymakers respond to the new situation. But those policy reactions will themselves be shaped by the priorities of older people to a greater extent than has previously been the case; they will be a bigger share of the population and in democracies they tend to vote more than younger people do.

On both sides of the Atlantic, recent budget decisions appear to reflect the priorities of the ageing and affluent. Annuities reform in Britain increased people's freedom to spend their pension pots; the disappearance of property-tax reform spared homeowning older Italians a new burden; America's budget slashed spending on the young and poor while failing to make government health and pension spending any less generous to the well-off. Few rich-country governments have shown any appetite for large-scale investment, despite low interest rates.

A set of forces pushing investment down and pushing saving **(savings)** up, with no countervailing policy response, makes the impact of ageing over the next few years look like the world that Hansen described: one of slower growth (albeit not as slow as it would have been if older folk were not working more), a surfeit of saving and very low interest rates. It will be a world in which ageing reinforces the changes in income distribution that new technology has brought with it: the skilled old earn more, the less-skilled of all ages are squeezed. The less-educated and jobless young will be particularly poorly served, never building up the skills to enable them to become productive older workers.

Compared with the dire warnings about the bankrupting consequences of a "grey tsunami", this is good news. But not as good as all that.²³

From *The Economist*, April 26, 2014

I. New Words

annuity	[əˈnjuːiti]	n.	年金,养老金
clutch	[klʌtʃ]	n.	a group
cognitive	[ˈkɔgnitiv]	adj.	认知的,感知的
countervailing	[ˈkauntəveiliŋ]	adj.	补偿的,抵消的
dearth	[dəːθ]	n.	lack
debt-laden	[detˈleidn]	adj.	债务缠身的
demography	[diˈmɔgrəfi]	n.	人口统计学
dependency	[diˈpendənsi]	n.	依赖,依靠他人扶养
diminished	[diˈminiʃt]	adj.	减弱的,减少的
fertility	[fəˈtiliti]	n.	繁殖(生育)力
fraction	[ˈfrækʃn]	n.	a small part or amount of sth
gerontology	[ˌdʒerənˈtɔlədʒi]	n.	老年医学;老人学

hark	[ha:k]	v.	~ back to sth to remind you of sth
lacklustre	[ˈlækˌlʌstə]	adj.	缺乏生气的,死气沉沉的
managerial	[ˌmæniˈdʒiəriəl]	adj.	管理(经营)上的
momentous	[məuˈmentəs]	adj.	very important
offset	[ˈɔfset]	v.	抵消
ossify	[ˈɔsifai]	v.	骨化；僵化
persistent	[pəˈsistənt]	adj.	continuing for a long period
projection	[prəˈdʒekʃn]	n.	预测；推断
prompt	[prɔmpt]	v.	to cause sth to happen
ruminate	[ˈru:mineit]	v.	*formal* to think deeply about sth
sanguine	[ˈsæŋgwin]	adj.	*formal* cheerful and confident
stagnation	[stægˈneiʃən]	n.	不景气,停滞
surfeit	[ˈsə:fit]	n.	an amount that is too large
trio	[ˈtri:əu]	n.	a group of three people
well-being	[ˈwelˈbi:ŋ]	n.	general health and happiness

II. Background Information

全球人口老龄化趋势

人口老龄化是指人口生育率降低或人均寿命延长导致的总人口中年轻人口比例减少而老年人口比例相应增长的动态趋势。人口老龄化可以指老年人口相对增多，在总人口中所占比例不断上升的过程，也可以指社会人口结构呈现老年状态，进入老龄化社会。按照国际标准，当一个国家或地区60岁以上老年人口占人口总数的10%，或65岁以上老年人口占人口总数的7%，即意味着这个国家或地区进入了老龄化社会（aging society）；当一个国家65岁以上人口占总人口比例达到14%的时候，这个国家便进入深度老龄化阶段（deep aging society）；如果一个国家或地区65岁以上人口占总人口比例达到20%，那么这个国家或地区便成为超级老龄化社会（super aging society）。

2020年世界年龄中位数为31岁。2022年全球年龄中位数最高的国家是摩纳哥。其年龄中位数为55.4，是全球唯一超过50岁的国家（或地区）。日本名列第二，年龄中位数为48.6。据统计，从1950—2021年，全球年龄中位数从22岁上升到30岁。联合国预测：到2050年全球年龄中位数将超过35岁。

从根本上讲，全球人口老龄化趋势是医疗进步、公共卫生事业发展、教育水平提高和经济增长的必然结果，例如很多国家和地区的饮用水卫生水平得到提高，人们营养更加均衡，传染病和寄生虫疾病得到有效控制，母婴死亡率大幅下降等。2020年，全世界60岁及以上老年人口总数已达10.5亿，人口老龄化的迅速发展引起了联合国及世界各国政府的高度关注。联合国多次召开老龄化问题世界大会，并将其列入历届联大的重要议题，先后通过《老龄问题国际行动计划》《联合国老年人原则》《1992至2001年解决人口老龄化问题全球目标》《世界老龄问题宣言》等一系列重要决议和文件。面对全球人口老龄化这一重大挑战,联合国呼吁设立老龄化问题国家级协调机构,在国家、区域和地方各级制定综合战略,把老龄问题纳入国家发展计划中,为老龄化社会的来临做好各项准备工作,以期增强人们对人口老龄化问题和老年人问题的重视。我国也在党的二十大报告中提出推进健康中国建设,实施积极应对人口老龄化国家战略,发展养老事业和养老产业,优化孤寡老人服务,推动实现全体老年人享有基本养老服务。

全球人口老龄化给人类社会方方面面都带来重大影响。在经济领域,人口老龄化将对经济增长、储蓄、投资与消费、劳动力市场、养恤金和税收政策等方面产生巨大冲击。在社会层面,人口老龄化给医疗保险、家庭组成和住房问题等方面带来较大影响。在政治方面,人口老龄化将直接影响投票竞选方式和选区选民的构成。

美国1950年就进入了老龄化阶段,2015年又进入了深度老龄化阶段。根据全球著名的商业市场研究和咨询服务机构盖洛普公司(Gallup)的调查,74%的美国成年人希望年龄达到65岁后继续工作。根据美国劳工统计局的统计数据,目前920万65岁以上的美国老人继续着全职或兼职工作,而十年前保持在岗工作的老人只有560万。抵达退休年龄后还坚持工作的情况已经成为全美普遍的文化现象,其原因是多方面的,最主要的原因是美国人均寿命的延长。根据美国社会保障局的预测,达到65岁的美国男性平均还有19年的寿命,女性则更长,达到21.5年。4名65岁的美国老人中就有一人会活到90岁以上,十分之一的老人寿命将超过95岁。随着"婴儿潮"(baby boom)向"银发海啸"(silver tsunami)的转变,美国社会迫切需要更多的政策支持和社会化的服务以适应人口老龄化的社会需求。

III. Notes to the Text

1. This is a natural corollary of the dropping birth rates that are slowing overall population growth; they mean there are proportionally fewer young people around. ——这是出生率下滑导致整体人口增速放缓的自然结果,意味着年轻人口的比例更小。(corollary——a natural consequence)

2. old-age dependency ratio ——老年人口赡养比率(通常以65岁以上人口数除以20—64岁人口数来计算,联合国所定的标准是用65岁以上人口数除以15—64岁人口数)

3. The received wisdom is that a larger proportion of old people means slower growth and, because the old need to draw down their wealth to live, less saving; that leads to higher interest rates and falling asset prices. ——公认的看法是老年人口比例增大造成经济增长减缓,并且由于老人需要花费自己的钱财以维持生活还会造成储蓄量的减少,这就导致利率上升和房价下跌。(the received wisdom ——the generally accepted view)

4. The answer depends on examining the three main channels through which demography influences the economy: changes in the size of the workforce; changes in the rate of productivity growth; and changes in the pattern of savings. 问题的答案是基于对人口影响经济三个主要途径的考察:劳动力规模的变化、生产力增长率的变化、储蓄模式的变化。

5. Credit Suisse — 瑞士信贷集团（2006年更名为瑞士瑞信银行,是一家投资银行和金融服务公司）

6. life expectancy — 预期寿命

7. statutory retirement age — 法定退休年龄（statutory — fixed by law）

8. the 2008 financial crisis—2008年的金融危机（又称世界金融危机,由次级房屋信贷危机最终引发）

9. The move away from corporate pension plans that provided a fraction of the recipient's final salary in perpetuity will also have kept some people working longer. — 取消原先为员工所设的提供金额相当其在职期最终薪金一小部分的公司养老金计划也会使一些人延迟退休。

10. the Brookings Institution — 布鲁金斯学会（美国著名智库之一,该学会历史悠久,规模较大,影响较大。）

11. In Europe, where workers of all sorts are soldiering on into their 60s more than they used to, the effect is not quite as marked, but still striking. — 在欧洲,各行业工作者都比以前工作时期要长,继续干到六十多岁,（教育促使工作人员延迟退休的）效果不（如美国）那么显著,但依然引人注目。(soldier on — to continue bravely with one's work, etc despite difficulties)

12. public pension — 公共养老金（由政府发起的养老保险）

13. ...people who go straight from unemployment to retirement experience a startling increase in their sense of well-being. — 从失业状态直接步入退休状态的人们感受到幸福感骤然增加。

14. With no surge in employment among women, and little appetite for mass immigration, in most of the rich world the workforce looks likely to shrink even if skilled oldies stay employed. — 大部分富裕国家,由于女性劳动力没有急剧增长,政府不愿引入大批移民,即使年老的技术人员继续工作,劳动力也很可能会减少。(① surge — a sudden increase; ② appetite — a strong desire; ③ shrink — to become smaller; ④ oldie — informal an old person)

15. "Star Craft II"— "星际争霸2"（该电子游戏是暴雪娱乐公司推出的一款即时战略游戏）

16. ...raw brainpower peaks at 24. — 大脑的原始智能在24岁达到顶峰。

17. But Japan's slowed productivity growth can also be ascribed to its burst asset bubble, and Germany's to reforms meant to reduce unemployment... — 但是日本生产力增长减缓还可以归咎于其房地产泡沫的破灭,德国则是归因于旨在减少失业率的改革。(① bubble — a good or lucky situation that is unlikely to last long; ② ascribe — to consider that sth is caused by a particular thing)

18. the World Economic Forum — 世界经济论坛（该机构是以研究和探讨世界经济领域存在的问题、促进国际经济合作与交流为宗旨的非官方国际性机构,总部设在瑞士日内瓦。因为每年年会在达沃斯召开,故又被称为达沃斯论坛。）

19. capital-intensive technology — 资本密集型技术（指生产消耗物化劳动或需要投入资金较多的资本密集型产品所需要的技术,如重化工业等。其特点是占用资金较多,周转较慢,投资回收期较长,容纳劳动力较少。）

20. In an age of ever-smarter machines, the attributes that enhance productivity may have less to do with pure cognitive oomph than motivation, people skills and managerial experience. — 在机器日益智能化的时代,提升生产力的因素不再是纯认知能力,而是驱动力、人工技术和

管理经验。(oomph — *informal* energy; a special good quality)

21. the International Institute for Applied Systems Analysis —国际应用系统分析研究所（即IIASA，成立于1972年，位于奥地利维也纳，是国际非政府研究机构。IIASA强调跨学科和系统性分析思路，旨在研究全球范围内的自然和社会问题，为各国提供合理政策导向。）

22. Demographic trends will shape the future, but they do not render particular outcomes inevitable. —人口趋势严重影响未来，但不会使特定结果成为必然。(render — to cause to be)

23. Compared with the dire warnings about the bankrupting consequences of a "grey tsunami", this is good news. But not as good as all that. —与"银发海啸"带来经济破产后果的严重警告相比，这是好消息，但并不是非常好。(① grey tsunami — a term used to refer to the impending retirement from the workforce of the baby boom generation, which will pose a great challenge to the economy; ② dire—very serious; ③ not all that — not very)

IV. Language Features

报刊英语翻译常见错误

阅读报刊译文时常常发现误译情况，造成误译的因素主要有以下四点：

1. 语法概念不清

例：At the same time that commercial loans are becoming harder to get, the developing nations' own funding has been devastated by the slump in commodity prices.

原译：与此同时，商业信贷越来越难以得到了，发展中国家本身的资金由于商品价格下跌而受重创。

改译：商业信贷越来越难以得到，与此同时……

2. 词义理解偏差

例：After a 10-year bender of gaudy dreams and Godless consumerism, Americans are starting to trade down.

原译：经过10年绚丽的梦和不信神的消费的大转弯，美国人开始减少消费。

改译：经过10年妖艳的梦和罪恶的无节制消费，美国人开始减少消费。

本句中bender是俚语，表示"狂热"。外刊中俚语常常出现，应引起译者的注意。

3. 有关知识缺乏

例：The radio broadcast patriotic messages and coded orders for military personnel.

原译：电台广播了爱国发言和给军事人员命令。

改译：电台播送激发爱国情绪的讲话和给军事人员加密的命令。

4. 语言知识缺乏

例：The Libyan strongman flashed hot and cold, warning that the waters off Tripoli would become "a red gulf of blood" if the Nimitz stayed too close—yet protesting that he had no intention of attacking his neighbor...

原译：利比亚铁腕人物大为恼怒。他警告：假如"尼米兹号"舰驶得太近,那么,的黎波里的近海流域将成为"血腥的海湾"——然而,他又抗议说,他没有袭击邻国的意图……

改译：这个利比亚铁腕人物反复无常,……然而,他又声称,……

这里,作者活用习语 blow hot and cold。习语活用在美英报刊中较为常见。

第一、二类错误是英语基本功问题,第三、四类错误是知识结构问题。上述例子说明：要想提高外刊理解和翻译水平,就得做到语法概念清晰,词义理解准确,文化知识广博,语言知识丰富。

V. Analysis of Content

1. Which of the following is NOT a natural consequence of dropping birth rates?

    A. A larger proportion of old people.

    B. A slowdown in population growth.

    C. Faster growth of old-age dependency ratio.

    D. Faster growth of old workers' income.

2. Which of the following continents goes against the global demographic trend?

    A. Europe.

    B. America.

    C. Africa.

    D. Asia.

3. Which of the following is NOT one of the main channels through which demography influences the economy according to the author?

    A. Changes in the size of the workforce.

    B. Changes in the rate of productivity growth.

    C. Changes in the income distribution.

    D. Changes in the pattern of savings.

4. Which of the following is the author's view on the impact of a larger proportion of old people on the economy?

    A. The situation won't be as bad as the dire warnings but not as good as all that.

    B. The future of an ageing world is bleak.

    C. The "grey tsunami" will lead to bankrupting consequences.

    D. Problems arising from it will be solved in the near future.

5. Which of the following does NOT shape the real size of the workforce according to the author?

    A. The age structure of the population.

    B. The number of women or immigrants in the labour force.

    C. The economy's potential growth rate.

    D. The average legal retirement age.

VI. Questions on the Article

1. What change in the structure of the population is more than enough to reshape the world economy?
2. According to the UN's population projections, what demographic estimates are remarkable but not different compared to what it was a few decades ago?
3. Is there any difference of old-age dependency ratio between rich countries and developing countries?
4. Will the high fertility rate in Asia and Africa reverse the overall rise of old-age dependency rate?
5. What accounts for the rise of retirement age since the turn of the century?
6. Why do people with higher education stay longer in the labour force?
7. According to the author, what can expand the workforce in rich countries?
8. What can offset much of the effect of a smaller workforce?
9. Why have the earnings of those over 50 risen relative to younger workers?
10. How do policymakers respond to the new situation?
11. What is the impact of ageing over the next few years?

VII. Topics for Discussion

1. Does higher ratio of old people's population slow down the growth of economy?
2. Should old people be encouraged to continue working?

Lesson 35

Lethal Blast Hits Jakarta Hotel

At least 13 dead, 149 wounded in attack ascribed to terror group[1]

By Ellen Nakashima

JAKARTA, Indonesia, Aug. 5 — A powerful car bomb exploded in front of the luxury JW Marriott Hotel[2] here during the lunchtime bustle[3] today, killing at least 13 people and injuring 149, according to the Indonesian Red Cross, in what officials said appeared to be a suicide attack. Two Americans were reported injured.

Explosives were hidden in a Toyota Kijang, an Indonesian-built minivan[4], which was moving slowly toward the lobby, said Gen. Da'i Bachtiar, the national police chief. The bomb went off at about 12:45 p.m., with the hotel's main restaurant filled to capacity.[5] Witnesses said they saw a fireball about 12 feet high, followed by billows of black smoke.

The 33-floor, 333-room Marriott, which is managed by the global chain based in Bethesda[6], has had a special relationship with the U.S. Embassy in Jakarta since it opened in September 2001. The embassy has held meetings and Fourth of July celebrations there and uses it to house temporary personnel. No Americans died in the attack; most of the victims were Indonesians.

There was no immediate claim of responsibility[7], but analysts said the attack was probably the work of the regional terror network Jemaah Islamiah[8], which intelligence agencies say cooperates with Osama bin Laden's al Qaeda organization[9].

Indonesian police have targeted Jemaah Islamiah in recent months, arresting more than 40 suspected members accused of involvement in October's nightclub bombings on the Indonesian island of Bali. The attack killed 202 people and was the most deadly act of terror since the Sept.11, 2001, attacks in the United States.

The Jakarta bombing "reminds us that we are still prosecuting the war against terrorists worldwide,"[10] Homeland Security Secretary Tom Ridge[11] told reporters in Washington. He cautioned against relating the bombing to any imminent attack in the United States.

Da'i, the police chief, said that police had found the minivan's engine, pieces of its radiator, its chassis registration number and its license plate and were trying to locate the vehicle's owner.

At the scene of the blast, broken glass, twisted metal, bloody body parts and singed shoes and clothing littered the area surrounding the hotel and the adjacent Mutiara Plaza shopping mall. The shells of at least eight burned cars and limousines smoldered in front of the plaza.

Windows in the hotel were shattered up to the 21st floor. Virtually an entire side of the high-rise Mutiara Plaza had lost its windows, and shredded draperies flapped in the wind.

Many of the victims were in the hotel's ground-floor restaurant, whose 250 seats were filled— prospective diners were wait-listed[12]. "I just heard an explosion and saw glass everywhere," said

Irna Fahrianti, 19, who was in training to be a waitress at the restaurant. "I covered my head with a tray. Everyone ran out, including me. I held my leg. My friend helped me."

Fahrianti, who spoke from her bed at Jakarta Hospital, where she was taken with an injured leg, said she ran to someone's car and that person drove her to Jakarta Hospital, one of several hospitals to treat the victims.

One waiter, I Gede Susriawawan, 27, was among the luckier ones. He heard the bomb, saw the restaurant's plate glass windows shatter and dove to the floor. He suffered a gash on his forehead from flying glass, but was otherwise unhurt. "Everybody was terrified," he said, standing in a hospital hallway as burn victims were wheeled by[13]. "They were running to get outside."

As in Bali last year, bulletins were posted outside hospital emergency rooms with the names— or sometimes just nationalities—of the wounded: Astrid Wikastri; Agus; USA; Oscar, 24; Pieter, 37.

 Simon Leunig, a marketing manager from Perth, Australia, had just showered in his seventh-floor room when he heard the explosion. "The windows blew in, throwing me across the room onto the bed," he said.

He said he grabbed his cell phone and passport, pulled on a pair of trousers and sneakers, ran to the elevator and "got out of there as fast as I could." He helped one wounded guest out from the lobby, he said, and saw two dead Indonesian limo or taxi drivers outside. He helped carry one badly injured man and was still clutching a piece of the man's burned clothing as he stood on a sidewalk cordoned off by police tape[14]. "I think he's going to make it," he said of the man he had helped.

About 100 yards from the hotel, on a sidewalk near Mutiara Plaza, lay a pair of scorched Fila sneakers and one black loafer, scraps of charred clothing and a bloody piece of human bone. Forensic workers carefully wrapped everything in gauze sheets and removed it to be examined as evidence.

One of the two Americans injured was treated and released, the U.S. Embassy said. The other was still being treated, according to U.S. Ambassador Ralph L. Boyce. "We extend our deepest condolences to the victims of this deplorable act of violence," Boyce said.

The attack occurred while a State Department travel warning for Indonesia is in effect, advising Americans to defer all non-essential trips to the country.[15] Britain and Australia have posted similar warnings. One Australian was wounded today, the Australian Embassy said.

 The explosion took place on the same day that Abubakar Baasyir, identified by intelligence agencies as the spiritual leader of Jemaah Islamiah, was testifying in his own defense in a trial here in Jakarta. He is accused of treason and seeking to overthrow the Indonesian government and of involvement in a series of church bombings across Indonesia on Christmas Eve 2000 that killed 19 people. Police have also said he participated in a plot to assassinate President Megawati Sukarnoputri.

 The blast came two days before the first verdict is expected in the Bali bombing trials, and Jemaah Islamiah had threatened retaliation if any of the three dozen suspects on trial were executed. It also came four days after Megawati publicly pledged to destroy the terror networks responsible for those attacks and others in the world's most populous Muslim nation. "This domestic branch of the international terrorism movement is a terrifying threat," she said.

 "It's clearly Jemaah Islamiah," said Zachary Abuza, a professor at Simmons College, Boston. "This shows these guys still have a lot of fight in them[16]. This is what they do. They're terrorists.

They commit attacks. This is not something you retire from. They also do it to justify, for morale's sake, their own organization.[17]"

A Western analyst in Jakarta, who spoke on condition of anonymity[18], called the bombing "part of a game to demonstrate that despite the series of arrests that have occurred, Jemaah Islamish is alive, living and well."

Abuza noted that last month police charged eight Jemaah Islamiah members in connection with the seizure of a large cache of explosives—including almost 2,000 pounds of potassium chloride, 350 pounds of TNT and 1,700 detonators—in central Java[19], Indonesia's main island and home to Jakarta and other large cities. But eight packages of explosives had already made it to Jakarta, he said.[20]

The suspects told police that their top three targets were shopping malls, churches and hotels, Abuza said.

From *The Washington Post*, Aug 6, 2003

I. New Words

adjacent	[əˈdʒeisnt]	adj.	lying near
billow	[ˈbiləu]	n.	great wave
cache	[kæʃ]	n.	a hiding place to store food, supplies, or treasures
chassis	[ˈʃæsi]	n.	（汽车等的）底盘，车架
chloride	[ˈklɔːraid]	n.	[化]氯化物
condolence	[kənˈdəuləns]	n.	sympathy for someone who had sth bad happen to him/her
cordon	[ˈkɔːdn]	v.	to enclose (with soldiers, police, etc.)
deplorable	[diˈplɔːrəbl]	adj.	regrettable, wretched
detonator	[ˈdetəneitə]	n.	雷管，起爆管
drapery	[ˈdreipəri]	n.	*plural* curtains of heavy material
flap	[flæp]	v.	拍动；飘动
forensic	[fəˈrensik]	adj.	法庭的，法医的
gash	[gæʃ]	n.	long and deep slash, cut or wound
gauze	[gɔːz]	n.	棉纱布
high-rise	[ˈhaiˈraiz]	adj.	(of a building) very tall, with many storeys
limousine	[ˈliməziːn]	n.	any large and luxurious sedan
litter	[ˈlitə]	v.	to scatter or to leave lying
loafer	[ˈləufə]	n.	AmE 休闲鞋
minivan	[ˈminivæn]	n.	小型货车
potassium	[pəˈtæsiəm]	n.	[化]钾
shredded	[ˈʃredid]	adj.	被撕成碎片的
singe	[sindʒ]	v.	烧焦或烫焦

II. Background Information

恐怖主义

恐怖主义是指通过暴力、破坏、恐怖等手段,制造社会恐慌,危害公共安全,侵犯人身、财产或者胁迫国家机关和国际组织,以实现其政治意识形态等目的的主张和行为。

震惊世界的9·11事件发生之后,国际恐怖主义活动一直层出不穷,范围在蔓延扩大。

2001年,印度新德里联邦议会遭到恐怖分子袭击;2002年,俄罗斯车臣共和国首府格罗兹尼市一警察分局大楼内发生一起严重爆炸事件,印度尼西亚旅游胜地巴厘岛发生系列爆炸;2003年,汽车炸弹袭击沙特利雅得一外国人居住区,巴基斯坦一座清真寺遭恐怖分子袭击,印度尼西亚雅加达万豪大酒店汽车炸弹爆炸。

近一些年全球发生的恐怖袭击出现以下三个趋势:

1. 恐怖主义活动范围已从西欧、中东、中亚向全球各地区扩散。
2. 攻击采取的手段由传统的绑架、劫持人质及暗杀等方式转向使用爆炸、袭击、劫持以及生物武器和网络恐怖主义等。
3. 攻击目标从政治机构、军事设施等硬目标(hard targets)转向娱乐、文化、餐饮、旅游等软目标(soft targets)。

当代恐怖主义类型除极右翼恐怖主义和极左翼恐怖主义之外,还有民族主义型和宗教型两种。民族主义型恐怖主义较为典型的是英国的爱尔兰共和军和俄罗斯车臣分裂分子。冷战之后,许多国家内部和国家间的民族和种族矛盾得以释放,泛化为狭隘的民族主义,长期得不到解决的历史问题更加激化,进而采取恐怖行动。宗教型恐怖主义是指打着宗教旗号实施恐怖活动的恐怖主义。特别值得一提的是"伊斯兰祈祷团"(Jemaah Islamiah, 简称J.I.)。这是活跃于东南亚的恐怖组织,该组织势力从泰国一直蔓延到印度尼西亚、澳大利亚。在印度尼西亚,该组织于2000年组织了圣诞夜系列爆炸案,2002年策划了巴厘岛爆炸案,2003年导演了万豪大酒店爆炸案。

"伊斯兰祈祷团"是印度尼西亚的恐怖组织,与很多恐怖袭击有牵连。其领导层和资金来源与"基地"有着密切联系。该组织的高层领导人在"基地"接受过培训,大部分经费也是从"基地"流入,其中8万美元用于巴厘岛和万豪大酒店爆炸案。面对现实的威胁,东南亚各国政府充分意识到反恐的必要性。这些国家加强了地区性的合作,采取了不少得力措施,在打击恐怖主义方面取得了一些成效。

III. Notes to the Text

1. attack ascribed to terror group — attack which is believed to have been caused by a terror group
2. JW Marriott Hotel — (位于雅加达市中心的五星级)万豪大酒店
3. the lunchtime bustle — 午餐繁忙时刻(bustle—busy, noisy activity)

4. a Toyota Kijang, an Indonesian-built minivan——印度尼西亚生产的丰田吉祥小型货车
5. The bomb went off at about 12:45 p.m., with the hotel's main restaurant filled to capacity.——炸弹在中午12时45分左右爆炸,当时饭店的主餐厅内坐满了用餐的人。(① go off —— to explode; ② filled to capacity —— completely full)
6. the global chain based in Bethesda —— 总部设在贝塞斯达的全球连锁业
7. There was no immediate claim of responsibility... —— No organization immediately said publicly that it was responsible for the attack.
8. the regional terror network Jemaah Islamiah —— 地区性恐怖组织"伊斯兰祈祷团"
9. Osama bin Laden's al Qaeda organization —— 奥萨马·本·拉登领导的"基地"组织
10. The Jakarta bombing "reminds us that we are still prosecuting the war against terrorists worldwide"... —— 雅加达的爆炸事件提醒我们世界范围的反恐战争仍在继续。(prosecute —— to continue doing sth)
11. Homeland Security Secretary Tom Ridge —— [美] 国土安全部部长汤姆·里奇
12. prospective diners were wait-listed——prospective diners were waiting for service (wait-list—— to put on a waiting list)
13. burn victims were wheeled by——烧伤病人的推车从旁边过去（wheel——to move someone in an object with wheels）
14. a sidewalk cordoned off by police tape——a sidewalk which is enclosed with police tape to prevent people from entering
15. The attack occurred while a State Department travel warning for Indonesia is in effect, advising Americans to defer all non-essential trips to the country. —— 袭击发生在国务院发布的印度尼西亚旅游警告有效期间,它建议美国人推迟所有到这个国家的非必需的旅行。
16. these guys still have a lot of fight in them——这些家伙还是非常好斗（fight——desire or ability to keep fighting）
17. They also do it to justify, for morale's sake, their own organization. ——他们这样做也是为了证明他们的组织具有战斗力,以此来鼓舞士气。
18. spoke on condition of anonymity——spoke only if his name would be kept secret
19. Java —— 爪哇岛(位于印度尼西亚南部,苏门答腊岛与巴厘岛之间,首都雅加达所在地)
20. But eight packages of explosives had already made it to Jakarta, he said. ——他说,但是已经有8包炸药运抵雅加达了。(make it to —— to arrive somewhere in time for sth)

IV. Language Features

倒金字塔结构

本文是纯新闻报道,篇章结构采用的是较为常见的"倒金字塔模式"(the Inverted Pyramid Form)。这种模式是按新闻事实重要性递降式进行布局。最重要的新闻事实安排在文章的开头(也称作新闻导语),较为次要的内容紧接导语之后,一般是导语中

的主要新闻要素的说明和扩展,最为次要的内容放在末尾。这样组合的文章便形成顶部大、底部小的倒三角形状,西方新闻学称此为"倒金字塔模式"。本文结构如下:

  I. 第1小段构成本文第一层次,即新闻导语。这一段交代了四个新闻要素:
  What — a powerful car bomb exploded
  Where — in front of the luxury J.W. Marriott Hotel
  When — lunch time today (August 5, 2003)
  How — a suicide attack

  II. 第2、3小段构成第二层次,这一部分补充说明导语中所提到的四个新闻要素:
  What — more details about the explosion
  Where — more details about the hotel
  When — 12:45 p.m.
  How — explosives were hidden in a Toyota Kijang

  III. 第4—6段构成第三层次,这一层交代了另一个新闻要素who,对这一爆炸事件尚无人声称负责,但分析家提出的看法是,爆炸肇事者是地区性的恐怖组织"伊斯兰祈祷团"。

  IV. 第7—9段构成第四层次,是新闻要素what的扩展,提供爆炸后的场景。

  V. 第10—16段构成第五层次,也是新闻要素what的扩展,提供爆炸时目击者的亲身经历。

  VI. 第17—18段构成第六层次,提供两名受伤美国人的情况。

  VII. 第19—22段构成第七层次,这一层次交代了最后一个新闻要素why。文中共列出可能导致这一恐怖事件发生的三个因素:(1)爆炸事件发生当日,"伊斯兰祈祷团"精神领袖Abubakar Baasyir出庭作证,自我辩护。(2)爆炸发生在法院对巴厘岛爆炸案做出第一次裁决之前两天。(3)恐怖组织显示自身战斗力,以此激励成员斗志。

  VIII. 文章最后两段构成第八层次。这一层次涉及爆炸案所用炸药的可能来源。"倒金字塔模式"具有以下三大优点:方便读者(读者可以从导语获得主要信息),方便写作(记者按此模式写作十分便捷),方便编辑(编辑排版根据篇幅自下而上删减不会漏掉文章重要内容)。由于"倒金字塔模式"具有这些优点,新闻撰写人员比较喜欢采用这种结构。它是纯新闻报道常用的篇章模式。

  然而,也有不少新闻学者反对这一模式,认为它是"头重脚轻"(Top-heavy form),指责"这种结构浪费篇幅,重要新闻事实重复三次(标题、导语、正文)"。还有的指出,这种模式已经不合时宜,面临电子新闻媒介的挑战,时新性不再是报刊长处,因为导语中的新闻事实读者已从广播电视中获悉。正因为如此,不少新的新闻写作模式已经出现。

V. Analysis of Content

1. The article is _____.
 A. a news comment   B. a straight news report
 C. an interpretative report   D. a news feature

2. The number of foreign victims in the explosion was _____.
   A. two   B. one
   C. three   D. unknown
3. Many of the victims were _____.
   A. those in the lobby   B. diners
   C. waiters and waitresses   D. car drivers
4. Marriott Hotel has a special relationship with _____.
   A. the Indonesian government   B. the American Embassy
   C. the British Embassy   D. the terror group
5. From the information provided by the suspects, we know that the top three targets of the terror group are _____.
   A. malls, churches and hotels
   B. schools, churches and hotels
   C. embassies, hotels and government buildings
   D. malls, theatres and schools

VI. Questions on the Article

1. When and where did the explosion take place?
2. What kind of relationship has Marriott Hotel had with the American Embassy?
3. How were the explosives moved near the hotel's lobby?
4. What kind of organization is the Jemaah Islamiah according to intelligence agencies?
5. What crimes is Abubakar Baasyir accused of?
6. What are the possible reasons for the attack according to the article?

VII. Topics for Discussion

1. Do you think that terrorist attacks are preventable?
2. What, do you think, is the proper way to deal with terrorist groups which use a religion as cover?